2026 국가직·지방직 공무원 시험 대비

실전동형 봉투모의고사
Vol. 1

영 어

■ 제1회 ~ 제12회 ■

실전동형 봉투모의고사

Vol.1

영 어

제1회 ~ 제12회

2026 공무원 시험 대비 실전동형 모의고사
영 어
▌제1회 ▐

<table>
<tr><td>응시번호

성 명</td><td>문제책형
</td></tr>
</table>

제1과목	국어	제2과목	영어	제3과목	한국사
제4과목		제5과목			

응시자 주의사항

1. **시험시작 전 시험문제를 열람하는 행위나 시험종료 후 답안을 작성하는 행위를 한 사람은** 「공무원임용시험령」 제51조에 의거 **부정행위자로 처리됩니다.**
2. **답안지 책형 표기는 시험시작 전 감독관의 지시에 따라 문제책 앞면에 인쇄된 문제책형을 확인**한 후, 답안지 책형란에 해당 책형(1개)을 '●'로 표기하여야 합니다.
3. **답안은 문제책 표지의 과목 순서에 따라 답안지에 인쇄된 순서(제1·2·3·4·5과목)에 맞추어 표기해야**하며, 과목 순서를 바꾸어 표기한 경우에도 문제책 표지의 과목 순서대로 채점되므로 유의하시기 바랍니다.
4. 시험이 시작되면 문제를 주의 깊게 읽은 후, 문항의 취지에 가장 적합한 하나의 정답만을 고르며, 문제내용에 관한 질문은 할 수 없습니다.
5. 답안지의 모든 기재 및 표기 사항은 **컴퓨터용 흑색 싸인펜을 사용**하며, 반드시 <보기>의 **올바른 표기 방식으로 답안을 작성해야** 합니다.

   <보기> 올바른 표기: ●　잘못된 표기: Ⓥ ⊗ ◑ ◉ ⊙ ⦵ ⊖ ③
6. **답안을 잘못 표기하였을 경우에는 답안지를 교체하여 작성하거나 수정할 수 있으며, 표기한 답안을**수정할 때는 응시자 본인이 가져온 **수정테이프만을 사용**하여 해당 부분을 완전히 지우고 부착된 수정테이프가 떨어지지 않도록 손으로 눌러주어야 합니다. (수정액 또는 수정스티커 등은 사용 불가)
   - **불량한 수정테이프의 사용과 불완전한 수정처리로 발생하는 모든 문제는 응시자 본인에게 책임이 있습니다.**
7. **법령, 고시, 판례 등에 관한 문제는 2026년 2월 28일 현재 유효한 법령, 고시, 판례 등을 기준**으로 정답을 구해야 합니다. 다만, 개별 과목 또는 문항에서 별도의 기준을 적용하도록 명시한 경우에는 그 기준을 적용하여 정답을 구해야 합니다.
8. **시험시간 관리의 책임은 응시자 본인에게 있습니다.**
   ※ 문제책은 시험종료 후 가지고 갈 수 있습니다.

정답공개 및 이의제기 안내

1. 정답공개: 정답가안 4.4.(토) 13:30 / 최종정답 4.13.(월) 18:00 / 사이버국가고시센터
2. 이의제기: 4.4.(토) 18:00 ~ 4.7.(화) 18:00 / 사이버국가고시센터
   - 구체적인 이의제기 방법은 정답가안 공개 시 공지 예정
3. 가산점 등록기간: 4.4.(토) 13:30 ~ 4.6.(월) 21:00
4. 가산점 등록방법: 사이버국가고시센터 ➜ [원서접수 → 가산점 등록/확인]

영　어

[1~5] 밑줄 친 부분에 들어갈 말로 가장 적절한 것을 고르시오.

1. The company requires thorough ___________ for every new process so that employees can follow each step consistently and avoid costly mistakes in daily operations.

① expense
② transaction
③ documentation
④ reservation

2. Although the committee is _________ concerns about the proposal's financial risks, several executives believe it could create unexpected opportunities if implemented strategically.

① raising
② mitigating
③ resolving
④ stabilizing

3. ___________ the contract was officially signed by both parties did the legal team begin preparing the necessary papers for the upcoming corporate merger.

① No longer
② Not only
③ No sooner
④ Not until

4.
A: I just finished watching the new sci-fi movie, Cosmic Drift. Have you seen it?
B: Not yet. I've heard mixed reviews. What did you think?
A: I loved it! The visual effects were breathtaking. The story was a bit complex, though.
B: I see. Who's in it?
A: It stars famous actors like Tom Vance and Maria Flores.
B: Oh, I'm a big fan of Tom Vance. ___________
A: He plays the lead role, an astronaut trying to find a new home for humanity.
B: That sounds captivating. I might have to watch it this weekend.

① What character does he play?
② What motivated him to accept the role?
③ Why did he decide to join the cast of this film?
④ What genre does he usually prefer to perform in?

5.

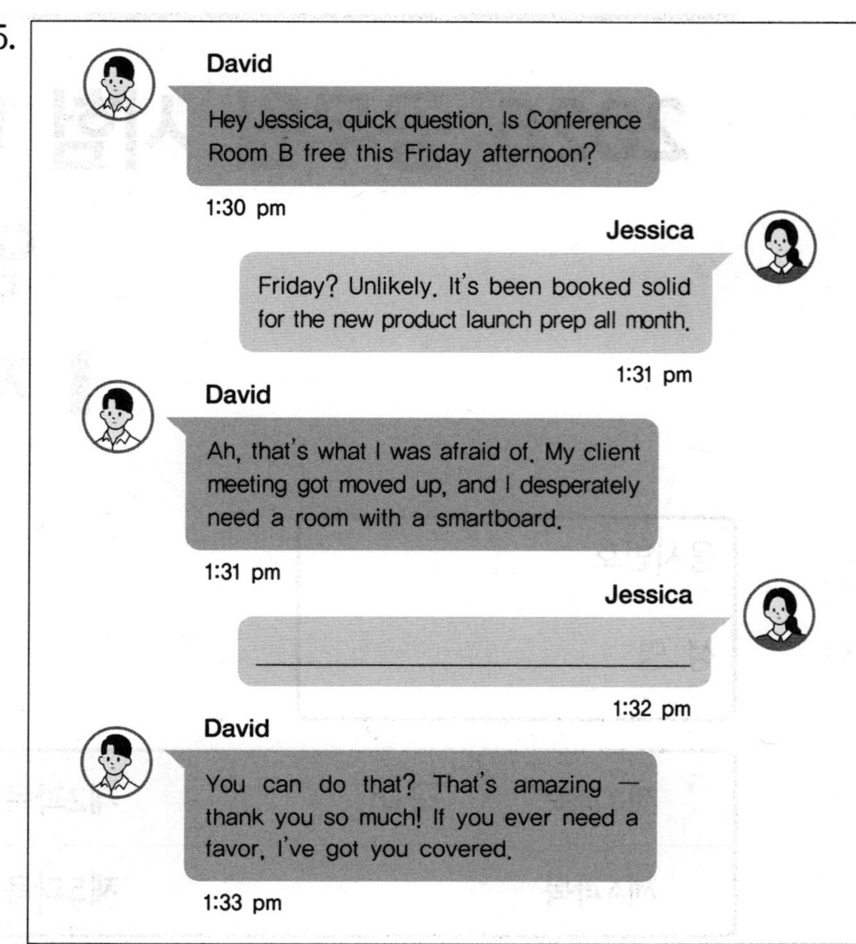

① I will check whether the smartboard is functioning properly.
② There might be a temporary workspace available, but I'm not sure it includes digital equipment.
③ Hold on. My team's booking on Friday was just canceled. I can switch the reservation to your name.
④ I can try finding another room, though it may not include a smartboard.

[6~7] 밑줄 친 부분 중 어법상 옳지 않은 것을 고르시오.

6. The new extensive international climate accord places a significant responsibility on signatory nations, requiring them ① <u>to invest</u> heavily in renewable energy infrastructure ② <u>as well as</u> to implement stricter emissions standards and ③ <u>communicated</u> their long-term strategies transparently to the global community. This comprehensive approach ④ <u>is deemed</u> essential for achieving the ambitious targets set forth in the agreement.

7. The ancient ruins, ① <u>discovered</u> deep in the jungle, offered clues about a civilization ② <u>disappeared</u> long ago. Archaeologists found pottery fragments and stone tools, items that suggest a complex society ③ <u>thrived</u> in the area. Studying these artifacts is helping researchers ④ <u>better</u> understand how the ancient society developed its cultural identity.

[8~9] 다음 글을 읽고 물음에 답하시오.

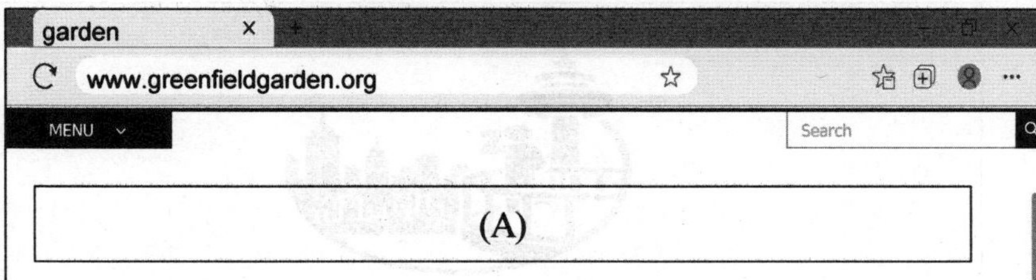

(A)

The Greenfield Community Garden is excited to announce that we are accepting applications for the 2026 gardening season. Located behind the public library, our garden offers a wonderful opportunity for residents to grow their own organic vegetables, flowers, and herbs. It's a great way to enjoy the outdoors, learn about sustainable agriculture, and connect with your neighbors.

Membership is open to all Greenfield residents. The annual fee is $30 per plot, which covers the cost of water, tool maintenance, and shared supplies. No prior gardening experience is necessary! We host free workshops on the first Saturday of each month, from May to September, covering topics like composting and pest control.

☐ **Plot Size**: Plots are approximately 10 feet by 10 feet.
☐ **Plot Allocation**: Plots are assigned on a first-come, first-served basis.

Due to high demand, we recommend applying early. Please visit our website at greenfieldgarden.org to download the application form. Join us in making our community greener!

8. (A)에 들어갈 윗글의 제목으로 가장 적절한 것은?

① Organic Composting: Tips for Community Gardeners
② Application Process for Prospective Gardeners
③ Membership Benefits for Local Residents
④ Guidelines for Maintaining Shared Garden Tools

9. 윗글의 내용과 일치하지 않는 것은?

① The location of the garden is described in relation to the public library.
② The annual fee includes the cost of purchasing personal gardening tools.
③ People who have never gardened before are welcome to join.
④ Garden plots are assigned in the order that applications are received.

[10~11] 다음 글을 읽고 물음에 답하시오.

Commitment to Better Travels

Thank you for choosing SwiftRide for your transportation needs. To ensure a smooth and safe experience for everyone, we ask that you follow a few simple guidelines. These measures are designed to protect both passengers and drivers throughout the journey.

Please confirm your pickup location is accurate on the map before requesting a ride. While waiting, stay in a safe, visible area away from traffic. Upon your driver's arrival, match the license plate and car model with the information provided in the app to <u>verify</u> you're getting into the right vehicle. For safety reasons, the number of passengers must not exceed the number of seatbelts available. Following these guidelines helps reduce risks and ensures a safer ride for all users.

10. 밑줄 친 verify의 의미와 가장 가까운 것은?

① ventilate   ② request
③ modify   ④ confirm

11. 윗글의 목적으로 가장 적절한 것은?

① 업데이트된 안전 수칙을 잘 따라준 것에 대해 감사를 표하려고
② 운전자와 사용자 간의 공식적인 분쟁 해결을 조력하려고
③ 고객들에게 서비스를 안전하게 이용하기 위한 수칙을 알리려고
④ 현재의 차량 유지보수 정책 수정을 요청하려고

12. 다음 글의 내용과 일치하는 것은?

World Wildlife Fund (WWF)

Mission Statement
The mission of the World Wildlife Fund (WWF) is to conserve nature and reduce the most pressing threats to the diversity of life on Earth. Founded in 1961, WWF seeks to ensure a sustainable future where people and nature can thrive together.

Organizational Structure
WWF operates as a global conservation organization in nearly 100 countries, supported by more than five million members worldwide. It is an independent, non-governmental organization managed through regional and national offices that coordinate efforts across continents to achieve conservation goals.

① WWF aims to mitigate urgent risks to various species.
② WWF's operations are limited to a few specific countries.
③ WWF requires all members to participate in annual global conferences.
④ WWF is a government-funded environmental agency.

13. 다음 글의 목적으로 가장 적절한 것은?

	Send	Preview	Save
To	manager@apex-electronics.com		
From	emily.jones@email.com		
Date	September 22, 2026		
Subject	Regarding my recent online purchase		

Dear Manager,

I am writing in reference to a product I purchased through your online store. The item, a "Noise-Cancelling Headphone Pro" delivered yesterday, unfortunately arrived with a malfunction: the right side produces no sound at all, even when connected to multiple devices. I have attached my receipt along with a video that documents the issue in detail.

I would appreciate information on how your company handles such defects, as I am interested in returning the product for a full refund. I look forward to hearing about the specific procedures I should follow regarding this defective product.

Sincerely,
Emily Jones

① to clarify whether the product is still eligible for its warranty coverage
② to ask for a refund after reporting a flawed product
③ to inquire about compensation options for delivery-related damages
④ to obtain technical support for a digital accessory

14. 다음 글의 주제로 가장 적절한 것은?

Most of the 24 billion plastic soft drink bottles sold every year in the United States are made of PET, which can be melted and remanufactured into carpet, fleece clothing, plastic strapping, and nonfood packaging. However, even a tiny amount of vinyl — a single PVC bottle in a truckload, for example — can make PET useless. Although most bottles are now marked with a recycling number, it's hard for consumers to remember which is which. Another worry is the prospect of plastic beer bottles. These bottles are made of PET but are colored amber to block sunlight and have a special chemical coating to keep out oxygen. Due to the special color, interior coating, and vinyl cap lining, these bottles should be separated from regular PET, and it costs more to remove them from the waste stream than the reclaimed plastic is worth.

① why plastic recycling matters in the u.s.
② factors that make recycling pet bottles difficult
③ environmental benefits of recycling plastic bottles
④ pros and cons of specialized plastic containers

15. 다음 글의 내용과 일치하지 않는 것은?

Welcome to the Skyline Observation Deck! Here, you can enjoy a breathtaking 360-degree view of the city from 800 feet above the ground.

Hours of Operation
- Monday - Thursday: 10:00 AM - 9:00 PM
- Friday - Sunday: 10:00 AM - 11:00 PM
- Last entry is permitted 1 hour before closing.

Ticket Prices
- Adults (18-64): $25
- Seniors (65+): $20
- Children (6-17): $18
- Children under 6: Free
- Tickets can be purchased online at a 10% discount. No discount is offered for on-site purchases.

Rules and Regulations
- Food and drinks, except for bottled water, are not allowed on the deck.
- Large bags, backpacks, and tripods are prohibited. Small personal bags are subject to search.
- For the safety of all visitors, running and leaning over the railings are strictly forbidden.

We hope you enjoy your visit!

① Visitors can enter the observation deck up to one hour before closing.
② Tickets for seniors are cheaper than those for adults.
③ All food and drinks are prohibited on the observation deck.
④ Bags are either prohibited or subject to inspection depending on their size.

16. 주어진 문장이 들어갈 위치로 가장 적절한 것은?

Rather, it is about consistently making small, manageable choices that align with your long-term goals.

It is a common misconception that getting fit requires a complete transformation of one's daily life. (①) In fact, living a healthy lifestyle does not mean making drastic, overnight changes. (②) This sustainable approach is far more effective. (③) For instance, instead of eliminating all junk food, you could start by replacing one sugary drink with water each day. (④) Similarly, instead of committing to a two-hour daily workout, you could begin with a 15-minute walk. These minor adjustments build momentum and become habits over time.

17. 다음 글의 흐름상 어색한 문장은?

Urbanization offers significant economic and social benefits, such as enhanced access to jobs, education, and healthcare. ① By concentrating people and resources, cities can foster innovation and increase productivity. ② To manage the rapid growth of urban areas sustainably, city planners are developing smart city initiatives that use technology to improve services and reduce environmental impact. ③ These initiatives often include intelligent transportation systems, energy-efficient buildings, and digital public services. ④ Rural areas often suffer from a lack of infrastructure and investment compared to their urban counterparts. By integrating these technologies, cities can become more livable and resilient, ensuring a higher quality of life for their residents.

18. 주어진 글 다음에 이어질 글의 순서로 가장 적절한 것은?

After years of thorough training inside simulators and metal mock-ups, I finally approached the exit door for my first space walk. Excitement tightened in my stomach.

(A) What impressed me first was not the darkness but the sun's intense light, reflecting off the station's hull in a harsh white that erased all detail.

(B) The red light above the exit turned green, indicating the outer space was ready. I stepped into the vacuum, gripping the handrail, my motions slow and cautious before the vast space.

(C) Hovering there, the Earth below—silent and swirling in blue and white—reshaped my sense of scale. All the procedures I had practiced felt small beside the overwhelming awe.

① (A)—(C)—(B)　　　　② (B)—(A)—(C)
③ (B)—(C)—(A)　　　　④ (C)—(B)—(A)

[19~20] 밑줄 친 부분에 들어갈 말로 가장 적절한 것을 고르시오.

19.

In today's interconnected world, the spread of misinformation has become a significant societal problem. False or inaccurate information can spread rapidly through social media and other digital platforms, often faster than verified facts. This phenomenon occurs partly because misinformation is frequently designed to be emotionally provocative, tapping into people's fears, anger, or excitement. Such content is more likely to be shared without critical evaluation. The consequences can be severe, leading to public health crises, social division, and erosion of trust in institutions. Therefore, it is crucial for individuals to develop media literacy skills. This means learning not just how to consume information, but how to question its source, verify its claims, and understand the potential motives behind it, because ＿＿＿＿＿＿＿＿＿＿＿＿＿＿＿.

① unchecked information can have harmful real-world impacts

② most digital platforms lack strict fact-checking systems

③ emotionally charged content often feels convincing even when false

④ people often share content quickly to maintain social connection

20.

The prevailing model of perception, long dominated by a bottom-up framework, is undergoing a radical shift. A groundbreaking synthesis of recent neuroscientific findings, featured this week in TIME, posits that the brain operates not as a passive receiver of sensory data, but as a proactive prediction machine. According to this "predictive processing" model, the brain constantly generates a rich, hierarchical model of the world to anticipate incoming sensory signals. What we experience as perception is not the raw data from our eyes and ears. Rather, it is the brain's best guess, a kind of "controlled hallucination," that is only updated when there is a mismatch—a prediction error— between the expectation and actual input from the outside. This reframes the very nature of consciousness, suggesting that reality is something ＿＿＿＿＿＿＿＿＿＿＿＿＿＿＿.

① our consciousness perceives as a mirror of the physical world

② our eyes and ears dictate through constant external signals

③ we must observe objectively to avoid any prediction errors

④ we actively and continuously construct from within

수고하셨습니다.
당신의 합격을 응원합니다.

합격까지 **박문각**

2026 공무원 시험 대비 실전동형 모의고사
영 어
▌ 제2회 ▌

<table>
<tr><td>응시번호

성 명</td><td>문제책형
</td></tr>
</table>

제1과목	국어	제2과목	<u>영어</u>	제3과목	한국사
제4과목		제5과목			

영 어

[1~3] 밑줄 친 부분에 들어갈 말로 가장 적절한 것을 고르시오.

1.

The novel illustrates how _________ can unravel even the closest relationships and slowly corrupt those who were once considered good.

① sympathy   ② outlet
③ greed   ④ novelty

2.

Because the meeting minutes were written in a very _________ manner, several departments interpreted the new guidelines differently and ended up following inconsistent procedures.

① administrative   ② vague
③ cumulative   ④ durable

3.

Regions of space _________ astronomers once thought were empty are often teeming with faint, distant galaxies detectable only with the most powerful telescopes.

① that   ② whichever
③ where   ④ how

[4~5] 밑줄 친 부분 중 어법상 옳지 않은 것을 고르시오.

4.

The psychologist explained that procedural memory, which involves the recall of skills and routines, ① is distinct from declarative memory, which concerns facts and events. Declarative memory is consciously recalled, whereas procedural memory works unconsciously. This is ② why a skilled cyclist can navigate a complex trail without thinking about every muscle movement. Such skills, ③ once learning, become so automatic that trying to control them consciously can hurt performance, a phenomenon known ④ as "choking under pressure."

5.

In the late 19th century, urban planners had to manage fast-growing cities. Among the most visionary figures of this era ① was Ebenezer Howard, who proposed the concept of the "Garden City." He envisioned self-contained communities ② surrounded by greenbelts, combining the best of town and country living. His ideas, detailed in his 1898 book, aimed ③ to solve the problems of urban ④ crowded and poor sanitation.

[6~7] 다음 글을 읽고 물음에 답하시오.

Design Inspired by Nature

Humanity continues to face complex environmental and technological challenges. The concept of biomimicry provides a sustainable path forward by drawing wisdom from the natural world.

Nature, through billions of years of evolution, has already developed solutions to many of the problems we struggle with today. From self-healing materials modeled after biological <u>tissues</u> to energy-efficient buildings inspired by termite mounds, innovators are turning to nature's design principles for answers.

The essence of biomimicry lies not in copying nature's appearance, but in learning from the resilience, efficiency, and sustainability of its systems. By adopting this approach, designers and engineers can create technologies that coexist harmoniously with the planet — making biomimicry a pivotal strategy for a sustainable future.

6. 밑줄 친 tissues의 의미와 가장 가까운 것은?

① vessels   ② organs
③ textures   ④ components

7. 윗글의 목적으로 가장 적절한 것은?

① 자연과 인간 기술의 차이를 비교하려고
② 생체 모방의 원리와 가능성을 소개하려고
③ 지속 가능한 기술의 이점을 설명하려고
④ 생물학적 기술 공학 분야의 연구 성과를 알리려고

8. 밑줄 친 부분에 들어갈 말로 가장 적절한 것은?

A: Have you had a chance to review the report I sent this morning?
B: Yes, I looked it over briefly, but I noticed a few typos and some formatting issues.
A: I see. ____
B: The headings on page two aren't consistent, and there are spelling errors in the conclusion.
A: Thanks for letting me know. I'll revise those parts and send you the updated version.
B: Sounds good. I'll review it one last time once you send it over.

① Then, could you let me know when you'll be available to review it?
② Would a two-page report be too short in terms of content?
③ Could you point out which sections need correction?
④ Do you have any tips for reducing spelling errors?

9. 밑줄 친 부분에 들어갈 말로 가장 적절한 것은?

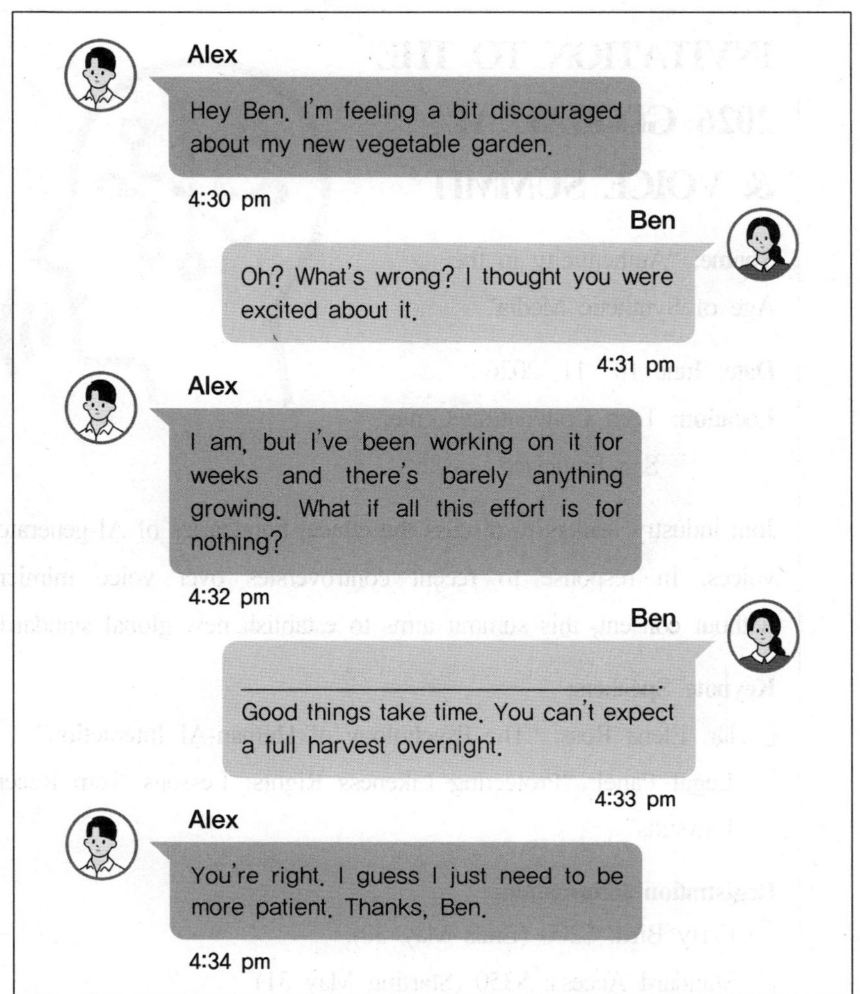

① You should have thought of that sooner
② Well, that's a definite possibility
③ Rome wasn't built in a day
④ Don't count your chickens before they hatch

10. 다음 글의 주제로 가장 적절한 것은?

The distinction between "practice" and "play" is essential in skill acquisition. Practice is a structured activity with clear goals and immediate feedback, aimed at improving specific aspects of performance. Because it requires sustained concentration and effort, it can be mentally and physically demanding. Play, in contrast, is unstructured and driven by intrinsic motivation, allowing learners to explore, experiment, and enjoy the activity without pressure. Although it may appear less productive, play nurtures creativity, strengthens long-term interest, and helps prevent burnout. For these reasons, effective learning does not rely on choosing one approach over the other, but on balancing both — using structured practice to build core skills and unstructured play to maintain motivation and inspire innovation.

① the importance of deliberate practice in professional fields
② play as a source of creativity and motivation
③ the synergy of practice and play for effective skill development
④ how to overcome burnout in high-stakes competitions

[11~12] 다음 글을 읽고 물음에 답하시오.

(A)

Every year, thousands of companion animals in our city end up in shelters, waiting for a second chance. The "Paws for a Cause" adoption campaign, hosted by the Liberty Animal Shelter, aims to connect these loving animals with caring families. This special event will run from October 14th to October 20th.

During the campaign week, we are reducing our standard adoption fee to $50 for all cats and dogs to ease the financial burden on new pet owners. All adopted animals are microchipped, vaccinated, and have undergone a health check. Our goal is not just to find them homes, but to ensure they find the right homes. Therefore, all potential adopters are required to complete a short counseling session with our staff to ensure a good match.

Join us and open your heart to a new friend. Your decision can change a life forever.

11. (A)에 들어갈 윗글의 제목으로 가장 적절한 것은?

① Financial Benefits for New Pet Owners
② Essential Requirements for Successful Adoption
③ A Guide to Animal Health Checks
④ Find Your Furry Family Member

12. 윗글의 내용과 일치하는 것은?

① This event begins on October 20th.
② The campaign is strictly limited to the adoption of cats.
③ All animals available for adoption have been vaccinated.
④ Staff consultations are optional for those who want to adopt.

13. 다음 글의 목적으로 가장 적절한 것은?

✎	Send	Preview	Save

To	planning.department@cityhall.gov
From	sunrise.neighborhood.assoc@email.org
Date	October 1, 2026
Subject	Regarding Parcel 7B

Dear City Planning Department,

On behalf of the Sunrise Neighborhood Association, I am writing to request clarification on the proposed zoning change for Parcel 7B at Oak Street and 12th Avenue. We reviewed the public notice posted last week, but it does not explain how the property will be used.

Our community values the residential character and green spaces of our neighborhood. The notice refers to a possible "mixed-use development," but the term is too broad for us to understand its impact.

Could you please provide more specific information, such as building height, permitted commercial uses, and expected effects on traffic and parking?

We look forward to your timely response.

Sincerely,
David Chen

① to protest the approval of a recent project
② to propose a new design for a local building
③ to seek details regarding a zoning change
④ to report an error in a government document

14. 다음 글의 흐름상 어색한 문장은?

Circadian rhythms are 24-hour cycles that are part of the body's internal clock, running in the background to carry out essential functions and processes. ① One of the most important and well-known circadian rhythms is the sleep-wake cycle, which is heavily influenced by light and darkness in the environment. ② When functioning properly, the circadian rhythm promotes consistent and restorative sleep, but when it's thrown off, it can create significant sleeping problems. ③ Individuals suffering from these sleeping problems often find that financial stress and job insecurity are the primary catalysts for their inability to rest at night. ④ This internal clock also regulates various other bodily functions, including hormone release, body temperature, and metabolism. And all of them fluctuate in a predictable pattern throughout the day.

15. 다음 글의 내용과 일치하지 않는 것은?

INVITATION TO THE 2026 GLOBAL AI & VOICE SUMMIT

Theme: "Authenticity in the Age of Synthetic Media"

Date: June 10 - 11, 2026
Location: Tech Convention Center, San Francisco

Join industry leaders to discuss the ethical boundaries of AI-generated voices. In response to recent controversies over voice mimicry without consent, this summit aims to establish new global standards.

Keynote Speakers:
☐ Dr. Elena Ross: "The Psychology of Human-AI Interaction"
☐ Legal Panel: "Protecting Likeness Rights: Lessons from Recent Lawsuits"

Registration Information:
☐ Early Bird: $200 (Ends May 30).
☐ Standard Access: $350 (Starting May 31)
☐ Virtual Pass: $100 (Includes live streaming of keynote sessions only)

Attendees will receive a digital certificate of participation.

All sessions will be recorded and made available to in-person attendees for up to 30 days after the event.

① 이 행사는 AI로 생성된 음성의 윤리적 문제를 중심으로 다룬다.
② 법률 전문가들이 참여하는 연설도 진행된다.
③ 조기 등록 할인은 5월 31일부터 적용된다.
④ 행사의 모든 시간은 녹화되어 다시 시청할 수 있다.

16. 주어진 글 다음에 이어질 글의 순서로 가장 적절한 것은?

The Fermi paradox refers to the contradiction between the high likelihood of extraterrestrial civilizations and the absence of evidence or contact.

(A) One well-known idea is the "Great Filter" theory, which argues that somewhere between simple life and advanced civilizations, there exists an extremely difficult barrier that most life cannot pass.

(B) The paradox is named after physicist Enrico Fermi, who famously asked, "Where is everybody?" — a question that captures the strange silence in a universe expected to host abundant life.

(C) Many explanations have been proposed, ranging from the rarity of intelligent life to the possibility that civilizations destroy themselves before making contact.

① (A) － (C) － (B)　　② (B) － (A) － (C)
③ (B) － (C) － (A)　　④ (C) － (B) － (A)

17. 다음 글에서 The Phoenix Project에 대한 내용과 일치하는 것은?

The Phoenix Project: Igniting Hope for At-Risk Youth

The Phoenix Project is a non-profit organization that supports at-risk youth through mentorship and vocational training. Our mission is to equip individuals aged 16 - 24 with the skills and confidence to overcome challenges and pursue successful futures.

Our Core Programs:

— **Mentorship**: Each participant is paired with a trained adult mentor who provides guidance and support for at least one year. The mentors work in a variety of professional fields and have joined this project to offer their support.

— **Vocational Training**: We offer hands-on training in high-demand fields such as culinary arts, information technology, and green construction. These programs are offered free of charge to all participants.

We operate primarily through private donations and corporate sponsorships, with less than 10% of our funding coming from government grants.

① It was established by the government to support young people.
② All mentors in the project are retired educators.
③ Participants in the training program pay part of the cost.
④ The project is also funded through individual donations.

18. 주어진 문장이 들어갈 위치로 가장 적절한 것은?

On the contrary, it requires a disciplined and systematic approach to problem-solving, where creativity is channeled to produce novel yet functional outcomes.

Brainstorming is often misunderstood as a chaotic, unstructured free-for-all where any and all ideas are welcome. (①) While the generation of a wide range of ideas is indeed a goal, effective brainstorming is far from chaotic. (②) The initial phase, known as divergence, encourages participants to think broadly and without judgment to generate as many ideas as possible, no matter how outlandish they may seem. (③) This phase is then followed by a crucial second stage: convergence. (④) Here, the team must critically evaluate, combine, and refine the generated ideas to select the most promising ones that align with the project's goals and constraints.

[19~20] 밑줄 친 부분에 들어갈 말로 가장 적절한 것을 고르시오.

19.

Many developed nations are standing on a demographic precipice, defined by rapidly falling fertility rates. This is not merely a social shift but an impending economic crisis, fundamentally altering the arrangement between generations. For decades, many economies benefited from a "demographic dividend"—a large, youthful workforce supporting a small elderly population. This fueled productivity and high tax revenues. Now, ___________________.
As the baby boomer generation retires, the workforce shrinks, and the dependency ratio—the ratio of non-workers to workers—skyrockets. This "demographic tax" places an unsustainable burden on public finances, straining pensions, healthcare, and social security. Governments are thus forced to choose between raising taxes, cutting benefits, or accepting massive debt.

① higher tax revenues are stabilizing the economy
② the workforce continues to expand at a steady pace
③ this trend is gaining momentum
④ this dynamic is reversing

20.

Behavioral economics offers a clear explanation for chronic overspending. It highlights a cognitive flaw called "present bias": we tend to overvalue immediate gratification and undervalue long-term goals. The pleasure of buying something now is vivid and emotionally strong, whereas saving for retirement or paying off debt feels abstract and distant. Our brain processes these choices differently—the impulsive system reacts to immediate rewards, while the rational system that supports future goals is easily ignored. This results in "time inconsistency," where our present self makes decisions that ___________________________________.
Thus, maintaining financial health requires not only budgeting but also creating systems that make future consequences feel more immediate.

① prioritize essential needs over luxury goods
② our future self will inevitably regret
③ are heavily influenced by social pressure and marketing
④ align our long-term goals with short-term desires

2026 공무원 시험 대비 실전동형 모의고사
영어
▌제3회▐

응시번호

성 명

제1과목	국어	제2과목	영어	제3과목	한국사
제4과목		제5과목			

응시자 주의사항

1. 시험시작 전 시험문제를 열람하는 행위나 시험종료 후 답안을 작성하는 행위를 한 사람은 「공무원임용시험령」 제51조에 의거 부정행위자로 처리됩니다.
2. 답안지 책형 표기는 시험시작 전 감독관의 지시에 따라 문제책 앞면에 인쇄된 문제책형을 확인한 후, 답안지 책형란에 해당 책형(1개)을 '●'로 표기하여야 합니다.
3. 답안은 문제책 표지의 과목 순서에 따라 답안지에 인쇄된 순서(제1·2·3·4·5과목)에 맞추어 표기해야 하며, 과목 순서를 바꾸어 표기한 경우에도 문제책 표지의 과목 순서대로 채점되므로 유의하시기 바랍니다.
4. 시험이 시작되면 문제를 주의 깊게 읽은 후, 문항의 취지에 가장 적합한 하나의 정답만을 고르며, 문제내용에 관한 질문은 할 수 없습니다.
5. 답안지의 모든 기재 및 표기 사항은 **컴퓨터용 흑색 싸인펜**을 사용하며, 반드시 <보기>의 올바른 표기 방식으로 답안을 작성해야 합니다.

   <보기> 올바른 표기: ● 잘못된 표기: ⨼ ⊗ ◐ ⊙ ⦷ ⑴ ○ ③

6. 답안을 잘못 표기하였을 경우에는 답안지를 교체하여 작성하거나 수정할 수 있으며, 표기한 답안을 수정할 때는 응시자 본인이 가져온 수정테이프만을 사용하여 해당 부분을 완전히 지우고 부착된 수정테이프가 떨어지지 않도록 손으로 눌러주어야 합니다. (수정액 또는 수정스티커 등은 사용 불가)
   ■ 불량한 수정테이프의 사용과 불완전한 수정처리로 발생하는 모든 문제는 응시자 본인에게 책임이 있습니다.
7. 법령, 고시, 판례 등에 관한 문제는 **2026년 2월 28일 현재 유효한 법령, 고시, 판례 등을 기준**으로 정답을 구해야 합니다. 다만, 개별 과목 또는 문항에서 별도의 기준을 적용하도록 명시한 경우에는 그 기준을 적용하여 정답을 구해야 합니다.
8. 시험시간 관리의 책임은 응시자 본인에게 있습니다.
   ※ 문제책은 시험종료 후 가지고 갈 수 있습니다.

정답공개 및 이의제기 안내

1. 정답공개: 정답가안 4.4.(토) 13:30 / 최종정답 4.13.(월) 18:00 / 사이버국가고시센터
2. 이의제기: 4.4.(토) 18:00 ~ 4.7.(화) 18:00 / 사이버국가고시센터
   ■ 구체적인 이의제기 방법은 정답가안 공개 시 공지 예정
3. 가산점 등록기간: 4.4.(토) 13:30 ~ 4.6.(월) 21:00
4. 가산점 등록방법: 사이버국가고시센터 ➜ [원서접수 → 가산점 등록/확인]

영　어

[1~5] 밑줄 친 부분에 들어갈 말로 가장 적절한 것을 고르시오.

1.

The rapid advancement of generative AI has created deepfake technologies with such stunning ＿＿＿＿＿ that they are nearly indistinguishable from reality, threatening information integrity.

① inventory
② credibility
③ consumption
④ deficiency

2.

As research into solid-state batteries progresses, the vision of electric vehicles with a 1,000-kilometer range might soon ＿＿＿＿ from a theoretical possibility into a commercial reality.

① stagnate
② retreat
③ evolve
④ deposit

3.

＿＿＿＿＿ his extensive experience in international negotiations, Mr. Lopez is considered the ideal candidate to lead the upcoming trade talks.

① Given
② Provided
③ As soon as
④ Aside from

4.

A: This smart planter is amazing! It says it automates watering and lighting cycles based on the plant type.
B: That's brilliant. So you just input that you're growing basil, and it handles the rest?
A: Pretty much. But I'm wondering, what happens if there's a power outage? Will all my settings be lost?
B: ＿＿＿＿＿＿＿＿＿＿＿. It usually stores your custom profiles in non-volatile memory.
A: Oh, that's a relief. So when the power comes back on, it will just resume its schedule?
B: Exactly. Your basil will be safe.

① You'll have to reconfigure it from scratch
② I doubt it has any backup system
③ That's a valid concern, but most modern devices have a fail-safe
④ The device will likely switch to a default low-power mode

5.

① We should focus exclusively on task-oriented communication
② The company should mandate a full return to the office
③ Being intentional about creating virtual social spaces could be key
④ I think we just need to accept that team dynamics will suffer

6. 다음 글의 주제로 가장 적절한 것은?

The "right to repair" movement, a growing consumer advocacy effort, challenges the prevailing business model of many electronics manufacturers. This model often involves designing products that are difficult or impossible for consumers or independent technicians to repair, for instance, by using proprietary screws, gluing components together, or restricting access to spare parts and repair manuals. Proponents of the right to repair argue that these practices are anti-competitive, generate unnecessary electronic waste, and infringe on the consumer's right to own and modify their property. However, manufacturers counter that such restrictions are necessary to protect intellectual property, ensure user safety from improper repairs, and maintain the quality and performance of their devices. The resulting legislative battles in various countries reflect a fundamental conflict between consumer autonomy and corporate control.

① the environmental impact of e-waste
② the barriers that limit consumer access to device repairs
③ the core arguments in the conflict over the right to repair
④ corporate limits on repairability in modern electronics

[7~8] 다음 글을 읽고 물음에 답하시오.

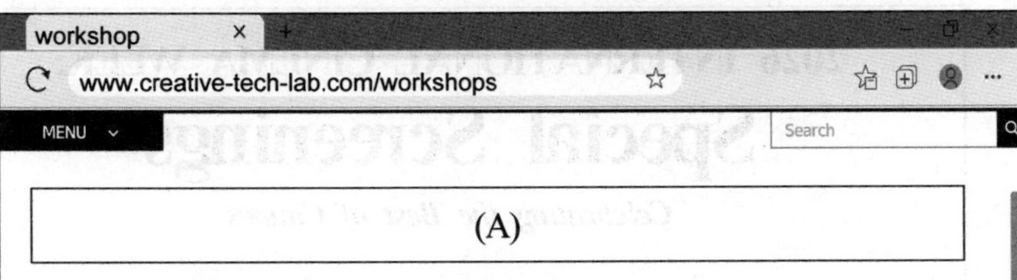

Are you interested in creating your own mobile applications but don't know where to start? This weekend workshop is tailored for beginners with no prior coding experience, guiding you from concept to launch.

Participants will learn the basics of user interface (UI) design and block-based coding. Please check the schedule below to choose the session that best fits your learning goals.

Workshop Sessions

Session	Focus Area
Morning Introduction	Introduction to app logic and screen layout design
Afternoon Production	Adding features like buttons, maps, and camera access
Evening Review	Testing the app on real devices and fixing bugs

All participants must bring their own laptops. Lunch and refreshments are provided free of charge. Registration closes two days before the event, so sign up early to secure your spot.

7. (A)에 들어갈 윗글의 제목으로 가장 적절한 것은?

① Marketing and Launch Strategies for Mobile Apps

② Advanced Programming Skills for App Developers

③ How Smartphones Changed Modern Technology

④ An Introductory Mobile App Workshop

8. 윗글의 내용과 일치하지 않는 것은?

① The workshop is designed for beginners with no prior coding experience.

② Participants are required to attend all sessions from morning to evening.

③ The evening session focuses on testing the app on real devices.

④ Each participant must provide their own laptop.

[9~10] 다음 글을 읽고 물음에 답하시오.

Guidance on AI Model Hazard Reporting

We welcome all submissions regarding the auditing of generative AI models, whether from internal compliance teams or designated third-party evaluators. It is imperative that we ensure that these models do not perpetuate systemic biases or generate <u>prohibited</u> content.

If you wish to file a complaint about a model's non-compliance with the AI Safety Act, we will review it as quickly as possible. If the report is submitted by an external auditor on behalf of a developer, a certified document authorizing the disclosure of proprietary model data is required before review can begin.

Submit all relevant documentation, including original source records and safety testing results, through our secure reporting portal. We will log and carefully review your complaint, and the AI Safety Commission's oversight board will respond.

9. 밑줄 친 prohibited의 의미와 가장 가까운 것은?

① forbidden   ② unprecedented

③ sustained   ④ fasten

10. 윗글의 내용과 일치하는 것은?

① Third-party evaluators are excluded from the initial auditing process.

② A primary goal is to prevent AI systems from reinforcing unfair social prejudices.

③ Review results will be sent within 24 hours.

④ Documentation should be delivered in person to the safety commission.

[11~12] 밑줄 친 부분 중 어법상 옳지 않은 것을 고르시오.

11.

A recent study on microplastics revealed that ① <u>these</u> tiny particles have become ubiquitous, infiltrating everything from marine ecosystems to human tissues. The research, ② <u>which</u> methodology involved analyzing samples from remote Arctic ice cores, ③ <u>provides</u> compelling evidence of their pervasive nature. What is most alarming is not just their presence, but ④ <u>that</u> they can act as vectors for harmful pollutants.

12.

The international community has struggled to establish a ① <u>binding</u> treaty on cyber warfare, leaving the digital realm in a state of perpetual low-level conflict. ② <u>Unlike</u> traditional warfare, where attribution is often clear, the anonymity of cyberspace makes ③ <u>it</u> difficult to identify perpetrators definitively. This ambiguity provides a convenient shield for state-sponsored actors, ④ <u>allowed</u> them to engage in espionage and sabotage with a degree of plausible deniability.

13. 다음 글의 목적으로 가장 적절한 것은?

✎	**Send**	Preview	Save

To	citycouncil@woodville.gov
From	ConcernedResident@community.org
Date	October 31, 2026
Subject	Regarding a Proposed Development

📎　[My PC]　[Browse]

[Times New ▾]　[10pt ▾]　[G G *G* G̲ G]

Dear Members of the City Council,

I am writing to express my profound disappointment and strong protest regarding your recent approval of the "Evergreen Tower" development project. This decision, which will eliminate the last significant green space in our downtown core, is a massive mistake.

Your focus on tax revenue and jobs overlooks the park's environmental and social value. This green space supports clean air, community use, and wildlife, and replacing it with a luxury condo harms the city's long-term well-being.

I would like to call upon the council to reconsider its decision immediately and to prioritize sustainable, community-focused urban planning over short-sighted commercial interests. Your prompt action is essential to ensure the well-being of our city.

Sincerely,
A Concerned Downtown Resident

① to complain about the poor maintenance of a public park

② to present concerns about the Evergreen Tower project

③ to protest a development decision and advocate for its reversal

④ to provide an ecological survey of the downtown green space

14. 주어진 문장이 들어갈 위치로 가장 적절한 것은?

> This shift transforms the internet from a static library of information into a dynamic, intelligent partner in creation and discovery.

The evolution of the internet is often categorized into distinct phases. Web 1.0 was the era of the "read-only" web, where a small number of creators provided content for a large audience of consumers. (①) Then came Web 2.0, the "read-write" web, characterized by social media and user-generated content, which turned users into active participants. (②) We are now entering the era of Web 3.0, often termed the "semantic" or "intelligent" web. (③) Such evolution is underpinned by a decentralized infrastructure and advanced artificial intelligence, which allow the network to understand context rather than just process keywords. (④) As a result, the internet moves beyond simple information delivery to actively supporting more meaningful, efficient, and personalized human interaction with knowledge.

15. 다음 글의 내용과 일치하지 않는 것은?

2026 INTERNATIONAL CINEMA WEEK:
Special Screenings
Celebrating the Best of Cannes

Join us at the Downtown Art Theater for a showcase of award-winning films straight from the festival.

Schedule ─────────
(May 24, Saturday):
☐ 2:00 PM: *The Apprentice* (Drama)
 - Followed by a panel discussion with film critics.
☐ 7:00 PM: *Megalopolis* (Sci-Fi) — *Sold Out.*

(May 25, Sunday): ─────────
☐ 3:00 PM: *Kinds of Kindness* (Anthology)
 - Directed by Yorgos Lanthimos.
☐ 6:00 PM: *Furiosa* (Action) — IMAX screening.
 - Surcharge of $5 applies.

(May 26, Monday) (Memorial Day Special) ─────────
☐ 11:00 AM: Short Film Compilation.
 - Free entry for students with valid ID.
☐ 5:00 PM: *The Apprentice* (Encore Screening).

Notes:
• Tickets can be purchased at the box office or via our app.
• Doors open 30 minutes before showtime. No late entry allowed.

① 토요일 오후 2시 상영 후에는 영화 평론가들과의 토론이 진행된다.

② 일요일 오후 6시 상영은 IMAX로 진행되며 추가 요금이 부과된다.

③ 월요일 오후 5시 상영은 처음으로 상영되는 작품이다.

④ 상영 시작 30분 전부터 입장이 가능하다.

16. 다음 글의 흐름상 어색한 문장은?

The global food system is facing a trilemma: it must provide nutritious food for a growing population, reduce its significant environmental footprint, and adapt to the increasing volatility of a changing climate. ① <u>One promising avenue is the development of cellular agriculture, which involves producing meat, milk, and eggs from cell cultures rather than from whole animals.</u> ② <u>In response to rising costs, many farmers are looking for ways to broaden the variety of grains used in livestock feed to improve animal health.</u> ③ <u>This approach could drastically reduce land use, water consumption, and greenhouse gas emissions associated with traditional livestock farming.</u> ④ <u>Consumer acceptance, however, remains a significant hurdle, as public perception of "lab-grown" food is often skeptical.</u> Furthermore, scaling up production to be cost-competitive with conventional agriculture presents formidable technological and economic challenges that need to be overcome.

17. 다음 글의 내용과 일치하는 것은?

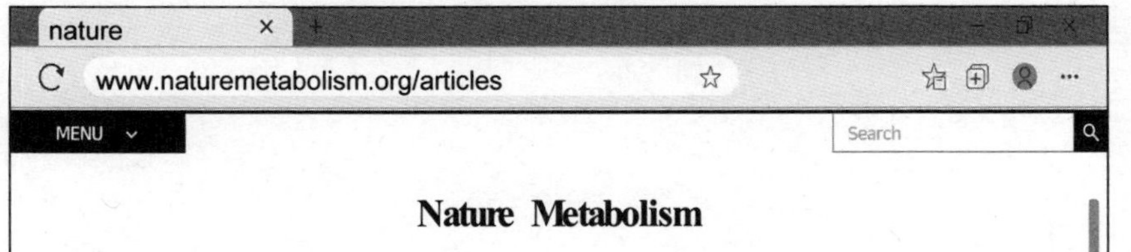

Nature Metabolism

A Recent Study on Intermittent Fasting

A recent meta-analysis published in Nature Metabolism examined the efficacy of various intermittent fasting (IF) regimens. The study synthesized data from over fifty clinical trials, concluding that while most IF protocols — including alternate-day fasting and time-restricted eating — do result in modest weight loss and improved metabolic markers, their effects are not significantly superior to those of traditional caloric restriction diets when overall calorie intake is matched.

The researchers suggest that the primary benefit of IF may not be metabolic magic, but rather its role as a simpler, more intuitive behavioral tool for reducing total energy consumption. They noted, however, that the long-term adherence rates and health effects of IF beyond two years remain largely unstudied and require further investigation.

① The study did not include as many as fifty clinical trials.

② It concludes that intermittent fasting shows no particular advantage when total calorie intake is the same.

③ The researchers note that the main benefits of intermittent fasting have not yet been clearly identified.

④ Long-term studies on intermittent fasting are complete.

18. 주어진 글 다음에 이어질 글의 순서로 가장 적절한 것은?

Deglobalization, the process of diminishing interdependence and integration between nations, is increasingly becoming a defining feature of the 21st-century geopolitical landscape, reversing decades of global economic convergence.

(A) In response to these pressures, governments have begun prioritizing national security and supply chain resilience over pure economic efficiency, giving rise to policies such as on-shoring and friend-shoring.

(B) The COVID-19 pandemic further reinforced this shift by exposing the vulnerabilities of hyper-specialized global supply chains and demonstrating the risks of excessive foreign dependency.

(C) Several factors are driving this trend, most notably the escalating strategic competition between major world powers and a rise in economic nationalism.

① (A)－(C)－(B) 　② (B)－(C)－(A)

③ (C)－(A)－(B) 　④ (C)－(B)－(A)

[19~20] 밑줄 친 부분에 들어갈 말로 가장 적절한 것을 고르시오.

19.

The transition to a circular economy, which emphasizes reusing, repairing, and recycling materials, represents a fundamental departure from our current linear "take-make-dispose" model. This systemic shift is not merely an environmental strategy; it is increasingly viewed as an economic imperative. As resource scarcity and supply chain volatility become more pronounced, businesses that rely on a constant input of virgin materials face growing risks. In contrast, a circular model offers a pathway to long-term resilience by __________ __________________________________. This creates more stable, localized supply chains and insulates businesses from the price shocks of the global commodity markets.

① increasing the efficiency of resource extraction and distribution

② minimizing the dependence on a continuous supply of raw materials

③ expanding production capacities to meet the growing global demand

④ securing a more diverse range of global suppliers for virgin materials

20.

The phenomenon of "doomscrolling" — the tendency to compulsively surf through bad news — has been linked to significant increases in anxiety and stress. Psychologists theorize that this behavior stems from a primal, evolutionary instinct to monitor for threats. In an ancient environment, this vigilance was a survival mechanism. In the modern world of infinite information feeds, however, this same instinct becomes maladaptive. The constant stream of negative information activates the body's threat response system without resolution, leaving individuals in a sustained state of hypervigilance. This cycle is particularly pernicious because the very anxiety it creates fuels the desire to keep scrolling, in a futile attempt to ____.

① achieve a sense of control or closure

② briefly ease the anxiety triggered by negative news

③ find entertainment and distraction

④ connect with a supportive community

수고하셨습니다.
당신의 합격을 응원합니다.

2026 공무원 시험 대비 실전동형 모의고사
영어
▌ 제4회 ▐

응시번호

성 명

제1과목	국어	제2과목	영어	제3과목	한국사
제4과목		제5과목			

응시자 주의사항

1. **시험시작 전 시험문제를 열람하는 행위나 시험종료 후 답안을 작성하는 행위를 한 사람은** 「공무원임용시험령」 제51조에 의거 **부정행위자로** 처리됩니다.
2. **답안지 책형 표기는 시험시작 전 감독관의 지시에 따라 문제책 앞면에 인쇄된 문제책형을 확인한 후, 답안지 책형란에 해당 책형(1개)을 '●'로 표기하여야** 합니다.
3. **답안은 문제책 표지의 과목 순서에 따라 답안지에 인쇄된 순서(제1·2·3·4·5과목)에 맞추어 표기해야 하며, 과목 순서를 바꾸어 표기한 경우에도 문제책 표지의 과목 순서대로 채점되므로 유의하시기 바랍니다.**
4. 시험이 시작되면 문제를 주의 깊게 읽은 후, **문항의 취지에 가장 적합한 하나의 정답만을 고르며,** 문제내용에 관한 질문은 할 수 없습니다.
5. 답안지의 모든 기재 및 표기 사항은 **컴퓨터용 흑색 싸인펜을 사용**하며, 반드시 <보기>의 **올바른 표기 방식으로 답안을 작성해야** 합니다.

   <보기> **올바른 표기: ●   잘못된 표기: ⊘ ⊗ ◑ ⊙ ⦷ ◔ ③**

6. **답안을 잘못 표기하였을 경우에는 답안지를 교체하여 작성하거나 수정할 수 있으며,** 표기한 답안을 수정할 때는 **응시자 본인이 가져온 수정테이프만을 사용**하여 해당 부분을 완전히 지우고 부착된 수정테이프가 떨어지지 않도록 손으로 눌러주어야 합니다. **(수정액 또는 수정스티커 등은 사용 불가)**

   ■ **불량한 수정테이프의 사용과 불완전한 수정처리로 발생하는 모든 문제는 응시자 본인에게 책임이 있습니다.**
7. **법령, 고시, 판례 등에 관한 문제는 2026년 2월 28일 현재 유효한 법령, 고시, 판례 등을 기준으로 정답을 구해야** 합니다. 다만, 개별 과목 또는 문항에서 별도의 기준을 적용하도록 명시한 경우에는 그 기준을 적용하여 정답을 구해야 합니다.
8. **시험시간 관리의 책임은 응시자 본인에게 있습니다.**

   ※ 문제책은 시험종료 후 가지고 갈 수 있습니다.

ⓘ 정답공개 및 이의제기 안내

1. 정답공개: 정답가안 4.4.(토) 13:30 / 최종정답 4.13.(월) 18:00 / 사이버국가고시센터
2. 이의제기: 4.4.(토) 18:00 ~ 4.7.(화) 18:00 / 사이버국가고시센터

   ■ 구체적인 이의제기 방법은 정답가안 공개 시 공지 예정
3. 가산점 등록기간: 4.4.(토) 13:30 ~ 4.6.(월) 21:00
4. 가산점 등록방법: 사이버국가고시센터 ➜ [원서접수 → 가산점 등록/확인]

영 어

[1~5] 밑줄 친 부분에 들어갈 말로 가장 적절한 것을 고르시오.

1.

The company's financial situation remains __________, with rising debts and an uncertain market outlook threatening its survival.

① precarious
② exceptional
③ relieved
④ imminent

2.

The judge ruled that the lawsuit was based on __________ claims that lacked any factual evidence, ultimately deciding that it did not merit further consideration in court.

① authentic
② feasible
③ spurious
④ definite

3.

If Google's new quantum chip 'Willow' __________ earlier, the breakthrough in computational speed would have occurred much sooner than expected.

① was released
② had been released
③ had released
④ released

4.

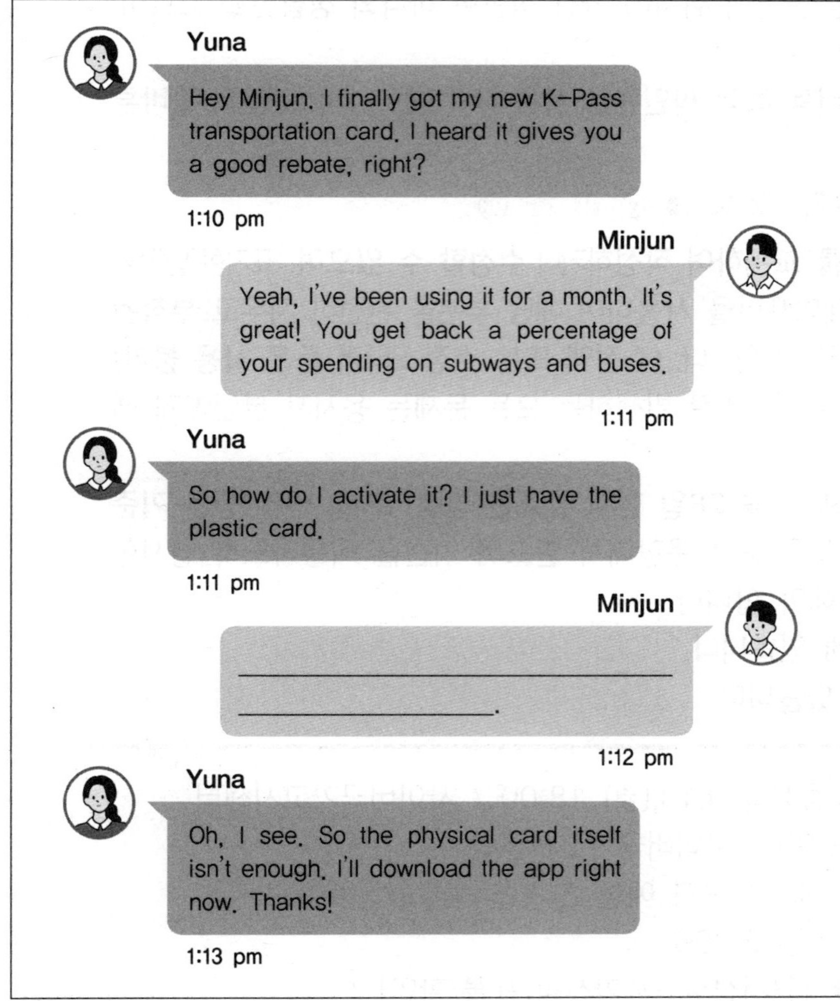

① The rebate is automatically applied when you tap the card
② You need to register the card in the K-Pass app
③ You have to visit the community center to prove your address
④ I think it's only available for people who live in Seoul

5.

A: Hi. You wanted to discuss your work plan? You mentioned something about working from abroad.

B: Yes, thank you for making time. I saw the company is now supporting the new 'Digital Nomad' visa. I'd like to apply to work from Spain for three months.

A: Spain is great. I'm open to the idea, as your performance has been excellent. Are there any specific concerns you've thought about?

B: __________

A: That's a valid point. Our core meeting hours are 2 PM to 5 PM KST. As long as you can guarantee your attendance for those, I'm fine with you managing the rest of your hours flexibly.

B: That's perfect. I can definitely manage that. Thank you!

① I'm worried that my salary might be cut significantly.
② I'm not sure if I can find a good apartment there.
③ My main concern is the time difference for team meetings.
④ I think I will be more productive working in a new environment.

[6~7] 다음 글을 읽고 물음에 답하시오.

The Hague Conference on Private International Law (HCCH) is a global inter-governmental organization. It serves as a nexus for various legal traditions, developing and servicing multilateral legal instruments that respond to global needs. The core mission of the HCCH is the <u>progressive</u> unification of the rules of private international law.

Unlike public international law, which governs relationships between States, private international law addresses cross-border legal issues between private persons and entities. The HCCH drafts international conventions and protocols that provide clarity and certainty in areas such as international child abduction, intercountry adoption, and the recognition of foreign judgments. This legal framework facilitates international trade, travel, and personal mobility by reducing the legal obstacles inherent in cross-border interactions.

6. 밑줄 친 progressive의 의미와 가장 가까운 것은?

① obstinate
② lavish
③ passive
④ gradual

7. 윗글의 목적으로 가장 적절한 것은?

① to present recent HCCH initiatives on cross-border family law
② to differentiate between public and private international law
③ to describe the fundamental mission and function of the HCCH
④ to explain the ongoing development of new HCCH conventions

[8~9] 다음 글을 읽고 물음에 답하시오.

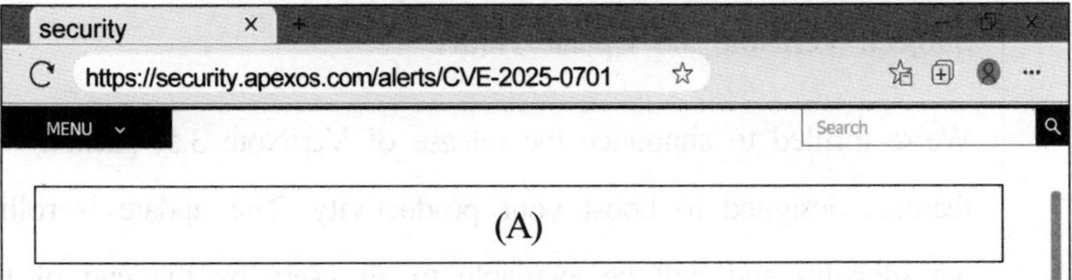

(A)

A critical zero-day vulnerability, designated CVE-2025-0701, has been identified in the kernel of the ApexOS enterprise operating system. This vulnerability allows for privilege escalation, enabling a local unprivileged attacker to gain root-level access. The exploit is currently being actively leveraged in the wild in targeted attacks. Due to the sophistication of the exploit, traditional heuristic-based detection systems may fail to identify the intrusion.

Immediate mitigation is imperative. While a permanent patch is under development, we have released an interim security script that restricts the system calls being exploited. System administrators are strongly advised to deploy this script without delay. It is crucial to understand that this is a temporary workaround, not a comprehensive solution. Organizations should also audit system logs for any anomalous activity indicative of a prior compromise.

8. (A)에 들어갈 윗글의 제목으로 가장 적절한 것은?

① Best Practices for Detecting Kernel-Level Intrusions

② New Features in the ApexOS Kernel

③ Emergence of a New Heuristic Detection System

④ Urgent Security Alert: ApexOS Kernel Vulnerability

9. 윗글의 내용과 일치하지 않는 것은?

① The vulnerability lets an attacker gain top-level access.

② The exploit hasn't been seen in real-world attacks yet.

③ A temporary security script is available to address the immediate threat.

④ A complete and permanent solution to this issue is still in preparation.

10. 밑줄 친 부분 중 어법상 옳지 않은 것은?

The number of tourists visiting the island ① <u>has increased</u> steadily over the past decade. This surge in tourism has boosted the local economy, creating numerous job opportunities for residents. However, environmentalists worry that the influx of visitors ② <u>is causing</u> damage to the delicate ecosystem. They argue that sustainable tourism practices ③ <u>should be implemented</u> to preserve the island's natural beauty. A number of strict regulations ④ <u>has been introduced</u> recently.

11. 다음 글의 내용과 일치하지 않는 것은?

Brooklyn Arts Council Presents: Art in the Park Fall Workshop

Date: Saturday, October 28, 2026
Time: 11:00 AM - 4:00 PM (Rain date: Sunday, Oct 29)
Location: Prospect Park (near the Boathouse)

Unleash your creativity this autumn! The Brooklyn Arts Council (BAC) invites families, students, and artists of all ages to our annual "Art in the Park" workshop. This year, we are focusing on natural materials and sustainable art.

Activities Include:
* Leaf Printing & Collage: Use fallen leaves to create stunning prints. (All materials provided).
* Clay Sculpting: Learn basic sculpting techniques using air-dry clay. (Suitable for ages 8+).
* Community Mural: Join us in creating large murals that will be on display in the park for a week.

Registration:
This event is FREE, but registration is required to ensure we have enough supplies. Please register on our website by October 25. On-site registration is only possible if the space allows it.

This program is supported, in part, by public funds from the NYC Department of Cultural Affairs.

① The event will be postponed to the following day in case of rain.

② This year's workshop theme includes the use of natural materials.

③ A large mural created by participants will be displayed in the park.

④ The program is supported by an individual artist.

12. 밑줄 친 부분 중 어법상 옳지 않은 것은?

Despite the heavy rain, the outdoor concert continued as scheduled, with thousands of fans ① <u>cheering</u> for their favorite band. The organizers ensured that safety measures ② <u>were in place</u> to prevent any accidents. However, some attendees complained that the sound quality was poor due to the weather conditions, ③ <u>making</u> it hard to hear the lyrics. The band promised to return next year when the weather ④ <u>will be</u> better.

13. 다음 글의 목적으로 가장 적절한 것은?

This notice is to inform the public regarding a change to a previously scheduled event.

On October 9, 2026, the Department of Transportation (DOT) published an official notice in the Federal Register (90 FR 48212). That earlier notice announced a public meeting of the United States Department of Transportation Advisory Board, which was scheduled to be held on Wednesday, October 22, 2026.

Due to unforeseen circumstances, this new notice serves to announce the cancellation of that specific public meeting. We apologize for any inconvenience caused to those who planned to attend or prepare materials for the session. Any future rescheduling will be announced separately, with updates provided through official DOT channels, including the Federal Register.

Please monitor these updates closely to ensure you catch new announcements as soon as they are released.

① to schedule a new Advisory Board meeting
② to announce the cancellation of a previously scheduled meeting
③ to publish the results of the October 22 meeting
④ to release the list of attendees who canceled their participation

14. 다음 글의 주제로 가장 적절한 것은?

Social sciences have been grappling with a "replication crisis," where findings from many foundational studies, particularly in social psychology, fail to be reproduced in subsequent experiments. This has cast doubt on the reliability of a significant body of published research. This crisis, however, has not been purely destructive; it has acted as a necessary catalyst for methodological reform. In response, a powerful movement toward "open science" has emerged. This movement champions robust practices such as pre-registering study protocols, sharing raw data and code publicly, and fostering collaborations to conduct large-scale replication studies. These practices aim to enhance transparency and rigor, ultimately rebuilding the credibility of the scientific process itself rather than just accepting published findings at face value.

① the destructive impact of the replication crisis on science
② the necessity of methodological reform via open science
③ the replication divide in social sciences
④ the specific psychological studies that failed to replicate

15. 다음 글의 내용과 일치하는 것은?

Subject: VeriNote 3.5 Update Notice

We're thrilled to announce the release of VeriNote 3.5, packed with features designed to boost your productivity. The update is rolling out globally and will be available to all users by the end of this week.

Key Feature: Smart Summaries

Tired of long meeting notes? Our new AI-powered "Smart Summaries" feature condenses any note into a concise, easy-to-read summary. This feature is immediately available to all Premium Plan subscribers. Standard (free) users are not provided access to the feature.

Additional Improvements:
* Stylus response time has improved, making writing smoother.
* More project management templates are now available.
* Archived notes now appear correctly in search results.

Important Information

To access these features, the application must be updated to version 3.5. Support for iOS 14 has been discontinued, and users on iOS 14 must upgrade their operating system to continue receiving updates.

① This update is available only in countries with strong internet connectivity.
② Access to the Smart Summaries tool is restricted to paid members.
③ The handwriting recognition feature in notes has not been improved in this update.
④ iOS 14 users can't use the features even after upgrading.

16. 다음 글의 흐름상 어색한 문장은?

Often overlooked in global climate models, tiny high-altitude ponds in the Andes mountains may play an outsized role in the global carbon cycle. ① Recent research indicates that these seemingly insignificant bodies of water are hotspots for microbial activity, processing large amounts of organic carbon from the surrounding landscape. ② The unique geology of the Andes features steep vertical slopes and diverse microclimates, which heavily influence local weather patterns. ③ Their cold temperatures and shallow depths cause carbon to decompose slowly, allowing these ponds to function as long-term carbon sinks. ④ As the region warms, scientists worry that this stored carbon could instead be released rapidly as methane, turning these sinks into major carbon sources. This discovery highlights the urgent need to incorporate these small-scale aquatic systems into future climate projections.

17. 주어진 문장이 들어갈 위치로 가장 적절한 것은?

> Researchers demonstrated that by inhibiting a specific enzyme, they could block short-term memory formation entirely, yet long-term memories still formed.

> The prevailing scientific theory of memory formation has long suggested a linear process. (①) This model holds that short-term memories (STM) are stored temporarily before being consolidated, over time, into stable long-term memories (LTM). (②) However, a late 2024 study from the Max Planck Florida Institute has fundamentally challenged this "single pathway" model. (③) This discovery is akin to finding a secret, parallel pathway to the brain's "permanent gallery" that bypasses the "temporary exhibit" of short-term memory. (④) This finding implies that LTM can be created independently, revising our entire understanding of how memory functions and potentially opening new avenues for treating memory disorders.

18. 주어진 글 다음에 이어질 글의 순서로 가장 적절한 것은?

> Psychologists have long studied the "Spotlight Effect," a phenomenon where individuals overestimate how much others notice their appearance or behavior.

> (A) To test this, researchers asked participants to wear an embarrassing t-shirt and enter a room full of strangers. The participants predicted that at least half of the people would notice the shirt.
>
> (B) In reality, less than 20 percent of the observers actually noticed. This discrepancy confirms that people are generally too focused on their own internal worlds to pay close attention to the minor details of others.
>
> (C) This cognitive bias stems from egocentricity. Since we are the center of our own universe, we instinctively assume we are the center of everyone else's, leading to unnecessary social anxiety.

① (A)—(C)—(B)   ② (B)—(A)—(C)

③ (B)—(C)—(A)   ④ (C)—(A)—(B)

[19~20] 밑줄 친 부분에 들어갈 말로 가장 적절한 것을 고르시오.

19.

> _________________________ is often far more complex for an adult than for a child. An adult learner typically possesses a highly structured cognitive framework and a native language that is deeply entrenched. This existing linguistic system often interferes with the acquisition of new phonological and grammatical rules. In contrast, a child's brain exhibits greater plasticity, absorbing linguistic patterns without the filter of a pre-existing language. Furthermore, social dynamics differ profoundly. Children are often immersed in play-based interactions where language errors are tolerated. Adults, however, face higher stakes; they require language for complex, meaningful exchanges and may feel social pressure to perform accurately, which can inhibit the natural learning process.

① The retention of specialized vocabulary

② The challenge of acquiring a second language

③ The motivation to engage in social interaction

④ The reliance on non-verbal cues in adult communication

20.

> A strategic pre-reading scan of a text, or 'skimming,' often reveals paratextual features that can significantly aid comprehension. Section headings, for instance, function as conceptual signposts, previewing the thematic contours of subsequent discussions. The typographical landscape itself is informative: paragraph length can imply the depth of topical treatment, while sentence complexity hints at the cognitive load the text will demand. Furthermore, visual highlighting — such as boldface, italics, or underlining — is a deliberate authorial intervention designed to direct the reader's attention to key concepts. Conversely, an absence of such aids suggests a greater onus on the reader to diligently excavate the core arguments. Illustrations and bibliographic references also provide metadata, indicating breaks for graphic information processing or _________________________.
> By internalizing these external cues, a reader can navigate even the most dense academic terrain with greater efficiency and insight.

① the scholarly rigor and academic grounding of the work

② instructions on how to purchase the next edition

③ simple summaries intended for a general audience

④ a quick way to skip the difficult core arguments

수고하셨습니다.
당신의 합격을 응원합니다.

2026 공무원 시험 대비 실전동형 모의고사
영 어
∎ 제5회 ∎

응시번호	
성 명	

제1과목	국어	제2과목	영어	제3과목	한국사
제4과목		제5과목			

⚠ 응시자 주의사항

1. **시험시작 전 시험문제를 열람하는 행위나 시험종료 후 답안을 작성하는 행위를 한 사람은** 「공무원임용시험령」 **제51조에 의거 부정행위자로 처리됩니다.**
2. **답안지 책형 표기는 시험시작 전 감독관의 지시에 따라 문제책 앞면에 인쇄된 문제책형을 확인한 후, 답안지 책형란에 해당 책형(1개)을 '●'로 표기하여야 합니다.**
3. **답안은 문제책 표지의 과목 순서에 따라 답안지에 인쇄된 순서(제1·2·3·4·5과목)에 맞추어 표기해야 하며, 과목 순서를 바꾸어 표기한 경우에도 문제책 표지의 과목 순서대로 채점되므로 유의하시기 바랍니다.**
4. **시험이 시작되면 문제를 주의 깊게 읽은 후, 문항의 취지에 가장 적합한 하나의 정답만을 고르며, 문제내용에 관한 질문은 할 수 없습니다.**
5. **답안지의 모든 기재 및 표기 사항은 컴퓨터용 흑색 싸인펜을 사용하며, 반드시 <보기>의 올바른 표기 방식으로 답안을 작성해야 합니다.**

   <보기> 올바른 표기: ● 잘못된 표기: ⓥ ⊗ ◑ ⊙ ⑾ ⊖ ③

6. **답안을 잘못 표기하였을 경우에는 답안지를 교체하여 작성하거나 수정할 수 있으며, 표기한 답안을 수정할 때는 응시자 본인이 가져온 수정테이프만을 사용하여 해당 부분을 완전히 지우고 부착된 수정테이프가 떨어지지 않도록 손으로 눌러주어야 합니다. (수정액 또는 수정스티커 등은 사용 불가)**
   - **불량한 수정테이프의 사용과 불완전한 수정처리로 발생하는 모든 문제는 응시자 본인에게 책임이 있습니다.**
7. **법령, 고시, 판례 등에 관한 문제는 2026년 2월 28일 현재 유효한 법령, 고시, 판례 등을 기준으로 정답을 구해야 합니다. 다만, 개별 과목 또는 문항에서 별도의 기준을 적용하도록 명시한 경우에는 그 기준을 적용하여 정답을 구해야 합니다.**
8. **시험시간 관리의 책임은 응시자 본인에게 있습니다.**
   ※ 문제책은 시험종료 후 가지고 갈 수 있습니다.

ⓘ 정답공개 및 이의제기 안내

1. 정답공개: 정답가안 4.4.(토) 13:30 / 최종정답 4.13.(월) 18:00 / 사이버국가고시센터
2. 이의제기: 4.4.(토) 18:00 ~ 4.7.(화) 18:00 / 사이버국가고시센터
   - 구체적인 이의제기 방법은 정답가안 공개 시 공지 예정
3. 가산점 등록기간: 4.4.(토) 13:30 ~ 4.6.(월) 21:00
4. 가산점 등록방법: 사이버국가고시센터 ➜ [원서접수 → 가산점 등록/확인]

영 어

[1~5] 밑줄 친 부분에 들어갈 말로 가장 적절한 것을 고르시오.

1.

Regular stretching and light exercise can help ___________ chronic back pain that gradually accumulates from prolonged hours of sedentary desk work.

① exacerbate
② alleviate
③ obscure
④ promote

2.

Because the initial symptoms were highly ___________ and resembled those of other disorders, clinicians struggled to make an accurate early diagnosis.

① plain
② coherent
③ equivocal
④ introverted

3.

Neither of the policies intended to improve public transportation by reducing traffic congestion and expanding access to affordable transit options ___________ the expected outcomes so far.

① have been produced
② having produced
③ have produced
④ has produced

4.

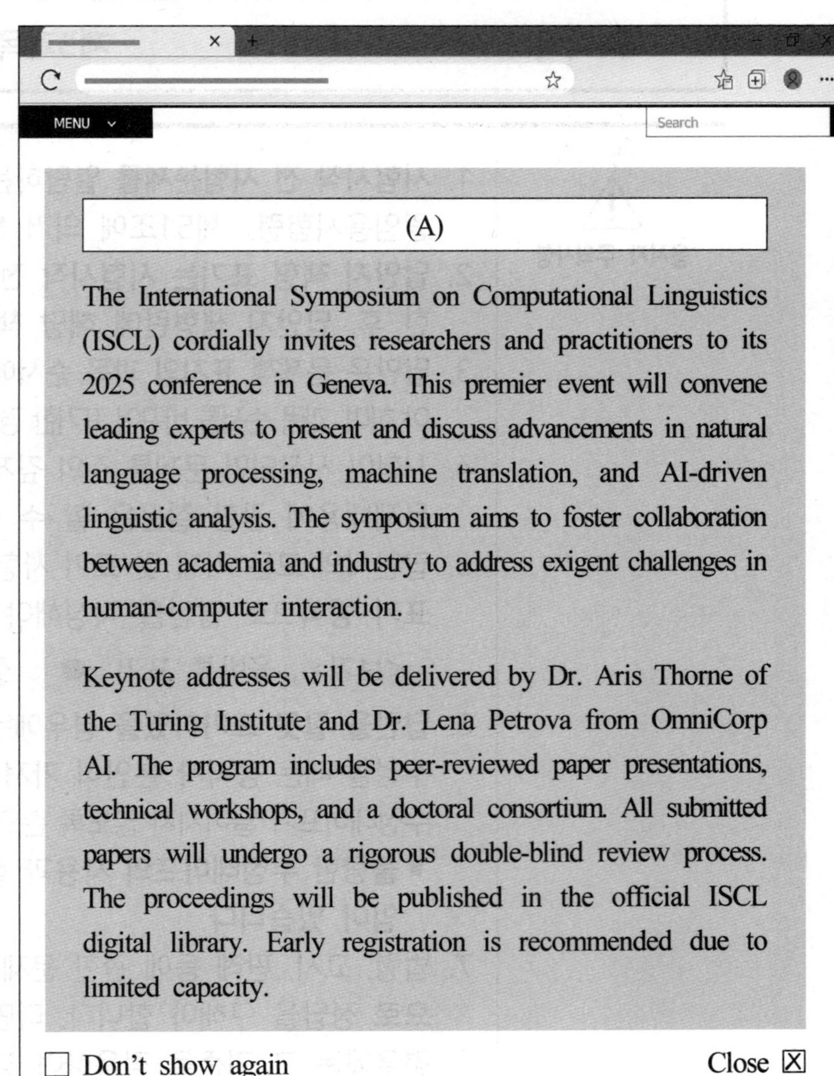

① Why couldn't you grade them properly?
② Please reprint the exam papers.
③ Please send me those answers.
④ I don't think the grading is really necessary.

5.

A: Your presentation was clear, but could you tell me where the data on the last slide came from? We need the exact source for the budget review.

B: I believe it's from the regional survey, but I'm not completely sure. ___________________________________.

A: Yes, having the exact source is essential to avoid any issues during the review.

B: I see. I'll verify it quickly and send it to you right away.

A: Great. Your presentation was solid, so the review should go smoothly.

① I'll check it and let you know the correct source
② Then I will conduct the survey again
③ I will prepare again and give a more polished presentation
④ Please let me know as soon as the review results are released

[6~7] 다음 글을 읽고 물음에 답하시오.

(A)

The International Symposium on Computational Linguistics (ISCL) cordially invites researchers and practitioners to its 2025 conference in Geneva. This premier event will convene leading experts to present and discuss advancements in natural language processing, machine translation, and AI-driven linguistic analysis. The symposium aims to foster collaboration between academia and industry to address exigent challenges in human-computer interaction.

Keynote addresses will be delivered by Dr. Aris Thorne of the Turing Institute and Dr. Lena Petrova from OmniCorp AI. The program includes peer-reviewed paper presentations, technical workshops, and a doctoral consortium. All submitted papers will undergo a rigorous double-blind review process. The proceedings will be published in the official ISCL digital library. Early registration is recommended due to limited capacity.

☐ Don't show again   Close ☒

6. (A)에 들어갈 윗글의 제목으로 가장 적절한 것은?

① A Review of Advances in Computational Linguistics
② The Societal Impact of New NLP Technologies
③ OmniCorp AI's New Machine Translation System
④ Call for Papers: The ISCL Conference in Geneva

7. 윗글에서 심포지엄에 관한 내용과 일치하는 것은?

① 계산언어학을 전공하는 학생들을 초대하고 있다.
② 박사과정 학생을 위한 별도의 프로그램은 제공되지 않는다.
③ 심사위원에게 저자의 신원 정보는 제공되지 않는다.
④ 학회 자료집은 실물 인쇄본으로만 제작되어 배포될 것이다.

8. 다음 글의 내용과 일치하지 않는 것은?

Echoes of the Future: Digital Art & Identity

Exhibition Run: October 18, 2025 – March 16, 2026
Location: Griffin Galleries (Main Building, 3rd Floor)

The MCA Chicago proudly presents "Echoes of the Future," a new major exhibition exploring how digital technology has radically reshaped contemporary identity. Featuring over 40 works by 25 international artists, the exhibition includes immersive installations, AI-generated art, and virtual reality experiences.

Admission:
- General Admission: $22 (Adults), $15 (Students/Seniors)
- Special Exhibition Surcharge: +$8
- MCA Members & Youth (18 and under): FREE (Both general admission and exhibition).

Special Exhibition:
- Artist Talk: Join artist Kenji Tanaka for a discussion on his AI-driven work. (Nov 1, 2025, 6 PM. Separate registration required).
- Members-Only Preview: MCA Members can preview the exhibition on October 17, 2025, one day before the public opening.

① More than 40 works by a total of 25 artists are on display.

② An additional fee is required to view the special exhibition.

③ MCA members receive free entry to both.

④ The special exhibition can be previewed by everyone on October 17.

[9~10] 밑줄 친 부분 중 어법상 옳지 않은 것을 고르시오.

9.

The novel, written in the 19th century, portrays the struggles of the working class. The author vividly describes the harsh conditions ① in which they lived. Readers can easily sympathize with the characters, ② whose lives are filled with hardship. The book, ③ despite its age, remains relevant today. It reminds us ④ of that social justice is an ongoing pursuit.

10.

The environmental organization is dedicated ① to protecting endangered species. They work tirelessly to preserve habitats ② destroying by human activity. Their efforts have led to the recovery of several populations. They believe that every creature plays a vital role in the ecosystem and deserves ③ to exist. Educating the public is also a key part of ④ their mission.

[11~12] 다음 글을 읽고 물음에 답하시오.

Monetary Policy Committee (MPC) Mandate

The Monetary Policy Committee (MPC) is entrusted with the formulation of national monetary policy, primarily aimed at maintaining price stability. This mandate requires a delicate balancing act: a policy stance that is too accommodative may curtail long-term growth by fueling inflationary pressures, whereas an excessively restrictive stance could <u>stifle</u> economic activity.

The Committee's decisions are grounded in a comprehensive analysis of a wide array of economic indicators, including but not limited to employment data, consumer price indices, and GDP growth projections. The MPC operates with a forward-looking perspective, anticipating future economic trends to preemptively adjust policy levers. The rationale behind each decision is communicated transparently to the public to manage expectations and bolster the credibility of the policy framework. This transparency is vital for anchoring inflation expectations, which is a key component of effective monetary policy.

11. 밑줄 친 stifle의 의미와 가장 가까운 것은?

① forfeit
② relinquish
③ hamper
④ augment

12. 윗글의 목적으로 가장 적절한 것은?

① to inform you of the latest rate adjustments announced by the MPC

② to explain the role and operational principles of the MPC

③ to evaluate the administration's monetary measures

④ to provide a detailed forecast of future economic trends

13. 다음 글의 주제로 가장 적절한 것은?

Recent advances in in vitro biotechnology have enabled the cultivation of cerebral organoids—three-dimensional clusters of human stem cells that self-assemble into brain-like tissue. While these "mini-brains" are valuable for studying neurodevelopment and testing new therapeutics, their increasing sophistication has pushed the field into an ethical gray zone. As they begin to show neural activity similar to that of fetal brains, scientists must confront a crucial question: what is the moral status of an entity that may be approaching a rudimentary form of sentience? Existing regulations, designed for far simpler tissue cultures, are inadequate, creating an urgent need for updated ethical guidelines.

① scientific breakthroughs behind cerebral organoids

② inadequacy of current scientific regulations

③ emerging ethical dilemma of sentient "mini-brains"

④ potential of organoids to cure neurodevelopmental disorder

14. 다음 글의 내용과 일치하는 것은?

As the temperature drops, the Greenwood Community Center will host its annual event, "Winter Warmth," from Nov. 10 to Dec. 15. The event will distribute new or clean winter coats, blankets, and gloves for families in need.

To ensure the drive's success, we are seeking volunteers for two key roles.

1. Donation-sorting (In-Center):
- Tasks: Receive, sort, and organize donated items at the community center.
- Shifts: Flexible 3-hour shifts, Monday - Friday (9 AM - 6 PM).
- Requirements: Must be able to lift up to 20 pounds. Training provided on-site.

2. Collection box operation (Remote/Community):
- Tasks: Set up and monitor a collection box at your local business, school, or organization.
- Commitment: The collection box must be operated for at least two weeks during the event.
- Note: Collected items should be delivered directly to the center once a week.

To sign up, please visit our website [link] by November 5th.

① This event accepts only monetary donations, not items.
② Donation sorting volunteers must lift the required weight.
③ One day is possible to participate in the operation of the collection box.
④ The collected items are picked up directly by the Center.

15. 다음 글의 목적으로 가장 적절한 것은?

	Send	Preview	Save
To	Valued Customer		
From	StreamZone Customer Support		
Date	April 8, 2026		
Subject	Important Update		

My PC | Browse

Times New | 10pt | G G G G G

Dear StreamZone User,

We are writing to inform you of an upcoming update to the StreamZone Privacy Policy, which will take effect on December 1, 2026.

This update is part of our ongoing commitment to transparency. We have reorganized the policy to make it easier to understand how we collect and use your data. Key changes include:
* There is a clearer explanation for data sharing with advertising partners.
* In the "Account Settings" menu, we have added a new option to manage your personal data preferences.

No action is required from you. Your continued use of the StreamZone service after December 1st signifies your agreement to the new policy. We encourage you to review the full policy [link] at your convenience. If you have questions, please contact our support team.

Thank you for being a part of StreamZone.

① to promote a newly released program
② to request that users update their personal information
③ to apologize for a data breach and compensation plan
④ to give prior notice of changes to the privacy policy

16. 주어진 문장이 들어갈 위치로 가장 적절한 것은?

> This involves developing an awareness of one's own cognitive load and emotional reactions to technology, rather than just focusing on the technical skills.

> As artificial intelligence becomes ubiquitous, media education systems are racing to incorporate "AI literacy." (①) Traditionally, this has meant focusing on the vital technical components of AI applications and innovation work. (②) However, recent pedagogical research from 2025 suggests this approach is incomplete, as it often disregards the psychological factors and anxieties students face. (③) To address this gap, educators are integrating "digital mindfulness" practices into the curriculum. (④) Studies show this integrated approach not only improves focus but also builds the self-confidence and collaboration skills necessary to master AI tools effectively.

17. 다음 글의 흐름상 어색한 문장은?

> In a novel blend of archaeology and conservation science, researchers are using ancient oyster shells to reconstruct past marine ecosystems and guide modern restoration. ① By analyzing the chemical composition and growth rings of millennia-old shells, scientists can trace historical changes in water conditions. ② This field, called zooarchaeology, offers essential baseline data on what coastal environments were like before major human impacts. ③ Such ancient data help set realistic goals for oyster reef restoration, a key strategy for improving water quality and protecting shorelines. ④ Oysters are filter feeders that consume plankton by drawing water over their gills, benefiting the surrounding ecosystem. This approach shows how archaeological records can serve as valuable tools in addressing today's environmental challenges.

18. 주어진 글 다음에 이어질 글의 순서로 가장 적절한 것은?

> The central dogma of molecular biology describes the flow of genetic information, summarized as "DNA makes RNA, and RNA makes protein."

> (A) The resulting messenger RNA (mRNA) then separates from the DNA, undergoes basic processing, and leaves the nucleus for the cytoplasm.
>
> (B) At a ribosome, the mRNA is read in translation as transfer RNA brings the appropriate amino acids, which are linked to form a polypeptide chain.
>
> (C) The process begins with transcription. In the nucleus, part of the DNA unwinds, allowing an enzyme to build a complementary RNA strand.

① (A)－(C)－(B)　　　　② (B)－(A)－(C)

③ (C)－(A)－(B)　　　　④ (C)－(B)－(A)

[19~20] 밑줄 친 부분에 들어갈 말로 가장 적절한 것을 고르시오.

19.

> In our society, transparency is a virtue, and we assume individuals accurately represent themselves. While digital communication has complicated this, historically, using a pseudonym was viewed with suspicion. Now, however, in cyberspace, the absence of physical cues like facial expressions and body language makes it difficult to assess character immediately. This lack of visual and auditory verification creates a high risk of being targeted by malicious actors. Therefore, users must recognize that virtual environments differ fundamentally from face-to-face encounters. Until trust is established through consistent interaction with the person behind the screen, _________________.
> This practice is not an act of deceit but a prudent measure of self-protection in an environment where verification is limited.

① revealing your real name is the best way to foster trust

② maintaining anonymity is both a reasonable and ethical choice

③ using a pseudonym should be avoided for social accountability

④ relying on digital instincts is enough to discern true nature

20.

> The evolution of human intelligence presents a compelling puzzle. Why are humans endowed with faculties for abstract thought, such as understanding calculus or composing symphonies, when such skills offered no apparent survival advantage in our primitive ancestral environment? The 'social brain hypothesis' offers a powerful solution. It posits that our intellect evolved not primarily to solve practical problems, but to navigate the complex web of social dynamics — to cooperate, deceive, detect deceit, and manage relationships. According to this view, the primary evolutionary pressure was ____________________________. Thus, what mattered most was not absolute cleverness, but being slightly more socially adept than one's rivals.

① the need to master the physical environment

② the ability to outwit and manipulate other humans

③ the pressure to share social knowledge

④ the rise of symbolic cultural communication

수고하셨습니다.
당신의 합격을 응원합니다.

2026 공무원 시험 대비 실전동형 모의고사
영어
▌제6회 ▌

응시번호

성 명

제1과목	국어	제2과목	<u>영어</u>	제3과목	한국사
제4과목		제5과목			

응시자 주의사항

1. **시험시작 전 시험문제를 열람하는 행위나 시험종료 후 답안을 작성하는 행위를 한 사람**은 「공무원임용시험령」 제51조에 의거 **부정행위자로 처리됩니다.**
2. **답안지 책형 표기는 시험시작 전 감독관의 지시에 따라 문제책 앞면에 인쇄된 문제책형을 확인**한 후, 답안지 책형란에 해당 책형(1개)을 '●'로 표기하여야 합니다.
3. **답안은 문제책 표지의 과목 순서에 따라 답안지에 인쇄된 순서(제1·2·3·4·5과목)에 맞추어 표기해야 하며, 과목 순서를 바꾸어 표기한 경우에도 문제책 표지의 과목 순서대로 채점되므로 유의하시기 바랍니다.**
4. 시험이 시작되면 문제를 주의 깊게 읽은 후, **문항의 취지에 가장 적합한 하나의 정답만을 고르며,** 문제내용에 관한 질문은 할 수 없습니다.
5. 답안지의 모든 기재 및 표기 사항은 **컴퓨터용 흑색 싸인펜을 사용**하며, 반드시 <보기>의 **올바른 표기** 방식으로 답안을 작성해야 합니다.

   <보기> 올바른 표기: ● 잘못된 표기: ⊘ ⊗ ◑ ⊙ ⑪ ⊖ ③

6. **답안을 잘못 표기하였을 경우에는 답안지를 교체하여 작성하거나 수정할 수 있으며,** 표기한 답안을 수정할 때는 응시자 본인이 가져온 수정테이프만을 사용하여 해당 부분을 완전히 지우고 부착된 수정테이프가 떨어지지 않도록 손으로 눌러주어야 합니다. (수정액 또는 수정스티커 등은 사용 불가)
   - **불량한 수정테이프의 사용과 불완전한 수정처리로 발생하는 모든 문제는 응시자 본인에게 책임이 있습니다.**
7. 법령, 고시, 판례 등에 관한 문제는 **2026년 2월 28일 현재 유효한 법령, 고시, 판례 등을 기준**으로 정답을 구해야 합니다. 다만, 개별 과목 또는 문항에서 별도의 기준을 적용하도록 명시한 경우에는 그 기준을 적용하여 정답을 구해야 합니다.
8. **시험시간 관리의 책임은 응시자 본인에게 있습니다.**

※ 문제책은 시험종료 후 가지고 갈 수 있습니다.

정답공개 및 이의제기 안내

1. 정답공개: 정답가안 4.4.(토) 13:30 / 최종정답 4.13.(월) 18:00 / 사이버국가고시센터
2. 이의제기: 4.4.(토) 18:00 ~ 4.7.(화) 18:00 / 사이버국가고시센터
   - 구체적인 이의제기 방법은 정답가안 공개 시 공지 예정
3. 가산점 등록기간: 4.4.(토) 13:30 ~ 4.6.(월) 21:00
4. 가산점 등록방법: 사이버국가고시센터 ➡ [원서접수 → 가산점 등록/확인]

영 어

[1~5] 밑줄 친 부분에 들어갈 말로 가장 적절한 것을 고르시오.

1.
> The researchers relied on high-resolution satellite imagery to conduct continuous surveillance of _________ regions that were largely inaccessible through conventional field methods.

① gloomy
② persistent
③ distant
④ varied

2.
> It required multiple rounds of deliberation to _________ the residents that the new policy would ultimately yield substantial benefits for the broader community.

① admire
② persuade
③ appoint
④ classify

3.
> Had the government implemented stricter regulations on carbon emissions a decade ago, we _____________ such extreme weather patterns today.

① would not face
② would not have faced
③ would not be facing
④ will not be facing

4.
> A: I'm really worried about our annual outdoor market this weekend.
> B: Why? All the vendors are confirmed, and the promotion is going well.
> A: I just checked the weather forecast. It says there's a 90% chance of a severe thunderstorm on Saturday afternoon.
> B: Oh, no. That's a disaster. All our setup is outdoors. What should we do?
> A: _______________________________________
> B: That seems like the best option for now. We can't just cancel everything.
> A: Exactly. I'll call the community center right now and see if their indoor hall is available.

① I think it's inevitable that we postpone the event until next month.
② Perhaps we can just provide extra tents to protect the products.
③ We should just take the risk. Forecasts are often wrong.
④ Let's ask about using the indoor hall as a backup.

5.

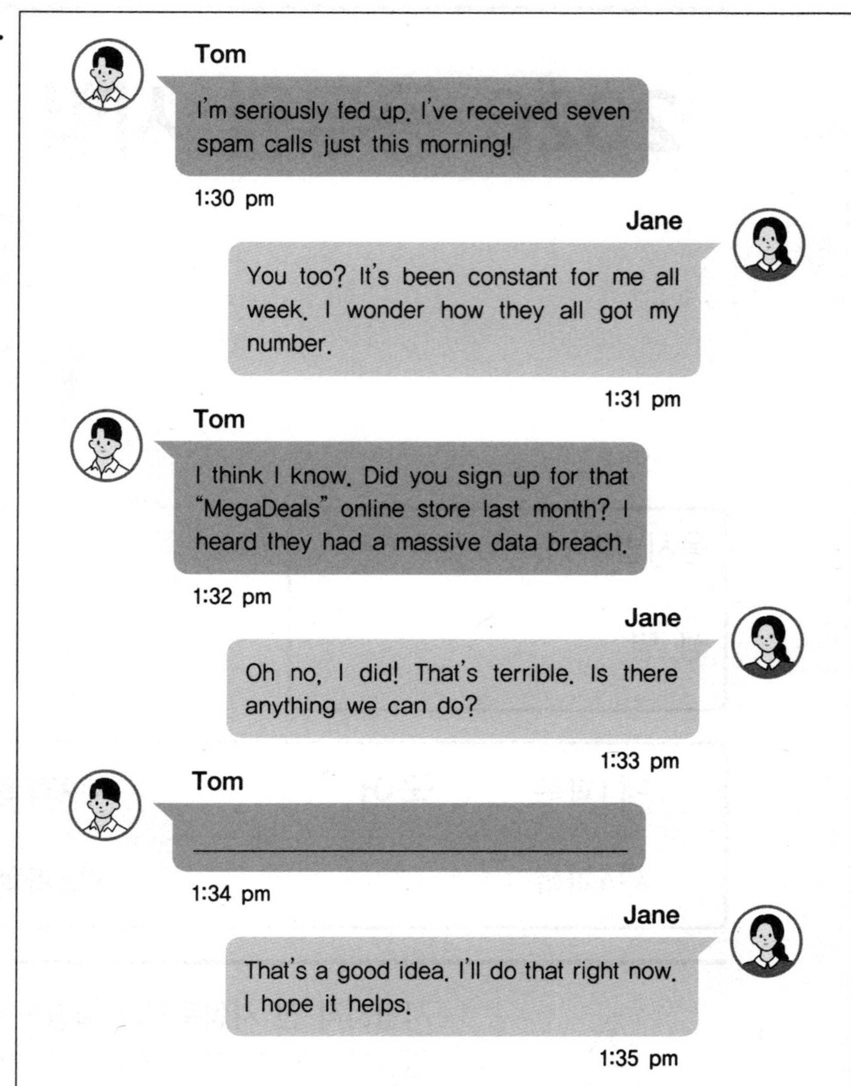

① I'm actually the one who leaked the data from that store.
② I'm going to install a good spam-blocking app right now.
③ You should probably just throw your phone away to stop the calls.
④ Why don't we call them back and sing opera until they hang up?

6. 다음 글의 목적으로 가장 적절한 것은?

> **The 25th Annual Destin Fall Festival**
>
> The City of Destin warmly invites all residents and visitors to join the 25th Annual Fall Festival, which will take place at the Destin Community Center on Monday, October 27, 2026, from 5:00 - 8:00 pm.
>
> To support our local food donation drive, we ask that each attendee bring one non-perishable food item for admission. The festival will feature booths with fun games and activities, a cakewalk, a costume contest, a jack-o'-lantern contest, and a variety of food available for purchase.
>
> Game and food tickets will be sold at 20 for $5. Registration for the costume contest will be held from 5:00 - 6:00 pm during the event. Carved pumpkins for the jack-o'-lantern contest must be dropped off before 3:00 pm for judging, which begins promptly at 5:00 pm.
>
> We look forward to seeing you there and celebrating the season together!

① to explain the purpose of the fall festival
② to provide guidelines for using the fall festival facilities
③ to offer tips on how to win the Halloween costume contest
④ to invite citizens to participate in the fall festival

[7~8] 다음 글을 읽고 물음에 답하시오.

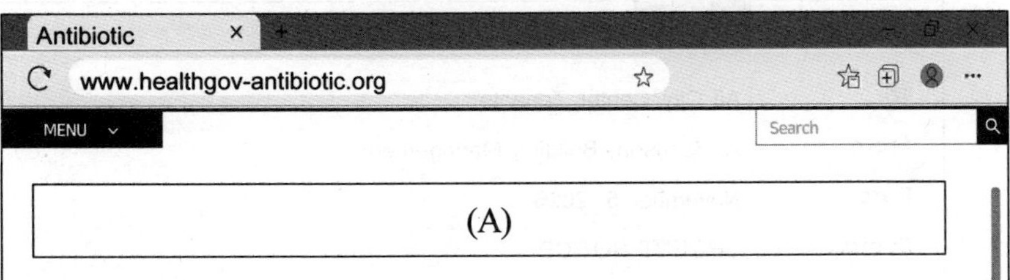

(A)

Our capacity to treat common infections is critically threatened by the rise of antimicrobial resistance (AMR). This phenomenon occurs when bacteria, viruses, and other pathogens evolve to defeat the drugs designed to kill them. A primary driver of AMR is the misuse and overuse of antibiotics. To preserve the efficacy of these life-saving medicines, a global shift in behavior is necessary.

The "Antibiotic Stewardship" campaign advocates for the responsible use of antibiotics among both healthcare providers and the public. This involves prescribing antibiotics only when necessary, based on diagnostic evidence, and completing the full prescribed course. For the public, it means understanding that antibiotics are ineffective against viral infections like the common cold and not pressuring physicians for prescriptions. This collective effort is paramount to slowing the emergence of drug-resistant strains.

7. (A)에 들어갈 윗글의 제목으로 가장 적절한 것은?

① The Hidden Threat Behind Everyday Antibiotic Use

② Preserving Our Last Defense Against AMR

③ Viral vs. Bacterial Infections: A Clinical Guide

④ Why Antibiotics Are Becoming Less Effective Over Time

8. 윗글의 내용과 일치하지 않는 것은?

① Modern medicine can still easily cure typical illnesses.

② Drug resistance stems mostly from improper medicine intake.

③ Medication should be given only based on lab results.

④ Both medical staff and laypeople must join this effort.

9. 밑줄 친 부분 중 어법상 옳지 않은 것은?

Telemedicine has become increasingly popular among the elderly population. However, many seniors are not used to ① handle digital devices, which creates a barrier to accessing care. To bridge this gap, community centers have started programs ② designed to educate them on digital literacy. These efforts are expected ③ to reduce the disparity in healthcare access ④ faced by older generations.

[10~11] 다음 글을 읽고 물음에 답하시오.

Annual Community Health Fair Notice

The Annual Community Health Fair is back to provide free medical services to local residents. Our goal is to promote early <u>detection</u> of diseases and encourage a healthy lifestyle for families.

The event will be held at the City Community Center this Saturday. Medical professionals will be on-site to offer consultations and perform various screenings. No insurance is required.

Screening Services

Service	Target Audience	Note
Vision Test	Children (Aged 5-12)	Includes free glasses prescription if needed
Blood Pressure	Adults (Aged 18+)	Consultation with a cardiologist available
Bone Density	Seniors (Aged 65+)	Results provided immediately on-site

While all services are free, registration is recommended to avoid long waiting times. Please bring a valid ID to check in at the front desk.

10. 밑줄 친 detection의 의미와 가장 가까운 것은?

① discovery   ② preservation

③ extraction   ④ screening

11. 윗글의 내용과 일치하지 않는 것은?

① 의료 전문가들이 현장에서 검진과 상담을 모두 제공한다.

② 7세 어린이는 시력 검사를 받을 수 있다.

③ 70세 노인이 골밀도 검사를 받더라도 결과를 즉시 확인할 수는 없다.

④ 서비스를 이용하기 위해 사전 등록이 권장된다.

12. 밑줄 친 부분 중 어법상 옳지 않은 것은?

The integration of AI in diagnostics ① <u>has significantly</u> improved accuracy. However, ② <u>remain</u> many ethical concerns about data privacy. This technology, which learns from vast datasets, ③ <u>is considered</u> a revolutionary tool by many experts, ④ <u>who</u> predict widespread adoption.

13. 다음 글의 내용과 일치하는 것은?

Bellingham Public Library: November 2026 Programs

Bellingham Public Library features special programs for children, teens and adults in November 2026, including a Stuffy Sleepover for children on Nov. 18, and a Book Club Social for adults on Nov. 15. The Library will also honor Native American Heritage Month. All Bellingham Public Library activities are free of charge.

* **Builders Club (Ages 4 ‑ 12):** Tuesday, November 4, 3:30 ‑ 5:00 pm. Join us for new monthly building challenges. All supplies are provided.
* **5th ‑ 8th Grade Book Group:** Meets on the second Thursday of each month. Snacks provided. Pre-registration is required as space is limited.
* **Sesame Street Workshop (Ages 3 ‑ 5 and caregivers):** Thursday, November 13, 5:00 ‑ 5:45 pm. A free, family-friendly workshop designed to help young children and their caregivers explore healthy digital habits together.

① The November programs are offered only for teens.
② All library activities are completely non-paid.
③ Participants in the Builders Club must bring their own materials.
④ Students can join the book group without signing up.

14. 다음 글의 주제로 가장 적절한 것은?

The concept of the "15-minute city," which envisions urban life where all essential amenities—work, shopping, education, and leisure—are accessible within a 15-minute walk or cycle, has gained significant traction globally. Proponents champion it as a paradigm for sustainability, fostering public health by reducing car dependency and enhancing community cohesion. This utopian vision, however, is encountering fierce backlash. Critics argue that the concept, particularly when enforced through zoning or digital monitoring, risks creating "urban enclosures" or "climate lockdowns." Concerns are mounting that this model could exacerbate socio-economic segregation, creating affluent, well-served bubbles while neglecting peripheral areas, and morphing a vision of convenience into a tool of surveillance and control.

① the benefits of reducing car dependency in urban areas
② the role of digital monitoring in modern city planning
③ the debate over the 15-minute city: livability vs. control
④ the historical evolution of sustainable urban design

15. 다음 글의 목적으로 가장 적절한 것은?

✎	**Send** Preview Save	

To	All City Center Tenants
From	A. Johnson, Building Management
Date	November 5, 2026
Subject	URGENT NOTICE

📎   [My PC] [Browse]

[Times New ▾] [10pt ▾] [G | G | *G* | G̲ | G]

Dear Tenants,

This is an important notification regarding the main passenger elevators (Elevators #1 and #2) in the City Center building. To ensure continued safety and reliability, we have scheduled mandatory annual maintenance. This work requires a complete shutdown of both main elevators.

* Date of Shutdown: Thursday, November 7, 2026
* Time: 10:00 AM to 4:00 PM (Estimated 6 hours)

During this period, all tenants and visitors must use the freight elevator (Elevator #3) located at the rear of the lobby. Please allocate extra time for your travel within the building, as this single elevator will service all floors. We have intentionally scheduled this work during mid-day hours to minimize disruption to morning and evening commutes.

We apologize for this unavoidable inconvenience and thank you for your understanding.

Sincerely,
A. Johnson

① to announce new elevator safety features
② to apologize for recent elevator malfunctions
③ to inform tenants of the scheduled elevator maintenance
④ to ask tenants to reduce their use of the main elevators

16. 다음 글의 흐름상 어색한 문장은?

The concept of "overeducation"—having more education than a job requires—is a growing issue in today's labor markets. ① Recent studies show that this problem is not random; a graduate's family background strongly affects the likelihood of being overeducated. ② Parental income and professional networks often give privileged graduates better access to jobs that match their skills. ③ Higher education institutions are increasingly revising curricula to emphasize practical skills and internships. ④ As a result, graduates from less affluent families, even with the same degrees, are more frequently pushed into positions that underuse their qualifications. This mismatch harms both individual career outcomes and the efficient use of human capital in the wider economy.

17. 주어진 문장이 들어갈 위치로 가장 적절한 것은?

> Evidence is also mounting from animal studies, with 2025 research on mice showing microplastics moving through their brains and blocking blood vessels.

> The pervasive nature of microplastic pollution is becoming increasingly clear, with new research highlighting its alarming penetration into the human body. (①) Scientists have now detected these tiny particles circulating in human blood, accumulating in the lungs, and even lodging deep within the liver. (②) Furthermore, recent studies have confirmed their presence in human placentas and testes, raising alarms about potential impacts on fetal development and reproductive health. (③) This accumulation has been linked to severe health issues, including increased risk of heart attacks, strokes, and inflammatory bowel disease. (④) While the full spectrum of these health risks is not yet fully categorized, the substantial data from recent clinical and laboratory findings provide a compelling case for urgent regulatory action.

18. 주어진 글 다음에 이어질 글의 순서로 가장 적절한 것은?

> The rapid rise of artificial intelligence—especially systems that mimic human conversation and reasoning—has pushed a once-philosophical question into urgent scientific focus: the nature of consciousness.

> (A) For this reason, scientists are intensifying efforts to find the neural signals linked to conscious experience. By identifying these patterns in humans, they aim to establish a measurable benchmark.
> (B) However, a major challenge remains. Even with such a benchmark, applying it to AI is difficult because silicon-based systems operate very differently from biological brains.
> (C) This question is no longer theoretical. As AI becomes more embedded in society, determining whether it could possess any form of subjective experience is essential for ethics and regulation. This requires understanding the biological basis of consciousness.

① (A)－(C)－(B)

② (B)－(A)－(C)

③ (C)－(A)－(B)

④ (C)－(B)－(A)

[19~20] 밑줄 친 부분에 들어갈 말로 가장 적절한 것을 고르시오.

19.

> _________________________ requires a profound level of cognitive discipline. Most individuals equate hearing with listening, but these are fundamentally different processes. Hearing is a passive physiological act, while true listening is an active psychological one. It demands that we momentarily suspend our own internal monologue—the constant stream of judgments, rebuttals, and associated memories that our brain naturally produces. This internal noise often drowns out the speaker's actual message. Therefore, achieving genuine comprehension involves silencing our own ego and cognitive biases, focusing entirely on the speaker's intended meaning rather than our interpretation of it. This deliberate act of self-suppression is far more taxing than simply processing auditory signals.

① Overcoming the anxiety of public speaking

② Building a consensus within a diverse group

③ Engaging in genuine, active listening

④ Formulating a persuasive argument

20.

> The end-of-year holiday season frequently triggers a paradoxical spike in consumer anxiety alongside festive cheer. While motivated by generosity, many individuals fall prey to an innate impulse to overspend. Experts note that the immediate, tangible gratification of gift-giving often overshadows the abstract, long-term goal of financial stability. This cognitive bias is exacerbated by external factors. Retailers strategically deploy promotions that create a sense of urgency, encouraging expenditures that exceed original budgets. Furthermore, there is an implicit societal expectation to demonstrate affection through material goods. Consequently, many consumers succumb to this blend of internal impulse and external pressure, leading them to _________________________________.

① prioritize experiences over material possessions

② adopt stricter budgeting practices for the new year

③ seek non-monetary ways to express affection

④ accumulate debt by prioritizing short-term social validation

수고하셨습니다.
당신의 합격을 응원합니다.

합격까지 **박문각**

2026 공무원 시험 대비 실전동형 모의고사
영어
▮ 제7회 ▮

응시번호

성 명

문제책형

가

제1과목	국어	제2과목	영어	제3과목	한국사
제4과목		제5과목			

응시자 주의사항

1. **시험시작 전 시험문제를 열람하는 행위나 시험종료 후 답안을 작성하는 행위를 한 사람은** 「공무원임용시험령」 제51조에 의거 **부정행위자로** 처리됩니다.
2. **답안지 책형 표기는 시험시작 전 감독관의 지시에 따라 문제책 앞면에 인쇄된 문제책형을 확인한 후, 답안지 책형란에 해당 책형(1개)을 '●'로 표기하여야** 합니다.
3. **답안은 문제책 표지의 과목 순서에 따라 답안지에 인쇄된 순서(제1·2·3·4·5과목)에 맞추어 표기해야 하며, 과목 순서를 바꾸어 표기한 경우에도 문제책 표지의 과목 순서대로 채점되므로 유의하시기** 바랍니다.
4. 시험이 시작되면 문제를 주의 깊게 읽은 후, 문항의 취지에 가장 적합한 하나의 정답만을 고르며, 문제내용에 관한 질문은 할 수 없습니다.
5. 답안지의 모든 기재 및 표기 사항은 **컴퓨터용 흑색 싸인펜을** 사용하며, 반드시 <보기>의 **올바른 표기 방식으로** 답안을 작성해야 합니다.

   <보기> 올바른 표기: ● 잘못된 표기: Ⓥ ⊗ ◑ ◉ ◍ ⊖ ③
6. **답안을 잘못 표기하였을 경우에는 답안지를 교체하여 작성하거나 수정할 수 있으며, 표기한 답안을** 수정할 때는 응시자 본인이 가져온 수정테이프만을 사용하여 해당 부분을 완전히 지우고 부착된 수정테이프가 떨어지지 않도록 손으로 눌러주어야 합니다. **(수정액 또는 수정스티커 등은 사용 불가)**
   - **■ 불량한 수정테이프의 사용과 불완전한 수정처리로 발생하는 모든 문제는 응시자 본인에게 책임이** 있습니다.
7. **법령, 고시, 판례 등에 관한 문제는 2026년 2월 28일 현재 유효한 법령, 고시, 판례 등을 기준으로** 정답을 구해야 합니다. 다만, 개별 과목 또는 문항에서 별도의 기준을 적용하도록 명시한 경우에는 그 기준을 적용하여 정답을 구해야 합니다.
8. **시험시간 관리의 책임은 응시자 본인에게** 있습니다.
   ※ 문제책은 시험종료 후 가지고 갈 수 있습니다.

정답공개 및 이의제기 안내

1. 정답공개: 정답가안 4.4.(토) 13:30 / 최종정답 4.13.(월) 18:00 / 사이버국가고시센터
2. 이의제기: 4.4.(토) 18:00 ~ 4.7.(화) 18:00 / 사이버국가고시센터
   - ■ 구체적인 이의제기 방법은 정답가안 공개 시 공지 예정
3. 가산점 등록기간: 4.4.(토) 13:30 ~ 4.6.(월) 21:00
4. 가산점 등록방법: 사이버국가고시센터 ➜ [원서접수 → 가산점 등록/확인]

영 어

[1~5] 밑줄 친 부분에 들어갈 말로 가장 적절한 것을 고르시오.

1.

Employees grew frustrated when they realized that promotions often depended on __________ criteria rather than objective performance metrics.

① logical
② impartial
③ arbitrary
④ cautious

2.

Many employees were __________ to embrace the new policy, fearing that it would increase their workload without offering any meaningful benefits.

① eager
② reluctant
③ qualified
④ composed

3.

A recent poll indicates 'quiet quitting' remains a trend, especially among younger employees __________ unrecognized by their managers.

① felt
② feels
③ which feels
④ who feel

4.

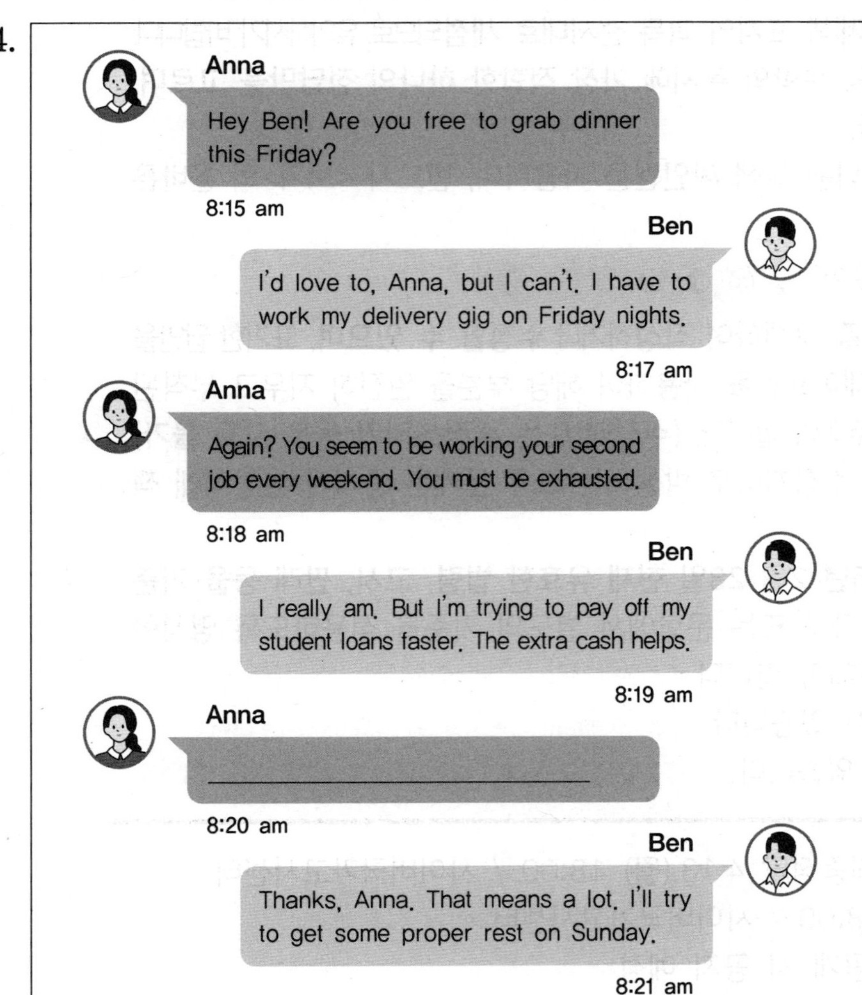

① You should quit your main job if the gig pays more.
② That's admirable, but please take care of yourself. Don't burn out.
③ Why don't you just ask your parents for the money?
④ I think you're just making excuses because you don't want to meet me.

5.

A: Did you see that article claiming scientists found a plant that cures cancer in just one week?
B: Wow, really? That's incredible! I'm going to share that with my family group chat right now.
A: Wait, hold on. I looked into it, and the source is a completely unknown blog. Every major medical journal says there's no evidence.
B: _______________________________________
A: It's easy to be fooled. These 'miracle' claims spread fast because people want them to be true. We just have to be more critical.
B: You're right. I'll delete the post.

① I should have subscribed to that medical journal earlier.
② That's impossible. My aunt already tried it and said it worked.
③ I don't trust mainstream media. The blog is probably right.
④ Oh, I was so caught up in the news that I didn't check it.

[6~7] 다음 글을 읽고 물음에 답하시오

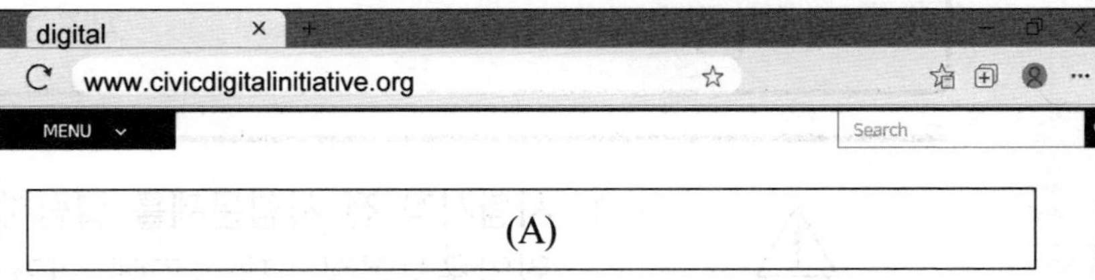

(A)

In an era dominated by digital information, the ability to critically evaluate online content is not merely a skill but a necessity for civic engagement. The proliferation of algorithmically curated newsfeeds often creates echo chambers, reinforcing existing beliefs and impeding exposure to diverse perspectives. This environment is a fertile ground for the spread of disinformation, which deliberately mimics the format of legitimate news sources to manipulate public opinion.

The "Civic Digital Initiative" is a campaign designed to equip citizens with the essential tools for digital discernment. Our workshops focus on source verification, cross-referencing claims with reputable outlets, and understanding the subtle indicators of propaganda. We contend that a digitally literate populace is the most robust defense against the erosion of democratic discourse. We do not advocate for censorship, but rather for the empowerment of the individual consumer of information.

6. (A)에 들어갈 윗글의 제목으로 가장 적절한 것은?

① The Role of Algorithms in Modern Media
② Civic Resilience Through Digital Literacy
③ Adapting to a Rapidly Changing Digital Era
④ Protecting Democracy from Digital Disinformation

7. 윗글에서 캠페인에 관한 내용과 일치하지 않는 것은?

① 온라인 콘텐츠를 비판적으로 평가하는 능력을 필수적인 것으로 본다.
② 알고리즘 기반 피드가 편향을 초래할 수 있다고 경고한다.
③ 시민들의 디지털 분별력을 강화하는 것을 목표로 한다.
④ 디지털 정보에 대한 검열은 현명한 정보 소비를 위해 필요하다.

8. 다음 글의 내용과 일치하지 <u>않는</u> 것은?

Bureau of Transportation Statistics News Release
Date: November 4, 2026

The Bureau of Transportation Statistics (BTS) released monthly motor fuels prices for October 2026. In October 2026, the national average price for regular motor gasoline was $3.06 per gallon. This price is down 3.3% from September 2026 and down 2.5% compared to October 2025.

Regionally, the average price for regular gasoline varied significantly. The West Coast had the highest average price at $4.18 per gallon, which is an increase of 3.9% from October 2025. In contrast, the Gulf Coast had the lowest average price at $2.62 per gallon, representing a 3.2% decrease from October 2025.

The average price for diesel no. 2 was $3.68 in October 2026, which was down 1.8% from September 2026.

① The national average price of gasoline in October 2026 was $3.06 per gallon.
② The national average gasoline price in October 2026 decreased compared to the previous month.
③ In the regional comparison, gasoline prices on the West Coast were the second highest.
④ The Gulf Coast was the region with the lowest average gasoline price.

[9~10] 밑줄 친 부분 중 어법상 옳지 <u>않은</u> 것을 고르시오.

9.
The new policy is ① <u>clearly</u> a significant improvement in the company's safety standards. ② <u>That</u> concerns the management most is how quickly employees will ③ <u>adapt</u> to the new guidelines. To ensure a smooth transition, the company is planning to provide additional training sessions for all newly ④ <u>hired</u> employees.

10.
Researchers are testing a new electrode material, ① <u>which</u> has shown early stability, and ② <u>despite</u> the project began only last year, the team has made progress difficult to achieve with conventional methods. This research, if ③ <u>successful</u>, could significantly reduce our reliance on fossil fuels. The new material is ④ <u>much</u> lighter than graphite.

[11~12] 다음 글을 읽고 물음에 답하시오.

Dear InnovateCorp Legal Team,

This email is to formally address a significant discrepancy we have identified concerning the service uptime metrics for the third quarter, as stipulated in Section 4.B of our Service Level Agreement (SLA) dated January 15, 2025. Our internal monitoring logs indicate a service availability of 99.5%, which falls short of the contractually mandated 99.9%.

This deviation constitutes a breach of the SLA and has tangibly impacted our operational workflow. We request that you <u>investigate</u> this matter and provide a formal report detailing the cause of the downtime and the remedial measures to prevent its recurrence. We appreciate your prompt attention and await your response.

Sincerely,
SynergyTech Contracts Department

11. 윗글의 목적으로 가장 적절한 것은?

① to confirm the accuracy of the quarterly service metrics
② to report a breach of contract and request corrective action
③ to request a revision of the Service Level Agreement's terms
④ to suggest improvements for future service performance

12. 밑줄 친 investigate의 의미와 가장 가까운 것은?

① assign　　　　　　② incorporate
③ calculate　　　　　④ examine

13. 다음 글의 주제로 가장 적절한 것은?

The rise of antibiotic-resistant "superbugs" has become a major global health threat, weakening the effectiveness of conventional treatments. This challenge has renewed interest in an older medical approach: phage therapy. Phages are viruses that specifically target and kill bacteria, unlike broad-spectrum antibiotics that harm both helpful and harmful microbes. This precision reduces unintended damage to the host's microbiome. Though once overlooked in the West, phage therapy was continually developed in Eastern Europe and is now being reconsidered worldwide as a promising tool against antimicrobial resistance.

① Superbugs Spreading Due to Increased Phage Application
② The Mechanisms of Antibiotic Resistance in Bacteria
③ How Phages Contribute to the Spread of Superbugs
④ The Re-emergence of Phage Therapy to Combat Superbugs

14. 다음 안내문의 내용과 일치하는 것은?

ISS Governance: Request for Public Comment

Date: November 3, 2026

ISS Governance has announced the commencement of the public comment period for its proposed benchmark policy changes for 2026. This follows the release of its 2026 Global Benchmark Policy Survey.

The comment period will remain open through 5:00 pm ET on November 11, 2026.

Submission Guidelines:

• Any comments should be submitted by email to policy@issgovernance.com.

• Please provide your name and your organization in your submission.

☐ Note: All comments may be published on ISS's website unless you specifically request confidentiality in the body of your email submission. ISS welcomes comments of any nature but suggests providing feedback on concerns with a proposed change.

① The public comment period began before the survey.

② Comments are accepted exclusively through email.

③ There is an option to send comments while remaining anonymous.

④ All submitted comments are treated as confidential without any conditions.

15. 다음 글의 내용과 일치하는 것은?>

SAFE CITY 2026: RESIDENT SAFETY WORKSHOP

When

Saturday, December 13, 2026
2:00 p.m. − 4:00 p.m.

Where

City Hall Council Chamber
1st Floor

What You Will Learn
■ How to use the new 'CitySafe' emergency app.
■ Cybersecurity tips for smart home devices.
■ Emergency evacuation routes for your neighborhood.

Registration
■ This event is strictly for residents of District 9.
■ Please register online at www.safecity.gov by December 10.
■ No walk-ins accepted. (Pre-registered guests only).

Refreshments
Light snacks and beverages will be served after the workshop.

① Attendance is limited to residents of District 9 who register in advance.

② The workshop will focus mainly on outdoor safety drills conducted at a local park.

③ On-site registration will be available for those who miss the online deadline.

④ A full meal will be served before the workshop begins for all attendees.

16. 다음 글의 흐름상 어색한 문장은?

Recent psychological studies are examining "vicarious trauma" among young adults heavily exposed to graphic conflict-related content on social media. ① Unlike direct trauma, vicarious trauma arises from empathizing with others' suffering, producing symptoms such as anxiety and emotional numbness. ② Social media platforms often amplify sensational or emotionally charged posts through engagement-driven algorithms. ③ Researchers warn that this constant, unfiltered crisis imagery undermines young users' sense of safety, making the world appear more threatening. ④ Such prolonged exposure without resolution can overwhelm emotional resources, resembling the psychological strain seen in frontline professions.

17. 주어진 문장이 들어갈 위치로 가장 적절한 것은?

This substitution is not uniform; it primarily affects tasks that are repetitive and do not require high emotional or social intelligence.

The economic impact of artificial intelligence on the labor market is a subject of intense debate, with some reports predicting massive job displacement. (①) Investment bank analyses suggest AI could replace the equivalent of 300 million full-time jobs, potentially automating a quarter of work tasks in the US and Europe. (②) For example, roles like customer service representatives, who often handle repetitive queries, are highly susceptible to this automation. (③) The same logic applies to many back-office and administrative functions where data entry and scheduling are primary duties. (④) However, this automation is also expected to create new jobs and fuel a significant productivity boom, complicating the net effect on employment.

18. 주어진 글 다음에 이어질 글의 순서로 가장 적절한 것은?

An Egyptian archaeological mission in North Sinai has announced a major discovery at the Tell al-Kharouba site: a New Kingdom‐era military fortress.

(A) As excavation continued, a secondary entrance was uncovered in the same wall, and a 75-meter zigzag wall on the west side was revealed, likely enclosing a housing area for soldiers.

(B) Initial work examined the southern wall, spanning about 105 meters and reinforced with eleven defensive towers, suggesting the fortress's strategic importance.

(C) This zigzag design is characteristic of New Kingdom military architecture and shows how builders adapted to desert conditions to defend Egypt's eastern borders.

① (A) － (C) － (B)　　　② (B) － (A) － (C)
③ (B) － (C) － (A)　　　④ (C) － (A) － (B)

[19～20] 밑줄 친 부분에 들어갈 말로 가장 적절한 것을 고르시오.

19.

_______________________________ is the cornerstone of strategic power. An immediate emotional response is the greatest impediment to influence, a tactical mistake that outweighs any brief relief gained from expressing one's feelings. Emotions cloud judgment, and once perception is distorted, one cannot act with proper control or foresight. Anger is especially corrosive, escalating tensions and strengthening an opponent's resolve. Maintaining an appearance of friendliness is often more effective than revealing hostility. Even positive emotions can be dangerous, as they may blind us to others' hidden motives. True mastery requires stepping back from the moment and assessing situations with the detached perspective of Janus.

① The immediate and transparent expression of one's feelings

② The cultivation of love and affection to build alliances

③ The willingness to act quickly based on one's judgment

④ The ability to subordinate emotional impulses to rational calculation

20.

The "Bandwagon Effect" is a cognitive bias describing the phenomenon whereby individuals adopt certain behaviors or beliefs primarily because many others are doing so. It stems from the "jump on the bandwagon" idiom, which implies joining a movement only once it appears successful. This tendency to "follow the crowd" often occurs without a critical examination of the underlying evidence or intrinsic merit of the choice. As adherence to an idea grows, its perceived validity increases, creating a feedback loop that draws in more people. This mechanism is particularly potent in politics, where momentum can be decisive. When a candidate gains perceived popular support, they attract voters whose decisions are swayed not by policy alignment but by the desire _______________________________.

① to align themselves with the successful or winning side

② to express their unique and independent political opinions

③ to critically examine the underlying evidence of the policies

④ to resist the growing momentum of the crowd

2026 공무원 시험 대비 실전동형 모의고사
영어
▌ 제8회 ▐

<table>
<tr><td>응시번호</td><td rowspan="2"></td><td rowspan="2">문제책형
가</td></tr>
<tr><td>성 명</td></tr>
</table>

제1과목	국어	제2과목	영어	제3과목	한국사
제4과목		제5과목			

응시자 주의사항

1. **시험시작 전 시험문제를 열람하는 행위나 시험종료 후 답안을 작성하는 행위를 한 사람은** 「공무원임용시험령」 제51조에 의거 **부정행위자로** 처리됩니다.
2. **답안지 책형 표기는 시험시작 전 감독관의 지시에 따라 문제책 앞면에 인쇄된 문제책형을 확인한 후, 답안지 책형란에 해당 책형(1개)을 '●'로 표기하여야** 합니다.
3. **답안은 문제책 표지의 과목 순서에 따라 답안지에 인쇄된 순서(제1·2·3·4·5과목)에 맞추어 표기해야 하며,** 과목 순서를 바꾸어 표기한 경우에도 **문제책 표지의 과목 순서대로 채점되므로 유의하시기 바랍니다.**
4. 시험이 시작되면 문제를 주의 깊게 읽은 후, 문항의 취지에 가장 적합한 하나의 정답만을 고르며, 문제내용에 관한 질문은 할 수 없습니다.
5. 답안지의 모든 기재 및 표기 사항은 **컴퓨터용 흑색 싸인펜을 사용**하며, 반드시 <보기>의 **올바른 표기 방식으로 답안을 작성해야** 합니다.

   <보기> **올바른 표기: ●   잘못된 표기: Ⓥ ⊗ ◐ ⊙ ◎ ◖ ◔ ③**

6. **답안을 잘못 표기하였을 경우에는 답안지를 교체하여 작성하거나 수정할 수 있으며,** 표기한 답안을 수정할 때는 **응시자 본인이 가져온 수정테이프만을 사용**하여 해당 부분을 완전히 지우고 부착된 수정테이프가 떨어지지 않도록 손으로 눌러주어야 합니다. **(수정액 또는 수정스티커 등은 사용 불가)**
   - ■불량한 수정테이프의 사용과 불완전한 수정처리로 발생하는 모든 문제는 응시자 본인에게 책임이 있습니다.
7. 법령, 고시, 판례 등에 관한 문제는 **2026년 2월 28일 현재 유효한 법령, 고시, 판례 등을 기준**으로 정답을 구해야 합니다. 다만, 개별 과목 또는 문항에서 별도의 기준을 적용하도록 명시한 경우에는 그 기준을 적용하여 정답을 구해야 합니다.
8. **시험시간 관리의 책임은 응시자 본인에게 있습니다.**
   ※ 문제책은 시험종료 후 가지고 갈 수 있습니다.

정답공개 및 이의제기 안내

1. 정답공개: 정답가안 4.4.(토) 13:30 / 최종정답 4.13.(월) 18:00 / 사이버국가고시센터
2. 이의제기: 4.4.(토) 18:00 ~ 4.7.(화) 18:00 / 사이버국가고시센터
   - ■구체적인 이의제기 방법은 정답가안 공개 시 공지 예정
3. 가산점 등록기간: 4.4.(토) 13:30 ~ 4.6.(월) 21:00
4. 가산점 등록방법: 사이버국가고시센터 ➜ [원서접수 → 가산점 등록/확인]

영   어

[1~3] 밑줄 친 부분에 들어갈 말로 가장 적절한 것을 고르시오.

1.

The company issued a carefully crafted apology to ________ public criticism after the data breach incident.

① clarify   ② belittle

③ fabricate   ④ mollify

2.

Because the construction company failed to comply with safety standards, the regional _________ ordered an immediate halt to all on-site operations.

① regulations   ② authorities

③ coverages   ④ components

3.

The manager approved the revised budget immediately, _________ the board members who had previously raised several concerns about it.

① neither did   ② so did

③ and so did   ④ and neither

4. 다음 글의 내용과 일치하는 것은?

Phoenix Public Library System ─ Maintenance Notice

The Phoenix Public Library (PPL) will be conducting essential system-wide maintenance to enhance and upgrade our online services. This scheduled outage will temporarily affect all PPL locations.

Maintenance Window:
All online and digital services will be unavailable for approximately 60 hours.

Services Unavailable During Maintenance:
- Online catalog (including search, renewals, and placing holds)
- Access to eBooks, eAudiobooks, and all digital databases
- Public computers and in-branch Wi-Fi

Services Available During Maintenance:
- Borrowing and returning physical materials (library card required)
- Library membership registration

For your information, all PPL branches will be open during regular operating hours on Saturday, November 15.

① Only some branches are affected during the maintenance.

② Online searches are available during the maintenance.

③ Access to digital databases will be suspended during the outage.

④ New registrations cannot be completed during the maintenance.

[5~6] 밑줄 친 부분에 들어갈 말로 가장 적절한 것을 고르시오.

5.

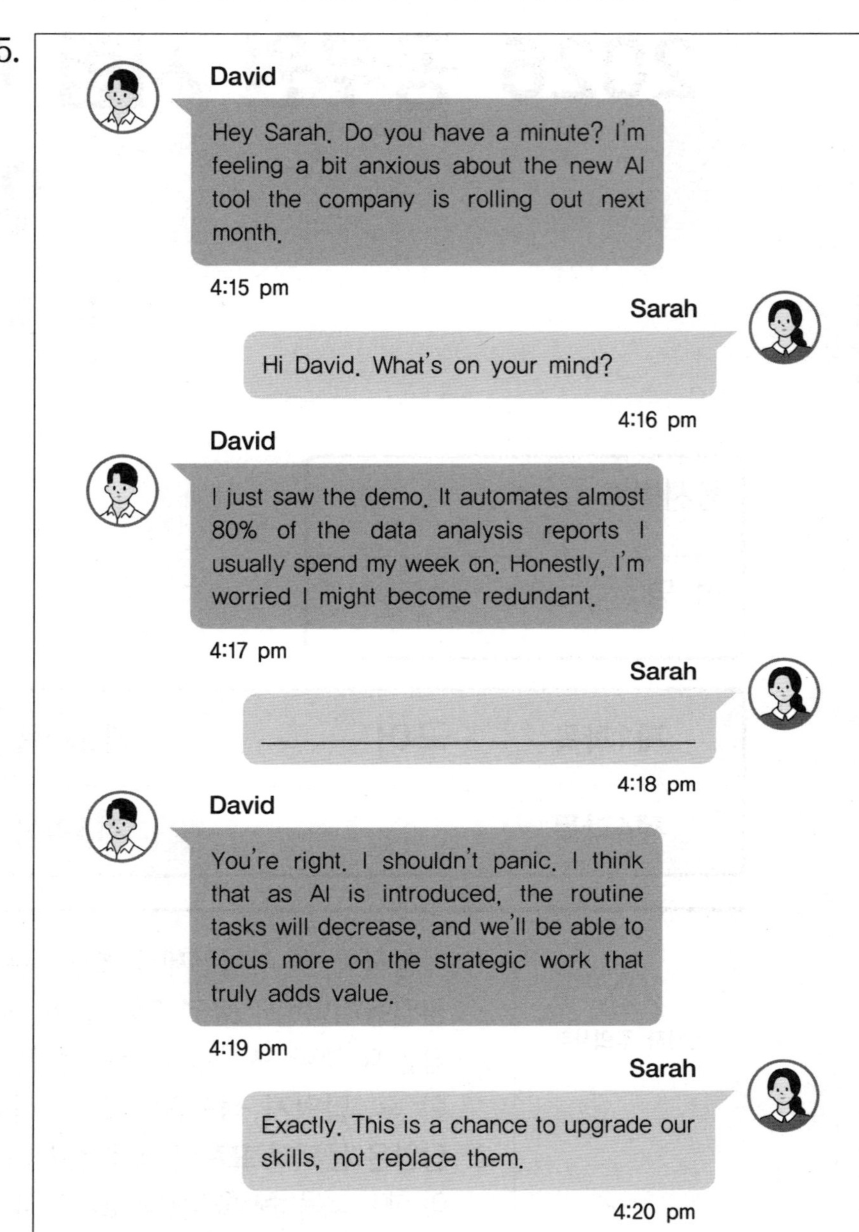

① I know it's stressful, but this change could seriously affect job security.

② Since the rollout is next month, we don't need to worry about its impact yet.

③ Automation has become an inevitable trend across many industries.

④ I get how you feel, but try seeing AI as a tool, not a replacement.

6.

A: Hey, you've been working late every night this week. Is everything okay with the new project?

B: Honestly, I'm overwhelmed. The deadline is tight, and the client keeps changing the requirements.

A: That sounds incredibly stressful. Make sure you're not skipping meals. You seem completely burned out.

B: _________________________________

A: I really think you should talk to the manager. Pushing yourself this hard isn't sustainable.

B: I guess you're right. I'll schedule a meeting with her tomorrow.

① I think I am. I feel exhausted all the time and I'm losing focus.

② Don't worry. I'll be finished by tomorrow morning.

③ I'm fine. I just need one more cup of coffee.

④ It's not a big deal. I'm used to this kind of pressure.

[7~8] 다음 글을 읽고 물음에 답하시오.

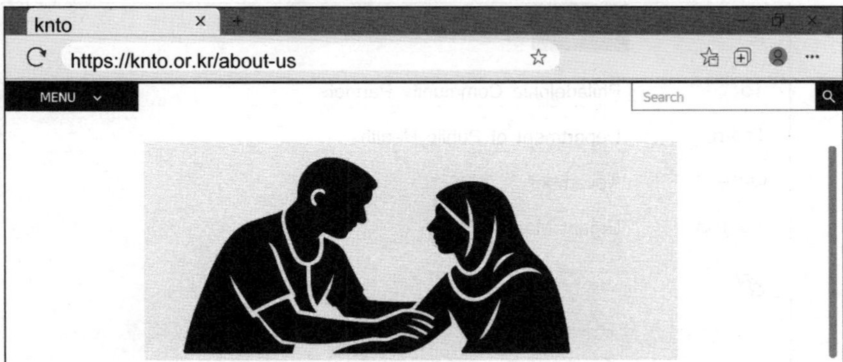

Médecins Sans Frontières (MSF)

Médecins Sans Frontières, or Doctors Without Borders, is an international humanitarian organization providing medical assistance to populations in distress, to victims of natural or man-made disasters, and to victims of armed conflict. The organization operates independently of any political, military, or religious agendas.

A core tenet of our work is impartiality. We provide assistance solely on the basis of need, irrespective of race, religion, gender, or political affiliation. Access to victims is our primary concern, and we strive to reach those who are beyond the reach of most other aid agencies. Furthermore, our principle of <u>neutrality</u> means we do not take sides in hostilities or engage in controversies of a political, racial, religious, or ideological nature. This commitment allows us to gain the trust of all parties to a conflict and to work in otherwise inaccessible areas.

7. 밑줄 친 neutrality의 의미와 가장 가까운 것은?

① accuracy   ② objectivity

③ proficiency   ④ liability

8. 윗글의 목적으로 가장 적절한 것은?

① to explain how MSF differs from other international aid organizations

② to emphasize the importance of providing medical aid in conflict zones

③ to inform readers of the reasons MSF avoids taking sides in conflicts

④ to clearly explain the fundamental principles of the organization

9. 밑줄 친 부분 중 어법상 옳지 않은 것은?

No sooner ① <u>has</u> the game started than it began to rain heavily. The players ran for cover, and the spectators opened their umbrellas. The referee decided to suspend the match ② <u>until</u> the rain stopped. Everyone waited anxiously, hoping the weather would clear up. Scarcely had the rain stopped ③ <u>when</u> the sun came out again. The game resumed, and the crowd cheered ④ <u>loudly</u>.

[10~11] 다음 글을 읽고 물음에 답하시오.

(A)

As the central bank of the Republic of Korea, the Bank of Korea's foremost mandate is to maintain price stability. The Monetary Policy Board determines the Base Rate through a comprehensive analysis of economic conditions, including inflationary pressures, economic growth trends, and financial market stability. This rate serves as a benchmark for market interest rates and is a crucial tool for managing liquidity in the financial system.

In periods of economic overheating, the central bank may raise the Base Rate to curtail excessive borrowing and cool down aggregate demand. Conversely, during economic downturns, a lower rate is implemented to stimulate investment and consumption. The ultimate objective of these policy adjustments is to foster sustainable economic growth within a framework of stability, thereby ensuring the long-term economic well-being of the nation.

10. (A)에 들어갈 윗글의 제목으로 가장 적절한 것은?

① The History of Korea's Central Banking System

② Flexible Base Rate Adjustment for Price Stability

③ Maintaining High Interest Rates in All Situations

④ The Role of Interest Rates in Supporting Economic Growth

11. 윗글에 관한 내용과 일치하는 것은?

① The Base Rate is primarily adjusted to stabilize employment levels.

② The Monetary Policy Board considers multiple economic indicators when setting the Base Rate.

③ In times of economic overheating, the Base Rate is lowered in response.

④ The primary purpose of interest rate adjustments is to respond to short-term market fluctuations only.

12. 밑줄 친 부분 중 어법상 옳지 않은 것은?

I am confident ① <u>that</u> my skills and experience make me a suitable candidate for the position. In particular, my previous work experience has contributed to my ability to adapt quickly to new challenges by ② <u>strengthening</u> my problem-solving skills. These strengths make me ③ <u>well</u> qualified to support your organization's objectives. Please do not hesitate to contact ④ <u>to</u> me if you need any additional information.

13. 다음 글의 내용과 일치하지 않는 것은?

WORLD PREMIERE:
HYPERLOOP ALPHA UNVEILING

Witness the Future of Transportation

When
Saturday, December 20, 2026
11:00 a.m. — 2:00 p.m.
Where
Nevada Desert Test Facility
(Shuttle buses depart from Las Vegas
City Hall at 9:30 a.m.)

Event Schedule
- ☐ 11:00 a.m.: CEO Keynote & Technology Presentation.
- ☐ 12:00 p.m.: Live Test Run (Watching from Observation Deck).
- ☐ 1:00 p.m.: Q&A with Engineering Team.

Admission
- ☐ Invited Media & VIPs: Priority Seating.
- ☐ General Public: $50 (Standing Room Only).

Important Information
- ☐ For safety reasons, no public rides will be offered during this event.
- ☐ Attendees must sign a safety waiver upon entry.
- ☐ Photography is allowed, but drone usage is strictly banned in the airspace.

① Shuttle buses will leave from Las Vegas City Hall before the event begins.
② Members of the general public will be provided with reserved seating during the event.
③ The event permits photography but under no circumstances is the operation of drones allowed.
④ The live test run can be viewed from a designated observation area.

14. 다음 글의 흐름상 어색한 문장은?

In the past, reading was primarily a solitary activity, often carried out in quiet spaces such as libraries or private homes. ① With the rise of digital technology, however, reading habits have undergone significant changes. ② Online platforms now allow readers to share opinions instantly and engage in discussions with others around the world. ③ As a result, many people today prefer printed books to digital formats because of their tactile experience. ④ This shift has transformed reading into a more social and interactive practice, reshaping how individuals consume and interpret written content. Reading today is no longer limited to private reflection but has become a shared and dynamic experience shaped by digital interaction.

15. 다음 글의 목적으로 가장 적절한 것은?

To	Philadelphia Community Partners
From	Department of Public Health
Date	November 3, 2026
Subject	Urgent Matter

This is an urgent reminder for our community partners.

The Department of Public Health has issued an application for the "One Philly SNAP Support Program," offering grant amounts from $5,000 to $50,000. This funding is intended to support organizations that assist Philadelphia residents using SNAP benefits. The application response deadline is 5:00 p.m. this Wednesday, November 4, 2026.

We are holding a final Zoom information session tomorrow morning, November 4, from 8:30 a.m. to 9:30 a.m. (registration required) to answer last-minute questions.

To be considered, all application questions must be completed by the deadline. We encourage all eligible partners to apply.

① to announce the creation of a new SNAP benefits program
② to ask residents for donations to a city food fund
③ to urge you to apply for a grant before the deadline
④ to postpone the application deadline for a funding opportunity

16. 다음 글의 주제로 가장 적절한 것은?

Dr. Keller and her research team discovered unexpectedly that a particular strain of bacteria improved nutrient absorption in laboratory animals commonly used in medical studies. Subsequent experiments involving related bacterial strains revealed similar effects in several other animal species as well. Dr. Keller is now conducting further research on additional microorganisms that appear to enhance immune responses in various hosts. She aims to gain a more comprehensive understanding of the benefits that different microorganisms may provide to the organisms they inhabit. Such findings would lend support to a growing view among biologists that many living beings depend on cooperative biological relationships rather than functioning entirely independently.

① biological independence of living organisms
② the role of interdependent relationships in sustaining life
③ factors influencing immune responses in living organisms
④ self-sufficiency of organisms in natural environments

17. 주어진 문장이 들어갈 위치로 가장 적절한 것은?

> However, this vulnerability to moisture and heat has historically been their primary commercial barrier, preventing widespread adoption.

> Perovskite solar cells are emerging as a major 2025 innovation, challenging traditional silicon panels. (①) Unlike rigid silicon, they are lightweight, flexible, and can be printed, offering revolutionary efficiency. (②) This allows them to be integrated into windows, vehicles, or even clothing. (③) Consequently, a primary research focus is now on developing protective coatings and encapsulation methods to enhance their durability. (④) If this stability challenge can be overcome, perovskites could unlock a new era of ubiquitous solar power.

18. 주어진 글 다음에 이어질 글의 순서로 가장 적절한 것은?

> The spread of misinformation, accelerated by social media and generative AI, poses a serious threat to democratic processes and public health. This has prompted research into effective countermeasures.

> (A) For example, recent studies have used short videos that teach viewers to recognize tactics like emotional appeals or false dichotomies, and the results show improved ability to distinguish truth from misinformation.
>
> (B) Unlike fact-checking, which happens after misinformation has spread, inoculation aims to prevent the "infection" in advance, similar to a vaccine.
>
> (C) One widely studied approach is "inoculation theory," which proposes that exposing people to a weakened form of misinformation — and explaining the techniques behind it — can build resistance.

① (A) − (C) − (B)

② (B) − (A) − (C)

③ (C) − (A) − (B)

④ (C) − (B) − (A)

[19~20] 밑줄 친 부분에 들어갈 말로 가장 적절한 것을 고르시오.

19.

> Psychological research shows a strong difference in motivation depending on how a task is framed. In one experiment, participants completed mazes under two conditions: one group worked toward a reward, while the other tried to avoid a threat. The group focused on gaining something positive showed noticeably higher speed and accuracy. This suggests that people generally perform better when pursuing a clear and desirable outcome. Although avoidance-based framing can trigger action, it often leads to scattered and less efficient behavior that is centered only on escaping what is negative. In contrast, having a specific goal provides a mental anchor that sharpens attention and enhances overall performance. Therefore, when designing incentives or setting personal goals, it is crucial to recognize that ________________________________.

① perceived threat can meaningfully influence motivation

② avoidance framing can still trigger strong engagement

③ cognitive framing has a negligible impact on task completion

④ pursuing a specific benefit yields better results than simply trying to evade a penalty

20.

> The human psyche is divided. The conscious mind relies on logic, while the unconscious governs raw emotions such as love, fear, jealousy, and joy. ________________________________, often overpowering rational intent and shaping much of our behavior before we realize it. This creates a strong inner conflict when conscious choices clash with deep subconscious drives. A person may logically decide to quit a harmful habit, yet find their resolve weakened by a persistent desire. This split — wanting to stop but desiring to continue — produces significant psychological strain. Neuroscience also shows the dominance of the subconscious; the brain begins preparing actions milliseconds before we consciously decide. Thus, what feels like deliberate choice often reflects decisions already formed in the unconscious.

① Logical reasoning can sometimes ease internal conflict

② It is this subconscious engine that drives our core emotions and desires

③ The conscious mind can exert limited control over emotions

④ The unconscious completely replaces conscious thought in all decisions

수고하셨습니다.
당신의 합격을 응원합니다.

2026 공무원 시험 대비 실전동형 모의고사
영 어
┃ 제9회 ┃

응시번호

성 명

제1과목	국어	제2과목	<u>영어</u>	제3과목	한국사
제4과목		제5과목			

응시자 주의사항

1. 시험시작 전 시험문제를 열람하는 행위나 시험종료 후 답안을 작성하는 행위를 한 사람은 「공무원임용시험령」 제51조에 의거 부정행위자로 처리됩니다.
2. 답안지 책형 표기는 시험시작 전 감독관의 지시에 따라 **문제책 앞면에 인쇄된 문제책형을 확인**한 후, 답안지 책형란에 해당 책형(1개)을 '●'로 **표기하여야** 합니다.
3. 답안은 문제책 표지의 과목 순서에 따라 답안지에 인쇄된 순서(제1·2·3·4·5과목)에 맞추어 표기해야 하며, 과목 순서를 바꾸어 표기한 경우에도 문제책 표지의 과목 순서대로 채점되므로 유의하시기 바랍니다.
4. 시험이 시작되면 문제를 주의 깊게 읽은 후, 문항의 취지에 가장 적합한 하나의 정답만을 고르며, 문제내용에 관한 질문은 할 수 없습니다.
5. 답안지의 모든 기재 및 표기 사항은 **컴퓨터용 흑색 싸인펜**을 사용하며, 반드시 <보기>의 **올바른 표기 방식**으로 답안을 작성해야 합니다.

    <보기> 올바른 표기: ●   잘못된 표기: ⓥ ⊗ ◑ ⊙ ◫ ⊖ ③

6. **답안을 잘못 표기하였을 경우**에는 답안지를 교체하여 작성하거나 수정할 수 있으며, 표기한 답안을 수정할 때는 응시자 본인이 가져온 수정테이프만을 사용하여 해당 부분을 완전히 지우고 부착된 수정테이프가 떨어지지 않도록 손으로 눌러주어야 합니다. (수정액 또는 수정스티커 등은 사용 불가)
 ■불량한 수정테이프의 사용과 불완전한 수정처리로 발생하는 모든 문제는 응시자 본인에게 책임이 있습니다.
7. 법령, 고시, 판례 등에 관한 문제는 **2026년 2월 28일 현재 유효한 법령, 고시, 판례 등을** 기준으로 정답을 구해야 합니다. 다만, 개별 과목 또는 문항에서 별도의 기준을 적용하도록 명시한 경우에는 그 기준을 적용하여 정답을 구해야 합니다.
8. **시험시간 관리의 책임은 응시자 본인에게 있습니다.**
 ※ 문제책은 시험종료 후 가지고 갈 수 있습니다.

정답공개 및 이의제기 안내

1. 정답공개: 정답가안 4.4.(토) 13:30 / 최종정답 4.13.(월) 18:00 / 사이버국가고시센터
2. 이의제기: 4.4.(토) 18:00 ~ 4.7.(화) 18:00 / 사이버국가고시센터
 ■구체적인 이의제기 방법은 정답가안 공개 시 공지 예정
3. 가산점 등록기간: 4.4.(토) 13:30 ~ 4.6.(월) 21:00
4. 가산점 등록방법: 사이버국가고시센터 ➡ [원서접수 → 가산점 등록/확인]

영　어

[1~5] 밑줄 친 부분에 들어갈 말로 가장 적절한 것을 고르시오.

1.

As living costs continue to rise while wage levels remain ________ over an extended period, a growing number of young professionals are leaving the city.

① stagnant
② insipid
③ competitive
④ versatile

2.

The accountant needs to ________ whether the reported figures accurately reflect quarterly revenue before filing documents.

① menace
② doubt
③ verify
④ diffuse

3.

We were surprised at ________ of the project ahead of schedule despite limited resources and staffing.

① him completed
② his completion
③ he completing
④ his complete

4.

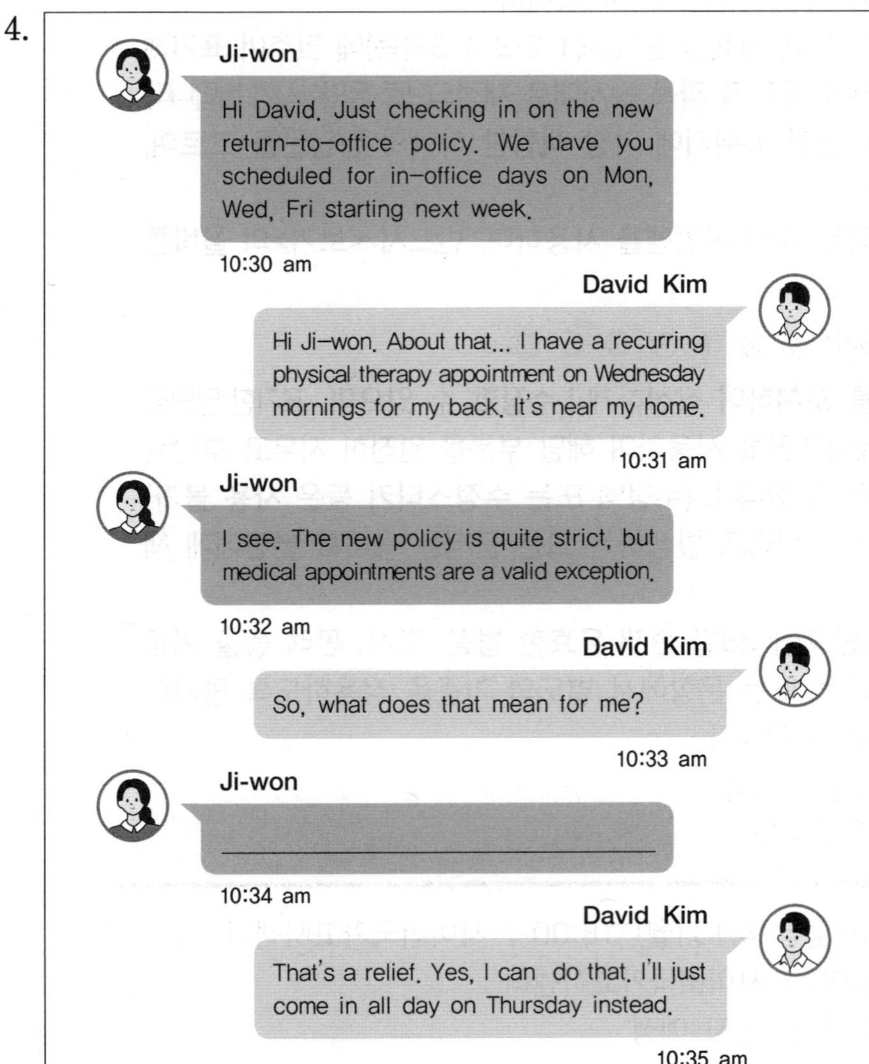

① You'll need to use your paid time off for Wednesdays.
② I'm afraid you must reschedule your therapy sessions.
③ How about adjusting your in-office days a bit?
④ You'll have to switch to a fully remote position.

5.

A: I just checked my credit card bill, and it's out of control.
B: I know what you mean. Inflation is driving up prices.
A: Exactly. I'm thinking of canceling my music streaming subscription to save some money.
B: Oh, which one do you use? I use 'TuneSphere'.
A: That's the one I have. It's great, but $15 a month just for me seems like a waste.
B: ________________________________
A: I didn't know they offered that. How does it work?
B: You can add up to five people. My friends and I share one, and it costs us only about $4 each.

① I agree, you should probably cancel it immediately.
② Why don't you check if they offer a family plan?
③ You should listen to the free version with ads instead.
④ I think $15 is actually a very reasonable price for music.

[6~7] 다음 글을 읽고 물음에 답하시오.

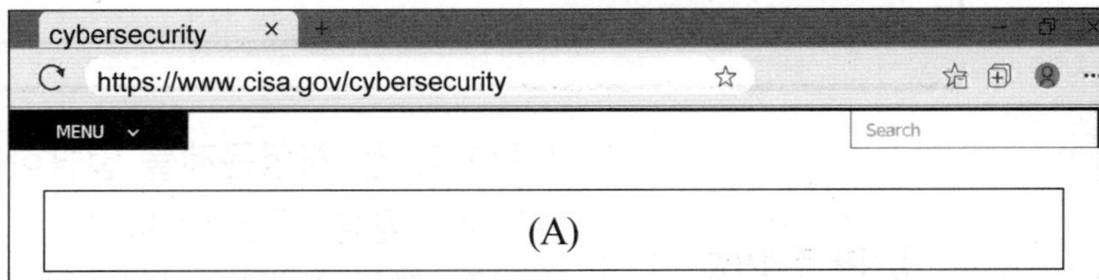

(A)

The Financial Security Agency has identified a surge in sophisticated spear-phishing campaigns targeting corporate executives. Unlike broad phishing attacks, these campaigns utilize meticulously researched information about the target to create a highly convincing pretext. The fraudulent emails often appear to originate from a trusted colleague or a reputable business partner.

The primary attack vector involves a malicious link disguised as a legitimate document, such as a "Quarterly Report" or "Confidential M&A Proposal." Clicking the link initiates a silent download of malware designed to exfiltrate sensitive corporate data, including financial records and intellectual property. Standard security filters may fail to detect these threats due to their tailored nature. A critical defense is fostering a culture of vigilant skepticism; employees should be trained to independently verify unexpected requests for sensitive information, especially those that convey a sense of urgency.

6. (A)에 들어갈 윗글의 제목으로 가장 적절한 것은?

① Preventing Data Loss in Corporate Email Systems
② Executive Training for Cyber Threat Response
③ Alert: Advanced Spear-Phishing Threat
④ Handling Sensitive Corporate Documents

7. 윗글의 내용과 일치하는 것은?

① There has been a recent surge in general mass phishing attacks.
② The phishing emails are disguised as attractive advertisements.
③ Clicking the link triggers an automatic download of malware.
④ Such attacks can be adequately detected by standard security filters.

[8~9] 다음 글을 읽고 물음에 답하시오.

Regulations for Government Research Grant Applications

This document delineates the official procedure for submitting proposals for the National Science Foundation grant. All submissions must conform strictly to the guidelines <u>stipulated</u> herein to be considered for review.

Proposals must be submitted electronically via the official portal before the deadline of 5:00 PM, November 30. The proposal must include a detailed research plan, a budget justification, and the curriculum vitae of all key personnel. The subsequent adjudication process will be conducted by a panel of independent experts.

Evaluation criteria include scientific merit, feasibility, and potential impact. Applicants will be notified of the outcome within 90 days of the submission deadline. Decisions made by the panel are final and not subject to appeal.

8. 밑줄 친 stipulated의 의미와 가장 가까운 것은?

  ① infringed   ② advocated
  ③ speculated   ④ prescribed

9. 윗글의 목적으로 가장 적절한 것은?

  ① to announce the recipients of a research grant
  ② to provide a formal protocol for a grant application
  ③ to appeal a decision made by a review panel
  ④ to recruit experts for a proposal evaluation committee

[10~11] 밑줄 친 부분 중 어법상 옳지 않은 것을 고르시오.

10.

Preparation is the most critical factor in ① <u>overcoming</u> exam anxiety. Many students spend sleepless nights memorizing every single detail, ② <u>fearing</u> that they might miss something important. However, if you have consistently followed a structured study plan and ③ <u>understood</u> the core concepts, you need not ④ <u>to worry</u> about the results of the test.

11.

The international community cannot afford ① <u>to delay</u> its response to these alarming climate shifts. We must take immediate action lest the situation ② <u>not worsen</u> beyond the point of no repair. Protecting the planet is ③ <u>not merely</u> an option, but a fundamental responsibility we owe to future generations. Only through collective and decisive measures ④ <u>can we</u> ensure a sustainable world.

12. 다음 글의 목적으로 가장 적절한 것은?

	Send	Preview	Save
To	All City of Valdosta Residents		
From	Valdosta Utilities Department		
Date	September 25, 2026		
Subject	Important Notice		

This is an important update regarding your city utility account.

In the aftermath of Hurricane Helene, the City of Valdosta temporarily paused late fees and service interruptions to support residents during the recovery period.

With critical services and infrastructure now stabilized, the City is announcing that standard billing policies, including late fees and service interruption notices for all past-due accounts, will resume effective October 1, 2026.

To avoid penalties, customers are strongly encouraged to make timely payments. The City offers payment arrangements and assistance programs for those experiencing financial hardship. Customers needing assistance are urged to contact the Utilities Customer Service team immediately.

  ① to offer residents a discount on utility bills
  ② to warn about the immediate arrival of Hurricane Helene
  ③ to announce the resumption of a temporarily paused billing policy
  ④ to introduce new payment assistance programs for all residents

13. 다음 글의 주제로 가장 적절한 것은?

The Ministry of Public Safety and Emergency Preparedness has issued a warning about the dangers of carbon monoxide (CO) poisoning, especially during the colder months when heating systems are in frequent use. Carbon monoxide is a colorless, odorless gas that can cause serious health issues or even death if inhaled in large amounts. The ministry highlighted that common sources of CO include malfunctioning furnaces, gas stoves, and portable generators. To prevent CO poisoning, the ministry advised residents to install carbon monoxide detectors in their homes, ensure proper ventilation, and have heating systems inspected annually by professionals. Additionally, the ministry emphasized the importance of never using portable generators or grills indoors, as they can produce lethal levels of CO.

  ① Limitations of safety sensors in detecting colorless gases
  ② The dangers of carbon monoxide poisoning and mitigation strategies
  ③ Assessing the environmental impact of carbon monoxide emissions
  ④ Proper maintenance procedures for indoor portable generators

14. 다음 글의 내용과 일치하지 <u>않는</u> 것은?

Call for Vendors: 2026 Old Town Holiday Market
Application Deadline: November 15, 2026

The Old Town Business Association (OTBA) invites artisans and food vendors to apply for our 10th Annual Holiday Market, running weekends from Dec. 6-22. We are seeking high-quality, unique, and handcrafted items. Mass-produced or resale items are not eligible and will be rejected.

Vendor Categories:
- Artisan/Craft (Jewelry, pottery, textiles, etc.)
- Specialty Food (Packaged goods like jams, baked items. No on-site meal prep.)

Application Process:
1. Submit the online application form by November 15.
2. Include a $25 non-refundable application fee.
3. Provide 3-5 high-resolution photos of your products.

All applications will be reviewed by a jury. Notifications of acceptance or rejection will be sent via email by November 20. Accepted vendors must pay the $150 booth fee by December 1.

---

① Only specific types of food items are allowed to be sold.
② Applicants will not receive a refund even if their submission is turned down.
③ Food vendors are permitted to cook and serve warm meals at their booths.
④ Selected vendors have to pay an additional fee for their booths.

15. 다음 글의 내용과 일치하는 것은?

IMPORTANT NOTICE

CITY SKYWATCH
PARTY CANCELLATION

We regret to inform you that the "Starliner Launch Viewing Party," originally scheduled for this Saturday, May 25, at the Observatory Park, has been indefinitely postponed.

Reason for Cancellation:
Due to technical delays with the spacecraft announced by the aerospace agency earlier today, the launch schedule is currently under review. Consequently, our local viewing event cannot proceed as planned.

Ticket Refunds:
☑ Those who purchased tickets online will receive a full automatic refund to their original payment method within 5−7 business days.
☑ No action is required on your part.

Alternative Plan:
Although the party is cancelled, Observatory Park will remain open for regular public stargazing this Saturday from 8 PM to 10 PM. Admission is free, but bring your own binoculars.

---

① The party will proceed as scheduled.
② The spacecraft's technical issues were resolved quickly.
③ Online ticket buyers will be refunded to their original method.
④ The stargazing event has also been cancelled.

16. 다음 글의 흐름상 어색한 문장은?

Recent research has identified betaine, a kidney-derived metabolite, as a key factor in cellular rejuvenation with effects similar to exercise. ① Betaine supplementation was shown to improve mitochondrial function and reduce inflammation—benefits typically associated with physical activity. ② Exercise remains the most effective way to improve cardiovascular health and build muscle mass. ③ This finding may offer a therapeutic option for individuals unable to exercise, providing a molecular alternative to some anti-aging effects of physical activity. ④ Further research is examining how betaine interacts with cellular pathways and whether its benefits are safe and long-lasting in humans.

17. 주어진 문장이 들어갈 위치로 가장 적절한 것은?

Establish a "digital-free zone" in your home where all electronic devices are strictly prohibited to ensure mental rest.

The constant stream of notifications from smartphones has made it increasingly difficult for modern individuals to achieve deep focus. (①) To regain control over your attention, you must proactively manage your physical environment rather than relying on willpower alone. (②) I am not suggesting that you should abandon technology entirely or live like a hermit in the woods. (③) Instead, the goal is to create intentional boundaries that protect your cognitive resources from constant interruption. (④) For instance, you could designate the dining table and the bedroom as areas where no phones are allowed, allowing for uninterrupted conversation or better sleep.

18. 주어진 글 다음에 이어질 글의 순서로 가장 적절한 것은?

The International Monetary Fund's recent World Economic Outlook projects that global growth will slow in the coming year, though the forecast varies across regions.

(A) In contrast, emerging market and developing economies are projected to grow at just over 4%, supported by strong domestic demand in several major countries, though they remain vulnerable to external shocks.

(B) Both groups still face notable risks. The IMF warns that geopolitical uncertainty, rising protectionism, and possible financial market corrections could undermine stability regardless of their current growth path.

(C) Advanced economies are expected to see modest growth of about 1.5%, mainly due to restrictive monetary policies aimed at controlling inflation and ongoing labor supply issues.

① (A) − (C) − (B)　　　② (B) − (A) − (C)
③ (C) − (A) − (B)　　　④ (C) − (B) − (A)

[19~20] 밑줄 친 부분에 들어갈 말로 가장 적절한 것을 고르시오.

19.

________________________ is a fundamental miscalculation in organizational and personal dynamics. Trust is not a passive trait one simply has, but the foundation of meaningful interactions, shaping the speed and quality of work and communication. It also serves as an economic driver by reducing friction and enabling collaboration. Far from being abstract, trust is a practical asset that can be intentionally built and carefully restored when damaged. In a climate of corporate scandals and growing skepticism, the ability to develop and sustain trust has become a defining leadership competency that distinguishes resilient organizations from the rest.

① Regarding trust merely as a soft, intangible ideal

② Assuming that trust is relevant in personal relationships

③ Believing that trust is actionable, renewable resource

④ Focusing on personal charm over structural trust

20.

Autoimmunity occurs when the immune system mistakenly identifies the body's own tissues as harmful. This abnormal response often begins subtly. When an environmental toxin or pathogen enters the body, a small, localized immune reaction is triggered. This initial process is usually balanced and not consciously noticeable. However, if it fails to remove the threat, the immune system escalates its response by releasing targeted antibodies. Although this stronger reaction is essential for protection, it can become harmful when sustained. If this heightened activity continues unchecked, the resulting chronic inflammation ________________________, leading to organ damage and the development of autoimmune disease.

① makes the initial immune reaction consciously noticeable

② begins to erode the very tissues it was meant to defend

③ focuses on eliminating environmental toxins more efficiently

④ triggers a temporary defense that leaves no lasting impact

수고하셨습니다.
당신의 합격을 응원합니다.

2026 공무원 시험 대비 실전동형 모의고사
영어
▌제10회 ▐

응시번호		문제책형
성 명		**가**

제1과목	국어	제2과목	<u>영어</u>	제3과목	한국사
제4과목		제5과목			

응시자 주의사항

1. 시험시작 전 시험문제를 열람하는 행위나 시험종료 후 답안을 작성하는 행위를 한 사람은 「공무원임용시험령」 제51조에 의거 **부정행위자로** 처리됩니다.
2. 답안지 책형 표기는 시험시작 전 감독관의 지시에 따라 **문제책 앞면에 인쇄된 문제책형을 확인**한 후, 답안지 책형란에 해당 책형(1개)을 '●'로 표기하여야 합니다.
3. 답안은 문제책 표지의 과목 순서에 따라 답안지에 인쇄된 순서(제1·2·3·4·5과목)에 맞추어 표기해야 하며, 과목 순서를 바꾸어 표기한 경우에도 문제책 표지의 과목 순서대로 채점되므로 유의하시기 바랍니다.
4. 시험이 시작되면 문제를 주의 깊게 읽은 후, 문항의 취지에 가장 적합한 하나의 정답만을 고르며, 문제내용에 관한 질문은 할 수 없습니다.
5. 답안지의 모든 기재 및 표기 사항은 **컴퓨터용 흑색 싸인펜을** 사용하며, 반드시 <보기>의 **올바른 표기** 방식으로 답안을 작성해야 합니다.

   <보기> 올바른 표기: ● 잘못된 표기: ⊘ ⊗ ◖ ⊙ ⦶ ○ ③

6. 답안을 잘못 표기하였을 경우에는 답안지를 교체하여 작성하거나 수정할 수 있으며, 표기한 답안을 수정할 때는 응시자 본인이 가져온 수정테이프만을 사용하여 해당 부분을 완전히 지우고 부착된 수정테이프가 떨어지지 않도록 손으로 눌러주어야 합니다. (수정액 또는 수정스티커 등은 사용 불가)
   ■ **불량한 수정테이프의 사용과 불완전한 수정처리로 발생하는 모든 문제는 응시자 본인에게 책임이 있습니다.**
7. 법령, 고시, 판례 등에 관한 문제는 **2026년 2월 28일 현재 유효한 법령, 고시, 판례 등을 기준**으로 정답을 구해야 합니다. 다만, 개별 과목 또는 문항에서 별도의 기준을 적용하도록 명시한 경우에는 그 기준을 적용하여 정답을 구해야 합니다.
8. **시험시간 관리의 책임은 응시자 본인에게 있습니다.**
   ※ 문제책은 시험종료 후 가지고 갈 수 있습니다.

정답공개 및 이의제기 안내

1. 정답공개: 정답가안 4.4.(토) 13:30 / 최종정답 4.13.(월) 18:00 / 사이버국가고시센터
2. 이의제기: 4.4.(토) 18:00 ~ 4.7.(화) 18:00 / 사이버국가고시센터
   ■ 구체적인 이의제기 방법은 정답가안 공개 시 공지 예정
3. 가산점 등록기간: 4.4.(토) 13:30 ~ 4.6.(월) 21:00
4. 가산점 등록방법: 사이버국가고시센터 ➜ [원서접수 → 가산점 등록/확인]

영　어

[1~5] 밑줄 친 부분에 들어갈 말로 가장 적절한 것을 고르시오.

1.

> The security system is designed to ___________ unauthorized access to the server room by requiring biometric verification at the entrance.

① infringe　　　　　② deter

③ depreciate　　　　④ authenticate

2.

> The board of directors expressed their ___________ about the proposed merger, citing concerns over potential cultural clashes between the two firms.

① transactions　　　② reservations

③ amenities　　　　④ credentials

3.

> The human resources director emphasized that there is much ___________ regarding the new benefit package, so an informative seminar will be held next Friday for clarification..

① confused　　　　　② confuse

③ confusion　　　　④ to be confused

4.

① I am in the immediate vicinity of the hospital right now.

② I have a prior medical record at this hospital.

③ My son is having trouble breathing right now.

④ There are no available beds in the emergency room at the moment.

5.

> A: Hey Clara, grabbing another coffee? That's your third disposable cup today.
>
> B: I know, I know. I feel a bit guilty about the waste.
>
> A: Why don't you use a tumbler, then? Most cafes even give you a discount.
>
> B: ____
>
> A: You should try putting a sticky note on your front door. It helps you remember.
>
> B: That's a good idea. I'll give it a shot tomorrow.

① I keep meaning to, but I always forget to bring it from home.

② I don't really like the taste of coffee from a tumbler.

③ Actually, these cups are fully biodegradable.

④ I have several tumblers, but none of them fit in my car's cup holder.

[6~7] 다음 글을 읽고 물음에 답하시오.

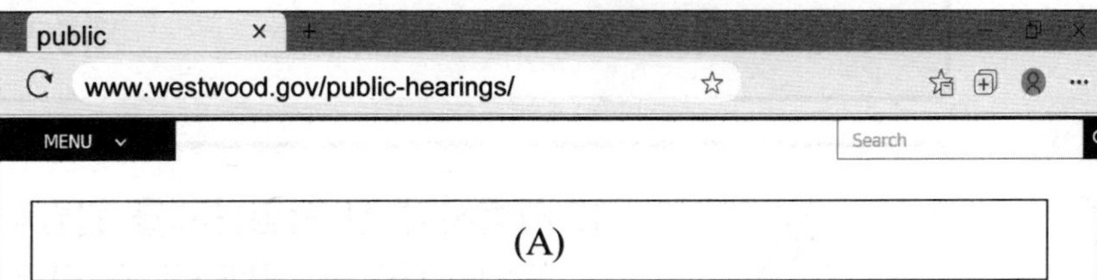

> **(A)**
>
> The Westwood Municipal Council announces a public hearing concerning the proposed rezoning of the Northwood industrial district for mixed-use residential and commercial development. The hearing is mandated by municipal ordinance 7.14 to ensure public discourse prior to any legislative action.
>
> The session will be held on October 28, at 7:00 PM in the City Hall chamber. Developers will present their master plan, followed by an environmental impact assessment from an independent consultant. Public commentary will be limited to three minutes per person and must pertain directly to the rezoning proposal itself, not to ancillary matters. Written submissions will be accepted until 5:00 PM on the day of the hearing and will be entered into the public record. This hearing is for informational and commentary purposes; no final vote will be taken at this meeting.

6. (A)에 들어갈 윗글의 제목으로 가장 적절한 것은?

① Environmental Guidelines for Industrial Zones

② Procedures for Business Proposal Submissions

③ Opportunities for Community Input on Land-Use Changes

④ Results of the Legislative Vote on Urban Plans

7. 윗글의 내용과 일치하지 않는 것은?

① 이번 공청회는 관련 시 조례에 의거하여 의무적으로 개최되는 절차이다.

② 외부 컨설턴트의 환경 영향 평가 발표 후, 개발자들이 마스터플랜을 공개할 예정이다.

③ 공청회 현장에서 개인이 발언은 시간 제한이 있다.

④ 이번 회의의 목적은 정보 공유 및 의견 수렴이며, 최종 투표는 진행되지 않는다.

8. 다음 글의 내용과 일치하지 않는 것은?

Summer Reading Challenge Information

The Metro Public Library invites readers of all ages to join the "Summer Reading Challenge." This program encourages the community to read more books during the summer holidays and offers exciting rewards for reaching reading milestones.

Participants can track their progress using our mobile app or a paper log. Upon completion of the challenge, everyone is invited to an awards ceremony at the end of August.

Challenge Categories:

Category	Requirement	Reward
Junior Readers	Read 10 picture books	A toy set and a certificate
Teens	Read 5 novels or 500 pages	A $20 book voucher
Adults	Read 3 books from different genres	A limited edition tote bag

Registration begins on June 1st. To sign up, simply visit the library website or stop by the main desk. Let's make this summer full of stories!

① The initiative is exclusively available throughout the summer season.

② Progress can be documented either digitally or via physical logs.

③ Youth participants must read five novels of at least 500 pages each.

④ The adult challenge does not allow reading books from only one genre.

9. 다음 글의 목적으로 가장 적절한 것은?

	Send　Preview　Save
To	All Residents of 'The Hamilton'
From	Hamilton Building Management
Date	November 5, 2026
Subject	Urgent Notice

[My PC] [Browse]

[Times New ▼] [10pt ▼] G G *G* G̲ G̲

This is a mandatory notice regarding annual fire alarm system testing, as required by city safety regulations. Our certified technicians will be testing the audible alarms (horns/strobes) inside every apartment unit.

Schedule:
- Floors 1-10: Wed, Nov 12 (9:00 AM - 5:00 PM)
- Floors 11-20: Thu, Nov 13 (9:00 AM - 5:00 PM)

Technicians require access to your unit for approx. 5-10 minutes. If you are not home, you must arrange access by either:
1. Leaving a key with the front desk (in a sealed, labeled envelope).
2. Ensuring a trusted neighbor is present.

Note: The common area alarms (hallways, lobby) will be tested separately on Friday, Nov 14, and will be very loud. This test does not require access to your unit.

① to provide residents with evacuation guidelines in case of a fire

② to request cooperation for the in-unit fire alarm inspection

③ to identify in advance the units that technicians will not be able to access

④ to gather residents' opinions on changes to city safety regulations

[10~11] 다음 글을 읽고 물음에 답하시오.

Invitation to a Symposium on Quantum Physics

The Institute for Advanced Physics cordially invites you to the International Symposium on Quantum Entanglement, a pivotal event for researchers and academics in the field. This symposium aims to <u>foster</u> collaboration and disseminate cutting-edge research findings.

The three-day event will feature keynote addresses by Nobel laureate Dr. Evelyn Reed and Dr. Kenji Tanaka, alongside numerous parallel sessions and poster presentations. All presentations will be conducted in English. Attendance is open to postgraduate students and professionals in quantum physics and related disciplines. A foundational knowledge of quantum mechanics is a prerequisite for all attendees to fully benefit from the technical sessions. Registration is mandatory and closes on November 1. Note that the symposium proceedings will be published in a peer-reviewed journal, but presentation at the symposium does not guarantee publication.

10. 밑줄 친 foster의 의미와 가장 가까운 것은?

① align
② repress
③ coerce
④ promote

11. 윗글의 심포지엄 안내와 일치하지 않는 것은?

① The event is intended to promote the sharing of advanced research.
② Postgraduate students in the field of quantum physics are eligible to attend.
③ Attendees must have a foundational knowledge of quantum mechanics.
④ All research presented at the event will be included in a journal.

[12~13] 밑줄 친 부분 중 어법상 옳지 않은 것을 고르시오.

12.

Linguistics in AI development ① <u>require</u> a sophisticated understanding of syntax and semantics. While some engineers argue that vast amounts of data are sufficient ② <u>for machines</u> to learn, most experts agree that structural knowledge is ③ <u>altogether</u> indispensable. Thus, ④ <u>to bridge</u> the gap between raw data and human-like understanding, a hybrid approach combining both methods is now the standard.

13.

The 2025 Emissions Gap Report finds that global warming projections ① <u>have fallen</u> slightly. However, delays in deep emission cuts driven by geopolitical tensions and economic instability ② <u>mean</u> the world will temporarily exceed the 1.5°C limit. The report ③ <u>argues</u> that action by the G20 will be pivotal in ④ <u>narrow</u> the emissions gap.

14. 다음 글의 내용과 일치하는 것은?

Holiday Shipping Deadlines: Order Now for Dec 24 Delivery

Date: November 5, 2026

To ensure your gifts arrive in time for the holiday, please place your orders by the following dates:

☐ Standard Shipping ($5.99 / Free on orders $50+):
　Order by 11:59 PM (EST), Monday, December 15.
☐ Expedited Shipping ($12.99):
　Order by 11:59 PM (EST), Thursday, December 18.
☐ Overnight Shipping ($24.99):
　Order by 1:00 PM (EST), Monday, December 22.

These deadlines apply only to addresses within the continental US. Shipments to Alaska, Hawaii, and international addresses will require an additional 5-7 business days and are not guaranteed for Dec 24 arrival.

Please note: Custom-monogrammed items require an extra 3 business days for processing and are not eligible for Overnight Shipping.

① Standard shipping is provided complimentary on orders over $50.
② Expedited shipping must be ordered by the morning of December 18.
③ An order placed at 2 PM on December 22 can use overnight shipping.
④ Orders shipped to Alaska are sure to arrive by December 24.

15. 다음 글의 주제로 가장 적절한 것은?

The dominant assumption in economics posits that efficiency will, in the long run, prevail. Suboptimal technologies, according to this view, should be swiftly replaced by superior alternatives. However, economic history is full of opposite examples, of which the QWERTY keyboard is the most cited. This phenomenon is termed "path dependency": the idea that initial, often trivial or accidental, choices can create powerful "lock-in" effects. High switching costs, established infrastructure, and network effects—where a product's value increases with the number of users—can entrench an inferior standard. Consequently, the trajectory of technological development is not always a rational march toward perfection but is often constrained by the contingent events of its own past.

① Reasons for the persistence of lower-quality technical standards
② How to replace suboptimal technologies quickly
③ The importance of being first in the technology market
④ Efficient ways to replace suboptimal technologies

16. 다음 글의 흐름상 어색한 문장은?

A growing concern in e-commerce is the rise of "surveillance pricing," a strategy where retailers use AI to analyze a customer's personal data and online behavior. ① This allows companies to set dynamic, individualized prices based on how much a shopper is likely to pay. ② Browsing history, location, device type, and even perceived income level can influence the price shown for the same product. ③ Supporters claim this is simply a more advanced form of market segmentation, rewarding loyal customers with discounts. ④ Many platforms also invest in cybersecurity to protect customer data. However, critics argue that this practice is discriminatory and creates an opaque market in which consumers cannot know if they are being treated fairly.

17. 주어진 문장이 들어갈 위치로 가장 적절한 것은?

However, according to Dr. John Dunlosky, this is far from the most effective way of retaining information.

Students instinctively rely on several popular study techniques. (①) When facing a thick textbook, you likely pick up a highlighter to mark important sentences. (②) While bright colors create a sense of achievement, they fail to embed knowledge, making active recall through self-testing a far superior strategy. (③) Your brain requires cognitive effort to strengthen neural pathways, triggered only during active retrieval. (④) Without this mental strain, the information remains at a superficial level, and your effort results in nothing more than a colorful but empty textbook.

18. 주어진 글 다음에 이어질 글의 순서로 가장 적절한 것은?

The World Meteorological Organization (WMO) reported a record leap in global carbon dioxide concentrations for 2024, raising fears of accelerating global heating.

(A) In addition to emissions from human activity, natural factors have exacerbated the problem. Expanding wildfires, fueled by drier and hotter conditions, released massive amounts of stored carbon into the atmosphere.

(B) This alarming increase, the largest since measurements began, is attributed to several factors. The most significant, according to the report, remains the continued and widespread use of fossil fuels for energy.

(C) Compounding this issue, the capacity of natural carbon sinks, such as oceans and forests, to absorb CO_2 appears to be diminishing. This reduced absorption means more of the emitted carbon remains in the atmosphere, driving temperatures higher.

① (A)−(C)−(B)   ② (B)−(A)−(C)

③ (B)−(C)−(A)   ④ (C)−(A)−(B)

[19~20] 밑줄 친 부분에 들어갈 말로 가장 적절한 것을 고르시오.

19.

We often judge communication by the eloquence of the speaker. We default to a mode of passive reception, ___________________. This passive stance is a critical error. The good listener operates differently; they treat listening as an active, extractive process, like mining for gold. They understand that a disorganized speaker or a flawed delivery may still conceal valuable insights. It is the listener's job to dig, to ask clarifying questions, and to connect disparate ideas. Rather than blaming the speaker for a lack of clarity, the effective listener interrogates their own understanding first. This assumption of responsibility is what separates a passive hearer from an active learner, ultimately determining how much value is gained from any interaction.

① shifting attention toward the speaker's delivery rather than the content

② actively seeking out the underlying message

③ relying on surface-level cues to make sense of the message

④ placing the burden of comprehension entirely on the one who is transmitting

20.

The influx of approximately 17,000 Chinese immigrants in the 1880s, pivotal for constructing the Canadian Pacific Railway, catalyzed a significant socio-economic backlash upon the project's completion. Amidst economic contraction and rising unemployment in 1885, a significant segment of the Canadian populace directed its anxieties toward the remaining immigrant laborers. The government, bending to this nativist pressure, instituted a discriminatory "head tax" of $50 −a formidable sum at the time. Despite this punitive measure, many immigrants stayed. This led the government to incrementally raise the tax to $500, a figure exceeding a full year's wages for most. This oppressive policy forced a large contingent of the Chinese community underground, seeking refuge in subterranean tunnels to evade the tax. These tunnels, rediscovered in the 1980s, now serve as a historical site, ___________________________.

① demonstrating the economic success of the railway project

② revealing the government's efforts to support immigrant laborers

③ reflecting the hardships faced by workers after the railway's completion

④ mirroring a significant rise in global urban dwellers

수고하셨습니다.
당신의 합격을 응원합니다.

2026 공무원 시험 대비 실전동형 모의고사
영 어
▌ 제11회 ▌

응시번호		문제책형
성 명		가

제1과목	국어	제2과목	영어	제3과목	한국사
제4과목		제5과목			

응시자 주의사항

1. **시험시작 전 시험문제를 열람하는 행위나 시험종료 후 답안을 작성하는 행위를 한 사람**은 「공무원임용시험령」 제51조에 의거 **부정행위자로 처리됩니다.**
2. 답안지 책형 표기는 시험시작 전 감독관의 지시에 따라 **문제책 앞면에 인쇄된 문제책형을 확인**한 후, 답안지 책형란에 해당 책형(1개)을 '●'로 표기하여야 합니다.
3. 답안은 문제책 표지의 과목 순서에 따라 답안지에 인쇄된 순서(제1·2·3·4·5과목)에 맞추어 표기해야 하며, 과목 순서를 바꾸어 표기한 경우에도 문제책 표지의 과목 순서대로 채점되므로 유의하시기 바랍니다.
4. 시험이 시작되면 문제를 주의 깊게 읽은 후, **문항의 취지에 가장 적합한 하나의 정답만을 고르며,** 문제내용에 관한 질문은 할 수 없습니다.
5. 답안지의 모든 기재 및 표기 사항은 **컴퓨터용 흑색 싸인펜을 사용**하며, 반드시 <보기>의 **올바른 표기 방식으로 답안을 작성해야** 합니다.

   <보기> 올바른 표기: ● 잘못된 표기: ⓥ ⊗ ◑ ◉ ◎ ⑪ ⊖ ③

6. 답안을 잘못 표기하였을 경우에는 답안지를 교체하여 작성하거나 수정할 수 있으며, 표기한 답안을 수정할 때는 응시자 본인이 가져온 **수정테이프만을 사용**하여 해당 부분을 완전히 지우고 부착된 수정테이프가 떨어지지 않도록 손으로 눌러주어야 합니다. (**수정액 또는 수정스티커 등은 사용 불가**)
   ■ 불량한 수정테이프의 사용과 불완전한 수정처리로 발생하는 모든 문제는 응시자 본인에게 책임이 있습니다.
7. 법령, 고시, 판례 등에 관한 문제는 **2026년 2월 28일 현재 유효한 법령, 고시, 판례 등을 기준**으로 정답을 구해야 합니다. 다만, 개별 과목 또는 문항에서 별도의 기준을 적용하도록 명시한 경우에는 그 기준을 적용하여 정답을 구해야 합니다.
8. **시험시간 관리의 책임은 응시자 본인에게 있습니다.**
   ※ 문제책은 시험종료 후 가지고 갈 수 있습니다.

정답공개 및 이의제기 안내

1. 정답공개: 정답가안 4.4.(토) 13:30 / 최종정답 4.13.(월) 18:00 / 사이버국가고시센터
2. 이의제기: 4.4.(토) 18:00 ~ 4.7.(화) 18:00 / 사이버국가고시센터
   ■ 구체적인 이의제기 방법은 정답가안 공개 시 공지 예정
3. 가산점 등록기간: 4.4.(토) 13:30 ~ 4.6.(월) 21:00
4. 가산점 등록방법: 사이버국가고시센터 ➡ [원서접수 → 가산점 등록/확인]

영 어

[1~5] 밑줄 친 부분에 들어갈 말로 가장 적절한 것을 고르시오.

1.

The official is _______ enough to not only pay attention to superficial problems, but also to grasp the fundamental problems underlying them.

① sharp
② conservative
③ reserved
④ spontaneous

2.

Human memory is highly _______, frequently reconstructing past events in response to emotional states or external suggestions.

① consistent
② enduring
③ mutable
④ persuasive

3.

The email reminded staff that _______ who participates in training sessions must sign attendance forms before leaving.

① every
② those
③ everyone
④ all

4.

A: Hey, did you hear about the flight delays due to the system outage yesterday?
B: Yeah, it was all over the news. Were you affected by it?
A: Unfortunately, yes. My flight from London was delayed by over 6 hours. I was stuck at the airport all day.
B: That sounds terrible. Did the airline offer any compensation?
A: Far from it. They said it was an "extraordinary circumstance" beyond their control.
B: That's a common excuse. You shouldn't give up, though.
____
A: You think so? I still have my boarding pass and the delay notification email.
B: Definitely. Under current regulations, you are entitled to compensation for delays over 3 hours, even for technical issues.

① Valid identification is required for all international travelers.
② You should file a formal claim with proof of the delay.
③ You had better confirm your reservation before departure.
④ The airport security should be held responsible for the delay.

5.

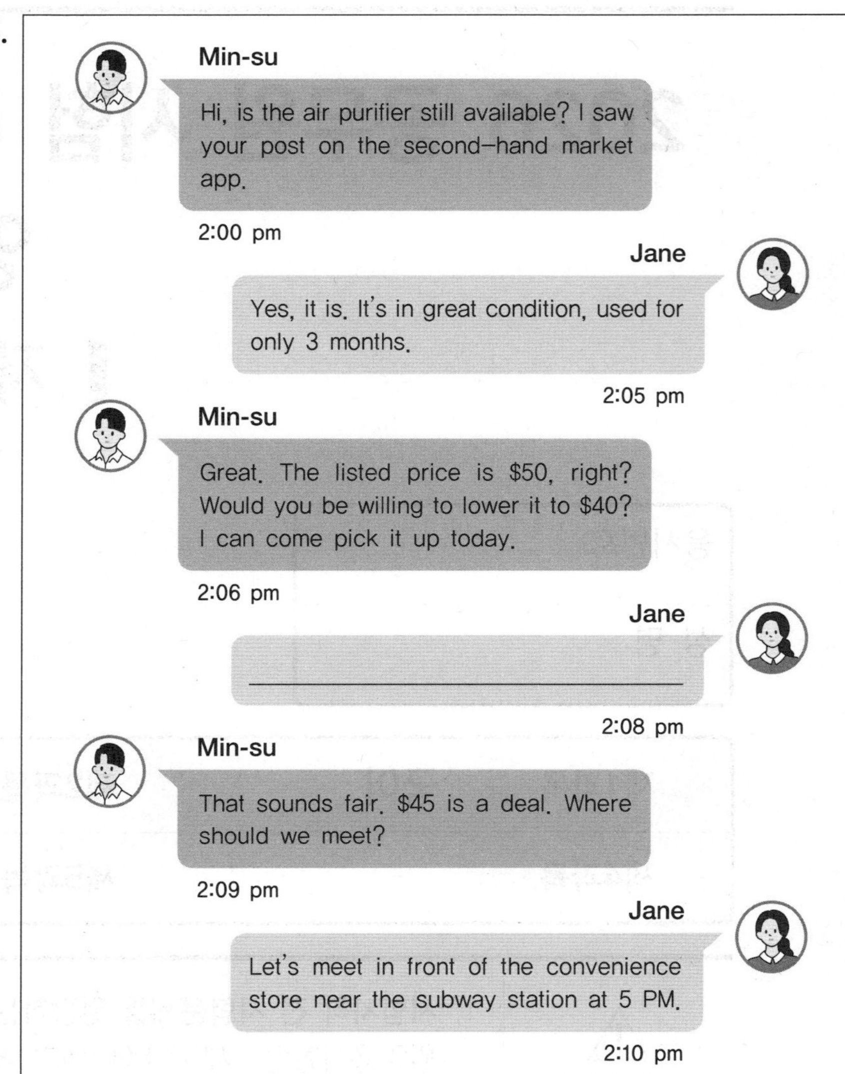

① Please refer to the original posting for the final asking price.
② You can check the product details again in the app description.
③ I'm firm on the price, but I'll make a one-time exception and meet you halfway.
④ The delivery driver is responsible for the final price.

6. 다음 글의 주제로 가장 적절한 것은?

Neuroscientists have recently mapped the precise brain circuits that govern the release of growth hormone (GH) during sleep. The study reveals a complex feedback system. During non-REM sleep, specific neurons in the hypothalamus are activated, triggering the pituitary gland to release GH. This hormone not only fuels growth and cellular repair but also, in turn, regulates neural pathways associated with wakefulness. This discovery illuminates a critical link between poor sleep patterns and a cascade of health issues. A disruption in this sleep-GH circuit—due to chronic insomnia or fragmented sleep— can lead to deficient hormone release. This deficiency is now strongly correlated not only with metabolic disorders like obesity and diabetes but also with accelerated cognitive decline, as GH plays a significant role in maintaining brain plasticity and memory consolidation.

① The Role of the Pituitary Gland in Cellular Repair
② The Primary Causes of Chronic Insomnia in Adults
③ The Neural Circuit Linking Sleep Quality to Metabolic and Cognitive Health
④ New Pharmaceutical Treatments for Growth Hormone Deficiency

[7~8] 다음 글을 읽고 물음에 답하시오.

U.S. Chemical Safety Board (CSB)

Mission

We investigate major chemical incidents at fixed industrial facilities to protect workers, the public, and the environment. Our mission is to drive chemical safety change by <u>uncovering</u> the root causes of accidents and issuing safety recommendations to plants, regulatory agencies, and industry groups. We don't impose fines or penalties directly.

Vision

We aim to be the global leader in chemical incident investigation, ensuring our findings and recommendations lead to systemic safety improvements. We facilitate this by ensuring objective, science-based analysis to the benefit of industry, workers, and the public.

Core Values

☐ Honesty & Integrity: We demand complete honesty and transparency in our findings.

☐ Independence & Objectivity: We act independently and objectively, free from regulatory or enforcement pressure, to create trust in our investigations.

---

7. 윗글의 내용과 일치하는 것은?

① It identifies underlying reasons of accidents and provides safety guidance.

② It is empowered to levy financial sanctions against violators.

③ It's primary goal is to lead the world in chemical manufacturing.

④ It must get approval from other agencies before beginning an investigation.

8. 밑줄 친 uncovering의 의미와 가장 가까운 것은?

① disclosing   ② concealing

③ recovering   ④ disregarding

9. 밑줄 친 부분 중 어법상 옳지 않은 것은?

Despite the recent economic downturn, our firm remains committed to ① <u>expand</u> its global market share. Should you require any assistance regarding the new project, please ② <u>feel</u> free to contact the planning department. We will provide necessary resources to ③ <u>whoever</u> is assigned to the task force. Furthermore, ④ <u>having completed</u> the preliminary market analysis, the team is now ready to present the final proposal to the board of directors.

[10~11] 다음 글을 읽고 물음에 답하시오.

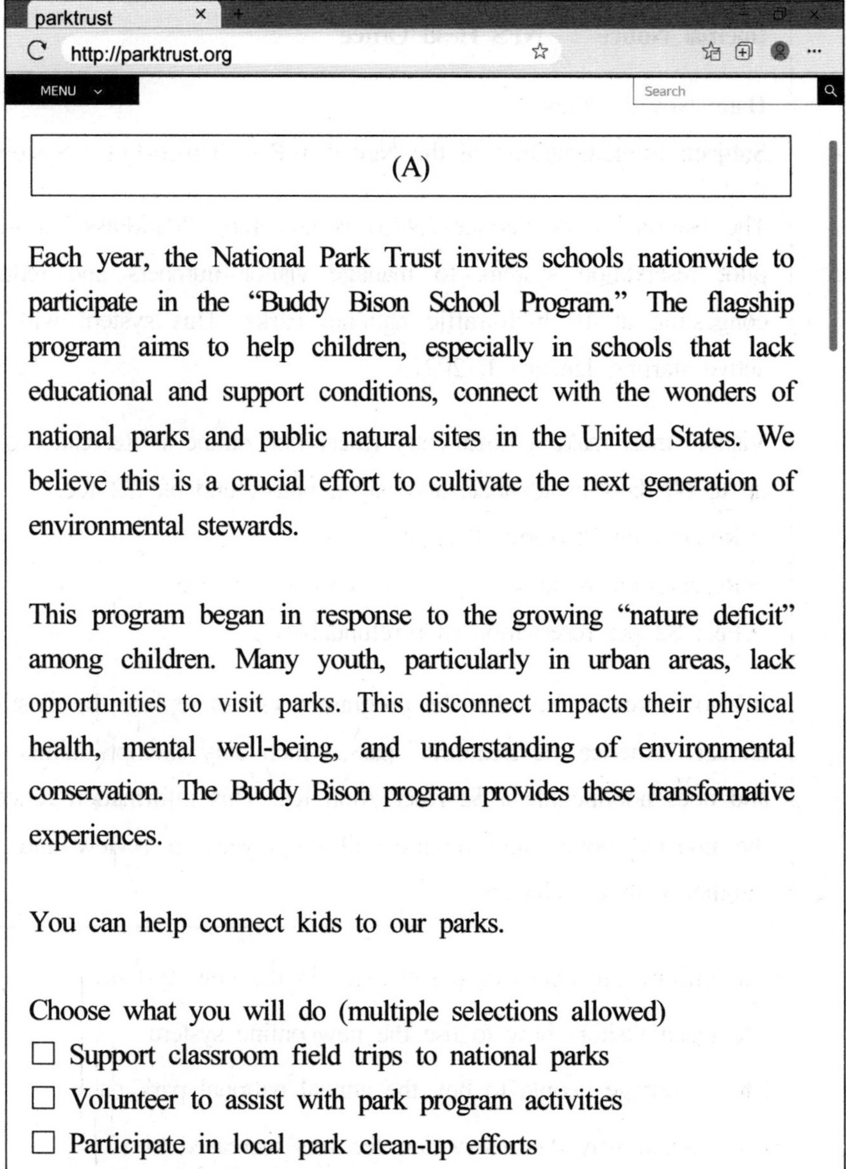

(A)

Each year, the National Park Trust invites schools nationwide to participate in the "Buddy Bison School Program." The flagship program aims to help children, especially in schools that lack educational and support conditions, connect with the wonders of national parks and public natural sites in the United States. We believe this is a crucial effort to cultivate the next generation of environmental stewards.

This program began in response to the growing "nature deficit" among children. Many youth, particularly in urban areas, lack opportunities to visit parks. This disconnect impacts their physical health, mental well-being, and understanding of environmental conservation. The Buddy Bison program provides these transformative experiences.

You can help connect kids to our parks.

Choose what you will do (multiple selections allowed)
☐ Support classroom field trips to national parks
☐ Volunteer to assist with park program activities
☐ Participate in local park clean-up efforts
☐ Fund transportation for the Kids to Parks Day event

10. (A)에 들어갈 윗글의 제목으로 가장 적절한 것은?

① Comparing Urban and Rural School Systems

② Bridging the Gap Between Urban Youth and the Great Outdoors

③ Professional Training for Environmental Stewards

④ Improving Physical Health Through Clean-up Events

11. 윗글에서 캠페인에 관한 내용과 일치하지 않는 것은?

① 교육 자원에 대한 접근이 제한적인 학생들을 대상으로 한다.

② 다음 세대의 환경 관리자들을 양성하는 것을 목표로 한다.

③ 국립공원을 위한 전문 여행 가이드를 교육하는 데 집중한다.

④ 프로그램에 기여하기 위해 한 가지 이상의 방법을 선택할 수 있다.

12. 밑줄 친 부분 중 어법상 옳지 않은 것은?

It is the transition to renewable energy sources ① <u>that</u> recent government initiatives aim to accelerate. This shift is considered ② <u>essential</u> for meeting climate goals. However, the investment required is ③ <u>very</u> larger than initial projections, posing a significant challenge for the budget. The authorities are seeking new strategies ④ <u>through</u> which they can manage the budget more efficiently.

13. 다음 글의 목적으로 가장 적절한 것은?

Internal Notice — **NPS Head Office**

Date: Nov 3, 2026

Subject: Implementation of the New ParkPass Timed-Entry System

The National Park Service (NPS) is launching "ParkPass," a new pilot reservation system, to manage visitor numbers and reduce congestion at 10 high-traffic national parks. This system will be active starting January 1, 2027.

Visitors must make a timed-entry reservation online at Recreation.gov, up to 60 days in advance, and pay a non-refundable $2 fee.
 • Reservation Platform: Recreation.gov
 • Reservation Window: Up to 60 days in advance
 • Fee: $2 per reservation (non-refundable)

It also makes it clear that the program does not replace the existing annual "America the Beautiful" pass, which only exempts admission and does not include a $2 reservation fee. This information reflects the updated policy and requires all employees to review and be familiar with the changes.

① to inform employees of the changes in the new system
② to teach visitors how to use the new online system
③ to encourage people to buy the annual national park pass
④ to explain why the reservation fee was increased to $2

14. 주어진 글 다음에 이어질 글의 순서로 가장 적절한 것은?

As organizations navigate the post-pandemic landscape, work is shifting toward greater flexibility and technology, reshaping how teams operate and stay connected.

(A) To facilitate the success of the integrated workspace, companies are investing in technologies like VR and AR to enhance virtual teamwork beyond standard video calls and create more engaging shared workspaces.

(B) Still, both remote and hybrid setups bring challenges, requiring organizations to address employee well-being and prevent burnout or isolation, which have become more visible in dispersed work environments.

(C) This evolution is best represented by the hybrid model, which combines office days with remote work to balance flexibility and collaboration while maintaining team cohesion.

① (A) − (C) − (B)　　　　② (B) − (A) − (C)
③ (C) − (A) − (B)　　　　④ (C) − (B) − (A)

15. 다음 글의 내용과 일치하지 않는 것은?

Austin Trail of Lights Returns for 61st Season
(Posted: Nov 2, 2026)

The 61st annual Austin Trail of Lights returns to Zilker Park, November 28 - December 23, 2026. This beloved community event will feature over 2 million lights, 90 holiday trees, and new interactive displays.

Hours: Open nightly from 7:00 PM – 10:00 PM.

Tickets: General admission is free for a total of seven nights (28-30 November, 1-4 December). For all other nights, advance ticket purchase is required ($10). Tickets must be purchased online via the official event website; no tickets will be sold at the gate.

Special Access: The "ZIP Fast Pass" ($25) allows early entry at 6:00 PM and access to an exclusive lounge.

Note: The annual Fun Run will take place on November 26, two days before the official opening.

① This announcement was posted two days before the festival opened.
② This year's festival is decorated with a vast number of lights.
③ General admission is not available for free on all days of the festival.
④ Visitors can buy a special early-entry pass for an extra fee.

16. 다음 글의 흐름상 어색한 문장은?

The global drive for decarbonization has increased interest in green hydrogen as a clean energy carrier. Green hydrogen is produced by using renewable energy to power electrolyzers that split water. ① Recent advancements aim to improve electrolyzer efficiency, shifting from older alkaline systems to Proton Exchange Membrane (PEM) and Solid Oxide technologies. ② These improvements focus on lowering the high production costs that limit green hydrogen's competitiveness. ③ In fact, many people prefer using green hydrogen because it is much cheaper to produce than other fuels. ④ Despite current challenges, green hydrogen remains essential for reducing emissions in sectors like steelmaking and heavy transport.

17. 다음 글의 목적으로 가장 적절한 것은?

	Send	Preview	Save
To	All Seattle Residents		
From	Seattle Department of Transportation		
Date	November 5, 2026		
Subject	the Draft Transportation Plan 2030		

Dear Seattle Residents,

The Seattle Department of Transportation (SDOT) has released the Draft Transportation Plan 2030, outlining our vision for the next decade. This plan focuses on safety, sustainability, and equity in mobility.

Before we finalize this important document, we need to hear from you. Your input is critical to ensuring the plan reflects the needs of all communities. We invite you to review the full draft plan on our official website. After reviewing, please complete our online public feedback survey, which will be open until November 30, 2026.

Your participation will directly influence the future of Seattle's transportation. We are also holding two virtual town hall meetings next week for live Q&A.

Thank you for your engagement.

① to announce the final version of the new transportation plan

② to gather public feedback on the Draft Transportation Plan 2030

③ to apologize for the cause of a recent traffic accident

④ to promote transportation safety policies through 2030

18. 주어진 문장이 들어갈 위치로 가장 적절한 것은?

This adverse reaction is caused by cucurbitacins, a class of bitter chemical compounds found naturally in gourds like squash and zucchini.

A recent medical case reported on November 12, 2025, highlighted a rare but severe danger associated with certain common vegetables. (①) A woman experienced life-threatening symptoms after consuming homemade juice made from gourds. (②) While these inherent substances normally exist in cultivated plants at harmless levels, factors like cross-pollination or environmental stress can cause them to increase dramatically. (③) The bitterness of the juice is a primary warning sign, but it can be easily masked when mixed with other ingredients like fruits. (④) Health officials advise that if a squash or zucchini tastes unusually bitter or "off," it should be discarded immediately to prevent poisoning.

[19~20] 밑줄 친 부분에 들어갈 말로 가장 적절한 것을 고르시오.

19.

Describing taste often challenges our language, so we bridge this gap by borrowing terms from other senses. For instance, we may describe a sour flavor as "high" or a bitter one as "low," using vocabulary typically reserved for musical pitch. This phenomenon, known as synesthetic metaphor, allows us to ______________________ to deepen our understanding of intangible experiences. Advertisers are particularly adept at leveraging this mechanism. By linking abstract shapes or sounds with specific products, they craft multi-dimensional experiences. A car with sleek lines is intuitively perceived as faster, not just visually but viscerally. By engaging multiple senses, marketers can appeal to consumers on a subconscious, almost primal level.

① isolate each sense to focus on pure perception

② use familiar sensory concepts to appreciate different experiences

③ confuse consumers with contradictory sensory signals

④ rely solely on literal descriptions to ensure clarity

20.

The narrative that technological progress inevitably leads to mass unemployment is a persistent historical fallacy. While automation can certainly displace manual workers in specific sectors, the macroeconomic evidence tells a counterintuitive story. Technological advancement boosts overall productivity and increases national income. This actual rise in collective wealth does not simply vanish; it ultimately translates into higher demand for a wide array of goods and services. To meet this new demand, firms must hire more workers, often in roles newly created by the technology itself, just as the rise of the automobile industry eventually created millions of jobs in suburban retail and tourism that didn't exist before. Consequently, while painful transitions exist, the long-term effect is not a net loss of jobs, but rather ______________________.

① a societal dependence on automated systems

② a growing wage gap between skilled and unskilled labor

③ a redistribution of the workforce into new industries

④ a permanent reduction in the overall demand for goods

수고하셨습니다.
당신의 합격을 응원합니다.

2026 공무원 시험 대비 실전동형 모의고사
영어
▌ 제12회 ▐

<table>
<tr><td>응시번호</td><td rowspan="2"></td><td rowspan="2">문제책형
</td></tr>
<tr><td>성 명</td></tr>
</table>

제1과목	국어	제2과목	<u>영어</u>	제3과목	한국사
제4과목		제5과목			

응시자 주의사항

1. **시험시작 전 시험문제를 열람하는 행위나 시험종료 후 답안을 작성하는 행위를 한 사람은** 「공무원임용시험령」 제51조에 의거 **부정행위자로 처리됩니다.**
2. **답안지 책형 표기는 시험시작 전 감독관의 지시에 따라 문제책 앞면에 인쇄된 문제책형을 확인한 후, 답안지 책형란에 해당 책형(1개)을 '●'로 표기하여야 합니다.**
3. **답안은 문제책 표지의 과목 순서에 따라 답안지에 인쇄된 순서(제1·2·3·4·5과목)에 맞추어 표기해야 하며, 과목 순서를 바꾸어 표기한 경우에도 문제책 표지의 과목 순서대로 채점되므로 유의하시기 바랍니다.**
4. 시험이 시작되면 문제를 주의 깊게 읽은 후, 문항의 취지에 가장 적합한 하나의 정답만을 고르며, 문제내용에 관한 질문은 할 수 없습니다.
5. 답안지의 모든 기재 및 표기 사항은 **컴퓨터용 흑색 싸인펜을 사용**하며, 반드시 <보기>의 **올바른 표기 방식으로 답안을 작성해야 합니다.**

   <보기>　올바른 표기: ●　　잘못된 표기: Ⓥ ⊗ ◐ ◉ ◍ ◯ ⊖ ③

6. **답안을 잘못 표기하였을 경우에는 답안지를 교체하여 작성하거나 수정할 수 있으며, 표기한 답안을 수정할 때는 응시자 본인이 가져온 수정테이프만을 사용하여 해당 부분을 완전히 지우고 부착된 수정테이프가 떨어지지 않도록 손으로 눌러주어야 합니다. (수정액 또는 수정스티커 등은 사용 불가)**
   ▪불량한 수정테이프의 사용과 불완전한 수정처리로 발생하는 모든 문제는 응시자 본인에게 책임이 있습니다.
7. 법령, 고시, 판례 등에 관한 문제는 **2026년 2월 28일 현재 유효한 법령, 고시, 판례 등을 기준**으로 정답을 구해야 합니다. 다만, 개별 과목 또는 문항에서 별도의 기준을 적용하도록 명시한 경우에는 그 기준을 적용하여 정답을 구해야 합니다.
8. **시험시간 관리의 책임은 응시자 본인에게 있습니다.**

   ※ 문제책은 시험종료 후 가지고 갈 수 있습니다.

정답공개 및 이의제기 안내

1. 정답공개: 정답가안 4.4.(토) 13:30 / 최종정답 4.13.(월) 18:00 / 사이버국가고시센터
2. 이의제기: 4.4.(토) 18:00 ~ 4.7.(화) 18:00 / 사이버국가고시센터
   ▪구체적인 이의제기 방법은 정답가안 공개 시 공지 예정
3. 가산점 등록기간: 4.4.(토) 13:30 ~ 4.6.(월) 21:00
4. 가산점 등록방법: 사이버국가고시센터 ➡ [원서접수 → 가산점 등록/확인]

영　어

[1~5] 밑줄 친 부분에 들어갈 말로 가장 적절한 것을 고르시오.

1.
Under the revised corporate policy, employees working at the remote branch are now eligible for a monthly housing ________ to offset higher living expenses.

① withdrawal
② compliance
③ subsidy
④ discrepancy

2.
The comprehensive insurance policy covers accidental damage to the building, although repairs caused by natural wear and tear are specifically ________ from coverage.

① excluded
② commended
③ adopted
④ expedited

3.
A legal document essential for the merger the CEO of both companies had carefully reviewed ________ during the private press conference.

① signed
② was signed
③ to be signed
④ would sign

4.
A: Hello, Customer Support. How may I assist you today?
B: Hi, I'm calling about the subscription fee for my music streaming service. I noticed a charge of $15 this month, but it used to be $10.
A: Ah, yes. We sent out an email last month regarding our price adjustment due to rising licensing costs. Didn't you receive it?
B: I must have missed it. To be honest, a 50% increase feels a bit too steep for me. I'm considering switching to another platform.
A: ____
B: Oh, really? That would maintain the original price for another year. In that case, I'll stay.

① I can guide you through the refund process prior to account termination.
② Unfortunately, the price hike applies to all users without exception.
③ We can offer you a long-term user discount that keeps your rate at $10 for 12 months.
④ You can upgrade to the family plan for an additional $5 per month.

5.

① Great, feel free to use the AI tool once you remove the names.
② I think you should ask the IT department to install the software.
③ Even so, company policy strictly forbids uploading internal data to public AI servers.
④ Why don't you hire a freelancer to process the data instead?

[6~7] 밑줄 친 부분 중 어법상 옳지 않은 것을 고르시오.

6.
The recent climate report emphasizes ① that rising sea levels are a direct consequence of global warming. Many coastal communities have ② already experienced severe flooding, and the situation ③ expects to worsen without immediate intervention. This challenge requires ④ a global response.

7.
Researchers ① investigating the ethics of AI argue that algorithms must be transparent, accountable, and ensure fairness. However, ensuring full compliance with the various legal frameworks and ethical guidelines recently established by international committees ② are incredibly difficult, as biases ③ can be deeply embedded in the training data, ④ leading to discriminatory outcomes.

[8~9] 다음 글을 읽고 물음에 답하시오.

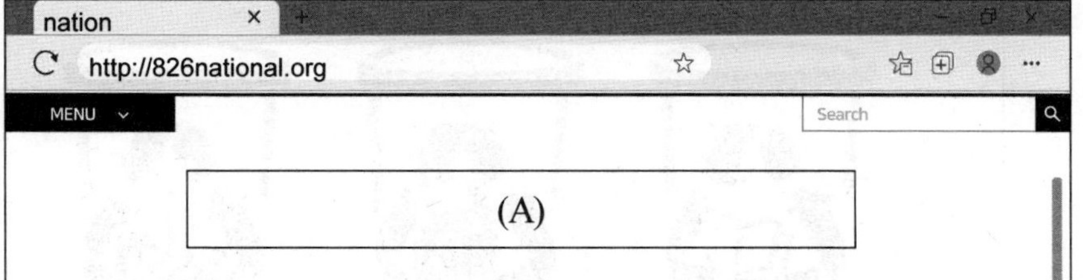

Each year in March, 826 National invites communities to celebrate the power of student writing. This initiative, "Amplify," aims to provide a platform for student voices and promote creative writing as a tool for self-empowerment. This is a critical step toward building a more empathetic and literate society.

Launched in response to funding cuts in arts education, this campaign supports students in under-resourced public schools. We aim to bridge the literacy gap by connecting students with adult mentors who provide personalized writing support and encourage creative expression.

Select Your Volunteer Role

☐ Writing Mentor: Provide 1:1 feedback on student work.
☐ Editorial Assistant: Edit manuscripts for publication.
☐ Event Coordinator: Organize community workshops.
☐ Guest Speaker: Share professional writing experience.

Preferred Session Type

☐ In-person (at a local school or center)
☐ Virtual (online mentorship via Zoom)

Availability

☐ Weekday Mornings (9 AM - 12 PM)
☐ Weekday Afternoons (1 PM - 5 PM)
☐ Weekend Sessions

8. (A)에 들어갈 윗글의 제목으로 가장 적절한 것은?

① How to Improve Your Creative Writing Skills
② Call for Volunteers to Support Student Writing
③ Strategies for Improving Student Writing Skills
④ Benefits of One-on-One Professional Mentorship

9. 윗글에서 캠페인에 관한 내용과 일치하지 않는 것은?

① The program is held on an annual basis every spring.
② It was established due to a reduction in financial support for arts programs.
③ Adult mentors are responsible for managing legal frameworks in public schools.
④ Volunteers can participate in the program regardless of their location.

[10~11] 다음 글을 읽고 물음에 답하시오.

The Hastings Center

People should be able to live healthy and prosperous lives, guided by sound ethical values. As medicine and technology advance, it is essential that these powerful tools be used responsibly. Ethical deliberation makes a critical contribution to societal well-being and ensures that scientific progress serves humanity.

But access to and the application of new medical technologies are not always equitable. These innovations raise <u>profound</u> ethical questions about life, death, and justice that society must address.

The Hastings Center is here to support this need. As a non-partisan bioethics research institute, it aims to frame and analyze the difficult ethical issues in health, science, and technology. The Center is committed to helping achieve this vision by partnering with diverse actors, including policymakers, philanthropists, and the scientific community, to inform public conversation and policy.

10. 밑줄 친 profound의 의미와 가장 가까운 것은?

① ingenuous   ② abstruse
③ explicit   ④ peripheral

11. 윗글의 목적으로 가장 적절한 것은?

① to highlight the need for more bioethics support
② to explain the role of this agency
③ to propose a new medical ethics campaign
④ to stress the need for medical-ethics training

12. 다음 글의 주제로 가장 적절한 것은?

Relying on reputation to judge integrity is a flawed strategy because it assumes character is static. Categorizing people as fundamentally "good" or "evil" based on past actions ignores the intricate complexity of human psychology. Most people act as pragmatists, making moral choices based on a delicate balance of potential gains and risks in a specific context. Therefore, an individual who is honest in one situation may act differently when faced with overwhelming pressures or tempting incentives. Consequently, honesty is not a fixed trait but a variable one. Integrity is not a fixed entity but a dynamic state that changes over time and under different circumstances.

① The role of personal gains in moral choices
② Why integrity is contextual, not permanent
③ Past reputation: a key to predicting integrity
④ The inherent complexity of human psychology

13. 다음 글의 내용과 일치하지 <u>않는</u> 것은?

> **Green Valley State Park: Winter Season Notice**
>
> As colder weather arrives, Green Valley State Park facilities are beginning to "winterize" for the safety of visitors and the protection of our infrastructure.
>
> **Facility Closures:**
> ☐ Campground: The main campground (Sites 1-50) is closed to all camping from November 10, 2025, to April 15, 2026.
> ※ Cabin rooms instead of campsites are available throughout the year.
> ☐ Modern Restrooms & Showers: All modern restroom buildings and shower facilities in the park are now closed. They will be drained and winterized.
> ☐ Water Systems: Water fountains and the RV dump station are shut off.
>
> **What Remains Open?**
> ☐ Trails: Park trails remain open for hiking. However, they will not be cleared of snow or ice. Visitors must use extreme caution and hike at their own risk.
> ☐ Lake Access: The boat ramp remains open, but the dock has been removed for the winter.

① The park is taking steps to prepare its facilities for the cold season.
② Water fountains are still accessible provided that visitors clean them after use.
③ Hiking routes stay open, although snow and ice will stay on the ground.
④ The boat ramp is accessible, although the dock is not in use.

14. 다음 글의 흐름상 어색한 문장은?

> A recent analysis by University of York researchers proposes a new hypothesis about dark matter. It challenges the belief that dark matter is completely "dark" and interacts only through gravity. ① <u>The theory suggests that dark matter may subtly interact with light, causing photons to gain or lose small amounts of energy.</u> ② <u>This would create a faint "tint" in the light from distant galaxies, shifting it slightly toward red or blue.</u> ③ <u>The exact percentage of dark matter in the early universe remains a subject of intense debate among cosmologists.</u> ④ <u>If confirmed, this hypothesis would provide the first non-gravitational "fingerprint" of dark matter and open a new way to study this mysterious substance.</u> Ultimately, it could help explain the universe's unseen mass.

15. 다음 글의 내용과 일치하는 것은?

> **New Residential Recycling Guidelines**
>
> To reduce landfill waste and promote sustainability, the City Council is implementing a new color-coded recycling system effective next month. All residents are required to sort their household waste according to the new guidelines.
>
> Correct sorting is essential for the recycling process to work effectively. Please refer to the chart below to ensure you are using the correct bin for each type of material.
>
> | Bin Color | Accepted Items | Notes |
> | --- | --- | --- |
> | Blue | Paper, Cardboard, Magazines | Must be clean and dry |
> | Green | Glass Bottles, Jars | Remove caps and rinse thoroughly |
> | Yellow | Aluminum Cans, Plastic Bottles | Crush items to save space |
>
> Collection days remain unchanged. However, bins containing mixed or contaminated items will not be collected.

① The new system begins officially next year.
② Always remove caps before using green bins.
③ Yellow bins accept all types of recyclables.
④ The collection schedule will change significantly.

16. 주어진 문장이 들어갈 위치로 가장 적절한 것은?

> This armored appearance led researchers to describe it as a "warrior" ancestor, differentiating it significantly from today's crocodiles.

> A remarkable fossil discovery from 240 million years ago, announced on November 12, 2025, is challenging our understanding of early crocodile ancestors. (①) The fossil reveals a creature that looked surprisingly like a dinosaur, equipped with plated armor covering its body. (②) Scientists note that this species lived on land millions of years ago, an environment vastly different from the aquatic habitats of modern crocodiles. (③) Its physical structure suggests it was likely a terrestrial predator, adapting to a life on land rather than in water. (④) The finding highlights the diverse evolutionary paths crocodile-line reptiles took before the familiar aquatic forms became dominant.

17. 다음 글의 목적으로 가장 적절한 것은?

✎	**Send** Preview Save
To	All Registered Attendees
From	The Organizing Team
Date	October 10, 2026
Subject	Important Notice

Dear Attendee,

We are pleased to welcome you to Innovate 2026 on Monday, November 10th. To enhance your conference experience, we have launched the official Innovate 2026 mobile app, which will serve as your primary guide throughout the event.

We are writing to strongly urge you to download the app before you arrive at the venue. The app will be your primary tool for:
- Checking In: Use the app's QR code for fast, digital check-in.
- Networking: Browse the attendee list and send messages.
- Schedule: Access the most up-to-date agenda, including any last-minute room changes.
- Live Q&A: Submit your questions to speakers directly through the app during sessions.

Please note that printed schedules will not be provided. All essential information, including maps and speaker details, will be available only on the app. You can download it from the Apple App Store or Google Play Store by searching "Innovate 2026."

Best,
The 'Innovate 2026' Team

① to announce a change in the conference registration fee
② to gather preliminary feedback from participants
③ to emphasize the paperless policy of the venue
④ to encourage the use of a digital event platform

18. 주어진 글 다음에 이어질 글의 순서로 가장 적절한 것은?

Astronomers using the James Webb Space Telescope (JWST) have created the first 3D atmospheric map of the exoplanet WASP-18b.

(A) These groundbreaking findings, including the detection of specific molecules, would have been impossible with earlier telescopes. They not only deepen understanding of WASP-18b but also showcase a new method for studying distant planets.

(B) The data showed dramatic temperature contrasts, including a dayside hotspot so extreme that it lies shifted from the point facing the star — evidence of powerful winds.

(C) The team accomplished this by using JWST's infrared instruments to track the planet over a full orbit. Changes in light as it passed behind its star and reappeared revealed its atmospheric temperature and composition.

① (A)－(C)－(B)　　　② (B)－(A)－(C)
③ (B)－(C)－(A)　　　④ (C)－(B)－(A)

[19～20] 밑줄 친 부분에 들어갈 말로 가장 적절한 것을 고르시오.

19.

The distinction between fear and anxiety is crucial, as their responses diverge significantly. While they often co-occur, they are by no means synonymous. Fear functions as an immediate signal of present danger, compelling swift action for survival. Anxiety, conversely, scans the murky horizon of the future, identifying potential threats that may not materialize. Consequently, ________________________________. We might struggle to pinpoint the exact source of our worry, and the unpredictability of the future makes it difficult to determine if a threat warrants attention. Nonetheless, by alerting us to possible catastrophes, anxiety prompts vital preparatory measures to mitigate future disasters.

① anxiety lacks the situational specificity of fear
② fear is a more prolonged state than anxiety
③ anxiety triggers a faster physiological response than fear
④ the dual alarm system implies their common evolutionary roots

20.

In experiments on time perception, Cassie Mogilner discovered a counterintuitive link between altruism and time. Subjects were divided into two groups: one spent time helping others, while the other engaged in self-serving or time-wasting tasks. Logically, giving away time should lead to a sense of depletion, yet the results showed the opposite. Those who assisted others felt as though they had more time available. This phenomenon suggests that giving boosts one's sense of competence and efficiency, creating a psychological expansion of time. When we feel effective, we feel less constrained by the clock. Thus, if you are overwhelmed, the best remedy is not to retreat into idleness but to help someone, as this sense of effectiveness makes you feel more in control of your schedule. Ironically, giving time away ________________________________ ________________________________.

① makes you feel more time-affluent than saving it for yourself
② causes you to neglect your own tasks due to exhaustion
③ provides a temporary distraction from your daily pressure
④ accelerates the clock by increasing your mental workload

수고하셨습니다.
당신의 합격을 응원합니다.

2026 국가직·지방직 공무원 시험 대비

실전동형 봉투모의고사

Vol. 1

영 어

제1회 ~ 제12회

정답 및 해설

박문각

영어 정답 및 해설

제1회 모의고사

01	02	03	04	05
06	07	08	09	10
11	12	13	14	15
16	17	18	19	20

01 [어휘　빈칸]　▶

난이도 중

정답 해설

직원들이 각 단계를 일관되게 따르고 일상적인 운영에서 비용이 많이 드는 실수를 피할 수 있도록 한다는 문맥으로 보아 새로운 절차에 대해 철저한 '문서 제작'을 요구한다는 내용이 적절하다. 따라서 밑줄 친 부분에 들어갈 말로 가장 적절한 것은 　이다.

해석

> 회사는 직원들이 각 단계를 일관되게 따르고 일상적인 운영에서 비용이 많이 드는 실수를 피할 수 있도록, 모든 새로운 절차에 대해 철저한 <u>문서 제작</u>을 요구한다.

어휘

documentation 문서 제작, 문서화, 서류
expense (어떤 일에 드는) 돈, 비용
transaction 거래, 매매, 처리
reservation 예약, 보류, 원주민[인디언] 보호 구역

02 [어휘　빈칸]　▶

난이도 중

정답 해설

주어진 문장은 역접을 나타내는 접속부사 although가 있으므로 예상치 못한 기회를 만들어 낼 수 있다는 긍정적인 내용과 반대되는 우려를 '제기한다'라는 부정적인 내용이 적절하다. 따라서 밑줄 친 부분에 들어갈 말로 가장 적절한 것은 　이다.

해석

> 비록 위원회가 그 제안의 재정적 위험성에 대해 우려를 <u>제기하고는</u> 있지만, 여러 임원들은 그것이 전략적으로 실행될 경우 예상치 못한 기회를 만들어 낼 수 있다고 믿고 있다.

어휘

raise 올리다, 제기하다, 키우다, 양육하다, 모으다
mitigate 완화하다, 진정시키다, 경감하다
resolve 해결하다, 결심하다, 분해[용해]하다
stabilize 안정시키다, 고정시키다

03 [문법　빈칸]　▶

난이도 중

정답 해설

[적중 포인트 038] 시제 관련 표현
& [적중 포인트 068] 부정부사와 도치구문
부정부사(no longer, not only, no sooner)가 문장 처음에 위치할 경우 바로 뒤에 '조동사　주어　'로 도치가 일어난다. 하지만 not until은 뒤에 명사 또는 주어와 동사가 나오고 나서 그 뒤에 도치가 일어난다. 따라서 밑줄 친 부분에 들어갈 말로 가장 적절한 것은 　이다.

해석

> 양측이 계약서에 공식적으로 서명하고 나서야 비로소, 법무팀은 다가오는 기업 합병에 필요한 서류 준비를 시작했다.

04 [생활영어　빈칸]　▶

난이도 하

정답 해설

새 공상과학 영화의 내용에 대해 이야기를 나누는 상황이다. 대화 흐름상, A가 "그는 인류의 새 보금자리를 찾는 우주비행사 주연을 맡았다"고 말한 것으로 보아, B는 그 배우가 영화에서 어떤 역할을 맡았는지 물어본 것이다. 따라서 밑줄 친 부분에 들어갈 말로 가장 적절한 것은 　이다.

해석

> A: 방금 새 공상과학 영화 'Cosmic Drift'를 다 봤어. 너 그거 봤어?
> B: 아직 안 봤어. 평이 엇갈린다고 들었는데, 어땠어?
> A: 난 정말 좋았어! 시각효과가 숨이 멎을 정도로 멋졌어. 다만, 줄거리가 좀 복잡하더라.
> B: 그렇구나. 누가 나와?
> A: Tom Vance랑 Maria Flores 같은 유명 배우들이 출연해.
> B: 오, 나 Tom Vance 팬이야. <u>그는 어떤 배역을 맡았어</u>
> A: 그는 인류의 새 보금자리를 찾으려는 우주비행사, 즉 주연을 맡았어.
> B: 흥미롭다. 이번 주말에 꼭 봐야겠네.

　그는 어떤 배역을 맡았어?
　그가 그 역할을 맡게 된 동기는 무엇이야?
　그가 왜 이 영화의 출연진에 합류하기로 결정한 거야?
　그는 보통 어떤 장르에서 연기하기를 선호해?

어휘

mixed (의견　생각 등이) 엇갈리는
effects (영화 속) 특수효과
astronaut 우주 비행사
captivating 마음을 사로잡는, 매혹적인
cast (어떤 연극이나 영화의) 출연자들[배역진]

05 [생활영어　빈칸]　▶

난이도 하

정답 해설

고객 미팅을 위해 회의실을 구하는 상황이다. David가 "회의실 B가 금요일 오후에 비어 있냐"고 묻자 Jessica는 "그건 이번 달 내내 예약되어 있다"고 답한다. 이후 David가 "스마트보드가 있는 방이 꼭 필요하다"고 말하며 도움을 요청하고, Jessica의 대답을 들은 David가 고맙다며 "다음에 도움이 필요하면 도와주겠다"고 말한 것으로 보아 Jessica가 스마트보드가 있는 방을 구해준 것을 알 수 있다. 따라서 밑줄 친 부분에 들어갈 말로 가장 적절한 것은 　이다.

해석

> David: 제시카, 잠깐 뭐 좀 물어볼게. 이번 주 금요일 오후에 B 회의실 비어 있어?
> Jessica: 금요일? 어려울걸. 이번 달 내내 신제품 출시 준비 때문에 예약이 꽉 차 있었어.
> David: 아, 그럴 줄 알았어. 고객 미팅이 앞당겨져서 스마트보드가 있는 방이 절실하게 필요하거든.
> Jessica: <u>잠깐만 우리 팀의 금요일 예약이 방금 취소됐어 내가 예약을 네 이름으로 바꿔줄 수 있어.</u>
> David: 네가 그걸 할 수 있다고? 정말 고마워, 혹시 다음에 내 도움이 필요하면 꼭 도와줄게.

　스마트보드가 제대로 작동하고 있는지 내가 확인해볼게.
　임시 작업공간이 이용 가능할 수도 있지만, 거기에 디지털 장비가 포함되어 있는지는 잘 모르겠어.
　잠깐만. 우리 팀의 금요일 예약이 방금 취소됐어. 내가 예약을 네 이름으로 바꿔줄 수 있어.
　다른 방을 찾아보려고는 하겠지만, 그 방에 스마트보드가 없을 수도 있어.

어휘

booked solid 모두 예약된
launch 출시, 개시

난이도 중

정답 해설

③ **[적중 포인트 078] 등위접속사와 병렬 구조 ★★★★☆**
등위접속사 and를 기준으로 communicated는 to implement와 병렬 구조를
이루고 있다. 따라서 밑줄 친 부분의 communicated를 communicate 또는 to
communicate로 고쳐야 한다.

오답 해설

① **[적중 포인트 025] to부정사를 목적격 보어로 취하는 대표 5형식 타동사 ★★★★☆**
동사 require는 5형식으로 쓰일 때 목적격 보어로 to부정사를 취한다. 따라서
밑줄 친 부분은 올바르게 쓰였다.

② **[적중 포인트 040] 상관접속사와 수 일치 ★★★☆☆**
상관접속사 as well as에 의해 to implement와 to invest가 병렬 구조를 이루고
있다. 따라서 밑줄 친 부분은 올바르게 쓰였다.

④ **[적중 포인트 049] 5형식 동사의 수동태 구조 ★★★★☆**
5형식 동사의 수동태 구조 be p.p. 뒤에는 목적격 보어가 남아 있다. deem은
'간주하다, 생각하다'라는 5형식 동사로 형용사나 명사 목적격 보어를 취할 수
있고 수동태로 쓰일 때 목적격 보어인 형용사나 명사 목적격 보어는 그대로
쓰인다. 따라서 밑줄 친 부분은 올바르게 쓰였다.

해석

새로운 포괄적인 국제 기후 협정은 서명국들에게 중대한 책임을 부과하고 있
으며, 그들에게 보다 엄격한 배출 기준을 시행할 뿐만 아니라, 재생에너지 인프
라에 대대적으로 투자하고, 장기 전략을 전 세계 공동체에 투명하게 전달하도
록 요구하고 있다. 이러한 종합적 접근은 협정에서 제시된 야심찬 목표를 달성
하는 데 필수적인 것으로 간주된다.

난이도 중

정답 해설

② **[적중 포인트 054] 분사 판별법 [현재분사 VS 과거분사] ★★★★★**
밑줄 친 부분인 disappeared를 포함한 문장의 구조가 완전한 구조를 이루고 있
으므로 disappeared는 과거시제 동사가 아닌 과거분사로 쓰인 것이다. 문맥상
'사라진' 문명이라는 능동의 의미가 적절하기 때문에 과거분사가 아닌 현재분
사로 써야 적절하다. 따라서 밑줄 친 부분의 disappeared를 disappearing으로
고쳐야 한다.

오답 해설

① **[적중 포인트 054] 분사 판별법 [현재분사 VS 과거분사] ★★★★★**
고대 유적지(ancient ruins)는 '발견된' 대상이므로 수동의 의미를 나타내는 과
거분사의 수식을 받아야 한다. 따라서 밑줄 친 부분은 올바르게 쓰였다.

③ **[적중 포인트 001] 문장의 구성요소 ★★★★☆**
suggest가 '제안하다'라는 의미일 경우에는, 목적어 자리에 오는 that절의 동사
는 '(should) 동사원형' 구조로 쓰여야 한다. 하지만 '암시하다, 보여주다'일 때
는 내용에 맞는 적절한 시제를 사용한 동사가 와야 한다. 문맥상 그 사회가 과
거에 '번성했다'는 사실을 나타내므로 과거 동사를 쓰는 것이 적절하다. 따라
서 밑줄 친 부분은 올바르게 쓰였다.

④ **[적중 포인트 091] 비교급 비교 구문 ★★★★☆**
better는 부사 well의 비교급 표현으로 동사를 수식할 수 있다. 따라서 밑줄 친
부분은 올바르게 쓰였다.

해석

정글 깊은 곳에서 발견된 고대 유적지는 오래전에 사라진 한 문명에 대한 단서
를 제공했다. 고고학자들은 토기 조각과 석기 도구를 발견했는데, 이는 이 지역
에서 번성했던 복잡한 사회가 존재했음을 시사하는 유물이었다. 이 유물들을
연구하는 것은 고고학자들이 그 고대 사회가 어떻게 자신들만의 문화적 정체
성을 형성해 갔는지를 더욱 잘 이해하는 데 도움이 되고 있다.

난이도 하

정답 해설

이 글은 그린필드 커뮤니티 가든이 2026년 정원 가꾸기 시즌을 맞아 새로운 회원
을 모집한다는 내용의 공지문이다. 첫 문장에서 '정원 가꾸기 시즌 신청을 받고
있다'고 명시하고 있으며, 이후에는 정원의 위치, 혜택, 참가비, 신청 방법 등을
구체적으로 안내하고 있다. 따라서 윗글의 제목으로 가장 적절한 것은 ②이다.

① 유기농 퇴비 만들기: 지역 정원사들을 위한 비법
② 예비 정원사들을 위한 신청 절차
③ 지역 주민들을 위한 회원 혜택
④ 공용 정원 도구 관리를 위한 지침

난이도 하

정답 해설

연회비는 구획당 30달러이며, 이 비용에는 물 사용료, 도구 관리비, 공동 비품 구
입비가 포함된다고 언급하고 있을 뿐, 개인용 농기구 구입 비용에 대한 내용은 언
급되지 않았다. 따라서 윗글의 내용과 일치하지 않는 것은 ②이다.

① 공공 도서관을 기준으로 정원의 위치가 안내되어 있다.
② 연회비에는 개인용 농기구 구입 비용이 포함되어 있다.
③ 정원 가꾸기를 한 번도 해 본 적 없는 사람들도 참여할 수 있다.
④ 정원 구획은 신청이 접수된 순서대로 배정된다.

오답 해설

① 우리 정원은 공공 도서관 뒤에 위치해 있다고 언급하고 있으므로 글의 내용과
　 일치한다.
③ 정원 가꾸기 경험이 없어도 참여할 수 있다고 언급하고 있으므로 글의 내용과
　 일치한다.
④ '배정 규칙' 부분에서 구획은 선착순으로 배정된다고 언급하고 있으므로 글의
　 내용과 일치한다.

해석

예비 정원사들을 위한 신청 절차

그린필드 커뮤니티 가든은 2026년 정원 가꾸기 시즌 참가 신청을 받게 되었음
을 기쁜 마음으로 알려드립니다. 우리 정원은 공공 도서관 뒤에 위치해 있으며,
주민들이 직접 유기농 채소, 꽃, 허브를 재배할 수 있는 멋진 기회를 제공합니
다. 이곳은 야외 활동을 즐기고, 지속 가능한 농업에 대해 배우며, 이웃과 교류
할 수 있는 훌륭한 장소입니다.

회원 자격은 모든 그린필드 주민에게 열려 있습니다. 연회비는 구획당 30달러
이며, 이 비용에는 물 사용료, 도구 관리비, 공동 비품 구입비가 포함됩니다.
정원 가꾸기 경험이 없어도 참여할 수 있습니다! 또한 5월부터 9월까지 매달
첫째 주 토요일에 퇴비 만들기, 해충 방제 등과 같은 주제를 다루는 무료 워크
숍을 개최합니다.

☐ **구역 크기:** 각 구역은 대략 가로 10피트, 세로 10피트입니다.
☐ **구역 배정:** 구역은 선착순으로 배정됩니다.

신청이 많을 것으로 예상되므로 가능한 한 빨리 신청할 것을 권장드립니다. 신
청서는 greenfieldgarden.org 홈페이지에서 다운로드할 수 있습니다. 우리 함께
더 푸른 공동체를 만들어 봅시다!

어휘

- agriculture 농업
- maintenance 유지, 지속
- supplies 비품, 용품
- composting 퇴비화, 퇴비 만들기
- approximately 대략, 거의
- assigned 배정된, 할당된
- demand 요구, 수요

10 [독해 – 세트형 문항(안내문 – 유의어)] ▶ ④

난이도 중

정답 해설

밑줄 친 verify는 '확인하다, 입증하다'라는 뜻으로, 문맥상 가장 가까운 의미는 ④ 'confirm(확인하다, 확증하다)'이다.

오답 해설

① ventilate 환기하다, 표출하다, 산소를 공급하다
② request 요청하다, 요구하다
③ modify 수정하다, 바꾸다

11 [독해 – 세트형 문항(안내문 – 목적)] ▶ ③

난이도 하

정답 해설

이 글은 SwiftRide 이용자들에게 안전하고 원활한 이용을 위한 지침을 안내하고 있다. 도입부에서 '모두의 안전하고 원활한 경험을 보장하기 위해' 지침 준수를 요청한 점과 본문에서 픽업 위치 확인, 차량 대조, 인원 제한 등 이용자가 실천해야 할 수칙을 상세히 나열한 점이 이를 뒷받침하고 있다. 따라서 글의 목적으로 가장 적절한 것은 ③이다.

해석

더 나은 이동을 위한 약속

SwiftRide를 이용해 주셔서 감사합니다. 모든 이용자가 안전하고 원활한 이동을 경험할 수 있도록, 아래의 간단한 안전 지침을 지켜주시기 바랍니다. 이러한 조치들은 이동하는 전 과정에서 승객과 운전자 모두를 보호하기 위해 마련된 것입니다.

차량을 호출하기 전에 지도에서 픽업 위치가 정확한지 반드시 확인하세요. 차량을 기다리는 동안에는 교통으로부터 떨어진, 잘 보이는 안전한 장소에서 대기하시기 바랍니다. 운전자가 도착하면, 차량 번호판과 차종이 앱에 표시된 정보와 일치하는지 확인하여 올바른 차량에 탑승하고 있는지 확인하세요. 안전상의 이유로, 탑승 인원은 이용 가능한 안전벨트의 수를 초과해서는 안 됩니다. 이러한 지침을 따르면 위험을 줄이고 모든 이용자에게 더 안전한 이동을 보장할 수 있습니다.

어휘

• ensure 보장하다, 확실하게 하다
• smooth 매끄러운, 문제없는
• accurate 정확한
• arrival 도착, 도래
• license plate 차량 번호판
• passenger 승객
• exceed 초과하다, 넘다

12 [독해 – 단일형 문항(홈페이지 게시글 – 내용 일치)] ▶ ①

난이도 하

정답 해설

세계자연기금의 사명은 자연을 보전하고 지구 생명 다양성에 대한 가장 심각한 위협을 줄이는 것이라고 언급하고 있다. 따라서 윗글의 내용과 일치하는 것은 ①이다.

오답 해설

② WWF는 전 세계 약 100개국에서 활동하는 국제 환경보전 단체로, 전 세계 500만 명 이상의 회원이 참여하고 있다고 언급하고 있으므로 글의 내용과 일치하지 않는다.
③ 회원이 많다는 언급은 있으나, 그들에게 연례 회의 참여 의무를 지우고 있다는 규칙은 언급되지 않았으므로 내용과 일치하지 않는다.
④ 이 단체는 지역사회와 협력하여 자원 이용의 지속 가능성을 촉진하고, 기업과 협력하여 환경 영향을 줄이며, 정부와 협력해 보전 정책을 시행한다고 언급하고 있을 뿐, 정부의 자금으로 운영된다고 언급되지 않았으므로 내용과 일치하지 않는다.

해석

세계 자연 기금(WWF)

사명

세계자연기금(WWF)의 사명은 자연을 보전하고 지구 생명 다양성에 대한 가장 심각한 위협을 줄이는 것입니다. 1961년에 설립된 WWF는 인간과 자연이 함께 번영할 수 있는 지속 가능한 미래를 보장하기 위해 노력하고 있습니다.

조직 구조

WWF는 전 세계 약 100개국에서 활동하는 국제 환경보전 단체로, 전 세계 500만 명 이상의 회원이 참여하고 있습니다. 비정부 독립 기구로서, 각 지역 및 국가 사무소를 통해 대륙 간 협력을 조정하며 환경보전 목표를 추진합니다.

① WWF는 다양한 생물 종에 닥친 긴급한 위험을 완화하는 것을 목표로 한다.
② WWF의 활동은 몇몇 특정 국가로 제한되어 있다.
③ WWF는 모든 회원들이 매년 열리는 세계 회의에 참가할 것을 요구한다.
④ WWF는 정부의 자금으로 운영되는 환경 기관이다.

어휘

• conserve 보존하다, 보호하다
• pressing 시급한, 긴급한
• diversity 다양성
• thrive 번성하다, 잘 자라다
• endangered 멸종 위기에 처한
• independent 독립적인
• coordinate 조정하다, 협력하다
• implement 시행하다, 실행하다
• practical 실질적인, 실용적인

13 [독해 – 단일형 문항(전자메일 – 목적)] ▶ ②

난이도 하

정답 해설

이 글은 구입한 헤드폰의 구체적인 결함 상태를 설명하며 시작되는데, 글의 중반부에서 작성자가 "이 제품을 반품하고 돈을 돌려받고 싶다"라고 자신의 최종적인 요구 사항을 명확하고 직접적으로 제시하고 있다. 마지막 문장에 언급된 '조치 사항' 역시 기기 자체의 고장을 고치는 수리 방법이 아니라, 앞서 언급한 '환불'을 완료하기 위해 필요한 행정적 절차를 의미하는 것이다. 따라서 글의 목적으로 가장 적절한 것은 ②이다.

해석

수신인: manager@apex-electronics.com
발신인: emily.jones@email.com
날짜: 2026년 9월 22일
제목: 최근 온라인 구매 건에 관하여

매니저님께,

제가 온라인 스토어에서 구입한 제품과 관련해 말씀드립니다. 어제 배송된 "Noise-Cancelling Headphone Pro"는 안타깝게도 고장이 난 채 도착했습니다. 여러 기기에 연결해 보았음에도 오른쪽 헤드폰에서는 전혀 소리가 나지 않습니다. 이에 대한 증거로 영수증과 문제 상황을 보여주는 영상을 함께 첨부했습니다.

저는 제품을 반품하고 전액 환불받기를 원하므로, 귀사에서 이와 같은 결함 사례를 보통 어떻게 처리하시는지 안내해 주시면 감사하겠습니다. 이 결함 제품과 관련하여 제가 진행해야 할 구체적인 절차에 대해 답변 기다리겠습니다.

진심으로,
Emily Jones

① 제품이 여전히 보증 적용 대상에 해당하는지 여부를 확인하려고
② 제품 결함을 알린 후 환불을 요청하려고
③ 배송 과정에서 발생한 손상에 대한 보상 방안이 무엇인지 문의하려고
④ 디지털 액세서리에 대한 기술 지원을 받으려고

- malfunction 오작동, 기능 이상
- defective 결함이 있는, 불량의
- refund 환불, 환불하다
- attach 첨부하다, 붙이다
- document 기록하다, 문서로 남기다
- warranty 보증, 품질 보증 기간
- coverage 적용 범위, 보장
- inquire 문의하다, 질문하다
- compensation 보상, 보상금

14 [독해 - 중심 내용 추론(주제)]　　　▶ ②

난이도 중

정답 해설

이 글은 미국에서 매년 판매되는 대부분의 플라스틱 병이 재활용되지만, PVC로 만들어진 병이나 특별한 코팅·색상을 가진 맥주병은 재활용 과정에서 큰 문제를 일으킨다는 점을 강조한다. 특히 마지막 문장에서 "이 병들은 일반적인 PET와 반드시 구분되어야 하며, 이를 폐기물 흐름에서 분리하는 데 드는 비용이 재생 플라스틱의 가치보다 더 크다"고 밝힘으로써, PET 병 재활용을 어렵게 만드는 여러 요인들에 있음을 알 수 있다. 따라서 글의 주제로 가장 적절한 것은 ②이다.

해석

미국에서 매년 판매되는 240억 개의 플라스틱 탄산음료 병의 대부분은 PET로 만들어지는데, PET는 녹여서 카펫, 플리스 소재의 의류, 플라스틱 끈, 비식품용 포장재로 다시 제조할 수 있다. 그러나 아주 소량의 비닐—예를 들어, 한 트럭 분량 안에 단 하나의 PVC 병만 섞여 있어도—PET 전체를 쓸모없게 만들 수 있다. 대부분의 병에는 이제 재활용 번호가 표시되어 있지만, 소비자들이 어떤 것이 어떤 것인지 기억하기는 어렵다. 또 다른 우려는 플라스틱 맥주병의 등장이다. 이 병들은 PET로 만들어지지만 햇빛을 차단하기 위해 호박색으로 착색되어 있으며, 산소 유입을 막기 위한 특수한 화학 코팅이 되어 있다. 이러한 특수한 색상, 내부 코팅, 그리고 뚜껑 안쪽의 비닐 라이닝 때문에 이러한 병들은 일반 PET와 구분하여 처리해야 하며, 폐기물 흐름에서 이를 따로 분리하는 데 드는 비용이 재생 플라스틱의 가치보다 더 많이 든다.

① 미국에서 플라스틱 재활용이 중요한 이유
② PET 병 재활용을 어렵게 만드는 요인들
③ 플라스틱 병 재활용의 환경적 이점들
④ 특수 플라스틱 용기의 장단점

- billion 10억
- remanufactured 재가공된, 다시 제조된
- vinyl 비닐(합성수지), 폴리염화비닐(PVC)
- prospect 가능성, 전망
- amber 호박색의
- chemical coating 화학적 코팅(표면 처리)
- interior 내부의, 안쪽의
- lining 안감, 안쪽 덧댐
- separated 분리된
- reclaimed 재활용된, 회수된

15 [독해 - 단일형 문항(안내문 - 내용 불일치)]　　　▶ ③

난이도 하

정답 해설

'규칙 및 규정' 부분에서 '병에 든 생수를 제외한 음식과 음료는 전망대에 반입할 수 없다'고 명시하고 있을 뿐, 모든 음식과 음료가 반입된다는 내용은 적절하지 않다. 따라서 윗글의 내용과 일치하지 않는 것은 ③이다.

오답 해설

① '운영 시간' 부분에서 '마감 1시간 전까지만 입장 가능하다'라고 명시하고 있으므로 글의 내용과 일치한다.
② '입장권 요금' 부분에서 '성인은 $25, 노인은 $20'으로 명시되어 있으므로 글의 내용과 일치한다.
④ '규칙 및 규정' 부분에서 '큰 가방, 배낭, 삼각대는 금지되어 있고, 작은 개인 가방은 검색 대상'이라고 명시하고 있으므로 글의 내용과 일치한다.

해석

스카이라인 전망대에 오신 것을 환영합니다! 이곳에서는 지상 800피트 상공에서 도시의 숨막히는 360도 전망을 감상할 수 있습니다.

운영 시간
- 월요일 ~ 목요일: 오전 10시 ~ 오후 9시
- 금요일 ~ 일요일: 오전 10시 ~ 오후 11시
- 마감 1시간 전까지만 입장 가능합니다.

입장권 요금
- 성인(18~64세): $25
- 노인(65세 이상): $20
- 어린이(6~17세): $18
- 6세 미만 어린이: 무료
- 티켓은 10% 할인된 가격으로 온라인에서 구매할 수 있습니다. 현장 구매 시 할인은 제공되지 않습니다.

규칙 및 규정
- 병에 든 생수를 제외한 음식과 음료는 전망대에 반입할 수 없습니다.
- 큰 가방, 배낭, 삼각대는 금지되어 있습니다. 작은 개인 가방은 검색 대상입니다.
- 모든 방문객의 안전을 위해 난간 위를 달리고 기울이는 것은 엄격히 금지됩니다.

즐거운 방문 되시길 바랍니다!

① 전망대는 마감 1시간 전까지만 입장이 가능하다.
② 입장권은 성인 요금보다 노인 요금이 더 저렴하다.
③ 모든 음식과 음료는 전망대에 반입할 수 없다.
④ 가방은 크기에 따라 반입이 금지되거나 검색 대상이 된다.

- observation deck 전망대
- breathtaking 숨이 (턱) 막히는[멋진 듯한]
- permit 허용[허락]하다
- senior 노인, 연장자
- personal 개인의, 사적인
- forbidden 금지된
- discount 할인, 할인하다
- depending on ~에 따라

16 [독해 - 문장 삽입]　　　▶ ②

난이도 상

정답 해설

이 글은 건강한 생활 방식은 급격한 변화가 아니라 작은 습관에서 비롯된다는 점을 강조한다. 주어진 문장은 '오히려'라는 단어로 ②번 앞 문장에서 말한 내용을 반박하며, 건강한 생활의 진정한 핵심은 장기적인 목표에 맞는 작고 실천 가능한 선택을 꾸준히 해 나가는 것임을 제시하고 있다. 또한 ②번 뒤 문장에서 사용된 "이러한 지속 가능한 접근법"이 바로 주어진 문장의 내용을 가리키고 있어, 논리적으로 자연스럽게 이어진다. 따라서 주어진 문장이 들어갈 위치로 가장 적절한 것은 ②이다.

해석

건강해지는 것이 일상의 완전한 변화를 요구한다는 것은 흔한 오해이다. (①) 사실, 건강한 삶을 산다는 것은 극단적이거나 하루아침에 모든 것을 바꾸는 것을 의미하지 않는다. (② 오히려 핵심은 장기적인 목표에 부합하는 작고 관리 가능한 선택을 지속적으로 하는 것이다.) 이러한 지속 가능한 접근 방식이 훨씬 더 효과적이다. (③) 예를 들어, 모든 정크 푸드를 한꺼번에 끊는 대신, 매일 설탕이 든 음료 한 잔을 물로 바꾸는 것부터 시작할 수 있다. (④) 마찬가지로, 매일 2시간 운동을 결심하기보다는 15분 걷기부터 시작해 보라. 이러한 작은 변화들이 점차 추진력을 만들어 내며 습관으로 자리 잡게 된다.

17 [독해 – 문장 제거]　▶④

난이도 하

정답 해설

이 글은 도시화의 이점과 그 지속가능성을 높이기 위한 스마트 시티 기술을 긍정적으로 설명하고 있다. ①, ②, ③번 문장과 마지막 문장은 모두 도시와 스마트 기술이라는 핵심 주제와 긴밀하게 연결되어 있다. 그러나 ④번 문장은 시골 지역의 문제점을 언급하며 도시와 농촌을 비교하고 있어, 글의 중심 주제인 '지속 가능한 도시 발전을 위한 스마트 시티'라는 흐름에서 벗어난다. 따라서 글의 흐름상 어색한 문장은 ④이다.

해석

도시화는 일자리, 교육, 의료 서비스에 대한 접근성을 높여주는 등 경제적·사회적으로 중요한 이점을 제공한다. ① 사람과 자원을 한곳에 집중함으로써, 도시는 혁신을 촉진하고 생산성을 높일 수 있다. ② 도시 지역의 급격한 성장을 지속 가능한 방식으로 관리하기 위해, 도시 계획가들은 기술을 활용해 서비스를 개선하고 환경 영향을 줄이는 스마트 시티 구상을 개발하고 있다. ③ 이러한 구상에는 지능형 교통 시스템, 에너지 효율적인 건물, 디지털 공공 서비스 등이 포함된다. (④ 농촌 지역은 도시 지역에 비해 인프라와 투자 부족으로 어려움을 겪는 경우가 많다.) 이러한 기술들을 통합함으로써 도시는 더 살기 좋고 회복력 있는 공간으로 발전할 수 있으며, 주민들의 삶의 질을 높일 수 있다.

18 [독해 – 순서 배열]　▶②

난이도 상

정답 해설

이 글은 우주비행사가 수년간의 훈련 끝에 마주한 첫 우주 유영의 경이로운 순간을 '물리적 진입'에서 '존재적 성찰'로 이어지는 심리적 흐름에 따라 서술하고 있다. 주어진 글에서 화자가 우주선 출구 앞에 서서 느끼는 팽팽한 긴장감은, 실제 우주 공간으로 발을 내딛는 행동적 전환이 나타난 (B)로 자연스럽게 연결된다. (B)에서 신호등이 초록색으로 바뀌며 진공 상태의 우주로 나가는 장면은 사건의 본격적인 시작을 알린다. 이어지는 (A)에서는 우주 밖으로 나간 직후 마주한 감각적 충격이 묘사되는데, 화자는 예상 밖의 강렬한 태양빛이 정거장 선체에 반사되는 광경을 통해 우주의 생경함을 체감한다. 이러한 시각적 자극은 마지막 단계인 (C)에서 내적인 변화와 성찰로 확장된다. '그곳에 떠 있는' 상태로 마주한 푸른 지구의 장엄한 모습은 화자로 하여금 그동안 연습했던 모든 기술적 절차를 사소하게 느끼게 만들며, 거대한 우주 앞에서 느끼는 압도적인 경외감으로 글의 흐름을 완성한다. 따라서 글의 순서로 가장 적절한 것은 ②이다.

해석

수년 동안 시뮬레이터와 금속 모형 안에서 철저한 훈련을 거친 끝에, 나는 마침내 첫 우주 유영을 위해 출구 문으로 다가갔다. 흥분으로 복부가 꽉 조여지는 기분이었다.

(B) 출구 위의 빨간 불이 초록색으로 바뀌며, 외부 우주가 준비되었음을 알렸다. 나는 손잡이를 꽉 잡고 진공 속으로 한 발 내디뎠다. 끝없이 펼쳐진 우주 앞에서 내 모든 동작은 느리고 조심스러웠다.

(A) 나에게 가장 먼저 깊은 인상을 준 것은 어둠이 아니라 태양의 강렬한 빛이었다. 그 빛은 정거장의 선체에 반사되어 모든 세부 형태를 지워버릴 만큼 거친 흰색으로 빛나고 있었다.

(C) 그곳에 떠 있자, 아래 펼쳐진 푸르고 하얀색으로 소용돌이치며 고요하게 빛나는 지구가 나의 규모에 대한 감각을 완전히 재정의했다. 그동안 내가 연습했던 모든 절차는 이 압도적인 경외감 옆에서는 작게만 느껴졌다.

19 [독해 – 빈칸 추론]　▶①

난이도 중

정답 해설

이 글은 허위 정보의 빠른 확산이 공중 보건 위기나 사회 분열 등 심각한 사회적 문제를 초래한다고 설명하고 있다. 이에 대한 해결책으로, 정보의 출처와 의도를 비판적으로 검토하는 '미디어 문해력' 기술의 필요성을 제시한다. 빈칸은 왜 미디어 문해력이 중요한지를 설명하는 자리이다. 본문에서 이미 언급된 허위 정보의 부정적 결과들을 고려하면, '확인되지 않은 정보가 현실 세계에 해로운 영향을 미칠 수 있기 때문'이라는 이유가 가장 적절하다. 따라서 밑줄 친 부분에 들어갈 말로 가장 적절한 것은 ①이다.

해석

오늘날 서로 연결된 세상에서 잘못된 정보의 확산은 심각한 사회적 문제가 되었다. 허위 또는 부정확한 정보는 소셜 미디어 및 기타 디지털 플랫폼을 통해 빠르게 확산될 수 있으며, 종종 확인된 사실보다 더 빠르다. 이러한 현상은 부분적으로 잘못된 정보가 감정적으로 도발적으로 설계되어 사람들의 두려움, 분노 또는 흥분을 자극하기 때문에 발생한다. 이러한 콘텐츠는 비판적인 평가 없이 공유될 가능성이 높다. 그 결과는 심각할 수 있으며 공중 보건 위기, 사회 분열, 기관에 대한 신뢰 약화로 이어질 수 있다. 따라서 개인이 미디어 문해력 능력을 개발하는 것은 매우 중요하다. 이는 단순히 정보를 소비하는 방법뿐만 아니라 정보 출처에 의문을 제기하고 주장을 검증하며 그 잠재적 동기를 이해하는 방법을 배우는 것을 의미하며, 이는 <u>확인되지 않은 정보가 실제에 해로운 영향을 미칠 수 있기</u> 때문이다.

① 확인되지 않은 정보가 실제에 해로운 영향을 미칠 수 있기
② 대부분의 디지털 플랫폼은 엄격한 사실 검증 시스템이 부족하기
③ 감정적으로 자극적인 콘텐츠는 거짓일 때조차 그럴듯하게 느껴지는 경우가 많기
④ 사람들은 사회적 연결을 유지하기 위해 콘텐츠를 빠르게 공유하는 일이 흔하기

[난이도] 상

[정답 해설]

이 글은 인식이 외부 감각 정보를 수동적으로 받아들이는 과정이 아니라, 뇌가 세상을 예측하는 모델을 끊임없이 생성하고, 실제 감각 정보는 이러한 예측을 수정하는 '오류 신호'로만 사용된다는 '예측 처리' 이론을 설명한다. 우리가 경험하는 현실은 외부 세계의 단순한 복사본이 아니라, 뇌가 만들어낸 '최선의 추측'이라는 것이다. 이 이론에 따르면, 현실은 우리가 수동적으로 관찰하는 대상이 아니라 '내부로부터 능동적이고 지속적으로 구성해내는 것'이라는 결론이 적절하다. 따라서 밑줄 친 부분에 들어갈 말로 가장 적절한 것은 ④이다.

[해석]

오랫동안 상향식 프레임워크가 지배적이었던 지각 모델이 급진적인 변화를 겪고 있다. 이번 주 TIME에 실린 최근 신경과학적 발견을 획기적으로 종합한 결과, 뇌는 감각 데이터를 수동적으로 수신하는 것이 아니라 능동적으로 예측하는 기계로 작동한다고 주장한다. 이 '예측 처리' 모델에 따르면 뇌는 들어오는 감각 신호를 예측하기 위해 끊임없이 풍부하고 계층적인 세계 모델을 생성한다. 우리가 지각으로서 경험하는 것은 눈과 귀의 원시 데이터가 아니다. 오히려 이것은 뇌의 최선의 추측, 일종의 '통제된 환각'이며, 이는 기대와 외부로부터 들어오는 실제 입력값 사이에 불일치, 즉 '예측 오류'가 있을 때에만 업데이트된다. 이는 의식의 본질 자체를 재정의하여 현실이란 <u>우리가 내부로부터 능동적이고 지속적으로 구성해내는</u> 무엇인가임을 시사한다.

① 우리의 의식이 물리적 세계의 거울로서 지각하는
② 우리의 눈과 귀가 끊임없는 외부 신호를 통해 지시하는
③ 우리가 어떠한 예측 오류도 피하기 위해 객관적으로 관찰해야 하는
④ 우리가 내부로부터 능동적이고 지속적으로 구성해내는

[어휘]

- prevailing 지배적인, 우세한
- perception 지각, 인지
- bottom-up 상향식의
- radical 급진적인, 획기적인
- neuroscientific 신경과학의
- posit (이론 등을) 제기하다, 주장하다
- passive 수동적인
- afferent 구심성의, 감각 신호를 전달하는
- hierarchical 계층적인
- consciousness 의식
- passively 수동적으로

영어 정답 및 해설

✅ 제2회 모의고사

01 ③	02 ②	03 ①	04 ③	05 ④
06 ②	07 ②	08 ③	09 ③	10 ③
11 ④	12 ③	13 ③	14 ③	15 ③
16 ③	17 ④	18 ②	19 ④	20 ②

---

01 [어휘 – 빈칸]　　　▶ ③

난이도 중

정답 해설

소설의 내용이 가장 가까운 인간관계는 물론, 한때 선하다고 여겨졌던 이들마저 서서히 타락시키는 모습으로 그려진 점을 보면, 작품이 말하고자 하는 핵심 요소로 '탐욕'의 내용이 적절하다. 따라서 밑줄 친 부분에 들어갈 말로 가장 적절한 것은 ③이다.

해석

그 소설은 <u>탐욕</u>이 가장 가까운 인간관계마저 무너뜨리고, 한때 선하다고 여겨졌던 이들조차 서서히 타락시킬 수 있음을 보여준다.

어휘

★ greed 탐욕, 욕망
● sympathy 공감, 동정, 연민
● outlet 발산[배출] 수단, 직판점, 할인점
● novelty 새로움, 참신함, 신기함

02 [어휘 – 빈칸]　　　▶ ②

난이도 중

정답 해설

여러 부서가 회의에서 정해진 새 지침을 제각기 다르게 해석하고, 결과적으로 절차가 일관되지 못하게 진행된 점을 고려하면 회의록이 '모호하게' 작성되었다는 내용이 적절하다. 따라서 밑줄 친 부분에 들어갈 말로 가장 적절한 것은 ②이다.

해석

회의록이 매우 <u>모호한</u> 방식으로 작성되었기 때문에, 여러 부서가 새 지침을 서로 다르게 해석했고 결국 일관되지 않은 절차를 따르게 되었다.

★ vague 모호한, 흐릿한
● administrative 관리[행정]상의
● cumulative 누적되는, 누계의
● durable 내구성이 있는, 오래가는, 튼튼한

03 [문법 – 빈칸]　　　▶ ①

난이도 중

정답 해설

① **[적중 포인트 079] 명사절 접속사의 구분과 특징** ★★★☆☆
　빈칸 뒤에는 주어가 없는 불완전한 절을 이끌고, 앞의 명사 Regions of space를 수식할 주격 관계대명사가 들어가야 한다. 따라서 밑줄 친 부분에 들어갈 말로 가장 적절한 것은 ①이다.

해석

천문학자들이 한때 비어 있다고 여겼던 우주의 영역들이, 사실은 가장 강력한 망원경으로만 관측 가능한 희미하고 먼 은하들로 가득 차 있는 경우가 흔하다.

04 [문법 – 밑줄]　　　▶ ③

난이도 중

정답 해설

③ **[적중 포인트 054] 분사 판별법[현재분사 VS 과거분사]** ★★★★★
　once가 이끄는 분사구문이다. 이때 분사구문의 의미상의 주어는 주절의 주어인 Such skills이다. '기술'은 스스로 배우는 주체가 아니라, 사람에 의해 습득되는 대상이므로 수동 의미의 과거분사로 써야 한다. 이는 원래 형태인 once they are learned에서 '주어+be동사'가 생략된 구조로 이해할 수 있다. 따라서 밑줄 친 부분의 once learning을 once learned로 고쳐야 한다.

오답 해설

① **[적중 포인트 039] 현재시제 동사와 be동사의 수 일치** ★★★★★
　문장의 주어(procedural memory)는 단수 명사이므로 동사도 단수 형태로 써야 한다. 따라서 밑줄 친 부분은 올바르게 쓰였다.

② **[적중 포인트 086] 관계부사의 선행사와 완전 구조** ★★★☆☆
　관계부사 why는 이유를 나타내는 명사 the reason을 수식하는데 이때 the reason이 생략되고 'why + 주어 + 동사 ~' 완전 구조가 남아 있을 수 있다. 따라서 밑줄 친 부분은 올바르게 쓰였다.

④ **[적중 포인트 050] 전치사에 유의해야 할 수동태** ★★★☆☆
　'~로서 알려져 있다'의 의미로 쓰이며 뒤에 자격, 신분, 이름이 쓰인다면 전치사 as로 쓸 수 있다. 따라서 밑줄 친 부분은 올바르게 쓰였다.

해석

심리학자는 절차기억이 기술과 절차를 회상하는 데 관여하며, 사실과 사건을 다루는 서술기억과 구별된다고 설명했다. 서술기억은 의식적으로 회상되는 반면, 절차기억은 무의식적으로 작동한다. 숙련된 자전거 타는 사람은 일일이 근육의 움직임을 의식하지 않고도 복잡한 코스를 헤쳐 나갈 수 있는 이유가 바로 이것이다. 이러한 기술은 일단 습득되고 나면 너무 자동화되어, 오히려 그것을 의식적으로 통제하려 하면 수행 능력이 떨어질 수 있는데, 이러한 현상을 '압박 상황에서의 경직'으로 알려져 있다.

05 [문법 – 밑줄]　　　▶ ④

난이도 상

정답 해설

④ **[적중 포인트 078] 등위접속사와 병렬 구조** ★★★★☆
　& [적중 포인트 001] 문장의 구성요소 ★★★★☆
　뒤에 등위접속사 and로 명사구(poor sanitation)가 이어지고 있으므로, 앞부분 역시 병렬 구조에 맞게 명사구가 와야 한다. 따라서 형용사 urban은 뒤의 명사를 수식하는 역할로 쓰여 '혼잡, 과밀'의 뜻으로 쓰이는 명사를 써서 명사형 구조를 이루어야 한다. 따라서 밑줄 친 부분의 crowded를 crowding으로 고쳐야 한다. 따라서 밑줄 친 부분은 올바르게 쓰였다.

오답 해설

① **[적중 포인트 070] 양보 도치 구문과 장소 방향 도치 구문** ★★★☆☆
　문장 처음에 장소나 방향 부사구가 쓰이면 그 뒤에 1형식 자동사와 주어 순서로 도치가 된다. 따라서 문장의 주어(Ebenezer Howard)는 단수형이므로 동사도 단수 형태로 써야 한다. 따라서

② **[적중 포인트 054] 분사 판별법[현재분사 VS 과거분사]** ★★★★★
　surrounded는 '둘러싸인'이라는 의미의 과거분사로, 앞의 명사(self-contained communities)를 수식한다. 문맥상 공동체가 그린벨트에 의해 둘러싸이는 수동 의미이므로 과거분사로 써야 한다. 따라서 밑줄 친 부분은 올바르게 쓰였다.

③ **[적중 포인트 060] to부정사의 명사적 역할** ★★★★☆
　'~을 목표로 하다'의 의미로 쓰이는 aim은 to부정사를 목적어로 취하는 3형식 타동사이다. 따라서 밑줄 친 부분은 올바르게 쓰였다.

19세기 말, 도시 계획가들은 빠르게 성장하는 도시들을 관리해야 했다. 이 시대의 가장 선견지명을 가진 인물 중 한 명이 바로 Ebenezer Howard였으며, 그는 '정원 도시' 개념을 제안했다. 그는 녹지대로 둘러싸인 자족적 공동체를 구상했는데, 이는 도시와 농촌 생활의 장점을 결합한 것이었다. 그의 아이디어는 1898년에 출간한 저서에서 자세히 설명되었으며, 도시 혼잡과 열악한 위생 문제를 해결하는 것을 목표로 했다.

06 [독해 − 세트형 문항(홈페이지 게시글 − 유의어)] ▶ ②

난이도 하

정답 해설

밑줄 친 tissue는 '조직, 화장지'라는 뜻으로, 문맥상 가장 가까운 의미는 ② 'organ(조직, 장기, 오르간)'이다.

오답 해설

① vessel 선박, 배, 그릇
③ texture 감촉, 질감
④ component 부품, (구성) 요소

07 [독해 − 세트형 문항(홈페이지 게시글 − 목적)] ▶ ②

난이도 상

정답 해설

이 글은 '생체 모방'이라는 개념을 정의하고, 자연의 설계 원리를 활용해 지속 가능한 기술을 창조하는 방향성을 제시하고 있다. 따라서 글의 목적으로 가장 적절한 것은 ②이다.

해석

자연에서 영감을 받은 설계

인류는 여전히 복잡한 환경적 · 기술적 도전 과제에 직면해 있다. 생체 모방의 개념은 자연 세계로부터 지혜를 얻어, 지속 가능한 미래로 나아갈 수 있는 길을 제시한다.

자연은 수십억 년의 진화를 거치며, 오늘날 우리가 씨름하는 많은 문제들에 대한 해답을 이미 개발해 왔다. 생물 조직을 본뜬 자가 치유 물질에서부터, 흰개미집 구조를 참고한 에너지 효율적인 건축물에 이르기까지, 혁신가들은 자연의 설계 원리에서 해답을 찾고 있다.

생체 모방의 본질은 자연의 겉모습을 단순히 복제하는 것이 아니라, 그 체계가 지닌 회복력, 효율성, 지속 가능성에서 배우는 것에 있다. 이러한 접근 방식을 채택함으로써, 디자이너와 엔지니어들은 지구와 조화를 이루며 공존할 수 있는 기술을 창조할 수 있다. 따라서 자연 모방은 지속 가능한 미래를 위한 중요한 전략이 된다.

어휘

- biomimicry 생체 모방, 자연 모방
- material 재료, 물질
- tissue (생물의) 조직
- inspired 영감을 받아 한, 직관에 따른
- resilience 회복력
- coexist 공존하다
- harmoniously 조화롭게
- pivotal 중추적인, 매우 중요한

08 [생활영어 − 빈칸] ▶ ③

난이도 중

정답 해설

A는 B에게 보고서의 검토 여부를 묻고, B는 간단히 검토한 결과 오타와 형식상의 문제가 있음을 지적한다. 이어지는 B의 발화에서 해당 문제들이 어느 쪽의 제목이 일관되지 않고 결론 부분에 철자 오류가 있는지 구체적으로 설명하고 있으며, A 또한 이에 대해 감사 인사를 전하며 해당 부분들을 수정하겠다고 말한다. 이로 인해 A가 오타와 형식상의 문제가 있는 구체적인 위치를 물어봤음을 짐작할 수 있다. 따라서 밑줄 친 부분에 들어갈 말로 가장 적절한 것은 ③이다.

해석

A: 오늘 아침에 제가 보낸 보고서를 검토해 보셨나요?
B: 네, 간단히 살펴봤는데 오타 몇 군데와 형식상의 문제가 있었습니다.
A: 알겠습니다. 어느 부분을 수정해야 하는지 짚어 주실 수 있을까요?
B: 2쪽의 제목들이 서로 일관되지 않고, 결론 부분에 철자 오류가 있습니다.
A: 알려주셔서 감사합니다. 그 부분들을 수정해서 업데이트된 버전을 보내겠습니다.
B: 좋아요. 보내주시면 최종으로 한 번 더 검토하겠습니다.

① 그럼 검토가 가능한 시간을 알려주실 수 있을까요?
② 보고서를 2쪽 분량으로 하면 내용이 부족할까요?
③ 어느 부분을 수정해야 하는지 짚어 주실 수 있을까요?
④ 철자 오류를 줄이는 요령이 있을까요?

어휘

- review 검토하다, 되새기다
- briefly 간단히
- typo 오타
- consistent 일관된, 한결같은
- conclusion 결론, 결말

09 [생활영어 − 빈칸] ▶ ③

난이도 중

정답 해설

빈칸 바로 뒤에 이어지는 Ben의 응답이 결정적인 단서가 된다. Alex가 즉각적인 성과가 없어 낙담하자, Ben은 "좋은 것들은 시간이 걸린다"라고 말하며 인내심의 중요성을 강조한다. 이에 같이 할 대답은 '큰일은 하루아침에 이루어지지 않으며, 꾸준한 노력과 시간이 필요하다'는 의미의 속담이 들어가는 것이 가장 자연스럽다. 따라서 밑줄 친 부분에 들어갈 말로 가장 적절한 것은 ③이다.

해석

Alex: 안녕, 벤. 새로 시작한 텃밭 때문에 좀 낙담했어.
Ben: 어? 왜 그래? 엄청 기대하고 있었잖아.
Alex: 기대하긴 했는데, 몇 주 동안 가꿨는데 자라는 게 거의 없어. 이 모든 노력이 헛수고가 되면 어떡하지?
Ben: 로마는 하루아침에 이루어지지 않았어. 좋은 것들은 시간이 걸리는 법이야. 하룻밤 사이에 풍성한 수확을 기대할 순 없잖아.
Alex: 네 말이 맞아. 그냥 좀 더 인내심을 가져야겠어. 고마워, Ben.

① 진작에 그 생각을 했어야 해
② 음, 그것은 확실히 가능성이 있는 일이야
③ 로마는 하루아침에 이루어지지 않았어
④ 김칫국부터 마시지 마

어휘

- discouraged 낙담한, 실망한
- barely 거의 ~없다, 간신히
- definite 확실한, 명확한
- possibility 가능성

10 [독해 – 중심 내용 추론(주제)] ▶ ③

난이도 하

정답 해설

이 글은 '연습'과 '놀이'의 개념을 대비하여 설명하고, 각각이 기술 습득 과정에서 어떤 역할을 하는지를 분석한다. 연습은 목표와 피드백이 분명한 구조적 활동으로, 집중적인 노력을 통해 수행 능력을 향상시키는 데 효과적이다. 반면 놀이는 압박 없이 자유롭게 탐색하고 즐기는 비구조적 활동으로, 창의성 발휘와 장기적 동기 유지에 기여한다. 결국 이 두 방식을 어느 하나로 선택하는 것이 아니라, 균형 있게 결합하는 것이 효과적인 기술 습득의 핵심이라고 결론짓는다. 따라서 글의 주제로 가장 적절한 것은 ③이다.

해석

'연습'과 '놀이'를 구분하는 것은 기술 습득에서 매우 중요한 요소이다. 연습은 명확한 목표와 즉각적인 피드백을 갖춘 구조화된 활동으로, 수행 능력의 특정 부분을 향상시키기 위해 이루어진다. 지속적인 집중과 노력이 필요하기 때문에 정신적·신체적으로 부담이 될 수 있다. 반면 놀이는 구조화되어 있지 않고 내적 동기에 의해 이루어지며, 학습자가 압박 없이 탐색하고 시도하며 활동 자체를 즐길 수 있게 한다. 겉보기에는 생산성이 낮아 보일지라도, 놀이는 창의성을 키우고 장기적인 흥미를 강화하며 번아웃을 예방하는 데 중요한 역할을 한다. 이러한 이유로 효과적인 학습은 어느 하나를 선택하는 것이 아니라, 두 요소의 균형을 맞추는 데 있다. 즉, 구조화된 연습을 통해 핵심 기술을 쌓고, 자유로운 놀이를 통해 동기와 혁신을 유지하는 것이다.

① 전문 분야에서 의도적 연습의 중요성
② 창의성과 동기의 원천으로서의 놀이
③ 효과적인 기술 습득을 위한 연습과 놀이의 시너지
④ 고위험 경쟁 상황에서 번아웃을 극복하는 방법

어휘

- distinction 구별, 차이
- acquisition 습득, 획득
- structured 구조화된, 체계적인
- immediate 즉각적인
- sustained 지속된, 한결같은, 일관된
- intrinsic 내적인, 고유한, 본질적인
- productive 생산적인
- nurture 양성하다, 키우다

11 [독해 – 세트형 문항(안내문 – 제목)] ▶ ④

난이도 중

정답 해설

이 글은 자유 동물 보호소에서 주최하는 입양 캠페인 'Paws for a Cause'를 홍보하는 안내문이다. 보호소의 유기된 동물들이 따뜻한 가정에 입양되도록 장려하는 것이며, 입양 절차와 혜택을 안내하고 있다. 따라서 글의 제목으로 가장 적절한 것은 ④이다.
① 새로운 반려동물 주인들을 위한 경제적 혜택
② 성공적인 입양을 위한 필수 요건들
③ 동물 건강 검진 안내서
④ 당신의 털 뭉치 가족(반려동물)을 찾으세요

12 [독해 – 세트형 문항(안내문 – 내용 일치)] ▶ ③

난이도 중

정답 해설

입양되는 모든 동물은 마이크로칩 삽입, 백신 접종 및 건강 검진을 마친 상태라고 언급하고 있다. 따라서 윗글의 내용과 일치하는 것은 ③이다.
① 이번 행사는 10월 20일부터 시작된다.
② 이 캠페인은 고양이 입양에만 엄격히 제한된다.
③ 입양 대상 동물들은 예방 접종을 모두 마친 상태이다.
④ 입양 희망자들에게 직원 상담은 선택 사항이다.

오답 해설

① 이 특별 행사는 10월 14일부터 10월 20일까지 진행된다고 명시되어 있으므로 글의 내용과 일치하지 않는다.
② 캠페인 주간 동안, 저희는 새로운 반려동물 주인들의 경제적 부담을 덜어드리기 위해 모든 고양이와 개에 대한 표준 입양비를 50달러로 인하한다고 언급하고 있으므로 글의 내용과 일치하지 않는다.

④ 모든 잠재적 입양 희망자들은 적절한 매칭을 보장하기 위해 저희 직원과 함께 짧은 상담 시간을 완료해야 한다고 언급하고 있으므로 글의 내용과 일치하지 않는다.

해석

당신의 털 뭉치 가족(반려동물)을 찾으세요

매년 우리 시의 수천 마리 반려동물들이 보호소로 오게 되며, 두 번째 기회를 기다립니다. 자유 동물 보호소가 주최하는 "Paws for a Cause" 입양 캠페인은 이 사랑스러운 동물들을 보살펴 줄 가족과 연결해 주는 것을 목표로 합니다. 이 특별 행사는 10월 14일부터 10월 20일까지 진행됩니다.

캠페인 주간 동안, 저희는 새로운 반려동물 주인들의 경제적 부담을 덜어드리기 위해 모든 고양이와 개에 대한 표준 입양비를 50달러로 인하합니다. 입양되는 모든 동물은 마이크로칩 삽입, 백신 접종 및 건강 검진을 마친 상태입니다. 저희의 목표는 단순히 동물들에게 집을 찾아주는 것이 아니라, 그들이 적합한 집을 찾도록 보장하는 것입니다. 따라서 모든 잠재적 입양 희망자들은 적절한 매칭을 보장하기 위해 저희 직원과 함께 짧은 상담 시간을 완료해야 합니다.

우리와 함께하여 새로운 친구에게 마음을 열어주세요. 여러분의 결정이 한 생명을 영원히 바꿀 수 있습니다.

어휘

- companion animal 반려동물
- adoption 입양, 채택
- ensure 보장하다
- counseling 상담, 조언

13 [독해 – 단일형 문항(전자메일 – 목적)] ▶ ③

난이도 중

정답 해설

이 전자메일은 공개된 구획 변경 공고가 지나치게 포괄적이고 세부 정보가 부족해 그 영향을 평가할 수 없으므로, 건물 높이, 허용될 사업체의 종류 등 더 구체적인 정보를 제공해 달라고 요청하는 데 있다. 따라서 글의 목적으로 가장 적절한 것은 ③이다.

해석

수신인: planning.department@cityhall.gov
발신인: sunrise.neighborhood.assoc@email.org
날짜: 2026년 10월 1일
제목: 7B 구역에 관하여

시 도시계획부에게,

Oak Street와 12번가 모퉁이에 위치한 7B 구획의 용도 변경안에 대해 명확한 설명을 요청드리고자, 선라이즈 이웃 협회를 대표해 연락드립니다. 지난주에 게시된 공지문을 확인했으나, 해당 부지가 어떻게 활용될 것인지에 대한 구체적인 내용이 없었습니다.

우리 지역사회는 주거 지역의 특성과 녹지 공간을 매우 중요하게 생각합니다. 공지문에는 "혼합 용도 개발" 가능성이 언급되어 있었지만, 이 표현만으로는 그 영향이 무엇인지 판단하기 어렵습니다.

건물 높이, 허용되는 상업 용도, 그리고 교통과 주차에 미칠 것으로 예상되는 영향 등과 같은 보다 구체적인 정보를 제공해 주실 수 있습니까?

빠른 시일 내에 답변을 받을 수 있기를 바랍니다.

진심으로,
David Chen

① 최근 프로젝트 승인에 항의하려고
② 지역 건물의 새로운 디자인을 제안하려고
③ 용도 구역 변경에 관한 세부 정보를 구하려고
④ 정부 문서의 오류를 보고하려고

어휘

- formally 공식적으로
- request 요청하다
- clarification 설명, 해명
- zoning 용도 지역 지정(도시 계획 용어)
- parcel (토지의) 구획

• **residential** 주거용의
• **assess** 평가하다
• **permitted** 허용된
• **projected** 예상된, 추정된
• **timely** 시기적절한

14 [독해 – 문장 제거]　　　　▶ ③

난이도 하

정답 해설

이 글은 일주기 리듬의 정의와 그것이 조절하는 다양한 신체 기능을 설명하고 있다. 도입부에서 일주기 리듬을 정의한 뒤, ①번과 ②번 문장에서는 대표적인 기능인 '수면-기상 주기'를 다루고 있다. ④번 문장은 수면 외에도 호르몬 분비, 체온, 신진대사 등 다른 기능들을 조절한다는 내용을 덧붙인다. 글의 전체적인 흐름은 '일주기 리듬이 조절하는 기능의 나열'에 초점을 두고 있다. 그러나 ③번 문장은 재정적 스트레스나 고용 불안정 같은 사회·경제적 요인을 수면 문제의 원인으로 지목하고 있다. 이는 생체 시계의 작동 원리를 다루는 글의 흐름에서 벗어난다. 따라서 글의 흐름상 어색한 문장은 ③이다.

해석

> 일주기 리듬은 신체의 내부 시계의 일부인 24시간 주기로, 필수적인 기능과 과정을 수행하기 위해 배경에서 실행된다. ① 가장 중요하고 잘 알려진 일주기 리듬 중 하나는 수면-기상 주기인데, 이는 환경의 빛과 어둠에 의해 크게 영향을 받는다. ② 제대로 기능할 때, 일주기 리듬은 일관되고 회복적인 수면을 촉진하지만, 그것이 흐트러지면 심각한 수면 문제를 일으킬 수 있다. (③ 이러한 수면 문제를 겪는 개인들은 흔히 재정적 스트레스와 고용 불안정이 밤에 잠을 이루지 못하게 하는 주요 기폭제라는 점을 깨닫는다.) ④ 이 내부 시계는 또한 호르몬 분비, 체온, 그리고 신진대사를 포함한 다양한 다른 신체 기능을 조절한다. 그리고 이 모든 것들은 하루 동안 예측 가능한 패턴으로 변동한다.

어휘

• **circadian** 생물학적 주기의, 24시간 주기의
• **internal** 내부의, 내적인
• **process** 과정, 절차
• **influence** 영향을 주다
• **consistent** 일관된, 지속적인
• **restorative** 회복시키는, 원기를 돋우는
• **regulate** 조절하다, 통제하다
• **metabolism** 신진대사
• **fluctuate** 변동하다, 오르내리다
• **predictable** 예측 가능한, 예상되는

15 [독해 – 단일형 문항(안내문 – 내용 불일치)]　　▶ ③

난이도 중

정답 해설

'등록 안내' 중 조기 등록 요금은 200달러이며 5월 30일에 마감된다고 명시되어 있다. 따라서 글의 내용과 일치하지 않는 것은 ③이다.

오답 해설

① AI로 생성된 음성의 윤리적 한계에 대해 논의하기 위해 업계 리더들이 한자리에 모인다고 언급하고 있으므로 글의 내용과 일치한다.
② '기조 연설자' 항목에서 법률 위원단이 참여하여 "초상권 보호: 최근 소송 사례에서의 교훈"을 주제로 연설한다고 언급하고 있으므로 글의 내용과 일치한다.
④ 모든 시간은 녹화되며, 현장 참석자는 행사 종료 후 최대 30일 동안 다시 시청할 수 있다고 언급하고 있으므로 글의 내용과 일치한다.

해석

> **2025 글로벌 AI & 음성 회담 초대**
>
> **주제:** "합성 미디어 시대의 진정성"
> **일정:** 2025년 6월 10일 - 11일
> **장소:** 샌프란시스코 테크 컨벤션 센터
>
> AI로 생성된 음성의 윤리적 한계에 대해 논의하기 위해 업계 리더들이 한자리에 모입니다. 동의 없는 음성 모방과 관련된 최근의 논란에 대응하여, 이번 회담은 새로운 글로벌 기준을 확립하는 것을 목표로 합니다.

> **기조 연설자:**
> ☐ Elena Ross 박사: "인간 - AI 상호작용의 심리학"
> ☐ 법률 위원단: "초상권 보호: 최근 소송 사례에서의 교훈"
>
> **등록 안내:**
> ☐ 조기 등록: 200달러 (5월 30일 마감)
> ☐ 일반 등록: 350달러 (5월 31일부터 적용)
> ☐ 가상 통행증: 100달러 (기조 시간 라이브 스트리밍만 포함)
>
> 참가자에게는 디지털 참가 증명서가 제공됩니다.
>
> 모든 시간은 녹화되며, 현장 참석자는 행사 종료 후 최대 30일 동안 다시 시청할 수 있습니다.

어휘

• **authenticity** 진정성, 진짜임
• **synthetic** 합성의, 인조의
• **ethical** 윤리적인, 도덕에 관계된
• **consent** 동의, 허락
• **early bird** 조기 등록
• **certificate** 증명서, 자격증

16 [독해 – 순서 배열]　　　　▶ ③

난이도 중

정답 해설

주어진 글은 먼저 '페르미 역설'을 정의하며 글을 시작한다. 이어지는 (B)는 'The paradox'를 받아, 이 용어가 물리학자 엔리코 페르미의 질문에서 유래했음을 밝히고, 그의 "Where is everybody?"라는 물음이 역설의 핵심 의미를 상징적으로 드러낸다는 점을 설명한다. (C)는 다시 'this paradox'를 이어받아, 이 역설에 대해 제시된 다양한 해결책들을 포괄적으로 소개한다. 마지막으로 (A)는 (C)에서 언급된 여러 설명들 가운데 대표적인 하나인 '대여과기(Great Filter)' 이론을 구체적으로 설명한다. 따라서 글의 순서로 가장 적절한 것은 ③이다.

해석

> 페르미의 역설은 외계 문명이 존재할 가능성은 매우 높은데도, 그에 대한 증거나 접촉이 전혀 없다는 모순을 가리킨다.
> (B) 이 역설은 물리학자 엔리코 페르미의 이름을 따서 붙여졌으며, 그는 한 대화 중 "도대체 모두 어디에 있는가?"라고 물었다. 이 질문은 생명으로 가득해야 할 우주가 유난히 조용하다는 점을 잘 드러낸다.
> (C) 지성을 가진 생명체가 매우 드물다는 견해부터, 문명들이 접촉하기도 전에 스스로를 파괴한다는 가설에 이르기까지, 이 역설을 설명하기 위한 다양한 해답들이 제시되어 왔다.
> (A) 잘 알려진 설명 중 하나가 '대(大)여과기' 이론인데, 이는 단순한 생명 단계에서 고도로 발전된 문명으로 가는 과정 중 어딘가에 대부분의 생명이 넘지 못하는 극도로 어려운 장벽이 존재한다고 주장한다.

어휘

• **paradox** 역설
• **contradiction** 모순, 상충
• **extraterrestrial** 지구 밖의, 외계의
• **absence** 부재, 없음
• **civilization** 문명
• **physicist** 물리학자
• **captures** 포착하다, 정확히 표현하다
• **abundant** 풍부한, 많은
• **rare** 드문, 희귀한

17 [독해 – 단일형 문항(안내문 – 내용 일치)]　▶ ④

난이도 중

정답 해설

마지막 부분에서 이 프로젝트는 주로 개인 기부와 기업 후원을 통해 운영되며, 자금의 10% 미만이 정부 보조금에서 나온다고 언급하고 있다. 따라서 윗글의 내용과 일치하는 것은 ④이다.

오답 해설

① 피닉스 프로젝트는 멘토링과 직업 훈련을 통해 위험에 처한 청소년들을 지원하는 비영리 단체라고 언급하고 있으므로 글의 내용과 일치하지 않는다.

② 멘토들은 다양한 전문 분야에서 활동하고 있으며, 이번 프로젝트를 돕기 위해 참여했다고 언급하고 있으므로 글의 내용과 일치하지 않는다.

③ 직업 훈련 프로그램들은 모든 참가자에게 무료로 제공된다고 언급하고 있으므로 글의 내용과 일치하지 않는다.

해석

피닉스 프로젝트: 위기 청소년을 위한 희망의 불씨

피닉스 프로젝트는 멘토링과 직업 훈련을 통해 위험에 처한 청소년들을 지원하는 비영리 단체입니다. 우리의 사명은 16세에서 24세 사이의 젊은이들이 어려움을 극복하고 성공적인 미래를 향해 나아갈 수 있도록 필요한 기술과 자신감을 갖추게 하는 것입니다.

저희의 핵심 프로그램:

- 멘토링: 각 참가자는 훈련된 성인 멘토와 짝을 이루어 최소 1년 동안 지도와 지원을 받습니다. 멘토들은 다양한 전문 분야에서 활동하고 있으며, 이번 프로젝트를 돕기 위해 참여했습니다.

- 직업 훈련: 저희는 요리 예술, 정보 기술, 친환경 건설과 같은 수요가 많은 분야에서 실무 훈련을 제공합니다. 이 프로그램들은 모든 참가자에게 무료로 제공됩니다.

저희는 주로 개인 기부와 기업 후원을 통해 운영되며, 자금의 10% 미만이 정부 보조금에서 나옵니다.

---

① 청년들을 지원하기 위해 정부에 의해 설립되었다.
② 이 프로젝트의 모든 멘토들은 은퇴한 교육자들이다.
③ 직업 훈련 프로그램의 참가자들은 일부 비용을 부담한다.
④ 이 프로젝트는 개인 기부를 통해서도 운영된다.

어휘

- at-risk 위험에 처한
- youth 청소년, 젊은이들
- vocational 직업과 관련된
- equip 준비시키다, 갖추게 하다
- confidence 자신감
- affordable 저렴한, 감당할 수 있는
- operate 운영되다, 작동되다
- grant 보조금

18 [독해 – 문장 삽입]　▶ ②

난이도 상

정답 해설

이 글은 브레인스토밍이 무질서하고 비구조적인 과정이라는 일반적인 오해를 바로잡고, 실제로는 체계적인 절차를 통해 기능적인 결과물을 만들어내는 과정임을 설명한다. ①번 뒤 문장에서는 브레인스토밍이 결코 혼란스러운 것이 아니라고 선언하며 오해를 일차적으로 차단한다. 이어지는 위치에 주어진 문장이 들어가면, 강한 역접 표현인 "On the contrary"를 통해 '혼란'과 정반대되는 개념인 '훈육되고 체계적인 접근'을 제시함으로써 앞선 선언을 구체적으로 뒷받침한다. 이렇게 브레인스토밍의 체계적 성격을 먼저 정의해 주어야만, 이후 ②번과 ③번 뒤 문장에서 구체적인 두 단계가 브레인스토밍이라는 전체 시스템 안에서 조화롭게 설명될 수 있다. 따라서 주어진 문장이 들어갈 위치로 가장 적절한 것은 ②이다.

해석

브레인스토밍은 종종 어떤 아이디어나 환영받는 무질서하고 구조화되지 않은 자유로운 판으로 오해받곤 한다. (①) 광범위한 아이디어를 생성하는 것이 실제로 하나의 목표이기는 하지만, 효과적인 브레인스토밍은 결코 무질서하지 않다. (② <u>그와는 반대로, 그것(브레인스토밍)은 문제 해결에 대한 훈련되고 체계적인 접근을 요구하며, 여기서 창의성은 새로우면서도 기능적인 결과물을 생산하도록 조절된다.</u>) '발산'이라고 알려진 초기 단계는 참가자들이 아무리 기발해 보일지라도 가능한 한 많은 아이디어를 생성하기 위해 판단 없이 폭넓게 생각하도록 독려한다. (③) 이 단계는 수렴이라는 중요한 두 번째 단계로 이어진다. (④) 여기에서 팀은 프로젝트의 목표와 제약 조건에 부합하는 가장 유망한 아이디어를 선택하기 위해 생성된 아이디어들을 비판적으로 평가하고, 결합하고, 정제해야 한다.

어휘

- disciplined 규율 있는, 훈련된
- channel (어떤 방향으로) 돌리다, 전하다
- novel 새로운, 참신한
- chaotic 혼란스러운, 무질서한
- free-for-all 무질서[혼란] 상태, 무한 경쟁
- divergence 발산, 분기
- outlandish 기이한, 터무니없는
- refine 정제하다, 다듬다, 개선하다
- promising 유망한, 전망 있는
- constraint 제약, 제한 조건

19 [독해 – 빈칸 추론]　▶ ④

난이도 중

정답 해설

이 글은 인구 구조의 변화가 경제에 미치는 영향을 설명하며 크게 두 부분으로 나뉘는데, 빈칸을 기점으로 과거와 현재의 상황이 극명하게 대조됩니다. 빈칸 앞부분은 인구 배당 효과의 긍정적인 역학 관계(풍부한 젊은 노동력, 높은 세수, 생산성 증대)를 설명하는 반면, 빈칸 뒤의 'Now'부터는 베이비붐의 퇴직, 노동 인구의 감소, 부양비의 급증 등 공공 재정에 심각한 부담을 주는 부정적인 상황을 열거하고 있다. 따라서 과거의 유리했던 경제 구조가 현재에 이르러 정반대로 뒤집히고 있다는 논리적 흐름이 들어가야 자연스럽다. 따라서 밑줄 친 부분에 들어갈 말로 가장 적절한 것은 ④이다.

해석

많은 선진국이 급격히 하락하는 출산율로 정의되는 인구 절벽 위에 서 있다. 이것은 단순한 사회적 변화가 아니라 임박한 경제 위기이며, 세대 간의 합의를 근본적으로 뒤바꾸고 있다. 수십 년 동안, 많은 경제가 '인구 배당금' – 적은 노인 인구를 부양하는 많은 젊은 노동력 – 으로부터 혜택을 받았다. 이것은 생산성을 높이고 높은 세수를 뒷받침했다. 이제, <u>이러한 역학 관계가 뒤바뀌고 있다</u>. 베이비붐 세대가 은퇴함에 따라, 노동력은 줄어들고, 부양 비율 – 노동자 대비 비노동자의 비율 – 이 급증한다. 이 '인구세'는 공공 재정에 지속 불가능한 부담을 지우며, 연금, 의료, 그리고 사회 보장 제도를 압박한다. 따라서 정부는 세금 인상, 수당 삭감, 또는 막대한 부채 수용 사이에서 선택을 강요받는다.

---

① 세수 증가가 경제를 안정시키고 있다
② 노동 인구가 꾸준한 속도로 계속 확장되고 있다
③ 이러한 추세가 탄력을 받고 있다
④ 이러한 역학 관계가 뒤바뀌고 있다

어휘

- developed nation 선진국
- demographic 인구 통계의
- precipice 벼랑, 극도의 위기 상황
- fertility rate 출산율, 출생률
- impending 임박한, 곧 닥칠
- demographic dividend 인구 배당 효과
- dependency ratio 부양 비율
- skyrocket 급증하다, 치솟다
- pension 연금
- retirees 은퇴자, 퇴직자
- pact 협약, 약속, 계약

난이도　상

정답 해설

이 글은 만성적 과소비의 원인을 단순한 의지력 문제가 아니라 '현재 편향'이라는 인지적 결함으로 설명한다. 현재 편향은 추상적이고 감정적으로 먼 미래의 목표보다, 즉각적이고 가시적인 만족을 과대평가하는 경향을 의미한다. 우리의 뇌는 즉각적 보상은 충동적 시스템으로, 미래 목표는 이성적 시스템으로 처리하는데, 충동적 시스템이 쉽게 우세해진다고 지문은 말한다. 이로 인해 현재의 자아가 미래의 자아의 이익에 어긋나는 결정을 내리는 '시간 불일치'가 발생한다. 따라서 밑줄 친 부분에 들어갈 말로 가장 적절한 것은 ②이다.

해석

행동경제학은 지속적인 과소비를 명확하게 설명해 준다. 행동경제학은 이를 "현재 편향"이라는 인지적 결함으로 설명하는데, 우리는 즉각적인 만족을 과대평가하고 장기적 목표는 과소평가하는 경향이 있다. 지금 무언가를 사는 즐거움은 생생하고 감정적으로 크게 느껴지는 반면, 은퇴를 위한 저축이나 부채 상환은 추상적이고 정서적으로 멀게 느껴진다. 우리의 뇌는 이 두 선택을 다르게 처리하는데, 즉각적 보상은 충동적 시스템을 자극하는 반면, 미래의 목표를 지원하는 이성적 시스템은 쉽게 무시된다. 이로 인해 현재의 자아가 <u>미래의 자아가 불가피하게 후회할</u> 결정을 내리는 '시간 불일치'가 발생한다. 따라서 재정적 건강을 유지하기 위해서는 단순히 예산을 세우는 것을 넘어, 미래의 결과를 더 즉각적으로 느낄 수 있게 하는 시스템을 마련하는 것이 필요하다.

① 사치품보다 필수적인 욕구를 우선시할
② 미래의 자아가 불가피하게 후회할
③ 사회적 압력과 마케팅의 큰 영향을 받을
④ 우리의 장기적인 목표를 단기적인 욕구에 맞춰 조정할

어휘

- behavioral 행동의, 행동 관련의
- economics 경제학
- chronic 만성적인, 지속적인
- overspending 과소비, 과도한 지출
- undervalue 과소평가하다
- abstract 추상적인, 막연한
- impulsive 충동적인
- rational 이성적인, 합리적인
- override 무시하다, 억누르다
- inconsistency 불일치, 모순

영어 정답 및 해설

✅ 제3회 모의고사

01 ②	02 ③	03 ①	04 ③	05 ③
06 ③	07 ④	08 ②	09 ①	10 ②
11 ②	12 ④	13 ②	14 ④	15 ③
16 ②	17 ②	18 ④	19 ②	20 ①

01 [어휘 – 빈칸]　　▶②

난이도 중

정답 해설

딥페이크 기술이 현실과 거의 구별하기 어려울 정도로 정교하며, 그로 인해 정보의 진실성까지 위협받고 있다는 점을 고려하면, 딥페이크 기술이 놀라운 '신빙성'을 지닌다는 내용이 적절하다. 따라서 밑줄 친 부분에 들어갈 말로 가장 적절한 것은 ②이다.

해석

> 생성형 AI의 급속한 발전은 너무나도 놀라운 <u>신빙성</u>을 지닌 딥페이크 기술을 만들어냈고, 그 결과 그것들은 현실과 거의 구별할 수 없어서 정보의 진설성이 위협받고 있다.

어휘

- ★ credibility 신빙성, 신뢰성
- ● inventory 물품 목록, 재고(품)
- ● consumption 소비, 소모, 섭취
- ● deficiency 결핍, 부족, 결함

02 [어휘 – 빈칸]　　▶③

난이도 중

정답 해설

전고체 배터리 연구가 점차 진전되고 있다는 점으로 보아, 전기차의 비전이 단순한 이론적 가능성을 넘어 상업적 현실로 발전할 수 있음을 짐작할 수 있다. 따라서 밑줄 친 부분에 들어갈 말로 가장 적절한 것은 ③이다.

해석

> 전고체 배터리 연구가 진전되면서, 1,000km 주행 전기차의 비전이 이론적 가능성에서 상업적 현실로 <u>발전할</u> 수 있다.

어휘

- ★ evolve 발전하다, 진화하다
- ● stagnate 정체되다, 침체되다, 고이다
- ● retreat 후퇴하다, 철수하다, 물러서다
- ● deposit 맡기다, 두다, 예금하다

03 [문법 – 빈칸]　　▶①

난이도 상

정답 해설

① [적중 포인트 058] 분사를 활용한 표현 및 구문 ★★★★☆

빈칸 뒤에는 'his extensive experience in international negotiations'라는 명사구가 이어지고 있다. 문맥상 '국제 협상에서의 폭넓은 경험을 고려할 때'라는 의미가 들어가야 자연스럽다. Given은 분사에서 파생된 전치사로, '~을 고려해 볼 때'라는 뜻으로 쓰이며, 뒤에 명사나 명사구를 목적어로 취할 수 있다. 따라서 밑줄 친 부분에 들어갈 말로 가장 적절한 것은 ①이다.

해석

> 국제 협상에서의 폭넓은 경험을 고려할 때, Lopez 씨는 다가오는 무역 협상을 이끌기에 가장 적합한 후보로 여겨진다.

04 [생활영어 – 빈칸]　　▶③

난이도 중

정답 해설

A는 정전 시 스마트 화분의 설정이 초기화될 것을 걱정하고 있다. 이에 B는 비휘발성 메모리를 통해 설정이 유지된다고 설명하며 안심시킨다. 이때 상대방의 우려를 인정하면서도 해결책이 있음을 암시하는 말이 앞서 나오는 것이 가장 자연스럽다. 따라서 밑줄 친 부분에 들어갈 말로 가장 적절한 것은 ③이다.

해석

> A: 이 스마트 화분 정말 대단해! 식물 종류에 따라 자동으로 물 주기랑 조명 주기를 조절한대.
> B: 멋진데? 그러면 그냥 "바질을 키운다"고 입력만 하면 나머지는 알아서 다 해주는 거야?
> A: 거의 그래. 그런데 정전이 나면 어떻게 될까? 내 설정들이 다 사라지는 건 아닐까?
> B: <u>그건 타당한 걱정이지만 대부분의 최신 기기에는 안전장치가 있어.</u> 보통 사용자 설정은 비휘발성 메모리에 저장돼.
> A: 다행이다. 그럼 전기가 다시 들어오면 일정이 그대로 이어지는 거네?
> B: 맞아. 네 바질은 안전할 거야.

① 처음부터 다시 설정해야 할 거야
② 그 기기에 백업 시스템이 있을 것 같진 않아
③ 그건 타당한 걱정이지만 대부분의 최신 기기에는 안전장치가 있어
④ 그 기기는 아마 기본 저전력 모드로 전환될 거야

어휘

- input 입력하다, 넣다
- power outage 정전
- non-volatile 비휘발성의(전원이 꺼져도 데이터가 남는)
- valid 타당한, 근거 있는
- fail-safe 안전장치

05 [생활영어 – 빈칸]　　▶③

난이도 중

정답 해설

동료와의 자연스러운 만남을 통해 형성되던 유대감이 하이브리드 근무로 약화될 것을 우려하는 상황이다. 이에 대해 Tom은 '가상 커피 브레이크'라는 구체적인 해결책을 제시한다. 이 아이디어의 핵심은 '자연스럽지 않다면 의도적으로라도 교류의 장을 만들자'는 것이다. 따라서 밑줄 친 부분에 들어갈 말로 가장 적절한 것은 ③이다.

해석

> Sarah: 이봐 Tom, 새로운 하이브리드 근무 정책 읽어봤어? 우리 팀 분위기가 좀 걱정되네.
> Tom: 응, 봤어. 출퇴근이 줄어드는 건 좋은데, 커피 머신 옆에서 나누던 잡담이 그리울 거야.
> Sarah: 맞아! 우리가 즉흥적으로 서로를 보지 못할 때 어떻게 팀의 유대감을 유지할 수 있을까?
> Tom: <u>가상의 사교 공간을 의도적으로 만드는 것이 핵심이 될 수 있어.</u> 만약 우리가 매주 가상 '커피 브레이크'를 위해 특정 시간을 할애한다면, 도움이 될지도 몰라.
> Sarah: 그거 좋은 생각이다. 시도해 볼 가치가 있겠어!

① 우리는 업무 중심의 소통에만 집중해야 해
② 회사는 전면적인 사무실 복귀를 의무화해야 해
③ 가상의 사교 공간을 의도적으로 만드는 것이 핵심이 될 수 있어
④ 팀의 결속력이 약해질 수밖에 없다는 사실을 그냥 받아들여야 한다고 생각해

어휘

- spontaneously 자발적으로, 즉흥적으로
- exclusively 오로지, 독점적으로
- task-oriented 일 중심의
- mandate 명령하다, 지시하다

06 [독해 - 중심 내용 추론(주제)] ▶ ③

난이도 | 하

정답 해설

이 글은 '수리할 권리'라는 사회적 운동을 중심으로, 이를 지지하는 소비자 옹호론자들의 주장과 이에 반대하는 제조업체들의 주장을 명확히 대조하여 설명하고 있다. 찬성 측은 반경쟁적 관행, 환경 문제, 소비자 소유권 침해를 근거로 들고, 반대 측은 지적 재산권 보호, 사용자 안전, 제품 품질 유지를 주장한다. 따라서 글의 주제로 가장 적절한 것은 ③이다.

해석

> 성장하는 소비자 옹호 운동인 "수리할 권리" 운동은 많은 전자제품 제조업체의 지배적인 비즈니스 모델에 도전한다. 이 모델은 종종 독점적인 나사를 사용하거나, 부품들을 접착제로 붙이거나, 예비 부품 및 수리 설명서에 대한 접근을 제한하는 등의 방법으로 소비자들이나 독립적인 기술자들이 수리하기 어렵거나 불가능하게 제품을 설계하는 것을 포함한다. 수리할 권리의 지지자들은 이러한 관행이 반경쟁적이고, 불필요한 전자 폐기물을 생성하며, 자신의 재산을 소유하고 수정할 소비자의 권리를 침해한다고 주장한다. 그러나, 제조업체들은 그러한 제한이 지적 재산권을 보호하고, 부적절한 수리로부터 사용자 안전을 보장하며, 자신들의 기기의 품질과 성능을 유지하기 위해 필요하다고 반박한다. 여러 국가에서 벌어지는 그 결과적인 입법 공방은 소비자 자율성과 기업 통제 사이의 근본적인 갈등을 반영한다.

① 전자 폐기물이 환경에 미치는 영향
② 소비자가 기기 수리에 접근하는 것을 제한하는 장벽들
③ '수리할 권리'를 둘러싼 갈등의 핵심 논점들
④ 현대 전자 기기의 수리 가능성에 대한 기업의 제한들

어휘

- advocacy 옹호, 지지, 변호
- prevailing 지배적인, 우세한, 일반적인
- restrict 제한하다, 금지하다
- spare part 예비 부품
- proponent 지지자, 옹호자
- anti-competitive 경쟁을 저해하는, 반경쟁적인
- infringe 침해하다, 위반하다
- modify 수정하다, 변경하다
- legislative 입법의, 법률 제정과 관련된
- autonomy 자율성, 자치권
- corporate 기업의, 회사의

07 [독해 - 세트형 문항(홈페이지 게시글 - 제목)] ▶ ④

난이도 | 하

정답 해설

이 글은 모바일 앱을 처음 만들어보는 초보자를 위한 주말 워크숍 안내문이다. 첫 문장에서 대상이 코딩 경험이 없는 입문자임을 분명히 한다. 일정표에서도 오전에는 앱 로직·화면 구성의 기초 소개, 오후에는 버튼·지도·카메라 등 기능 추가, 저녁에는 실제 기기 테스트와 버그 수정을 다루고 있다. 따라서 글의 제목으로 가장 적절한 것은 ④이다.
① 모바일 앱을 위한 마케팅 및 출시 전략
② 앱 개발자를 위한 고급 프로그래밍 기술
③ 스마트폰이 현대 기술을 어떻게 변화시켰는가
④ 모바일 앱 입문 워크숍

08 [독해 - 세트형 문항(홈페이지 게시글 - 내용 불일치)] ▶ ②

난이도 | 하

정답 해설

워크숍 일정표를 제시하며, 아래의 일정을 확인한 뒤 자신의 학습 목표에 가장 잘 맞는 시간을 선택하라고 안내하고 있다. 따라서 글의 내용과 일치하지 않는 것은 ②이다.
① 워크숍은 코딩 경험이 전혀 없는 초보자를 대상으로 설계되었다.
② 참가자들은 오전부터 저녁까지 모든 시간에 반드시 참여해야 한다.
③ 저녁 시간은 실제 기기를 사용해 앱을 테스트하는 데 중점을 둔다.
④ 각 참가자는 개인 노트북을 직접 준비해야 한다.

오답 해설

① 이 주말 워크숍은 코딩 경험이 전혀 없는 초보자를 위해 마련되었다고 언급하고 있으므로 글의 내용과 일치한다.
③ 워크숍 일정표에 저녁은 '검토' 과정으로 실제 기기에서 앱을 테스트하고 오류 수정한다고 언급하고 있으므로 글의 내용과 일치한다.
④ 모든 참가자는 개인 노트북을 지참해야 한다고 언급하고 있으므로 글의 내용과 일치한다.

해석

> **모바일 앱 입문 워크숍**
>
> 모바일 앱을 직접 만들어 보고 싶지만 어디서부터 시작해야 할지 모르시나요? 이 주말 워크숍은 코딩 경험이 전혀 없는 초보자를 위해 마련되었으며, 아이디어 구상부터 앱 출시까지의 전 과정을 안내합니다.
>
> 참가자들은 사용자 인터페이스(UI) 디자인의 기초와 블록 기반 코딩을 배우게 됩니다. 아래의 일정을 확인한 뒤, 자신의 학습 목표에 가장 잘 맞는 시간을 선택해 주세요.
>
> **워크숍 시간**
>
> | 시간 | 중점 내용 |
> | --- | --- |
> | 오전 입문 | 앱의 기본 로직과 화면 레이아웃 설계 소개 |
> | 오후 제작 | 버튼, 지도, 카메라 접근 기능 등 다양한 기능 추가 |
> | 저녁 검토 | 실제 기기에서 앱을 테스트하고 오류 수정 |
>
> 모든 참가자는 개인 노트북을 지참해야 합니다. 점심과 다과는 무료로 제공됩니다. 등록은 행사 이틀 전 마감되므로, 자리를 확보하려면 서둘러 신청하시기 바랍니다.

어휘

- beginner 초보자, 초심자
- fit 맞다, 적합하다
- refreshment 다과, 가벼운 식사
- free of charge 무료로

09 [독해 - 세트형 문항(안내문 - 유의어)] ▶ ①

난이도 | 하

정답 해설

밑줄 친 prohibited는 '금지된, 금하고 있는'이라는 뜻으로, 문맥상 가장 가까운 의미는 ① 'forbidden(금지된)'이다.

오답 해설

② unprecedented 전례 없는
③ sustained 지속된, 한결같은, 일관된
④ fasten 매다, 채우다, 잠그다, 고정시키다

10 [독해 - 세트형 문항(안내문 - 내용 일치)] ▶ ②

난이도 | 중

정답 해설

이러한 모델들이 체계적인 편향을 영속화하거나 금지된 콘텐츠를 생성하지 않도록 보장하는 것은 매우 시급하고 중요한 사안이라고 언급하고 있다. 따라서 글의 내용과 일치하는 것은 ②이다.
① 제3자 평가 기관은 초기 감사 과정에서 제외된다.
② 주요 목표는 AI 시스템이 불공정한 사회적 편견을 강화하는 것을 방지하는 것이다.
③ 검토 결과는 24시간 이내에 전송될 것이다.
④ 서류는 안전 위원회에 직접 방문하여 제출해야 한다.

오답 해설

① 내부 규정 준수 팀이나 지정된 제3자 평가 기관 등, 생성형 AI 모델의 감사와 관련된 모든 제출물을 환영한다고 언급하고 있으므로 글의 내용과 일치하지 않는다.
③ 만약 특정 모델의 'AI 안전법' 불이행에 대해 민원을 제기하고자 하신다면, 저희는 이를 가능한 한 신속하게 검토할 것이라고 언급하고 있을 뿐, 구체적인 시간은 명시하지 않았으므로 글의 내용과 일치하지 않는다.
④ 모든 관련 서류를 당사의 보안 보고 포털을 통해 제출해 달라고 언급하고 있으므로 글의 내용과 일치하지 않는다.

AI 모델 위험 보고 지침

우리는 내부 규정 준수 팀이나 지정된 제3자 평가 기관 등, 생성형 AI 모델의 감사와 관련된 모든 제출물을 환영합니다. 이러한 모델들이 체계적인 편향을 영속화하거나 <u>금지된</u> 콘텐츠를 생성하지 않도록 보장하는 것은 매우 시급하고 중요한 사안입니다.

만약 특정 모델의 'AI 안전법' 불이행에 대해 민원을 제기하고자 하신다면, 저희는 이를 가능한 한 신속하게 검토할 것입니다. 외부 감사인이 개발자를 대신하여 보고서를 제출하는 경우, 검토를 시작하기 전에 독점적인 모델 데이터의 공개를 승인하는 인증된 문서가 반드시 필요합니다.

원본 소스 기록과 안전성 테스트 결과를 포함한 모든 관련 서류를 당사의 보안 보고 포털을 통해 제출해 주십시오. 저희는 귀하의 민원을 기록하고 신중하게 검토할 것이며, AI 안전 위원회의 감독 위원회가 이에 대해 응답할 것입니다.

- submission 제출, 진술
- auditing (회계) 감사
- imperative 필수적인, 반드시 해야 하는
- perpetuate 영속시키다, 지속하게 하다
- compliance 준수, 규정 따름
- certified 보증된, 공인의
- document 문서, 서류
- authorize 승인하다, 허가하다
- proprietary 소유주[자]의, 독점적인

11 [문법 – 밑줄] ▶②

② **[적중 포인트 082] 관계대명사의 선행사와 문장 구조 ★★★★☆**
밑줄 친 부분의 which는 주격 또는 목적격 관계대명사로 뒤에 주어나 목적어 없는 불완전 구조를 취한다. 하지만, 밑줄 친 부분 뒤에는 완전한 구조이므로 완전한 구조를 이끌 수 있는 소유격 관계대명사가 필요하다. 따라서 밑줄 친 부분의 which를 whose로 고쳐야 한다.

① **[적중 포인트 012] 지시대명사 this와 that ★★★★☆**
뒤에 주어와 동사가 모두 복수 형태로 쓰였다. 가까이 있는 명사를 지칭할 때 복수형이면 지시대명사 these를 쓴다. 따라서 밑줄 친 부분은 올바르게 쓰였다.

③ **[적중 포인트 039] 현재시제 동사와 be동사의 수 일치 ★★★★★**
문장의 주어(The research)는 단수형이므로 동사도 단수 형태로 수 일치한다. 따라서 밑줄 친 부분은 올바르게 쓰였다.

④ **[적중 포인트 078] 등위접속사와 병렬 구조 ★★★★☆**
not just A but (also) B 구문에서 A(their presence)와 B(that they can act)는 보어 자리에서 병렬 구조를 이루고 있다. 명사절을 이끄는 접속사 that은 적절하다. 따라서 밑줄 친 부분은 올바르게 쓰였다.

최근의 미세플라스틱 연구는 이 작은 입자들이 이제 어디에나 퍼져 있으며, 해양 생태계에서부터 인체 조직에 이르기까지 모든 것을 침투하고 있다는 사실을 밝혀냈다. 이 연구는 외딴 북극의 빙핵 시료를 분석하는 방법론을 사용한 것으로, 미세플라스틱의 광범위한 확산을 보여주는 강력한 증거를 제공한다. 가장 우려스러운 점은 단순히 그 존재 자체가 아니라, 이들이 유해 오염 물질의 매개체 역할을 할 수 있다는 사실이다.

12 [문법 – 밑줄] ▶④

④ **[적중 포인트 054] 분사 판별법 [현재분사 VS 과거분사] ★★★★★**
콤마 뒤는 주절의 내용을 부연하는 분사구문 자리이다. 주절의 주어(This ambiguity)가 국가 배후 행위자들이 스파이 활동을 하도록 '허용하는' 능동의 의미이므로 현재분사로 써야 한다. 따라서 밑줄 친 부분의 allowed를 allowing으로 고쳐야 한다.

① **[적중 포인트 014] 형용사와 부사의 차이 ★★★★★**
binding은 '구속력 있는'의 의미인 형용사로 쓰였고, 뒤의 명사(treaty)를 수식하고 있다. 따라서 밑줄 친 부분은 올바르게 쓰였다.

② **[적중 포인트 088] 전치사와 명사 목적어 ★★★☆☆**
Unlike는 '~와 달리'의 의미를 가진 전치사이며, 뒤에 명사구(traditional warfare)를 목적어로 취해 주절과 자연스럽게 대비시키고 있다. 따라서 밑줄 친 부분은 올바르게 쓰였다.

③ **[적중 포인트 060] to부정사의 명사적 역할 ★★★★☆**
동사 make가 5형식으로 쓰여, '가목적어 it+형용사+진목적어 to identify'의 구문을 이루고 있다. 따라서 밑줄 친 부분은 올바르게 쓰였다.

국제 사회는 사이버 전쟁에 대한 구속력 있는 조약을 마련하는 데 계속 어려움을 겪고 있으며, 이로 인해 디지털 영역은 끊임없는 저강도 분쟁 상태에 놓이게 되었다. 전통적 전쟁에서는 공격 주체가 비교적 명확한 반면, 사이버 공간의 익명성은 가해자를 확정적으로 식별하기 어렵게 만든다. 이러한 모호성은 국가가 후원하는 행위자들에게 그럴듯한 부인 가능성을 제공하여, 그들이 첩보 활동과 파괴 행위를 벌이도록 사실상 방패막이 역할을 한다.

13 [독해 – 단일형 문항(전자메일 – 목적)] ▶③

이 글은 시의회가 도심의 마지막 녹지 공간을 없애는 '에버그린 타워' 개발을 승인한 것에 대해, 한 주민이 강한 항의와 깊은 실망을 표하기 위해 작성한 것이다. 시의회가 주민의 장기적 복지보다 상업적 이익을 우선시했다고 지적하며, 이 결정을 즉시 재고하고 철회한 뒤 지속 가능한 도시 계획을 우선해야 한다고 강력히 촉구하고 있다. 따라서 글의 목적으로 가장 적절한 것은 ③이다.

수신인: citycouncil@woodville.gov
발신인: ConcernedResident@community.org
날짜: 2026년 10월 31일
제목: 제안된 개발 사업에 관하여

존경하는 시의회 의원님들께,

저는 최근 시의회가 승인한 '에버그린 타워' 개발 사업에 대해 깊은 실망과 강한 항의의 뜻을 전하고자 이 글을 씁니다. 이 결정은 우리 도심 중심부에 남아 있는 마지막 주요 녹지를 없애는 것으로, 매우 중대한 실수입니다.

세수와 일자리에 집중하는 것은 공원의 환경적, 사회적 가치를 간과하는 것입니다. 이 녹지 공간은 깨끗한 공기, 커뮤니티 이용, 야생동물을 지원하며, 고급 콘도로 대체하면 도시의 장기적인 복지에 해를 끼칩니다.

본인은 의회의 결정을 즉각 재고할 것과, 근시안적인 상업적 이익보다 지속 가능하고 지역사회 중심적인 도시 계획을 우선시할 것을 강력히 촉구합니다. 우리 도시의 안녕을 보장하기 위해서는 귀측의 신속한 조치가 필수적입니다.

진심으로,
한 명의 우려하는 도심 주민 드림

① 공공 공원의 열악한 유지 관리 상태에 대해 항의하려고
② 에버그린 타워 사업에 관한 우려를 제기하려고
③ 개발 결정에 항의하고 그 결정을 철회하도록 촉구하려고
④ 도심 녹지의 생태학적 조사를 제공하려고

- profound 심오한, 깊이 있는
- protest 항의, 반대, 이의를 제기하다
- approval 승인, 허가
- justification 정당화, 타당한 이유
- irreversible 되돌릴 수 없는, 회복 불가능한
- vacant 비어 있는, 사용되지 않는
- habitat 서식지, 생태 환경
- flagrant 명백한, 눈에 띄는, 노골적인
- disregard 무시하다, 경시하다
- short-sighted 단기적인, 근시안적인
- reversal 철회, 뒤바꿈, 전환

14 [독해 - 문장 삽입] ▶④

난이도 | 상

정답해설

이 글은 인터넷의 발전 단계를 Web 1.0에서 Web 3.0으로 이어지는 흐름에 따라 단계적으로 설명하고 있다. 주어진 문장은 인터넷이 '정적인 정보 도서관'에서 '창조와 발견의 역동적이고 지능적인 파트너'로 변모한다는 내용을 담고 있다. 지문에서 ②번 뒤 문장은 Web 3.0(지능형 웹) 시대의 도래를 언급하고 있으며, ③번 뒤 문장은 이를 뒷받침하는 기술적 기반(분산형 인프라 및 첨단 AI)과 그 기능(문맥 이해)을 구체적으로 설명한다. 따라서 기술적 배경 설명이 마무리된 후, 그 기술이 가져온 근본적인 성격의 변화를 요약하는 주어진 문장이 ④번에 위치하는 것이 가장 자연스럽다. 이러한 변화는 ④번 뒤에 이어지는 문장의 내용, 즉 인터넷이 단순한 정보 전달을 넘어 '개인화된 상호작용을 적극적으로 지원'하게 되었다는 결과론적 설명과 논리적으로 직결된다. 따라서 주어진 문장이 들어갈 위치로 가장 적절한 것은 ④이다.

해석

인터넷의 진화는 종종 여러 뚜렷한 단계로 구분된다. 웹 1.0은 소수의 창작자가 다수의 소비자에게 콘텐츠를 제공하던 '읽기 전용' 웹의 시대였다. (①) 그 후 소셜 미디어와 사용자 생성 콘텐츠로 특징지어지는 '읽기-쓰기' 웹, 즉 웹 2.0이 등장하여 사용자들을 적극적인 참여자로 바꾸어 놓았다. (②) 이제 우리는 흔히 '시맨틱 웹' 또는 '지능형 웹'이라고 불리는 웹 3.0의 시대로 접어들고 있다. (③) 이러한 진화는 분산형 인프라와 첨단 인공지능에 의해 뒷받침되며, 이는 네트워크가 단순히 키워드를 처리하는 것을 넘어 문맥을 이해할 수 있게 해준다. (④ <u>이 변화는 인터넷을 정적인 정보 도서관에서 창조와 발견의 역동적이고 지능적인 파트너로 변모시킨다.</u>) 그 결과, 인터넷은 단순한 정보 전달을 넘어 지식과 인류 사이의 더욱 의미 있고 효율적이며 개인화된 상호작용을 적극적으로 지원하는 단계로 나아간다.

어휘

- transform 변형시키다, 바꾸다
- static 정적인, 고정된
- dynamic 역동적인, 활발한
- evolution 진화, 발전, 변화 과정
- distinct 뚜렷한, 별개의, 확실한
- era 시대, 시기
- characterize 특징짓다, ~의 특징을 이루다
- semantic 의미론의, 의미 기반의
- decentralized 분산적인, 분산형의
- process 처리하다, 가공하다
- meaningful 의미 있는, 중요한

15 [독해 - 단일형 문항(안내문 - 내용 불일치)] ▶③

난이도 | 중

정답해설

5월 26일 월요일 오후 5시에 상영되는 'The Apprentice'는 5월 24일 토요일 오후 2시에 이미 상영된 작품으로, 이후 앙코르 상영으로 다시 진행되는 드라마이다. 따라서 글의 내용과 일치하지 않는 것은 ③이다.

오답해설

① 5월 24일 토요일 오후 2시에 'The Apprentice'가 상영되고 이후 영화 평론가들과의 패널 토론 진행이 된다고 명시되어 있으므로 글의 내용과 일치한다.
② 5월 25일 일요일 오후 6시에 상영되는 'Furiosa'는 IMAX 상영이며 추가 요금 5달러가 부과된다고 명시되어 있으므로 글의 내용과 일치한다.
④ '안내 사항' 부분에서 상영 시작 30분 전부터 입장이 가능하며, 지각 입장은 허용되지 않는다고 명시되어 있으므로 글의 내용과 일치한다.

해석

2026 국제 영화 주간:
특별 상영회
칸 영화제 최고의 작품들을 기념하며

다운타운 예술 극장에서 영화제에서 바로 선보이는 수상작들을 감상할 수 있는 상영회에 여러분을 초대합니다.

일정
(5월 24일, 토요일):
☐ 오후 2시: The Apprentice (드라마) - 상영 후 영화 평론가들과의 패널 토론 진행
☐ 오후 7시: Megalopolis (SF) - 매진

(5월 25일, 일요일):
☐ 오후 3시: Kinds of Kindness (명화집) - 감독: Yorgos Lanthimos
☐ 오후 6시: Furiosa (액션) - IMAX 상영. 추가 요금 5달러가 부과됩니다.

(5월 26일, 월요일) (현충일 특별 상영)
☐ 오전 11시: 단편 영화 모음 상영. 유효한 학생증을 지참한 학생은 무료 입장.
☐ 오후 5시: The Apprentice (앙코르 상영)

안내 사항:
- 티켓은 매표소 또는 앱을 통해 구매할 수 있습니다.
- 상영 시작 30분 전부터 입장이 가능하며, 지각 입장은 허용되지 않습니다.

어휘

- award-winning 수상한, 상을 받은
- critics 평론가, 비평가
- sold out 표가 매진된, 다 팔린
- anthology 명화, 명곡, 선집
- surcharge 추가 요금
- compilation 모음집, 편집본

16 [독해 - 문장 제거] ▶②

난이도 | 중

정답해설

이 글은 미래 식량 문제를 해결하기 위한 혁신적인 대안으로 '세포 농업'을 소개하며, 이 기술의 잠재적 장점과 해결해야 할 현실적인 과제들을 논리적으로 제시하고 있다. 지문의 도입부와 ①번, ③번 문장, 그리고 마지막 문장은 모두 '동물을 기르지 않고 세포를 배양하여 식량을 생산'한다는 세포 농업이라는 일관된 주제를 중심으로 전개된다. 그러나 ②번 문장은 세포 농업이라는 혁신적 대안과는 거리가 먼, 기존 축산업의 틀 안에서 '가축 사료용 곡물 다양화'를 통해 비용을 절감하려는 전통적인 농가 관리 방식을 다루고 있다. 따라서 글의 흐름상 어색한 문장은 ②이다.

해석

전 세계 식량 시스템은 삼중고에 직면해 있다. 즉, 늘어나는 인구에게 영양가 있는 음식을 제공해야 하고, 막대한 환경 발자국을 줄여야 하며, 변동성이 커지는 기후 변화에 적응해야 한다는 것이다. ① 한 가지 유망한 방안은 세포 농업의 발전인데, 이는 동물을 통째로 사육하는 대신 세포 배양을 통해 고기, 우유, 계란을 생산하는 것을 포함한다. (② 상승하는 비용에 대응하여, 많은 농부들은 가축의 건강을 개선하기 위해 가축 사료에 사용되는 곡물의 종류를 넓힐 수 있는 방법을 찾고 있다.) ③ 이러한 접근법은 전통적인 축산업과 관련된 토지 사용, 물 소비, 그리고 온실가스 배출을 급격히 줄일 수 있다. ④ 그러나 소비자의 수용성이 여전히 큰 장벽으로 남아 있는데, 이는 "실험실에서 배양된" 식품에 대한 대중의 인식이 종종 회의적이기 때문이다. 게다가, 기존 농업과 비교해 비용 경쟁력을 갖출 수 있을 만큼 생산 규모를 확대하는 것은 극복해야 할 만만치 않은 기술적, 경제적 과제를 안겨준다.

어휘

- trilemma 삼중고, 삼도 논법, 3자 택일의 궁지
- nutritious 영양가 있는, 영양이 풍부한
- environmental footprint 환경 발자국
- volatility 변동성, 불안정성
- promising 유망한, 전망이 좋은
- cell culture 세포 배양
- drastically 급격히, 과감하게
- acceptance 수용, 수락, 동의
- skeptical 회의적인, 의심 많은
- conventional 기존의, 관습적인

17 [독해 – 단일형 문항(홈페이지 게시글 – 내용 일치)]   ▶ ②

난이도 중

정답 해설

대부분의 IF 프로토콜이 적당한 체중 감량과 대사 지표 개선을 초래하지만, 전체 칼로리 섭취량을 일치시킬 때 그 효과는 기존 칼로리 제한 식단에 비해 크게 우수하지 않다는 결론을 내렸다고 언급하고 있다. 따라서 윗글의 내용과 일치하는 것은 ②이다.

오답 해설

① 이 연구는 50개 이상의 임상 시험에서 얻은 데이터를 종합한다고 언급하고 있으므로 글의 내용과 일치하지 않는다.

③ 연구진은 IF의 주요 이점이 대사 마법이 아니라 총 에너지 소비를 줄이는 더 간단하고 직관적인 행동 도구로서의 역할일 수 있다고 제안한다고 언급하고 있으므로 글의 내용과 일치하지 않는다.

④ 연구진은 2년 이상의 IF의 장기 순응도와 건강 영향에 대해서는 아직 대부분 연구되지 않았으며 추가 연구가 필요하다고 지적했다고 언급하고 있으므로 글의 내용과 일치하지 않는다.

해석

> **Nature Metabolism**
>
> 간헐적 단식에 관한 최근 연구
>
> 최근 Nature Metabolism에 발표된 메타 분석에서는 다양한 간헐적 단식(IF) 요법의 효능을 조사했습니다. 이 연구는 50개 이상의 임상 시험에서 얻은 데이터를 종합하여, 교대 단식과 시간 제한 식사를 포함한 대부분의 IF 프로토콜이 적당한 체중 감량과 대사 지표 개선을 초래하지만, 전체 칼로리 섭취량을 일치시킬 때 그 효과는 기존 칼로리 제한 식단에 비해 크게 우수하지 않다는 결론을 내렸습니다.
>
> 연구진은 IF의 주요 이점이 대사 마법이 아니라 총 에너지 소비를 줄이는 더 간단하고 직관적인 행동 도구로서의 역할일 수 있다고 제안합니다. 그러나 연구진은 2년 이상의 IF의 장기 순응도와 건강 영향에 대해서는 아직 대부분 연구되지 않았으며 추가 연구가 필요하다고 지적했습니다.

① 그 연구는 50개만큼이나 많은 임상 시험을 포함하지는 않았다.
② 간헐적 단식은 총 칼로리 섭취량이 같을 경우, 특별한 이점을 보이지 않는다고 결론짓고 있다.
③ 연구진은 간헐적 단식의 주요 이점이 아직 명확히 밝혀지지 않았다고 언급한다.
④ 간헐적 단식에 대한 장기 연구가 완료되었다.

어휘

- examine 조사하다, 검토하다
- efficacy 효능, 효과성
- regimen 운동 및 식이 요법
- synthesize 종합하다, 통합하다
- clinical trial 임상 시험
- alternate-day 격일의, 하루 걸러
- modest 적당한, 크지 않은, 보통의
- metabolic 신진대사의
- intuitive 직관적인, 이해하기 쉬운
- identify 규명하다, 밝히다, 알아내다
- complete 완료하다, 끝내다

18 [독해 – 순서 배열]   ▶ ④

난이도 중

정답 해설

주어진 글은 탈세계화가 21세기의 중요한 특징으로 부상하고 있음을 제시한다. (C)는 이러한 추세를 이끄는 근본적 요인으로 강대국 간의 전략적 경쟁 심화와 경제 민족주의의 확산을 제시한다. 이어 (B)에서는 COVID-19 팬데믹이 글로벌 공급망의 취약성을 드러내며, 이러한 탈세계화 흐름을 추가적으로 강화했음을 설명한다. 마지막으로 (A)는 앞서 언급된 경쟁 심화와 팬데믹으로 인한 공급망 위기라는 압력들에 대응하여, 각국 정부가 경제적 효율성보다 국가 안보와 공급망 회복력을 우선시하는 정책(온쇼어링, 프렌드쇼어링 등)을 채택하고 있음을 제시하며 글을 마무리한다. 따라서 글의 순서로 가장 적절한 것은 ④이다.

해석

> 탈세계화는 국가 간 상호의존성과 통합이 줄어드는 과정으로, 수십 년간의 세계 경제 수렴을 뒤집으며 21세기 지정학적 지형의 결정적 특징이 되고 있다.
> (C) 몇 가지 요인이 이러한 추세를 이끌고 있는데, 가장 두드러지는 것은 주요 강대국 간의 고조되는 전략적 경쟁과 경제 민족주의의 부상이다.
> (B) 코로나19 팬데믹은 초전문화된 글로벌 공급망의 취약성을 노출하고 과도한 해외 의존의 위험성을 입증함으로써 이러한 변화를 더욱 강화했다.
> (A) 이러한 압력에 대응하여, 정부는 순수한 경제적 효율성보다 국가 안보와 공급망 회복력을 우선시하기 시작했으며, 이는 온쇼어링(생산 시설 국내 복귀) 및 프렌드쇼어링(동맹국 내 생산)과 같은 정책을 낳았다.

어휘

- deglobalization 탈세계화
- diminish 줄이다, 감소시키다
- geopolitical 지정학의, 지정학적인
- reverse 뒤집다, 뒤바꾸다
- convergence 수렴, 하나로 모임
- nationalism 민족주의, 국수주의
- reinforce 강화하다, 보강하다
- resilience 회복력, 탄력성
- efficiency 효율성

19 [독해 – 빈칸 추론]   ▶ ②

난이도 상

정답 해설

이 글은 기존의 경제 모델에서 탈피한 '순환 경제'의 경제적 필요성을 역설하고 있다. 기존의 선형 경제 모델은 '채취–제조–폐기'의 과정을 거치며 끊임없이 새로운 자원을 투입해야만 성장이 유지되는 구조이기에, 자원 고갈과 글로벌 공급망 불안정에 매우 취약할 수밖에 없다. 반면 순환 경제는 소재를 재사용, 수리, 재활용함으로써 이미 존재하는 자원을 지속적으로 순환시켜 새로운 가치를 창출한다. 이러한 체계적 변화의 핵심은 경제 성장을 자원 소비 및 환경 부하로부터 분리시키는 '탈동조화'에 있다. 지문에서 언급된 신규 원자재 의존에 따른 리스크를 극복하고 비즈니스의 회복탄력성을 확보하기 위해서는, 외부 자원 공급망에 매달리지 않는 자생적 구조가 필수적이다. 따라서 밑줄 친 부분에 들어갈 말로 가장 적절한 것은 ②이다.

해석

> 재사용, 수리, 재활용을 중시하는 순환경제로의 전환은 기존의 '채취-생산-폐기' 방식의 선형경제 모델에서 근본적으로 벗어나는 변화이다. 이러한 체계적 전환은 단순한 환경 전략이 아니라, 점점 더 경제적 필수 과제로 인식되고 있다. 자원 부족과 공급망의 불안정성이 심화됨에 따라, 끊임없이 새로운 원자재 투입에 의존하는 기업들은 점점 더 큰 위험에 직면하고 있다. 반면, 순환경제 모델은 <u>원자재의 지속적인 공급에 대한 의존도 최소화함으로써</u> 장기적인 회복력으로 가는 길을 제시한다. 이러한 접근은 보다 안정적이고 지역화된 공급망을 형성하고, 기업이 글로벌 원자재 시장의 가격 변동 충격으로부터 스스로를 보호할 수 있도록 돕는다.

① 자원 추출 및 배분의 효율성 증대함으로써
② 원자재의 지속적인 공급에 대한 의존도 최소화함으로써
③ 증가하는 글로벌 수요를 충족하기 위한 생산 능력 확대함으로써
④ 신규 원자재를 위한 더 다양한 글로벌 공급처 확보함으로써

어휘

- transition 전환, 이행
- circular economy 순환 경제
- emphasize 강조하다
- fundamental 근본적인, 핵심적인
- imperative 필수적인, 반드시 해야 하는
- scarcity 부족, 결핍
- volatility 변동성, 불안정성
- pronounced 뚜렷한, 두드러진, 단호한
- insulate 보호하다, 차단하다
- commodity 원자재, 상품
- extraction 채굴, 추출
- decouple 분리시키다
- outsourcing 외주 제작, 아웃소싱

난이도 상

정답 해설

이 글은 둠스크롤링이 '위협을 감시하려는' 인간의 원시적 본능에서 비롯된다고 설명한다. 인간은 불확실하고 위협적인 상황에 직면했을 때, 더 많은 정보를 얻음으로써 상황을 이해하고 통제하려는 심리적 동기를 갖는다. 둠스크롤링은 바로 이러한 동기가 현대의 정보 환경에서 왜곡된 형태로 나타난 것이다. 즉, 사람들은 끊임없이 나쁜 뉴스를 확인함으로써 자신이 처한 위협적인 세상에 대해 통제감을 얻거나, 문제의 끝을 확인해 종결감을 느끼려는 헛된 시도를 하게 된다. 그러나 이러한 행동은 불안을 줄이기는커녕 오히려 증폭시키는 악순환을 초래한다고 설명한다. 따라서 밑줄 친 부분에 들어갈 말로 가장 적절한 것은 ①이다.

해석

'둠스크롤링' 현상, 즉 나쁜 뉴스들을 강박적으로 끝없이 찾아보는 습관은 불안과 스트레스의 뚜렷한 증가와 관련이 있는 것으로 알려져 있다. 심리학자들은 이러한 행동이 위험을 감시하려는 원초적이고 진화적인 본능에서 비롯된다고 본다. 고대의 환경에서는 이러한 경계심이 생존을 위한 필수적인 메커니즘이었다. 하지만 무한한 정보가 넘쳐나는 현대 사회에서는 이 본능이 오히려 부적응적으로 작용한다. 끊임없이 쏟아지는 부정적인 정보가 해결되지 않은 채 신체의 위협 반응 시스템을 계속 자극하여, 사람들을 지속적인 과잉 각성에 머물게 만든다. 이 악순환이 특히 해로운 이유는, 그 자체가 만들어내는 불안이 오히려 사람들로 하여금 계속 스크롤을 하게 만들기 때문이다. 즉, 사람들은 <u>통제감이나 심리적 안정감을 얻으려는</u> 헛된 시도로 끝없이 뉴스를 내려보게 되는 것이다.

① 통제감이나 심리적 안정감을 얻으려는
② 부정적인 뉴스가 불러일으킨 불안을 잠시라도 완화하려는
③ 오락이나 일시적인 주의 전환을 찾는
④ 서로 지지해 주는 공동체와 연결되는

어휘

- doomscrolling 둠스크롤링(나쁜 상황에 대한 뉴스만을 강박적으로 확인하는 행위)
- compulsively 강박적으로, 충동적으로
- anxiety 불안, 걱정
- theorize 이론화하다, 가설을 세우다
- primal 원시의, 태고의
- vigilance 경계심, 주의 깊음
- maladaptive 부적응적인, 환경에 맞지 않는
- hypervigilance 과잉 각성(주변에 대한 경계 수준이 극도로 높은 상태)
- pernicious 해로운, 치명적인
- distraction 산만함, 주의 전환

영어 정답 및 해설

✅ 제4회 모의고사

01 ①	02 ③	03 ②	04 ②	05 ③
06 ④	07 ③	08 ④	09 ②	10 ④
11 ④	12 ④	13 ②	14 ②	15 ②
16 ②	17 ③	18 ④	19 ②	20 ①

---

01 [어휘 – 빈칸]　▶ ①

난이도 중

정답 해설

증가하는 부채와 불확실한 시장 전망이 회사의 존속을 위협하고 있는 점을 보면, 회사의 재정 상황이 '위태로운' 상태의 내용이 적절하다. 따라서 밑줄 친 부분에 들어갈 말로 가장 적절한 것은 ①이다.

해석

회사의 재정 상황은 여전히 <u>위태로운</u> 상태이며, 증가하는 부채와 불확실한 시장 전망이 존속을 위협하고 있다.

어휘

★ precarious 불안정한, 위태로운
● exceptional 예외적인, 특출한
● relieved 안심한, 안도한, 다행으로 여기는
● imminent 임박한, 목전의

02 [어휘 – 빈칸]　▶ ③

난이도 하

정답 해설

판사는 해당 소송이 사실적 증거가 전혀 없고 더 이상 법정에서 검토할 가치가 없다고 판단해 기각 판결을 내렸다는 문맥으로 보아 소송이 '허위' 주장에 기반한다는 내용이 적절하다. 따라서 밑줄 친 부분에 들어갈 말로 가장 적절한 것은 ③이다.

해석

판사는 그 소송이 어떠한 사실적 증거도 없는 <u>허위</u> 주장에 근거한 것이라고 판단하며, 더 이상 법정에서 검토할 가치가 없다고 보아 기각 판결을 내렸다.

어휘

★ spurious 가짜의, 위조의, 비논리적인
● authentic 진짜의, 정확한
● feasible 실행 가능한, 가능성 있는
● definite 확실한, 확고한, 분명한

03 [문법 – 빈칸]　▶ ②

난이도 중

정답 해설

② **[적중 포인트 074] 가정법 과거완료 공식 ★★★★★**
　& [적중 포인트 045] 능동태와 수동태의 차이 ★★★★★
　주절에 would have occurred(조동사 과거형 + have p.p.)가 사용된 것으로 보아, 이 문장은 과거 사실과 반대되는 상황을 가정하는 가정법 과거완료 구문이다. 가정법 과거완료에서는 If절에 'had + p.p.' 형태가 와야 한다. 또한 문장의 주어(Google's new quantum chip 'Willow')가 '출시되다'의 의미를 가지며, 뒤에 목적어가 없으므로 수동태로 써야 한다. 따라서 밑줄 친 부분에 들어갈 말로 가장 적절한 것은 ②이다.

해석

구글의 새로운 양자 칩 '윌로우'가 더 일찍 출시되었더라면, 계산 속도의 획기적인 발전은 예상보다 훨씬 더 빨리 일어났을 것이다.

04 [생활영어 – 빈칸]　▶ ②

난이도 하

정답 해설

Yuna는 K-패스 교통카드를 받은 뒤, 이를 어떻게 활성화하는지 Minjun에게 묻고 있다. Minjun의 설명을 듣고 Yuna가 "실물 카드만으로는 안 된다"며 앱을 바로 다운로드하겠다고 반응한 점을 보면, 활성화 방법이 앱 다운로드 및 등록 절차에 대해 대답했음을 짐작할 수 있다. 따라서 밑줄 친 부분에 들어갈 말로 가장 적절한 것은 ②이다.

해석

Yuna: Minjun 씨, 저 드디어 K-패스 교통카드 받았어요. 이거 환급 잘 해준다고 들었는데, 맞죠?
Minjun: 네, 저 한 달째 쓰고 있는데 정말 좋아요! 지하철이나 버스에서 쓴 돈의 일정 비율을 돌려받아요.
Yuna: 그래서 이거 어떻게 활성화해요? 전 그냥 실물 카드만 있는데요.
Minjun: <u>K-Pass 앱에서 그 카드를 등록해야 해요.</u>
Yuna: 아, 그렇군요. 그럼 실물 카드 자체로는 안 되는 거네요. 지금 바로 앱 다운로드할게요. 고마워요!

① 카드를 찍기만 하면 환급이 자동으로 적용돼요
② K-Pass 앱에서 그 카드를 등록해야 해요
③ 주소를 증명하려면 주민센터에 직접 가야 해요
④ 그건 서울에 사는 사람들만 사용할 수 있는 것 같아요

어휘

• rebate 환급, 환불, 할인
• physical card 실물 카드
• register 등록하다, 기재하다
• prove 증명하다, 입증하다

05 [생활영어 – 빈칸]　▶ ③

난이도 하

정답 해설

B가 '디지털 노마드' 비자를 활용해 스페인에서 3개월간 근무하고 싶다고 밝혔다. A는 긍정적인 입장을 보이며, 직원이 어떤 구체적인 우려가 있는지 물었다. 이어 B의 답변에 대해 A가 "타당한 지적"이라며 수긍하고, 한국 표준시 기준으로 '핵심 회의 시간'을 안내하고 있는 점을 보면, B가 제기한 걱정은 회의 시간에 대한 시차 문제였음을 알 수 있다. 따라서 밑줄 친 부분에 들어갈 말로 가장 적절한 것은 ③이다.

해석

A: 안녕하세요. 업무 계획에 대해 이야기하고 싶다고 했죠? 해외에서 일하는 것과 관련해 언급한 게 있다던데요.
B: 네, 시간 내주셔서 감사합니다. 회사가 새로 도입한 '디지털 노마드' 비자를 지원한다고 봤습니다. 그래서 스페인에서 3개월 동안 근무를 신청하고 싶습니다.
A: 스페인 좋죠. 당신의 업무 성과도 훌륭해서 저는 긍정적으로 생각하고 있어요. 혹시 고민하고 있는 부분이 있나요?
B: <u>제가 가장 걱정하는 건 팀 회의 때의 시차 문제입니다.</u>
A: 그건 충분히 이해됩니다. 우리 핵심 회의 시간은 한국 시간으로 오후 2시에서 5시예요. 그 시간에 참석만 보장할 수 있다면, 나머지 근무 시간은 유연하게 관리해도 괜찮습니다.
B: 정말 좋네요. 그건 충분히 가능할 것 같습니다. 감사합니다!

① 제 급여가 크게 삭감될까 봐 걱정됩니다.
② 그곳에서 좋은 아파트를 구할 수 있을지 잘 모르겠습니다.
③ 제가 가장 걱정하는 건 팀 회의 때의 시차 문제입니다.
④ 새로운 환경에서 일하면 생산성이 더 높아질 것 같습니다.

어휘

• discuss 논의하다, 상의하다
• abroad 해외에서, 해외로
• core 핵심의, 중심의
• guarantee 보장하다, 확약하다

06 [독해 – 세트형 문항(안내문 – 유의어)] ▶ ④

난이도 | 하

정답 해설

밑줄 친 progressive는 '점진적인, 꾸준히 진행되는, 진보적인'이라는 뜻으로, 문맥상 가장 가까운 의미는 ④ 'gradual(점진적인, 서서히 일어나는)'이다.

오답 해설

① obstinate 고집 센, 완강한
② lavish 풍성한, 호화로운, 아주 후한
③ passive 수동적인, 소극적인

07 [독해 – 세트형 문항(안내문 – 목적)] ▶ ③

난이도 | 중

정답 해설

이 글은 헤이그 국제사법회의(HCCH)가 어떤 기관인지 소개하면서, 그 핵심 사명인 국제사법 규칙의 점진적 통일을 설명하고 있다. 또한 국제 아동 탈취, 국가 간 입양, 외국 판결의 승인과 같은 분야에서 HCCH가 어떤 협약과 의정서를 마련해 국제적 법적 안정성을 제공하는지, 즉 구체적으로 어떤 기능을 수행하는지도 전반적으로 제시하고 있다. 따라서 글의 목적으로 가장 적절한 것은 ③이다.
① 국경 간 가족법 분야에서 HCCH의 최근 추진 사항을 제시하려고
② 공법적 국제법과 사법적 국제법을 구분하려고
③ HCCH의 근본적인 임무와 기능을 설명하려고
④ HCCH가 새 국제 협약을 개발 중임을 설명하려고

해석

헤이그 국제사법회의(HCCH)는 전 세계적 범위의 정부 간 국제기구입니다. 이 기구는 다양한 법적 전통이 만나는 중심 역할을 하며, 글로벌 수요에 대응하는 다자간 법적 문서를 개발하고 관리합니다. HCCH의 핵심 임무는 국제사법 규칙의 <u>점진적인</u> 통일입니다.

공법적 국제법이 국가 간의 관계를 규율하는 것과 달리, 사법적 국제법은 개인이나 법인 등 사인 간의 국경을 넘는 법적 문제를 다룹니다. HCCH는 국제적 아동 탈취, 국가 간 입양, 외국 판결의 승인과 같은 분야에서 명확성과 법적 안정성을 제공하는 국제 협약과 의정서를 작성합니다. 이러한 법적 틀은 국제 무역, 여행, 개인의 이동성을 촉진하며, 국경 간 상호작용에 내재된 법적 장벽을 줄여줍니다.

어휘

• nexus 결합, 연쇄
• legal tradition 법적 전통, 법 체계의 관습
• multilateral 다자간의, 여러 국가가 참여하는
• progressive 점진적인, 단계적으로 나아가는
• private international law 국제 사법
• govern 규율하다, 통제하다
• draft 초안을 작성하다
• convention 협약, 조약, 관습
• recognition 승인, 인정
• facilitate 촉진하다, 용이하게 하다
• inherent 내재된, 본질적인

08 [독해 – 세트형 문항(홈페이지 게시글 – 제목)] ▶ ④

난이도 | 하

정답 해설

이 글은 ApexOS 운영체제의 커널에서 심각한 제로데이 취약점이 발견되었으며, 현재 실제 공격에 활용되고 있다는 사실을 긴급하게 알리는 보안 경고이다. 또한 즉각적인 완화 조치가 필요하고, 임시 스크립트 배포 및 시스템 로그 점검을 강조하는 등 긴박한 대응을 요구하고 있다. 따라서 글의 제목으로 가장 적절한 것은 ④이다.
① 커널 단계 침해를 탐지하기 위한 모범 사례
② ApexOS 커널의 새로운 기능들
③ 새로운 휴리스틱(추론 기반) 탐지 시스템의 등장
④ 긴급 보안 경고: ApexOS 커널 취약점

09 [독해 – 세트형 문항(홈페이지 게시글 – 내용 불일치)] ▶ ②

난이도 | 하

발견된 취약점과 관련된 익스플로잇은 현재 실제 환경에서 표적 공격에 적극적으로 활용되고 있다고 언급하고 있다. 따라서 윗글의 내용과 일치하지 않는 것은 ②이다.
① 취약점은 공격자가 최고 수준의 접근 권한을 얻을 수 있게 한다.
② 해당 익스플로잇은 아직 실제 공격에서 발견된 적이 없다.
③ 즉각적인 위협에 대응하기 위한 임시 보안 스크립트가 제공되고 있다.
④ 이 문제에 대한 완전하고 영구적인 해결책은 아직 준비 중이다.

오답 해설

① 발견된 취약점은 권한 상승을 가능하게 하여, 로컬의 권한 없는 공격자가 루트 수준 접근 권한을 획득할 수 있게 만든다고 언급하고 있으므로 글의 내용과 일치한다.
③ 대응과 관련해서는, 현재 영구적인 패치를 개발 중이지만, 우리는 우선 악용되고 있는 시스템 호출을 제한하는 임시 보안 스크립트를 배포했다고 언급하고 있으므로 글의 내용과 일치한다.
④ 발표한 대응은 어디까지나 임시 우회 조치이며, 완전한 해결책이 아니라는 점을 반드시 이해해야 한다고 언급하고 있으므로 글의 내용과 일치한다.

해석

> **긴급 보안 경고: ApexOS 커널 취약점**
>
> ApexOS 기업용 운영체제의 커널에서 CVE-2025-0701로 지정된 심각한 제로데이 취약점이 발견되었습니다. 이 취약점은 권한 상승을 가능하게 하여, 로컬의 권한 없는 공격자가 루트 수준 접근 권한을 획득할 수 있게 만듭니다. 해당 익스플로잇은 현재 실제 환경에서 표적 공격에 적극적으로 활용되고 있는 중입니다. 익스플로잇의 정교함 때문에, 기존의 체험 기반 탐지 시스템은 침해를 식별하지 못할 가능성이 있습니다.
>
> 즉각적인 대응이 필수적입니다. 현재 영구적인 패치를 개발 중이지만, 우리는 우선 악용되고 있는 시스템 호출을 제한하는 임시 보안 스크립트를 배포했습니다. 시스템 관리자들은 이 스크립트를 지체 없이 적용할 것을 강력히 권고합니다. 이는 어디까지나 차선책이며, 완전한 해결책이 아니라는 점을 반드시 이해해야 합니다. 또한 기관들은 이전 침해의 흔적을 나타낼 수 있는 비정상적 활동이 있는지 시스템 로그를 점검해야 합니다.

어휘

• zero-day 컴퓨터 보안 담당자가 알기 전에 컴퓨터 보안의 취약한 부분을 이용하는
• designate 지정하다, 명명하다
• unprivileged 권한이 없는, 제한된 권한의
• heuristic 체험적인[스스로 발견하게 하는]
• intrusion 침입, 침해
• interim 임시의, 과도기의
• workaround 차선책
• anomalous 비정상적인, 이례적인

10 [문법 – 밑줄] ▶ ④

난이도 | 하

정답 해설

④ [적중 포인트 043] 혼동하기 쉬운 주어와 동사 수 일치 ★★★★☆
'a number of + 복수 명사'는 '많은 명사'라는 의미로 쓰이며, 복수 동사와 수 일치한다. 따라서 밑줄 친 부분의 has been introduced를 have been introduced로 고쳐야 한다.

오답 해설

① [적중 포인트 043] 혼동하기 쉬운 주어와 동사 수 일치 ★★★★☆
'the number of + 복수 명사'는 '명사의 수'라는 의미로 쓰이며, 단수 동사와 수 일치한다. 따라서 밑줄 친 부분은 올바르게 쓰였다.
② [적중 포인트 039] 현재시제 동사와 be동사의 수 일치 ★★★★★
주어(the influx)가 단수 형태이므로, 동사도 단수 형태로 써야 한다. 따라서 밑줄 친 부분은 올바르게 쓰였다.
③ [적중 포인트 066] 조동사 should의 3가지 용법과 생략 구조 ★★★★★
주장 동사 argue 뒤의 that절에서는 당위성을 나타내기 위해 '(should) 동사원형'의 형태로 쓸 수 있다. 따라서 밑줄 친 부분은 올바르게 쓰였다.

해석

지난 10년 동안 섬을 방문하는 관광객의 수가 꾸준히 증가했다. 이러한 관광 급증은 지역 경제를 활성화시켜 주민들에게 수많은 일자리를 창출했다. 그러나 환경론자들은 방문객의 유입이 섬세한 생태계에 피해를 주고 있다고 우려한다. 그들은 섬의 자연적 아름다움을 보존하기 위해 지속 가능한 관광 관행이 시행되어야 한다고 주장한다. 최근 많은 엄격한 규제들이 도입되었다.

11 [독해 – 단일형 문항(안내문 – 내용 불일치)] ▶ ④

난이도 하

정답 해설

마지막 부분에 이 프로그램은 뉴욕시 문화부의 공공 기금 지원을 받아 진행된다고 언급하고 있다. 따라서 윗글의 내용과 일치하지 않는 것은 ④이다.

오답 해설

① 시간 안내 부분에 '우천 시 10월 29일 일요일로 연기'된다고 명시되어 있으므로 글의 내용과 일치한다.
② 올해 워크숍은 자연 재료와 지속 가능한 예술을 주제로 진행된다고 언급하고 있으므로 글의 내용과 일치한다.
③ '활동' 항목에서 참가자가 함께 만드는 대형 벽화가 공원에 일주일간 전시된다고 설명하고 있으므로 글의 내용과 일치한다.

해석

브루클린 예술위원회 발표: Art in the Park Fall Workshop

날짜: 2026년 10월 28일 토요일
시간: 오전 11시 - 오후 4시 (비 오는 날: 10월 29일 일요일)
위치: 전망 공원 (보트하우스 근처)

올 가을, 여러분의 창의력을 마음껏 펼쳐보세요! 브루클린 예술위원회(BAC)는 가족, 학생, 모든 연령대의 예술가들을 연례 행사인 '아트 인 더 파크' 워크숍에 초대합니다. 올해는 천연 재료와 지속 가능한 예술을 주제로 진행됩니다.

활동에는 다음이 포함됩니다:
* 낙엽 프린트 & 콜라주: 떨어진 나뭇잎을 활용해 멋진 프린트 작품을 만들어 보세요. (모든 재료는 제공됩니다.)
* 점토 조각 기법: 완전히 건조된 점토를 사용한 기본 조각 기법을 배워보세요. (8세 이상 참여 가능)
* 커뮤니티 벽화: 공원에 일주일간 전시될 대형 벽화 제작에 함께 참여해 보세요.

등록:
이 행사는 무료이지만 충분한 재료를 확보하려면 등록이 필요합니다. 10월 25일까지 웹사이트에 등록해 주세요. 현장 등록은 공간이 허락하는 경우에만 가능합니다.

이 프로그램은 뉴욕시 문화부의 공공 기금 지원을 받아 진행됩니다.

① 비가 올 경우 행사는 다음 날로 연기된다.
② 올해 워크숍의 주제에는 자연 재료의 활용이 포함되어 있다.
③ 참가자들이 만든 대형 벽화가 공원에 전시될 예정이다.
④ 이 프로그램은 한 예술가의 지원을 받고 있다.

어휘
• collage 콜라주(붙이기 미술), 모음
• clay 점토, 찰흙
• sculpting 조각기법
• air-dry 완전히 건조된
• mural 벽화
• registration 등록, 신청
• on-site 현장 등록의, 현장에서 이루어지는
• fund 기금, 자금
• Department of Cultural Affairs 문화
• postpone 연기하다, 미루다

12 [문법 – 밑줄] ▶ ④

난이도 중

정답 해설

④ [적중 포인트 035] 미래를 대신하는 현재시제 ★★★★☆
when이 이끄는 시간 부사절에서는 비록 내용이 미래의 일을 가리키더라도 미래시제를 쓰지 않고 현재시제를 써야 한다. 따라서 밑줄 친 부분의 will be를 is로 고쳐야 한다.

오답 해설

① [적중 포인트 058] 분사를 활용한 표현 및 구문 ★★★★☆
'with + 명사 + 분사' 형태의 with 분사구문이다. 문맥상 팬들이 밴드를 향해 환호하는 능동적 상황을 나타내므로, 현재분사로 써야 한다. 따라서 밑줄 친 부분은 올바르게 쓰였다.
② [적중 포인트 037] 시제의 일치와 예외 ★☆☆☆☆
주절의 동사가 과거형이므로, 종속절에서도 과거형을 써서 시제를 일치시켜야 한다. 따라서 밑줄 친 부분은 올바르게 쓰였다.
③ [적중 포인트 056] 여러 가지 분사구문 ★★★★★
앞 문장의 내용 전체를 받아 결과적으로 발생한 상황을 설명하는 분사구문이다. 문맥상 날씨 조건이 가사를 듣기 어렵게 '만드는' 능동적 원인을 나타내므로 현재분사로 써야 한다. 따라서 밑줄 친 부분은 올바르게 쓰였다.

해석

폭우에도 불구하고 야외 콘서트는 예정대로 진행되었고, 수천 명의 팬들이 그들이 좋아하는 밴드를 위해 환호했다. 주최 측은 사고를 예방하기 위해 안전 조치가 마련되었는지 확인했다. 그러나 일부 참석자들은 날씨로 인해 음질이 좋지 않아 가사를 듣기 어렵다고 불평했다. 밴드는 날씨가 더 좋을 내년에 다시 오겠다고 약속했다.

13 [독해 – 단일형 문항(전자메일 – 목적)] ▶ ②

난이도 하

정답 해설

이 전자메일은 미국 교통부(DOT)가 발송한 공식 공지문으로, 본문에서 이전에 공지되었던 10월 22일 자문위원회 회의가 취소되었음을 명확히 알리고 있다. 즉, 이 문서의 핵심 목적은 기존에 예정된 공공 회의의 취소 사실을 전달하고, 향후 일정은 추후 별도로 안내하겠다는 점을 공지하고 있다. 따라서 글의 목적으로 가장 적절한 것은 ②이다.

해석

수신인: 관련자 여러분
발신인: 미 교통부(DOT)
날짜: 2026년 10월 20일
제목: 공공 회의

이번 공고는 이전에 계획된 행사의 변경 사항을 대중에게 알리기 위한 것입니다.

2026년 10월 9일, 교통부(DOT)는 연방 관보(90 FR 48212)에 공식 공고를 게재했습니다. 해당 이전 공고는 2026년 10월 22일 수요일에 개최될 예정이었던 미국 교통부 자문위원회의 공청회 개최를 알리는 내용이었습니다.

예기치 못한 사정으로 인해, 이번 새로운 공지는 해당 공공 회의가 취소되었음을 공식적으로 알리기 위한 것입니다. 이번 회의 참석 또는 자료 준비를 계획하셨던 분들께 불편을 끼쳐 드린 점 사과드립니다. 추후 재개최 일정이 정해질 경우 별도로 안내드릴 예정이며, 연방 관보를 포함한 교통부 공식 채널을 통해 업데이트가 제공될 것입니다.

새로운 공고가 나오는 대로 바로 확인하실 수 있도록, 업데이트되는 내용을 주의 깊게 살펴봐 주시기 바랍니다.

① 새로운 자문위원회 회의의 일정을 잡으려고
② 이미 예정된 회의의 취소를 알리려고
③ 10월 22일 회의의 결과를 발표하려고
④ 회의 참석 취소자 명단을 공개하려고

어휘
• inform 알리다, 통지하다
• previously 이전에, 앞서
• publish 공표하다, 발표하다, 발간하다

• Federal Register (연방 정부의) 공보
• announce 발표하다, 알리다
• unforeseen 예기치 못한, 예상 밖의
• circumstance 상황, 사정
• cancellation 취소, 무효화

14 [독해 – 중심 내용 추론(주제)]　　　　　▶ ②

정답 ②

난이도 중

정답 해설

이 글은 사회과학 분야에서 제기된 '재현성 위기'를 중심으로 논의를 전개한다. 여러 핵심 연구들이 후속 실험에서 재현되지 않으면서 기존 연구들의 신뢰성이 흔들리고 있다는 문제를 제기한다. 그러나 글은 '그러나' 이후에서 이 위기가 단순히 부정적인 현상에 그치는 것이 아니라, 오히려 '방법론적 개혁'을 이끄는 '필요한 촉매제'가 되었다는 점을 강조한다. 그 결과로 등장한 것이 '오픈 사이언스' 운동이며, 이는 연구 사전등록, 데이터·코드 공개, 대규모 재현 연구 협업과 같은 실천을 통해 투명성과 엄격성을 강화하고 과학의 '신뢰성'을 재건하는 데 목적이 있다. 따라서 글의 주제로 가장 적절한 것은 ②이다.

해석

> 사회과학 분야는 지금 '재현성 위기'를 해결하려고 노력한다. 특히 사회심리학을 중심으로 많은 기초 연구들의 결과가 후속 실험에서 재현되지 않으면서, 기존에 발표된 상당수 연구들의 신뢰성에 의문이 제기되고 있다. 그러나 이러한 위기가 완전히 부정적인 것만은 아니며, 오히려 방법론적 개혁을 촉진하는 필수적인 계기로 작용해 왔다. 이에 대한 대응으로 '개방 과학'이라 불리는 강력한 움직임이 등장했다. 이 운동은 연구 계획을 사전에 등록하고, 미가공 데이터와 코드 등을 공개하며, 대규모 재현 연구를 위한 협업을 촉진하는 등의 더 엄격하고 투명한 연구 관행을 지향한다. 이러한 실천은 단순히 기존 연구 결과를 액면 그대로 받아들이는 것이 아니라, 과학적 과정 자체의 신뢰성을 다시 구축하는 것을 목표로 한다.

① 재현성 위기가 과학에 미친 파괴적 영향
② 개방 과학을 통한 방법론적 개혁의 필요성
③ 사회과학에서 나타나는 재현성 격차
④ 재현에 실패한 특정 심리학 연구들

어휘

• grapple with ～을 해결하려고 노력하다
• replication crisis 재현성 위기(기존의 많은 과학 연구가 재현하기 어려워 다른 실험으로 뒷받침할 수 없어 문제가 됨을 의미)
• foundational 기초적인, 기반이 되는
• subsequent 이후의, 뒤따르는
• reliability 신뢰성, 믿음직함
• methodological 방법론의
• open science 개방 과학(네트워크를 통해 공유,발전하여 지식을 습득)
• champion 옹호하다, 싸우다
• robust 강건한, 튼튼한, 신뢰할 수 있는
• raw data 미가공 데이터
• rigor 엄밀함, 철저함
• at face value 액면 그대로
• divide 분열, 격차

15 [독해 – 단일형 문항(안내문 – 내용 일치)]　　　▶ ②

정답 ②

난이도 중

정답 해설

AI 기반의 새로운 "스마트 요약" 기능은 모든 프리미엄 플랜 가입자에게 즉시 제공되며, 표준(무료) 이용자는 해당 기능에 대한 접근 권한이 제공되지 않는다고 언급하고 있다. 따라서 윗글의 내용과 일치하는 것은 ②이다.

오답 해설

① 이 업데이트는 전 세계적으로 출시되며 이번 주말까지 모든 사용자가 이용할 수 있다고 언급하고 있으므로 글의 내용과 일치하지 않는다.
③ '추가 개선 사항' 항목 중 하나로 스타일러스 반응 속도가 향상되어 필기가 더 부드러워졌다고 언급하고 있으므로 글의 내용과 일치하지 않는다.
④ iOS 14 사용자는 계속해서 업데이트를 받기 위해 운영체제를 업그레이드해야 한다고 언급하고 있으므로 글의 내용과 일치하지 않는다.

해석

> 제목: VeriNote 3.5 업데이트 안내
>
> 생산성 향상을 위해 설계된 기능이 탑재된 VeriNote 3.5의 출시를 발표하게 되어 매우 기쁩니다. 이 업데이트는 전 세계적으로 출시되며 이번 주말까지 모든 사용자가 이용할 수 있습니다.
>
> 주요 기능: 스마트 요약
> 긴 회의 노트에 지치셨나요? AI 기반의 새로운 "스마트 요약" 기능은 모든 노트를 간결하고 읽기 쉬운 요약으로 압축합니다. 이 기능은 모든 프리미엄 플랜 가입자에게 즉시 제공됩니다. 표준 (무료) 이용자는 해당 기능에 대한 접근 권한이 제공되지 않습니다.
>
> 추가 개선 사항:
> * 스타일러스 반응 속도가 향상되어 필기가 더 부드러워졌습니다.
> * 프로젝트 관리를 위한 템플릿이 더 많이 제공됩니다.
> * 보관된 노트가 이제 검색 결과에 정상적으로 나타납니다.
>
> 중요 안내
> 이 기능들을 이용하려면 앱을 버전 3.5로 업데이트해야 합니다. 이번 업데이트부터 iOS 14 지원이 중단되며, iOS 14 사용자는 계속해서 업데이트를 받기 위해 운영체제를 업그레이드해야 합니다.

① 이번 업데이트는 인터넷 환경이 좋은 국가에서만 제공된다.
② 스마트 요약 도구에 대한 접근은 유료 회원에게만 제한된다.
③ 노트 필기 인식 기능은 이번 업데이트에서도 개선되지 않았다.
④ iOS 14 사용자는 업그레이드 후에도 해당 기능을 사용할 수 없다.

어휘

• announce 발표하다, 공지하다
• release 출시하다, 공개하다
• roll out 출시하다, 시작하다
• AI-powered 인공지능 기반의
• condense 압축하다, 요약하다
• concise 간결한, 명료한
• subscriber 이용자[가입자], 구독자
• stylus 스타일러스(특수 컴퓨터 화면에 글을 쓰거나 그림을 그리는 등의 표시를 할 때 쓰는 펜)
• archived 보관된
• discontinue 중단하다, 종료하다
• recognition 인식, 판별

16 [독해 – 문장 제거]　　　　　▶ ②

정답 ②

난이도 하

정답 해설

이 글은 안데스 산맥의 작은 고산 연못들이 지구 탄소 순환에서 예상보다 큰 역할을 한다는 점을 설명한다. ①번 문장은 이 연못들이 미생물 활동을 통해 유기 탄소를 처리한다는 점을, ③번 문장은 낮은 수온과 얕은 수심으로 인해 장기 탄소 흡수원으로 기능한다는 점을, ④번 문장은 기후 변화로 저장된 탄소가 메탄으로 방출될 위험을 제기한다. 그러나 ②번 문장은 안데스 지형과 미기후에 대한 일반적인 배경 설명에 그쳐, 연못이나 탄소 문제와 직접 연결되지 않아 흐름을 방해한다. 따라서 글의 흐름상 어색한 문장은 ②이다.

해석

> 세계 기후 모델에서 종종 간과되지만, 안데스 산맥의 고지대에 있는 작은 연못들은 지구 탄소 순환에서 예상보다 훨씬 큰 역할을 할 수 있다. ① 최근 연구에 따르면 이처럼 보잘것없이 보이는 물웅덩이들이 사실은 미생물 활동이 매우 활발한 곳으로, 주변 지형에서 유입되는 많은 양의 유기 탄소를 처리하고 있다고 한다. (② 그러나 안데스 지역의 독특한 지질은 가파른 경사와 다양한 미기후를 특징으로 하며, 지역 기상 패턴에 강한 영향을 미친다.) ③ 이러한 연못들은 낮은 온도와 얕은 수심 때문에 탄소가 천천히 분해되어, 장기간 탄소를 저장하는 저장고 역할을 한다. ④ 하지만 기후 변화로 이 지역이 따뜻해지면, 이렇게 저장된 탄소가 메탄 형태로 빠르게 방출되어 이러한 저장고가 오히려 주요 탄소 배출원으로 바뀔 수 있다는 우려가 제기된다. 이러한 발견은 앞으로의 기후 예측 모델에 이러한 소규모 수생 생태계를 반드시 포함해야 한다는 점을 강조한다.

- **overlook** 간과하다, 못 보고 지나치다
- **high-altitude** 고도가 높은
- **outsized** 매우 큰, 대형의
- **indicate** 보여주다, 나타내다
- **seemingly** 겉보기에는, 외견상
- **hotspot** 활발한 곳
- **microbial** 미생물의, 세균의
- **geology** 지질학
- **decompose** 분해되다, 부패하다
- **release** 방출하다, 풀어 주다
- **methane** 메탄
- **aquatic** 수생의, 물속의

17 [독해 – 문장 삽입] ▶ ③

난이도 상

정답 해설

이 글은 기억 형성과 관련한 새로운 과학적 발견을 소개하고 있다. 글은 먼저 단기기억이 장기기억으로 전환된다는 기존의 단일 경로 모델을 설명한 뒤, 2024년 말 연구가 이 이론에 근본적 의문을 제기했다고 밝힌다. 이어 이 도전이 어떤 실험적 사실에 기반하는지 제시하는데, 특정 효소를 억제해 단기기억 형성이 차단되었음에도 장기기억은 정상적으로 형성되었다는 연구 결과가 그 근거이다. 이후 글은 이 발견을 단기기억을 거치지 않는 '비밀의 병렬 경로'에 비유하며 의미를 부각한다. 마지막으로 이러한 결과가 장기기억이 단기기억과 독립적으로 형성될 수 있음을 시사하며, 기억 작용에 대한 기존 이해를 수정해야 함을 강조한다. 따라서 주어진 문장이 들어갈 위치로 가장 적절한 것은 ③이다.

해석

기억 형성에 관한 기존의 주요 과학 이론은 오랫동안 기억이 선형적인 과정을 통해 형성된다고 보아 왔다. (①) 이 모델에 따르면, 단기기억(STM)은 일시적으로 저장되었다가 시간이 지나면서 안정적인 장기기억(LTM)으로 통합되는 것으로 설명된다. (②) 그러나 2024년 말, 맥스 플랑크 플로리다 연구소에서 발표된 연구는 이러한 '단일 경로' 모델을 근본적으로 뒤흔드는 결과를 내놓았다. (③ <u>연구진은 특정 효소를 억제하면 단기기억 형성은 완전히 차단되지만, 장기기억은 여전히 형성될 수 있다는 사실을 입증했다.</u>) 이 발견은 마치 뇌의 '영구 전시관'으로 가는 비밀 통로가 있어, 단기기억이라는 '임시 전시 공간'을 우회할 수 있다는 것을 발견한 것과 같다. (④) 이는 장기기억이 단기기억과 독립적으로 형성될 수 있음을 시사하며, 기억이 어떻게 작동하는지에 대한 우리의 기존 이해를 수정하고 나아가 기억 장애 치료의 새로운 가능성을 열어줄 수 있다.

어휘

- **inhibit** 억제하다, 막다
- **enzyme** 효소
- **prevailing** 지배적인, 우세한, 널리 퍼진
- **linear** 선형의, 직선적인
- **consolidate** 통합하다, 굳히다, 강화하다
- **stable** 안정된, 변하지 않는
- **akin to** ~와 유사한, 비슷한
- **parallel** 평행하는, 병렬의, 동시에 존재하는
- **bypass** 우회하다, 건너뛰다
- **imply** 암시하다, 의미하다
- **independently** 독립적으로, 따로
- **revise** 수정하다, 개정하다
- **avenue** (나아갈) 길, 방안
- **disorder** 장애, 이상 상태, 엉망

18 [독해 – 순서 배열] ▶ ④

난이도 중

정답 해설

이 글은 심리학적 현상인 조명 효과를 소개하고 그 원인 분석과 실험을 통한 증명 과정을 설명한다. 우선 현상을 정의한 주어진 글 다음에, 이 현상을 이 인지적 편향으로 구체화하며 그 근본 원인이 자기중심성에 있음을 설명하는 (C)가 이어져 이론적 배경을 완성한다. 그 뒤에 이론을 검증하기 위해 이를 테스트하기 위해라는 연결어와 함께 구체적인 실험 과정 및 참가자들의 예측 수치를 소개하는 (A)가

연결된다. 마지막으로 '실제로'라는 표현을 통해 실제 수치가 예측과 달랐음을 보여주며, 이러한 차이를 근거로 사람들이 타인보다 자신의 내면세계에 더 집중한다는 결론을 내리는 (B)가 이어지는 것이 자연스럽다. 따라서 글의 순서로 가장 적절한 것은 ④이다.

해석

심리학자들은 개인이 자신의 외모나 행동을 다른 사람들이 얼마나 주목하는지 과대평가하는 현상인 '조명 효과'를 오랫동안 연구해 왔다.
(C) 이러한 인지적 편향은 자기중심성에서 비롯된다. 우리는 우리 자신의 우주에서 중심이기 때문에, 본능적으로 다른 모든 사람들의 우주에서도 우리가 중심이라고 가정하며, 이는 불필요한 사회적 불안으로 이어진다.
(A) 이를 테스트하기 위해, 연구원들은 참가자들에게 난처한 티셔츠를 입고 낯선 사람들로 가득 찬 방에 들어가도록 요청했다. 참가자들은 적어도 절반의 사람들이 그 티셔츠를 알아차릴 것이라고 예측했다.
(B) 하지만 실제로는 관찰자 중 20% 미만이 실제로 알아차렸다. 이러한 차이는 사람들이 일반적으로 자신의 내면세계에 너무 집중하느라 타인의 사소한 세부 사항에는 면밀한 주의를 기울이지 않는다는 사실을 확인시켜 준다.

어휘

- **spotlight effect** 조명 효과(자신이 언제나 불특정 다수에 의해 평가받고 있다고 여기는 경향)
- **overestimate** 과대평가하다
- **appearance** (겉)모습, 외모
- **embarrassing** 난처한, 쑥스러운
- **predict** 예측[예견]하다
- **at least** 적어도[최소한]
- **discrepancy** 차이, 불일치
- **internal** 내부의
- **egocentricity** 자기중심적임, 이기심
- **instinctively** 본능적인, 본능[직감]에 따른

19 [독해 – 빈칸 추론] ▶ ②

난이도 중

정답 해설

이 글은 성인 학습자와 아동 학습자를 대조하며, 성인이 새로운 언어를 배울 때 겪는 어려움을 구체적으로 설명한다. 성인의 복잡한 인지 구조, 깊이 자리 잡은 모국어 체계, 새로운 음운·문법 규칙 습득에 대한 간섭, 두뇌 가소성의 차이, 언어 오류에 대한 사회적 관용의 차이, 성인이 느끼는 수행 압박 등 모든 요소가 '새로운 언어를 배우는 과정', 즉 제2언어 습득의 어려움을 중심으로 전개된다. 따라서 밑줄 친 부분에 들어갈 말로 가장 적절한 것은 ②이다.

해석

<u>제2언어를 습득하는 데 따르는 어려움</u>은 종종 어린이보다 성인에게 훨씬 더 복잡하다. 성인 학습자는 대개 매우 정교하게 구조화된 인지 체계와 깊이 자리 잡힌 모국어 체계를 갖고 있다. 이러한 기존 언어 체계는 새로운 음운 규칙이나 문법 규칙을 익히는 데 간섭을 일으키곤 한다. 반면 아이의 뇌는 가소성이 더 높아, 이미 존재하는 언어의 필터 없이 언어적 패턴을 자연스럽게 흡수한다. 사회적 환경 또한 크게 다르다. 아이들은 언어적 실수가 허용되는 놀이 중심의 상호작용 속에 자주 놓여 있다. 그러나 성인은 상황이 훨씬 더 부담스럽다. 복잡하고 의미 있는 의사소통을 위해 언어가 필요하며, 정확하게 말해야 한다는 사회적 압박을 느끼기 때문에 자연스러운 학습 과정이 오히려 방해받을 수 있다.

① 전문 어휘를 유지하는 것
② 제2언어를 습득하는 데 따르는 어려움
③ 사회적 상호작용에 참여하려는 동기
④ 성인의 의사소통에서 비언어적 단서에 의존하는 경향

어휘

- **structured** 구조화된, 체계적인
- **cognitive** 인지의, 사고와 관련된
- **native language** 모국어
- **entrenched** 깊이 뿌리내린, 견고한, 확립된
- **interfere** 방해하다, 간섭하다
- **phonological** 음운의, 음성 체계의
- **grammatical** 문법의, 문법적인
- **plasticity** 가소성, 유연성
- **tolerate** 용인하다, 허용하다
- **inhibit** 억제하다, 방해하다

• retention 유지, 보유
• non-verbal 비언어적인

20 [독해 – 빈칸 추론]　　　　　　　　　　　　　▶ ①

난이도) 상

정답 해설

이 글은 독해 전에 텍스트를 훑어보며 파악할 수 있는 여러 '준텍스트적 요소'들을 설명하고 있다. 표제, 문단 길이, 강조 표기 등은 독자가 글의 구조와 핵심 내용을 빠르게 예측하도록 돕는 대표적 장치로 제시된다. 이어지는 마지막 문장은 삽화와 참고문헌이 제공하는 부가적 정보에 주목한다. 삽화가 시각적 자료 처리의 흐름을 자연스럽게 안내한다면, 참고문헌은 해당 텍스트가 어떤 학술적 전통과 연구 성과를 기반으로 작성되었는지를 드러내는 중요한 근거다. 이는 글의 신뢰도, 연구 깊이, 학술적 엄격함을 판단할 수 있게 해 주며, 독자가 텍스트의 성격과 수준을 미리 가늠하도록 돕는다는 점에서 핵심적인 메타데이터 역할을 한다. 따라서 밑줄 친 부분에 들어갈 말로 가장 적절한 것은 ①이다.

해석

> 텍스트를 전략적으로 미리 훑어보는 이른바 '훑어보기'는 이해를 돕는 다양한 주변 텍스트 요소들을 드러내 준다. 예를 들어, 소제목은 이후 전개될 논의의 주제적 윤곽을 미리 보여주는 개념적 이정표로 기능한다. 또한 지면의 조판 방식 자체도 중요한 정보를 담고 있다. 문단의 길이는 해당 주제가 어느 정도 깊이 있게 다뤄지는지를 암시하며, 문장의 복잡성은 독자가 요구받게 될 인지적 부담을 보여준다. 여기에 굵은 글씨, 이탤릭체, 밑줄과 같은 시각적 강조는 독자의 주의를 핵심 개념으로 이끄기 위해 저자가 의도적으로 사용하는 장치다. 반대로 이러한 도움 요소가 없다는 것은 독자가 핵심 논지를 스스로 더 적극적으로 파고들어야 함을 뜻한다. 삽화와 참고 문헌은 또한 메타데이터를 제공하여 그래픽 정보 처리의 휴식 지점이나 작품의 학문적 엄밀성과 학문적 근거를 나타낸다. 이러한 외부적 단서들을 내면화함으로써, 독자는 아무리 난해한 학술적 영역이라도 더 큰 효율성과 통찰력을 가지고 헤쳐 나갈 수 있다.

① 작품의 학문적 엄밀성과 학문적 근거
② 다음 판을 구매하는 방법에 대한 안내
③ 일반 독자를 위해 의도된 단순한 요약
④ 어려운 핵심 주장들을 건너뛰는 빠른 방법

어휘

• scan 훑어보다, 살피다
• conceptual 개념적인, 관념적인
• signpost 표지판, 이정표, 길잡이
• contour 윤곽, 개략
• typographical 인쇄상의
• deliberate 의도적인, 신중한
• authorial 저자[작가]의
• intervention 개입, 조정
• absence 부재, 없음
• onus 책임, 부담
• diligently 부지런히, 열심히
• excavate 발굴하다, 출토하다
• bibliographic 서지(학)의, 도서 목록의
• scholarly 학문적인, 학술적인
• interpretation 해석, 이해

영어 정답 및 해설

✓ 제5회 모의고사

01 ②	02 ③	03 ④	04 ③	05 ①
06 ④	07 ③	08 ④	09 ④	10 ②
11 ③	12 ②	13 ③	14 ②	15 ④
16 ④	17 ④	18 ③	19 ②	20 ②

01 [어휘 – 빈칸]　▶②

난이도 하

정답 해설

장시간 앉아서 하는 업무로 축적되는 만성적인 허리 통증은 규칙적인 스트레칭과 가벼운 운동을 통해 '완화하는' 데 도움이 된다는 의미가 자연스럽다. 따라서 밑줄 친 부분에 들어갈 말로 가장 적절한 것은 ②이다.

해석

규칙적인 스트레칭과 가벼운 운동은 오랜 시간 앉아서 하는 업무로 인해 서서히 축적되는 만성적인 허리 통증을 <u>완화하는</u> 데 도움이 된다.

어휘

★ alleviate 완화하다, 경감시키다
● exacerbate 악화시키다
● obscure 보기[듣기/이해하기] 어렵게 하다, 모호하게 하다
● promote 촉진하다, 홍보하다, 승진시키다

02 [어휘 – 빈칸]　▶③

난이도 중

정답 해설

임상의들이 초기에 정확한 진단을 내리는 데 어려움을 겪었다는 점에서, 초기 증상은 매우 '모호하고' 다른 질환들과도 유사하다는 의미가 자연스럽다. 따라서 밑줄 친 부분에 들어갈 말로 가장 적절한 것은 ③이다.

해석

초기 증상이 매우 <u>모호하고</u> 다른 질환의 증상과도 비슷해 임상의들은 초기 정확한 진단에 어려움을 겪었다.

어휘

★ equivocal 모호한, 애매한
● plain 분명한, 솔직한, 소박한
● coherent 일관성 있는, 논리[조리] 정연한
● introverted 내성[내향]적인

03 [문법 – 빈칸]　▶④

난이도 중

정답 해설

④ [적중 포인트 044] 주어 자리에서 반드시 단수 또는 복수 취급하는 특정 표현 ★★★★☆

빈칸은 동사 자리이므로 분사구문은 올 수 없다. 이 문장의 주어는 Neither of the policies로, 'neither of + 복수 명사'는 의미상 단수로 취급되므로 단수 동사와 수 일치를 이루어야 한다. 또한 타동사 뒤에 목적어를 취하고 있으므로 능동태로 써야 한다. 따라서 밑줄 친 부분에 들어갈 말로 가장 적절한 것은 ④이다.

해석

교통 혼잡을 완화하고 저렴한 대중교통 접근성을 확대하려는 목적의 정책들 중 어느 것도 지금까지 기대된 성과를 내지 못했다.

04 [생활영어 – 빈칸]　▶③

난이도 하

정답 해설

채점 과정에서 서술형 답안 중 채점 기준에 맞지 않는 부분이 있어 기준을 명확히 해달라는 요청이 있었고, Anna가 적절한 기준을 알려주겠다고 말한 점을 보면, 그에 앞서 해당 답안을 자신에게 보내 달라고 했음을 짐작할 수 있다. 따라서 밑줄 친 부분에 들어갈 말로 가장 적절한 것은 ③이다.

해석

Anna: 시험이 끝나고 시험지는 모두 회수된 건가요?
Min-su: 네. 그런데 서술형 답안을 채점하다 보니 채점 기준에 딱 맞지 않는 답들이 몇 개 있었습니다. 이런 경우 어떻게 점수를 줘야 하는지 설명해주실 수 있을까요?
Anna: 그 답안들을 저에게 보내주세요. 적절한 기준을 알려드릴게요.
Min-su: 기준을 알려주시면 채점을 마무리하겠습니다.
Anna: 좋아요. 도와줘서 고마워요.

① 왜 제대로 채점을 못 했나요?
② 시험지를 다시 인쇄해 주세요.
③ 그 답안들을 저에게 보내주세요.
④ 채점은 굳이 안 해도 될 거 같아요.

어휘

• grade 채점하다, 등급을 매기다
• match 일치하다, 부합하다, 조화를 이루다
• appropriate 적절한, 알맞은

05 [생활영어 – 빈칸]　▶①

난이도 하

정답 해설

예산 심사를 위해 발표 중 마지막 슬라이드에서 언급된 자료의 출처가 정확해야 한다고 말하고 있다. B는 그것이 지역 설문조사에서 나온 것으로 보이지만 확신하지 못한다고 답하며 이어서 대답하자, 이에 A가 "정확한 출처가 있어야 예산 심사에서 문제가 없다"고 강조한 점을 고려하면, B가 이어서 빠르게 출처를 확인하겠다고 말했음을 짐작할 수 있다. 따라서 밑줄 친 부분에 들어갈 말로 가장 적절한 것은 ①이다.

해석

A: 발표는 명확했지만, 마지막 슬라이드의 자료가 어디에서 나온 건지 알려주실 수 있을까요? 예산 심사를 위해 정확한 출처가 필요합니다.
B: 아마 지역 설문조사에서 나온 자료로 알고 있지만, 확실하지는 않습니다. <u>제가 그것을 확인한 후 정확한 출처를 알려드리겠습니다.</u>
A: 네, 정확한 출처가 있어야 예산 심사에서 문제가 없을 겁니다.
B: 그렇군요. 빠르게 확인하고 바로 전달하겠습니다.
A: 네, 발표 내용이 좋아서 심사도 잘 진행될 겁니다.

① 제가 그것을 확인한 후 정확한 출처를 알려드리겠습니다
② 그러면 설문조사를 다시 진행하겠습니다
③ 다시 준비해서 더 완성도 있는 발표를 하겠습니다
④ 심사 결과가 나오면 바로 알려주시기 바랍니다

어휘

• budget 예산
• regional 지역의, 지방의
• essential 필수적인, 꼭 필요한
• verify 검증하다, 확인하다

06 [독해 – 세트형 문항(홈페이지 게시물 – 제목)] ▶ ④

<u>난이도</u> 하

<u>정답 해설</u>

이 글은 2025년 제네바에서 열리는 국제 계산언어학 심포지엄(ISCL)에 연구자와 실무자를 초대하는 안내문이다. 행사 목적, 주요 프로그램, 그리고 논문 제출 및 엄격한 이중 블라인드 심사 절차까지 구체적으로 안내하고 있어, 전형적인 '논문 모집 공고' 형식에 해당한다. 따라서 글의 제목으로 가장 적절한 것은 ④이다.
① 컴퓨터 언어학 최신 발전에 대한 리뷰
② 새로운 자연어 처리 기술의 사회적 영향
③ OmniCorp AI의 새로운 기계 번역 시스템
④ 논문 모집: 제네바에서 열리는 ISCL 학술대회

07 [독해 – 세트형 문항(홈페이지 게시글 – 내용 일치)] ▶ ③

<u>난이도</u> 하

제출된 모든 논문은 엄격한 블라인드 2중 심사를 거친다고 언급하고 있다. 따라서 윗글의 내용과 일치하는 것은 ③이다.

<u>오답 해설</u>

① 국제 계산언어학 심포지엄(ISCL)은 연구자와 현역들을 제네바에서 열리는 2025년 학회에 정중히 초대한다고 언급하고 있으므로 글의 내용과 일치하지 않는다.
② 프로그램에는 동료 평가를 거친 논문 발표, 기술 워크숍, 박사과정 연구자 모임 등이 포함된다고 언급하고 있으므로 글의 내용과 일치하지 않는다.
④ 학회 자료집은 공식 ISCL 전자 도서관에 게재될 예정이라고 언급하고 있을 뿐, 실물 인쇄본으로 제작되어 배포된다는 내용은 언급되지 않았으므로 글의 내용과 일치하지 않는다.

<u>해석</u>

> **논문 모집: 제네바에서 열리는 ISCL 학술대회**
>
> 국제 계산언어학 심포지엄(ISCL)은 연구자와 현역들을 제네바에서 열리는 2025년 학회에 정중히 초대합니다. 이 세계적 행사에서는 자연어 처리, 기계 번역, AI 기반 언어 분석 분야의 발전을 발표하고 논의하기 위해 주요 전문가들이 모이게 됩니다. 이번 심포지엄은 인간-컴퓨터 상호작용 분야의 시급한 과제를 해결하기 위해 학계와 산업계 간의 협력을 촉진하는 것을 목표로 합니다.
>
> 기조연설은 튜링 연구소의 Aris Thorne 박사와 OmniCorp AI의 Lena Petrova 박사가 맡습니다. 프로그램에는 동료 평가를 거친 논문 발표, 기술 워크숍, 박사과정 연구자 모임 등이 포함됩니다. 제출된 모든 논문은 엄격한 블라인드 2중 심사를 거치게 됩니다. 학회 자료집은 공식 ISCL 전자 도서관에 게재될 예정입니다. 참가 인원이 한정되어 있으므로 조기 등록을 권장합니다.

<u>어휘</u>

- cordially 정중하게, 진심으로
- practitioner 현역, 실무자, 전문가
- convene 소집하다, 모이다
- foster 촉진하다, 증진하다
- exigent 긴급한, 시급한
- keynote 기조연설
- peer-reviewed 동료 평가를 받은
- publish 출판하다, 공개하다
- capacity 수용 인원, 용량

08 [독해 – 단일형 문항(홈페이지 게시글 – 내용 불일치)] ▶ ④

<u>난이도</u> 하

<u>정답 해설</u>

'특별 전시회' 안내 부분에서는 MCA 회원이 일반 공개 하루 전인 2025년 10월 17일에 전시회를 미리 볼 수 있다고만 언급할 뿐, 모두가 관람할 수 있다고는 되어 있지 않다. 따라서 윗글의 내용과 일치하지 않는 것은 ④이다.

<u>오답 해설</u>

① 이번 전시는 총 25명의 작가가 참여해 40여 점의 작품을 선보인다고 언급하고 있으므로 글의 내용과 일치한다.
② '입장 안내' 부분에서 특별 전시에 추가 요금이 부과된다고 명시되어 있으므로 글의 내용과 일치한다.
③ '입장 안내'에 MCA 회원과 18세 이하 청소년은 일반 입장과 특별 전시 모두 무료라고 명시되어 있으므로 글의 내용과 일치한다.

<u>해석</u>

> **미래의 메아리: 디지털 아트 & 정체성**
>
> **전시 기간:** 2025년 10월 18일 – 2026년 3월 16일
> **장소:** 그리핀 갤러리 (본관 3층)
>
> 시카고 현대미술관(MCA Chicago)은 디지털 기술이 현대인의 정체성을 어떻게 근본적으로 재구성했는지 탐구하는 새로운 대형 전시 "미래의 메아리(Echoes of the Future)"를 선보입니다. 이번 전시는 25명의 국제 작가의 작품 40여 점을 소개하며, 몰입형 설치 작품, AI 생성 예술, 가상현실(VR) 체험 등을 포함합니다.
>
> **입장 안내:**
> - 일반 입장료: $22(성인), $15(학생/시니어)
> - 특별 전시회 추가 요금: +$8
> - MCA 회원 및 청소년 (18세 이하): 무료 (일반 입장 및 전시 모두 가능).
>
> **특별 전시회:**
> - 아티스트 토크: 아티스트 Kenji Tanaka와 함께 AI 기반 작품에 대한 토론을 진행합니다. (2025년 11월 1일 오후 6시, 별도 등록 필요).
> - 회원 전용 미리보기: MCA 회원은 공개 개막 하루 전인 2025년 10월 17일에 전시회를 미리 볼 수 있습니다.

① 총 25명의 작가가 참여한 40점이 넘는 작품이 전시된다.
② 특별 전시를 관람하려면 추가 요금이 필요하다.
③ MCA 회원들은 두 곳 모두 무료로 입장할 수 있다.
④ 특별 전시회는 모두 10월 17일에 미리 볼 수 있다.

<u>어휘</u>

- present 소개하다, 제시하다
- contemporary 현대의
- installation 설치 작품, 설치물
- admission 입장료
- surcharge 추가 요금, 추가 요금을 부과하다
- display 전시하다, 보여주다

09 [문법 – 밑줄] ▶ ④

<u>난이도</u> 중

<u>정답 해설</u>

④ **[적중 포인트 023] 목적어 뒤에 특정 전치사를 수반하는 3형식 타동사 ★★★☆☆**
'상기시키다'의 의미를 가진 remind는 목적어 뒤에 오는 구조에 따라 'remind + 사람 + of 명사(구)' 또는 'remind + 사람 + that절'의 형태로 쓰인다. 이 문장에서는 뒤에 완전한 절(that절)이 목적어로 오고 있으므로, 전치사 of를 함께 쓸 수 없다. 따라서 밑줄 친 부분의 of를 삭제해야 한다.

<u>오답 해설</u>

① **[적중 포인트 083] 「전치사+관계대명사」 완전구조 ★★★★☆**
conditions를 선행사로 하여 뒤에서 이를 수식하는 관계절이다. 관계절 내부에서 lived는 전치사 in의 목적어가 필요하므로, in which는 적절한 '전치사+관계대명사' 구조이다. 따라서 밑줄 친 부분은 올바르게 쓰였다.

② **[적중 포인트 082] 관계대명사의 선행사와 문장 구조 ★★★★☆**
선행사 characters의 삶(their lives)을 나타내는 관계절이므로, 소유 관계를 나타내는 소유격 관계대명사 whose는 적절하다. 따라서 밑줄 친 부분은 올바르게 쓰였다.

③ **[적중 포인트 080] 부사절 접속사의 구분과 특징 ★★★☆☆**
despite는 전치사이므로 뒤에는 명사구를 써야 한다. 뒤에 its age는 명사구이므로 전치사를 쓸 수 있다. 따라서 밑줄 친 부분은 올바르게 쓰였다.

<u>해석</u>

> 19세기에 쓰인 그 소설은 노동 계급의 투쟁을 묘사한다. 작가는 그들이 살았던 가혹한 환경을 생생하게 묘사한다. 독자들은 삶이 고난으로 가득 찬 등장인물들에게 쉽게 공감할 수 있다. 그 책은 오래되었음에도 불구하고 오늘날에도 여전히 유의미하다. 그것은 우리에게 사회 정의가 계속 추구해야 할 것임을 상기시킨다.

10 [문법 – 밑줄]　▶ ②

정답 해설

② **[적중 포인트 054] 분사 판별법 [현재분사 VS 과거분사] ★★★★★**
분사의 수식을 받는 명사(habitats)가 인간 활동에 의해 파괴를 '당하는' 수동의 의미인 경우 과거분사로 써야 한다. 따라서 밑줄 친 부분의 destroying을 destroyed 로 고쳐야 한다.

오답 해설

① **[적중 포인트 053] 암기해야 할 동명사 표현 ★★★★★**
'~에 전념하다'의 의미인 'be dedicated to'에서 to는 부정사가 아닌 전치사이 므로, 뒤에는 동사 원형이 아닌 동명사를 써야 한다. 따라서 밑줄 친 부분은 올바르게 쓰였다.

③ **[적중 포인트 051] 동명사의 명사 역할 ★★★★★**
deserve는 목적어가 능동의 의미를 가질 때 to부정사를 쓴다. 따라서 밑줄 친 부분은 올바르게 쓰였다.

④ **[적중 포인트 010] 격에 따른 인칭대명사 ★★☆☆☆**
앞 문장에서 주어는 The environmental organization이지만 이를 They로 받아 이미 단체를 복수 대명사로 처리하고 있다. 문맥상 조직·단체를 구성원 집단 으로 보고 they 또는 their로 받는 것이 자연스럽다. 위치상 뒤에 명사를 수식하 는 형용사 자리로 소유격 인칭대명사를 써야 한다. 따라서 밑줄 친 부분은 올 바르게 쓰였다.

해석

> 그 환경 단체는 멸종 위기종을 보호하는 데 전념하고 있다. 그들은 인간 활동 에 의해 파괴된 서식지를 보존하기 위해 끊임없이 노력한다. 그들의 노력은 여 러 개체군의 회복으로 이어졌다. 그들은 모든 생물이 생태계에서 중요한 역할 을 하며 존재할 가치가 있다고 믿는다. 대중을 교육하는 것 또한 그들의 임무 중 핵심 부분이다.

11 [독해 – 세트형 문항(안내문 – 유의어)]　▶ ③

정답 해설

밑줄 친 stifle은 '억누르다, 억압하다, 숨이 막히다'라는 뜻으로, 문맥상 가장 가까 운 의미는 ③ 'hamper(방해하다, 애먹이다)'이다.

오답 해설

① forfeit 몰수당하다, 박탈당하다
② relinquish 포기하다
④ augment 늘리다, 증가시키다

12 [독해 – 세트형 문항(안내문 – 목적)]　▶ ②

정답 해설

이 글은 통화정책위원회(MPC)의 핵심 임무인 물가 안정을 위한 통화 정책 수립 이라는 역할을 설명하고, 경제 지표 분석, 선제적 정책 조정, 투명한 소통 등 위원 회의 운영 원칙을 구체적으로 제시하고 있다. 따라서 글의 목적으로 가장 적절한 것은 ②이다.
① 통화정책위원회(MPC)가 발표한 최근 금리 조정 내용을 안내하려고
② 통화정책위원회(MPC)의 역할과 운영 원칙을 설명하려고
③ 정부의 통화 정책 조치를 평가하려고
④ 미래 경제 동향에 대한 상세한 전망을 제공하려고

해석

> **통화정책위원회(MPC)의 임무**
>
> 통화정책위원회(MPC)는 국가의 통화정책을 수립하는 책임을 맡고 있으며, 그 핵심 목표는 가격 안정 유지에 있습니다. 이 임무는 매우 섬세한 균형 조정을 요구합니다. 지나치게 완화적인 정책 기조는 인플레이션 압력을 높여 장기적 성장을 줄일 수 있고, 반대로 지나치게 긴축적인 정책은 경제 활동을 억누를 수 있기 때문입니다.
>
> 위원회의 결정은 고용 지표, 소비자물가지수, GDP 성장 전망 등 폭넓은 경제 지표에 대한 종합적인 분석을 토대로 이루어집니다. MPC는 미래의 경제 동향 을 예측해 선제적으로 정책 수단을 조정하는 전향적 관점으로 운영됩니다. 또 한 각 결정의 배경과 논리는 대중에게 투명하게 전달되는데, 이는 기대를 관리 하고 정책 체계의 신뢰성을 강화하기 위함입니다. 이러한 투명성은 효과적인 통화정책의 핵심 요소인 인플레이션 기대를 안정시키는 데 필수적입니다.

- monetary 통화[화폐]의
- entrust 맡기다, 위임하다
- accommodative 완화적인, 순응적인
- curtail 줄이다, 축소하다
- fuel 부추기다, 촉발시키다
- grounded in ~에 기반한
- indicator 지표, 지수
- preemptively 선제적으로
- rationale 근거, 논리적 설명
- bolster 강화하다, 지지하다
- augment 증가시키다, 늘리다

13 [독해 – 중심 내용 추론(주제)]　▶ ③

정답 해설

이 글은 인간 줄기세포로 배양한 '뇌 오르가노이드', 즉 '미니 뇌'에 대해 다루고 있다. 이것이 질병 모델링에 유용하다는 내용을 언급한 뒤, '그러나'를 기점으로 심각한 윤리적 회색 지대에 들어섰음을 강조한다. 오르가노이드가 태아의 뇌와 유 사한 복잡한 신경 활동을 보이면서, 이것이 기초적인 지각력에 도달할 수 있는지 에 대한 존재론적 질문에 직면하게 되었음을 설명하고 있다. 따라서 글의 주제로 가장 적절한 것은 ③이다.

해석

> 최근 체외 생명공학 기술의 발전으로 인간 줄기세포가 스스로 조립되어 뇌와 유사한 조직을 형성하는 3차원 군집체인 '대뇌 오가노이드'를 배양하는 것이 가능해졌다. 이러한 '미니 뇌'는 신경 발달을 연구하고 새로운 치료제를 테스 트하는 데 귀중한 자원이 되지만, 이들의 정교함이 점점 더 높아지면서 이 분 야는 윤리적인 회색 지대로 밀려나고 있다. 이것들이 태아의 뇌와 유사한 신경 활동을 보이기 시작함에 따라, 과학자들은 중대한 질문에 직면해야만 한다. 즉, 초기 형태의 지각 능력에 도달하고 있을지도 모르는 존재의 도덕적 지위는 무 엇인가?라는 질문이다. 기존 규제는 훨씬 단순한 조직 배양을 기준으로 설계되 어 이러한 상황을 다루기에는 불충분하며, 그 결과 새로운 윤리 지침이 시급한 상태이다.

① 뇌 오르가노이드를 가능하게 한 과학적 혁신들
② 현행 과학 규제의 미비함
③ 감각성을 지닌 '미니 뇌'가 제기하는 새로운 윤리적 딜레마
④ 오르가노이드가 신경 발달 장애를 치료할 잠재력

- advance 발전, 진보, 향상
- enable 가능하게 하다, 허용하다
- cultivation 배양, 재배
- assemble 모이다, 조립되다
- sophistication 정교함, 복잡함
- confront 직면하다, 맞서다
- status 상태, 지위
- entity 존재, 실체
- inadequate 불충분한, 부적절한
- breakthrough 돌파구, 획기적 발전

14 [독해 – 단일형 문항(안내문 – 내용 일치)]　▶ ②

정답 해설

'기부품 분류' 항목의 요건에서 최대 20파운드(약 9kg)를 들 수 있어야 한다고 명 시되어 있다. 따라서 윗글의 내용과 일치하는 것은 ②이다.

오답 해설

① 본 행사는 도움이 필요한 가정을 위해 새것 또는 깨끗한 겨울 코트, 담요, 장갑 을 나눠 준다고 언급하고 있으므로 글의 내용과 일치하지 않는다.
③ 수거함 운영 봉사자는 행사 기간 중 최소 2주간 수거함을 관리해야 한다고 명 시되어 있으므로 글의 내용과 일치하지 않는다.
④ 수거된 물품은 봉사자가 주 1회 직접 센터에 전달해야 한다고 명시되어 있으므 로 글의 내용과 일치하지 않는다.

기온이 떨어짐에 따라 그린우드 커뮤니티 센터에서는 11월 10일부터 12월 15일까지 연례 행사인 "겨울 나눔(Winter Warmth)" 활동을 진행합니다. 이번 행사에서는 도움이 필요한 가정을 위해 새것 또는 깨끗한 상태의 겨울 코트, 담요, 장갑을 나눠줄 예정입니다.

이번 행사가 성공적으로 진행되기 위해 다음 두 가지 역할의 자원봉사자를 모집합니다.
1. 기부품 분류 (센터 내 활동):
• 업무: 센터에서 기부된 물품을 받고, 분류하고, 정리합니다.
• 근무 교대: 월~금 오전 9시~오후 6시 중 원하는 3시간 교대 근무.
• 요건: 최대 20파운드(약 9kg) 정도를 들 수 있어야 합니다. 현장에서 교육이 제공됩니다.
2. 수거함 운영 (원격/지역사회):
• 업무: 지역 내 사업장, 학교, 기관 등에 기부 수거함을 설치하고 관리합니다.
• 참여 기간: 행사 기간 중 최소 2주 이상은 수거함을 운영해야 합니다.
• 참고: 수거된 물품은 주 1회 센터에 직접 전달해야 합니다.

참여 신청은 11월 5일까지 저희 웹사이트 [링크]에서 가능합니다.

① 이번 행사는 물품이 아니라 금전만 지원받는다.
② 기부품 분류 봉사자는 필요한 무게를 들어 올려야 한다.
③ 하루 동안 수거함 운영에 참여할 수 있다.
④ 수거된 물품은 센터에서 직접 수거해 간다.

어휘
• distribute 나누어 주다, 배포하다
• ensure 보장하다, 확실하게 하다
• sort 분류하다, 정리하다
• organize 정리하다, 조직하다
• flexible 유연한, 탄력적인
• commitment 약속, 의무, 헌신
• sign up 등록하다, 신청하다

15 [독해 – 단일형 문항(전자메일 – 목적)]   ▶④

난이도 하

정답 해설

이 메일은 StreamZone 고객들에게 발송된 것으로, 개인정보 보호정책의 업데이트 소식을 안내하고 그 주요 변경 내용을 구체적으로 설명하고 있다. 따라서 글의 목적으로 가장 적절한 것은 ④이다.

해석

수신인: 소중한 고객 여러분
발신인: StreamZone 고객지원팀
날짜: 2026년 4월 8일
제목: 중요한 업데이트 안내

StreamZone 사용자 여러분께,

저희는 2026년 12월 1일부터 적용될 예정인 StreamZone 개인정보 보호정책 업데이트 사항을 안내드리고자 합니다.

이번 업데이트는 투명성을 강화하기 위한 지속적인 노력의 일환입니다. 고객님이 데이터가 어떻게 수집되고 활용되는지를 더 쉽게 이해할 수 있도록 정책 구조를 재정비했습니다. 주요 변경 사항은 다음과 같습니다.
* 광고 파트너와의 데이터 공유에 대한 더 명확한 설명이 있습니다.
* "계정 설정" 메뉴에서 개인 데이터 선호도를 관리할 수 있는 새로운 옵션을 추가했습니다.

고객님께서 따로 취하셔야 할 조치는 없습니다. 12월 1일 이후에도 StreamZone 서비스를 계속 이용하시면, 새로운 정책에 동의하는 것으로 간주됩니다. 정책 전문은 [링크]를 통해 언제든지 확인하시기를 권장드립니다. 궁금하신 점이 있다면 고객지원팀으로 문의해 주세요.

StreamZone과 함께해 주셔서 감사합니다.

① 새로 출시된 프로그램을 홍보하려고
② 사용자들에게 개인정보를 업데이트해 달라고 요청하려고
③ 데이터 유출 사고에 대해 사과하고 보상 방안을 알리려고
④ 개인정보 처리방침의 변경 사항을 사전에 안내하려고

어휘
• inform 알리다, 통지하다
• upcoming 다가오는, 곧 있을
• transparency 투명성, 명확성
• include 포함하다, 구성하다
• explanation 설명, 해설
• preference 선호, 선택 사항
• convenience 편의, 편리함
• compensation 보상, 배상

16 [독해 – 문장 삽입]   ▶④

난이도 상

정답 해설

이 글은 AI 시대의 'AI 문해력' 교육이 기술 중심을 넘어 '디지털 마음챙김'을 포함해야 한다는 점을 강조하고 있다. ③번 뒤 문장에서는 "이러한 격차를 해소하기 위해" 디지털 마음챙김을 교육 과정에 통합하고 있다고 제시한다. 이어지는 주어진 문장은 "This involves(이것은 ~을 포함한다)"로 시작하며, 앞에서 도입된 디지털 마음챙김이 구체적으로 무엇을 의미하는지 즉, 기술적 능력뿐 아니라 기술 사용 과정에서 자신의 인지적 부하와 감정적 반응을 인식하는 것임을 설명한다. 그 다음 ④번 뒤 문장은 "이러한 통합적 접근"의 효과를 언급하므로, '개념 도입'과 '효과 제시' 사이에 '개념 정의' 역할을 하는 주어진 문장이 들어가는 것이 가장 자연스럽다. 따라서 주어진 문장이 들어갈 위치로 가장 적절한 것은 ④이다.

해석

인공지능이 일상 곳곳에 퍼지면서, 미디어 교육 시스템은 "AI 문해력"을 교육 과정에 빠르게 도입하고 있다. (①) 전통적으로 이는 AI 활용과 혁신 작업에 필요한 핵심 기술 요소에 집중한다는 의미였다. (②) 그러나 2025년의 최근 교육 연구는 이러한 접근이 불완전하다고 지적하는데, 그 이유는 학생들이 겪는 심리적 요인과 불안을 종종 간과하기 때문이다. (③) 이러한 공백을 메우기 위해, 교육자들은 교육과정에 "디지털 마음챙김"을 도입하고 있다. (④ <u>이는 기술적 능력에만 집중하는 것이 아니라, 기술을 사용할 때 자신의 인지적 부하와 감정적 반응을 스스로 인식하는 능력을 기르는 것을 말한다.</u>) 연구에 따르면 이러한 통합적 접근은 집중력을 높일 뿐 아니라, AI 도구를 효과적으로 다루는 데 필요한 자신감과 협업 능력까지 강화해 준다.

어휘
• ubiquitous 도처에 존재하는, 흔한
• incorporate 포함하다, 통합하다
• vital 매우 중요한, 필수적인
• pedagogical 교육학의, 교수법의
• incomplete 불완전한, 미완성의
• disregard 무시하다, 소홀히 하다
• address 다루다, 해결하다
• confidence 자신감, 신뢰
• cognitive 인지적인, 사고의

17 [독해 – 문장 제거]   ▶④

난이도 중

정답 해설

이 글은 고대 굴 껍데기를 고고학과 보존 과학의 관점에서 분석해 현대 해양 생태계 복원에 활용하는 새로운 접근을 소개한다. ①번 문장은 굴 껍데기의 화학 성분과 성장 흔적을 통해 과거 수질 변화를 파악하는 방법을, ②번 문장은 이 분야가 산업화 이전의 '건강한' 연안 환경 기준을 제공함을, ③번 문장은 이러한 과거 데이터가 굴 암초 복원 목표 설정에 중요함을 설명한다. 그러나 ④번 문장은 굴의 먹이 섭취 방식이라는 일반적 생물학 정보를 제시할 뿐, 글의 흐름에서 벗어난다. 따라서 글의 흐름상 어색한 문장은 ④이다.

해석

고고학과 보전 과학을 결합한 새로운 연구에서, 학자들은 고대 굴 껍데기를 활용해 과거의 해양 생태계를 재구성하고 현대 복원 작업에 필요한 정보를 얻고 있다. ① 수천 년 된 굴 껍데기의 화학 성분과 성장 흔적을 분석함으로써, 과학자들은 과거 수질 변화를 추적할 수 있다. ② 동물고고학이라 불리는 이 연구 분야는 인간의 큰 영향이 미치기 이전 해안 환경이 어떠했는지에 대한 중요한 기준 자료를 제공한다. ③ 이러한 고대 자료는 수질 개선과 해안선 보호에 핵심적인 굴 암초 복원 목표를 현실적으로 설정하는 데 도움을 준다. (④ 굴은 아가미로 물을 흘려보내며 플랑크톤을 걸러 먹는 여과섭식 생물로, 주변 생태계에 이로움을 준다.) 이 접근 방식은, 정적인 자료로 여겨졌던 고고학 기록이 오늘날의 환경 문제를 해결하는 데 유용한 도구가 될 수 있음을 보여준다.

어휘

- novel 새로운, 참신한
- archaeology 고고학
- conservation 보존, 보호
- composition 구성, 성분
- realistic 현실적인
- surrounding 주변의

18 [독해 – 순서 배열] ▶ ③

난이도 중

정답 해설

주어진 글은 "DNA가 RNA를 만들고, RNA가 단백질을 만든다"로 요약되는 분자생물학의 중심 원리를 소개하고 있다. (C)에서는 "과정은 전사로 시작된다"는 문장처럼, 핵 속에서 DNA 일부가 풀리고 상보적인 RNA 가닥이 합성되는 첫 단계를 설명한다. (A)는 이렇게 만들어진 mRNA가 DNA에서 분리된 뒤 가공을 거쳐 핵을 빠져나갈 준비를 하는 전사 이후의 중간 단계를 제시한다. (B)는 이어서 핵을 떠난 mRNA가 세포질의 리보솜에 도달해 번역 과정을 거치며 아미노산을 연결해 단백질을 형성하는 마지막 단계를 설명한다. 따라서 글의 순서로 가장 적절한 것은 ③이다.

해석

분자생물학의 중심 원리는 "DNA가 RNA를 만들고, RNA가 단백질을 만든다"라는 표현으로 요약되듯, 유전 정보의 흐름을 설명한다.
(C) 이 과정은 복사로 시작된다. 핵 안에서 DNA의 일부분이 풀리고, 효소가 이에 상보적인 RNA 가닥을 합성한다.
(A) 이렇게 만들어진 메신저 RNA(mRNA)는 DNA에서 분리된 후 기본적인 가공을 거쳐 핵을 빠져나와 세포질로 이동한다.
(B) 리보솜에서, mRNA는 번역 과정을 통해 읽히며, 이때 운반 RNA(tRNA)가 적절한 아미노산을 가져오고, 이 아미노산들이 연결되어 폴리펩타이드 사슬을 형성한다.

어휘

- describe 설명하다, 묘사하다
- summarize 요약하다
- separate 분리되다, 떨어지다
- processing 처리, 가공
- cytoplasm 세포질
- unwind 풀리다, 이완되다
- enzyme 효소
- complementary 상보적인
- amino acid 아미노산

19 [독해 – 빈칸 추론] ▶ ②

난이도 중

정답 해설

이 글은 사이버 공간에서의 익명성이 기만행위가 아닌 자신을 지키기 위한 필수적 조치임을 설명한다. 과거에는 가명 사용을 불명예스러운 은폐로 여겨 의심했으나, 온라인은 표정이나 몸짓 같은 신체적 단서가 부족해 상대를 즉각 평가하기 어렵다는 특수성이 있다. 특히 시·청각적 검증의 부재는 악의적인 행위자에게 표적이 될 위험을 높이므로, 필자는 가상 환경이 대면 만남과 근본적으로 다름을 인정해야 한다고 강조한다. 따라서 충분한 신뢰가 쌓이기 전까지는 '익명성을 유지하는 것이 합리적이면서도 윤리적인 선택'이며, 이는 타인을 속이려는 의도가 아니라 검증이 제한된 환경에서의 신중한 자기 보호 수단이다. 따라서 밑줄 친 부분에 들어갈 말로 가장 적절한 것은 ②이다.

해석

우리 사회에서 투명성은 하나의 덕목이며, 우리는 개인이 자기 자신을 정확하게 나타낸다고 가정한다. 디지털 소통이 이를 복잡하게 만들긴 했지만, 역사적으로 가명을 사용하는 것은 의구심 어린 시선으로 여겨졌다. 그러나 이제 사이버 공간에서는 얼굴 표정이나 몸짓 언어와 같은 신체적 단서의 부재로 인해 인물의 됨됨이를 즉각적으로 평가하는 것이 어려워졌다. 이러한 시각적, 청각적 검증의 부족은 악의적인 행위자들의 표적이 될 높은 위험을 초래한다. 그러므로 사용자들은 가상 환경이 대면 만남과는 근본적으로 다르다는 것을 인식해야 한다. 화면 뒤에 있는 사람과 일관된 상호작용을 통해 신뢰 관계가 구축될 때까지, 익명성을 유지하는 것은 합리적이면서도 윤리적인 선택이다. 이러한 관행은 기만행위가 아니라 검증이 제한된 환경에서 자신을 보호하기 위한 신중한 조치이다.

① 당신의 실명을 밝히는 것이 신뢰를 촉진하는 가장 좋은 방법이다
② 익명성을 유지하는 것은 합리적이면서도 윤리적인 선택이다
③ 사회적 책무를 위해 가명 사용은 피해야 한다
④ 본성을 파악하기 위해 디지털 본능에 의존하는 것으로 충분하다

어휘

- transparency 투명성
- complicated 복잡한
- absence 부재, 없음, 결핍
- verification 검증, 입증
- consistent 한결같은, 일관된
- deceit 속임수, 사기, 기만
- prudent 신중한

20 [독해 – 빈칸 추론] ▶ ②

난이도 중

정답 해설

이 글은 겉보기에는 생존과 직접 관련 없어 보이는 인간의 고등 지성이 왜 진화했는지를 묻고, 그 해답으로 '사회적 뇌 가설'을 제시한다. 이 가설에 따르면 인간의 지성은 실용적 문제 해결이 아니라 복잡한 사회적 역학을 헤쳐 나가기 위해 발달했다. 글에서는 협력, 속임수, 속임수 간파, 관계 관리 등 다양한 사회적 능력이 그 예시로 제시된다. 빈칸은 이러한 과정 속에서 작용한 '주된 진화 압력'을 요약해야 하는 위치이며, 결국 "다른 인간들을 능가하고 조종하려는 필요성"이 이 사회적 경쟁의 본질을 가장 정확히 드러낸다. 따라서 밑줄 친 부분에 들어갈 말로 가장 적절한 것은 ②이다.

해석

인간 지능의 진화는 흥미로운 수수께끼를 제기한다. 왜 인간은 미적분을 이해하거나 교향곡을 작곡하는 것과 같은 추상적 사고 능력을 갖게 되었을까? 우리의 원시 조상 환경에서 그러한 기술들이 뚜렷한 생존 이점을 제공하지 않았는데도 말이다. '사회적 뇌 가설'은 이에 대한 강력한 해답을 제시한다. 이 가설에 따르면 인간의 지능은 실용적 문제를 해결하기 위해서가 아니라, 협력하고 속이고 속임수를 간파하며 관계를 관리하는 등 복잡한 사회적 역학을 헤쳐 나가기 위해 주로 진화했다는 것이다. 이 관점에서 가장 중요한 진화 압력은 다른 사람들을 능가하고 조종하는 능력이었다. 따라서 중요한 것은 절대적인 영리함이 아니라, 경쟁자들보다 사회적으로 조금 더 능숙해지는 것이었다.

① 물리적 환경을 정복해야 할 필요성
② 다른 사람들을 능가하고 조종하는 능력
③ 사회적 지식을 공유해야 했던 압력
④ 상징적 문화적 의사소통의 부상

어휘

- intelligence 지능
- compelling 설득력 있는, 주목할 만한
- endow 부여하다
- abstract 추상적인
- primitive 원시의, 초기의
- hypothesis 가설
- detect 감지하다, 탐지하다
- adept 능숙한, 숙련된
- manipulate 조종하다, 다루다

수고하셨습니다.
당신의 합격을 응원합니다.

영어 정답 및 해설

제6회 모의고사

01 ③	02 ②	03 ③	04 ④	05 ②
06 ④	07 ②	08 ①	09 ①	10 ①
11 ③	12 ②	13 ②	14 ③	15 ③
16 ③	17 ④	18 ③	19 ③	20 ④

01 [어휘 – 빈칸]　　▶ ③

난이도 하

정답 해설

연구자들이 기존 현장 조사 방식으로는 관측하기 어려워 고해상도 위성 영상에 의존했다는 점에서, 해당 지역이 직접 접근이 어려운 '먼' 지역임을 유추할 수 있다. 따라서 밑줄 친 부분에 들어갈 말로 가장 적절한 것은 ③이다.

해석

연구자들은 기존의 현장 조사 방식으로는 대부분 접근이 불가능한 먼 지역을 지속적으로 관측하기 위해 고해상도 위성 영상에 의존했다.

어휘

★ distant 먼, (멀리) 떨어져 있는
● gloomy 우울한, 침울한
● persistent 끈질긴, 집요한, 끊임없이 지속[반복]되는
● varied 다양한, 다채로운

02 [어휘 – 빈칸]　　▶ ②

난이도 중

정답 해설

새로운 정책과 관련해 여러 차례의 심도 있는 논의가 필요했다고 한 점에서, 주민들에게 해당 정책이 실질적인 이익을 가져올 것임을 '설득하려는' 목적이었음을 알 수 있다. 따라서 밑줄 친 부분에 들어갈 말로 가장 적절한 것은 ②이다.

해석

새로운 정책이 결국 지역 사회 전반에 실질적인 이익을 가져올 것임을 주민들에게 설득하기 위해서는 여러 차례의 심도 있는 논의가 필요했다.

어휘

★ persuade 설득하다, 납득시키다
● admire 존경하다, 칭찬하다
● appoint 임명하다, 지명하다
● classify 분류하다, 구분하다

03 [문법 – 빈칸]　　▶ ③

난이도 중

정답 해설

③ **[적중 포인트 075] 혼합 가정법 공식 ★★★★☆**

If가 생략되고 Had가 문두로 도치된 구문이고, 종속절은 a decade ago라는 표현에서 알 수 있듯이 과거 사실과 반대되는 가정을 나타낸다. 그러나 주절에는 today라는 현재 시점의 시간 부사가 제시되어 있어, 과거의 가정이 현재에 미치는 결과를 말하고 있음을 알 수 있다. 따라서 이 문장은 혼합 가정법이며, 혼합 가정법에서 주절은 '조동사의 과거형 + 동사원형'을 써야 한다. 따라서 밑줄 친 부분에 들어갈 말로 가장 적절한 것은 ③이다.

해석

만약 정부가 10년 전에 탄소 배출에 대해 더 엄격한 규제를 시행했더라면, 우리는 오늘날과 같은 극단적인 기상 패턴에 직면하고 있지 않을 것이다.

04 [생활영어 – 빈칸]　　▶ ④

난이도 하

정답 해설

A와 B는 주말 야외 행사를 앞두고 심각한 뇌우 예보 문제에 직면해 있다. B가 "어떻게 해야 하죠?"라고 묻고, A의 말을 들은 뒤 "그것이 현재로서는 최선의 방법 같다. 모든 일정을 취소할 수는 없다"고 반응한 점을 보면, A가 야외 행사 대신 실내에서 진행할 수 있는 대안을 제시했음을 알 수 있다. 따라서 밑줄 친 부분에 들어갈 말로 가장 적절한 것은 ④이다.

해석

A: 이번 주말에 열리는 연례 야외 시장 때문에 정말 걱정돼.
B: 왜? 모든 판매자들도 확정됐고, 홍보도 잘 되고 있잖아.
A: 방금 일기예보를 확인했어. 토요일 오후에 심한 폭풍우가 올 확률이 90%래.
B: 오, 안 돼. 큰일이네. 준비한 게 전부 야외에 있는데. 어떡하지?
A: 실내 홀을 예비 장소로 사용할 수 있는지 한번 물어보자.
B: 그것이 현재로서는 최선의 방법인 거 같네. 모든 걸 그냥 취소할 수는 없지.
A: 맞아. 지금 바로 커뮤니티 센터에 전화해서 실내 홀이 사용 가능한지 알아볼게.

① 우리는 그 행사를 다음 달까지 연기하는 것이 불가피하다고 생각해.
② 아마도 제품을 보호하기 위해 추가 텐트를 제공할 수도 있을 거야.
③ 그냥 위험을 감수하자. 일기 예보는 자주 틀리잖아.
④ 실내 홀을 예비 장소로 사용할 수 있는지 한번 물어보자.

어휘

• vendor 판매자, 노점상
• promotion 홍보, 판촉
• forecast 일기예보, 전망
• severe 심각한, 혹독한

05 [생활영어 – 빈칸]　　▶ ②

난이도 하

정답 해설

Tom과 Jane은 '데이터 유출'로 인해 스팸 전화가 급증한 문제를 논의하고 있다. Jane이 "우리가 할 수 있는 일이 있을까요?"라고 해결책을 묻고, Tom의 말에 "그거 좋은 생각이네요. 지금 바로 할게요."라고 응답한 점을 보면, Tom이 즉시 실행 가능한 현실적 해결책을 제시했음을 알 수 있다. 따라서 밑줄 친 부분에 들어갈 말로 가장 적절한 것은 ②이다.

해석

Tom: 정말 진절머리가 나네요. 오늘 아침에만 스팸 전화를 7통이나 받았어요!
Jane: 당신도요? 전 이번 주 내내 끊이지 않았어요. 다들 어떻게 제 번호를 아는지 모르겠어요.
Tom: 전 알 것 같아요. 혹시 지난달에 '메가딜' 온라인 스토어에 가입했어요? 거기서 대규모 데이터 유출이 있었다고 들었어요.
Jane: 아, 저 가입했는데! 끔찍하네요. 우리가 할 수 있는 일이 있을까요?
Tom: 나는 지금 당장 좋은 스팸 차단 앱을 설치하려고요.
Jane: 좋은 생각이네요. 지금 당장 할게요. 도움이 되면 좋겠네요.

① 사실 그 가게에서 데이터를 유출한 사람은 바로 저예요.
② 나는 지금 당장 좋은 스팸 차단 앱을 설치하려고요.
③ 전화를 그만 받으려면 아마 그냥 휴대폰을 버려야 할 거예요.
④ 그들에게 다시 전화를 걸어 끊을 때까지 오페라를 부르는 건 어때요?

어휘

• be fed up 진절머리 나다, 싫증나다
• constant 끊임없는, 지속적인
• wonder 궁금해하다
• massive 거대한, 대규모의
• probably 아마도, 대체로

06 [독해 - 단일형 문항(안내문 - 목적)] ▶④

난이도 하

정답 해설

이 글은 행사 안내 공지문으로서, 날짜·장소·입장 조건·프로그램·등록 시간 등을 소개하며, 마지막에는 주민과 방문객이 함께 참여해 축제를 즐기기를 기대한다고 밝히고 있다. 따라서 글의 목적으로 가장 적절한 것은 ④이다.

해석

제25회 Destin 가을 축제

Destin 시는 모든 주민과 방문객들이 2026년 10월 27일 월요일 오후 5시부터 8시까지 Destin 커뮤니티 센터에서 열리는 제25회 연례 가을 축제에 함께해 주시기를 진심으로 초대합니다.

지역 푸드 드라이브를 지원하기 위해, 참석자께서는 보관이 가능한 비상식품 1개를 지참해 주시기 바랍니다. 축제 현장에서는 다양한 게임 및 활동 부스, 케이크워크, 할로윈 코스튬 콘테스트, 잭오랜턴 콘테스트, 그리고 판매용 음식이 제공됩니다.

게임 및 음식 티켓은 20장에 5달러에 판매됩니다. 코스튬 콘테스트 등록은 행사 중 오후 5시부터 6시까지 진행됩니다. 잭오랜턴 콘테스트용 조각된 호박은 오후 3시 이전에 제출해야 하며, 심사는 오후 5시 정각에 시작됩니다.

축제에서 여러분을 만나 함께 가을을 즐길 수 있기를 기대합니다!

① 가을 축제의 목적을 설명하려고
② 가을 축제 시설 사용에 대한 지침을 제공하려고
③ 할로윈 코스튬 콘테스트에서 우승하는 방법에 대한 팁을 제공하려고
④ 가을 축제에 시민들을 초대하려고

어휘
• resident 주민, 거주자
• attendee 참석자, 참여자
• non-perishable 상하지 않는, 장기 보관 가능한
• registration 등록, 신청
• promptly 즉시, 제시간에

07 [독해 - 세트형 문항(홈페이지 게시글 - 제목)] ▶②

난이도 중

정답 해설

이 글은 항생제 내성(AMR)이라는 심각한 위협 속에서, 항생제라는 핵심 의약품의 효능을 보존해야 한다고 강조한다. 항생제는 감염병에 맞서는 인류의 중요한 방어선으로 비유될 수 있다. 따라서 글의 제목으로 가장 적절한 것은 ②이다.
① 일상적인 항생제 사용 뒤에 숨겨진 위협
② 항생제 내성에 대한 최후의 방어 유지하기
③ 바이러스 감염과 세균 감염: 임상 안내서
④ 항생제의 효과가 시간이 지남에 따라 감소하는 이유

08 [독해 - 세트형 문항(홈페이지 게시글 - 내용 불일치)] ▶①

난이도 하

정답 해설

항생제 내성(AMR)이 증가함에 따라, 우리는 흔한 감염병조차 제대로 치료하지 못할 심각한 위험에 놓이게 되었다고 경고하고 있다. 따라서 윗글의 내용과 일치하지 않는 것은 ①이다.
① 현대 의학은 여전히 일반적인 질병들을 쉽게 치료할 수 있다.
② 약물 내성은 주로 부적절한 약 복용에서 기인한다.
③ 약물은 오직 검사 결과에 기반해서만 투여되어야 한다.
④ 의료진과 일반인 모두 이 노력에 동참해야 한다.

오답 해설

② AMR은 박테리아와 바이러스 등 다양한 병원체가 자신들을 죽이기 위해 만들어진 약물을 무력화하도록 진화하면서 발생하는 현상이며, 그 주요 원인은 항생제의 오용과 남용이라고 제시되고 있으므로 글의 내용과 일치한다.
③ 이 캠페인의 목적은 항생제를 책임감 있게 사용하도록 권장하는 것이며, 이는 진단 근거에 따라 필요한 경우에만 항생제를 처방하고 처방된 복용 기간을 끝까지 준수하는 것을 의미한다고 언급되어 있으므로 글의 내용과 일치한다.

④ 이 캠페인은 일반 대중에게도 항생제는 감기와 같은 바이러스성 감염에는 효과가 없으며, 불필요하게 의사에게 항생제를 요구해서는 안 된다는 점을 이해하도록 한다고 설명하고 있으므로 글의 내용과 일치한다.

해석

항생제 내성에 대한 최후의 방어 유지하기

항생제 내성(AMR)이 증가함에 따라, 우리는 흔한 감염병조차 제대로 치료하지 못할 심각한 위험에 놓이게 되었습니다. AMR은 박테리아, 바이러스 등 다양한 병원체가 자신들을 죽이기 위해 만들어진 약물을 무력화하도록 진화하면서 발생하는 현상입니다. 이러한 AMR의 주요 원인은 항생제의 오용과 남용입니다. 생명을 구하는 이러한 약물의 효과를 지키기 위해서는 전 세계적인 행동 변화가 필요합니다.

'항생제 관리' 캠페인은 의료진과 일반 대중 모두에게 항생제를 책임감 있게 사용할 것을 권장합니다. 이는 진단 근거에 따라 꼭 필요한 경우에만 항생제를 처방하고, 처방된 복용 기간을 끝까지 지키는 것을 의미합니다. 일반 대중에게는 항생제가 감기 같은 바이러스성 감염에는 효과가 없다는 점을 이해하고, 불필요하게 의사에게 항생제를 요구하지 않는 것이 필요합니다. 이러한 공동의 노력이야말로 약물 내성을 지닌 균주의 출현을 늦추는 데 결정적으로 중요합니다.

어휘
• capacity 능력, 수용력
• preserve 보존하다, 유지하다
• responsible 책임 있는, 신중한
• prescribe 처방하다
• diagnostic 진단의
• paramount 가장 중요한, 으뜸가는
• strain (바이러스·세균의) 균주, 종류

09 [문법 - 밑줄] ▶①

난이도 중

정답 해설

① **[적중 포인트 064] to부정사의 관용 구문 ★★★★☆**
'~하는 데 익숙하다'의 의미를 나타낼 때는 'be used to + 동명사' 구조를 써야 한다. 문맥상 노인들이 디지털 기기를 다루는 데 익숙하지 않다는 의미이므로 동명사를 써야 한다. 따라서 밑줄 친 부분의 handle을 handling으로 고쳐야 한다.

오답 해설

② **[적중 포인트 054] 분사 판별법 [현재분사 VS 과거분사] ★★★★★**
분사의 수식을 받는 명사(programs)가 교육을 '하는' 것이 아니라 교육을 위해 설계된 대상이므로 수동 의미의 과거분사로 써야 한다. 따라서 밑줄 친 부분은 올바르게 쓰였다.
③ **[적중 포인트 049] 5형식 동사의 수동태 구조 ★★★★☆**
expect는 목적격 보어로 to부정사를 취하는 동사이며, 수동태(be expected)로 전환되더라도 to부정사는 뒤에 그대로 유지된다. 따라서 밑줄 친 부분은 올바르게 쓰였다.
④ **[적중 포인트 054] 분사 판별법 [현재분사 VS 과거분사] ★★★★★**
분사의 수식을 받는 명사(disparity)는 노년층이 '직면한' 대상이므로 수동 의미의 과거분사로 써야 한다. 따라서 밑줄 친 부분은 올바르게 쓰였다.

해석

원격 의료는 노인 인구 사이에서 점점 더 인기를 얻고 있다. 그러나 많은 노인들은 디지털 기기를 다루는 데 익숙하지 않아, 이는 의료 서비스 접근에 장벽이 되고 있다. 이 격차를 해소하기 위해 커뮤니티 센터들은 그들에게 디지털 리터러시를 교육하기 위해 고안된 프로그램을 시작했다. 이러한 노력은 노년층이 직면한 의료 접근성의 격차를 줄일 것으로 기대된다.

10 [독해 – 세트형 문항(홈페이지 게시글 – 유의어)] ▶ ①

 하

밑줄 친 detection는 '발견, 간파, 탐지'라는 뜻으로, 문맥상 가장 가까운 의미는 ① 'discovery(발견)'이다.

② preservation 보존, 보호, 유지
③ extraction 뽑아냄, 추출
④ screening 검사, 심사, 상영, 방영

11 [독해 – 세트형 문항(홈페이지 게시글 – 내용 불일치)] ▶ ③

 하

검진 서비스 항목 중 65세 이상의 노인들은 골밀도 검사를 받을 수 있고 검사 결과도 현장에서 즉시 제공한다고 명시되어 있다. 따라서 윗글의 내용과 일치하지 않는 것은 ③이다.

① 의료 전문가들이 현장에 상주하여 상담을 제공하고 다양한 건강 검진을 실시할 예정이라고 언급하고 있으므로 글의 내용과 일치한다.
② 검진 서비스 항목 중 5~12세 어린이가 시력 검사 대상자로 명시되어 있으므로 글의 내용과 일치한다.
④ 모든 검진 서비스는 무료이지만, 대기 시간을 줄이기 위해 사전 등록을 권장한다고 언급하고 있으므로 글의 내용과 일치한다.

연례 지역사회 건강 박람회 안내

연례 지역사회 건강 박람회가 다시 열려 지역 주민들에게 무료 의료 서비스를 제공합니다. 본 행사의 목적은 질병의 조기 발견을 촉진하고, 가족들이 건강한 생활 습관을 실천하도록 장려하는 것입니다.

이번 행사는 이번 토요일 시립 커뮤니티 센터에서 개최됩니다. 의료 전문가들이 현장에 상주하여 상담을 제공하고 다양한 건강 검진을 실시할 예정입니다. 보험은 필요하지 않습니다.

검진 서비스

서비스	대상	비고
시력 검사	어린이(5 - 12세)	필요 시 무료 안경 처방 제공
혈압 검사	성인(18세 이상)	심장병 전문의 상담 가능
골밀도 검사	노인(65세 이상)	검사 결과를 현장에서 즉시 제공

모든 서비스는 무료이지만, 대기 시간을 줄이기 위해 사전 등록을 권장합니다. 접수 시에는 유효한 신분증을 지참해 주시기 바랍니다.

- promote 촉진하다, 홍보하다
- encourage 장려하다, 권장하다
- professional 전문가, 전문직 종사자
- insurance 보험, 보험금
- vision 시력, 시야, 환상, 환영
- cardiologist 심장병 전문의
- bone density 골밀도

12 [문법 – 밑줄] ▶ ②

 중

② [적중 포인트 043] 혼동하기 쉬운 주어와 동사 수 일치 ★★★★☆
  remain은 '남아 있다'라는 의미의 자동사이며, 이 문장의 주어는 many ethical concerns이다. 그러나 문장에서는 동사 remain이 주어보다 먼저 나오는 비문법적 어순이 사용되어 있다. 정상 어순은 'many ethical concerns remain'이며, 도치를 사용하려면 'There remain many ethical concerns'와 같이 there 구문이 필요하다. 따라서 밑줄 친 부분의 remain을 there remain으로 고쳐야 한다.

① [적중 포인트 014] 형용사와 부사의 차이 ★★★★★
  동사구(has improved)를 수식하는 것은 형용사가 아닌 부사이다. 따라서 밑줄 친 부분은 올바르게 쓰였다.
③ [적중 포인트 049] 5형식 동사의 수동태 구조 ★★★★☆
  'consider A B'의 수동태인 'is considered+명사(보어)' 구조로 쓸 수 있다. 따라서 밑줄 친 부분은 올바르게 쓰였다.
④ [적중 포인트 082] 관계대명사의 선행사와 문장 구조 ★★★★☆
  선행사 many experts(사람)에 맞춰 주격 관계대명사 who를 사용하였고, 뒤의 predict가 문장에서 동사 역할을 하므로 적절하다. 따라서 밑줄 친 부분은 올바르게 쓰였다.

진단 분야에 AI가 도입되면서 정확도가 크게 향상되었다. 그러나 데이터 프라이버시와 관련된 윤리적 우려가 여전히 많이 남아 있다. 방대한 데이터셋을 기반으로 학습하는 이 기술은 많은 전문가들에 의해 혁신적인 도구로 간주되며, 그들은 이러한 기술이 널리 채택될 것이라고 예측한다.

13 [독해 – 단일형 문항(안내문 – 내용 일치)] ▶ ②

 중

Bellingham 공공도서관의 모든 활동은 무료라고 언급하고 있다. 따라서 윗글의 내용과 일치하는 것은 ②이다.

① Bellingham 공공도서관은 2026년 11월에 어린이, 청소년, 성인을 위한 다양한 프로그램을 제공한다고 명시되어 있으므로 글의 내용과 일치하지 않는다.
③ 'Builders Club' 항목에서 모든 재료가 제공된다고 명시되어 있으므로 글의 내용과 일치하지 않는다.
④ '5~8학년 독서 모임'은 공간이 제한되어 있어 사전 등록이 필요하다고 명시되어 있으므로 글의 내용과 일치하지 않는다.

Bellingham 공공도서관: 2026년 11월 프로그램 안내

Bellingham 공공도서관은 2026년 11월에 11월 18일 어린이들을 위한 'Stuffy Sleepover'와 11월 15일 성인들을 위한 'Book Club Social'을 포함하여 어린이, 청소년, 성인을 위한 특별 프로그램들을 선보입니다. 또한 도서관에서는 11월을 맞아 미국 원주민 유산의 달을 기념합니다. Bellingham 공공도서관의 모든 활동은 무료입니다.

* Builders Club (4~12세): 11월 4일 화요일, 오후 3:30 - 5:00. 새로운 월간 만들기 도전을 함께해 보세요. 모든 재료는 제공됩니다.
* 5~8학년 독서 모임: 매달 둘째 주 목요일에 모임이 열립니다. 간식이 제공되며, 공간이 제한되어 있어 사전 등록이 필요합니다.
* Sesame Street 워크숍 (3~5세 및 보호자): 11월 13일 목요일, 오후 5:00 - 5:45. 어린이와 보호자가 함께 건강한 디지털 습관을 탐색하도록 돕는 가족 친화적 무료 워크숍입니다.

① 11월 프로그램은 청소년만을 대상으로 운영된다.
② 모든 도서관 활동은 완전히 무료이다.
③ Builders Club 참가자는 필요한 재료를 직접 준비해 와야 한다.
④ 학생들은 등록 없이 독서 모임에 참여할 수 있다.

- honor 기리다, 기념하다
- free of charge 무료로, 비용 없이
- pre-registration 사전 등록, 미리 신청
- required 필수의, 요구되는
- caregiver 보호자, 돌보는 사람
- material 재료, 자료

14 [독해 – 중심 내용 추론(주제)] ▶ ③

난이도 중

정답 해설

이 글은 '15분 도시' 개념의 양면성을 중심으로 논의를 전개한다. 전반부에서는 15분 도시가 자동차 의존도를 줄이고 공동체를 강화하는 지속가능성의 새로운 패러다임으로 긍정적인 평가를 받는다고 설명한다. 그러나 However 이하에서는 이러한 유토피아적 비전이 격렬한 반발에 직면하고 있으며, 감시와 통제의 도구가 될 가능성, 그리고 부유한 지역만 혜택을 누리게 하는 사회경제적 분리 심화 등의 우려가 제기되고 있음을 강조한다. 따라서 글의 주제로 가장 적절한 것은 ③이다.

해석

'15분 도시' 개념은 일상에 필요한 모든 편의시설－직장, 쇼핑, 교육, 여가－을 도보 또는 자전거로 15분 안에 이용할 수 있는 도시 생활을 구상하는 것으로, 전 세계적으로 큰 주목을 받고 있다. 지지자들은 이 모델이 자동차 의존도를 줄이고 지역 공동체를 강화함으로써 지속 가능성과 공중 보건을 촉진하는 도시의 새로운 패러다임이라고 주장한다. 그러나 이러한 유토피아적 비전은 강한 반발에도 직면하고 있다. 비판자들은 특히 이 개념이 구역 지정이나 디지털 감시를 통해 강제될 경우, '도시 봉쇄'나 '기후 봉쇄'를 초래할 위험이 있다고 지적한다. 또한 이 모델이 사회·경제적 분리를 심화시켜, 잘 갖춰진 부유한 지역과 소외된 변두리 지역 간의 격차를 확대시키고, 편리한 도시를 향한 비전이 감시와 통제의 도구로 변질될 수 있다는 우려도 커지고 있다.

① 도시 지역에서 자동차 의존도를 줄이는 것의 장점
② 현대 도시 계획에서 디지털 감시의 역할
③ 15분 도시를 둘러싼 논쟁: 살기 좋은 도시인가, 통제 도구인가
④ 지속 가능한 도시 설계의 역사적 발전 과정

어휘

• envision 상상하다, 구상하다
• amenity 생활 편의 시설
• proponent 지지자, 옹호자
• dependency 의존, 종속
• cohesion 결속력, 응집력
• backlash 반발, 역풍
• enforced 강제된, 시행된
• segregation 분리, 차별
• affluent 부유한, 풍요로운
• peripheral 주변의, 주변부의
• surveillance 감시, 관찰

15 [독해 – 단일형 문항(전자메일 – 목적)] ▶ ③

난이도 하

정답 해설

이 글은 City Center 건물 관리실에서 입주자들에게 보낸 안내문으로, 핵심 내용은 필수 연례 유지보수 실시와 승강기 중단 날짜 및 시간을 구체적으로 알리는 것이다. 따라서 글의 목적으로 가장 적절한 것은 ③이다.

해석

수신인: 시티 센터 건물의 모든 임차인
발신인: 건물 관리부 A. Johnson
날짜: 2026년 11월 5일
제목: 긴급 공지

임차인 여러분께,

City Center 건물의 주요 승강기(1번 및 2번 승강기)에 관한 중요한 안내 사항입니다. 안전성과 안정적인 작동을 지속적으로 보장하기 위해, 의무적인 연례 점검을 진행할 예정입니다. 이 작업에는 두 대의 주요 승강기를 완전히 중단시키는 절차가 포함됩니다.

* 중단 날짜: 2026년 11월 7일 목요일
* 중단 시간: 오전 10시 ~ 오후 4시 (예상 6시간)

이 시간 동안, 모든 임차인과 방문객들은 로비 뒤편에 위치한 화물용 승강기(3번 승강기)를 이용해야 합니다. 한 대의 승강기가 모든 층을 운영하게 되므로, 건물 내부 이동 시 여유 시간을 충분히 확보해 주시기 바랍니다. 또한, 출퇴근 시간의 불편을 최소화하기 위해 점검 작업을 낮 시간대에 진행하도록 일정을 조정하였습니다.

불가피한 불편에 대해 사과드리며, 여러분의 양해에 감사드립니다.

진심으로,
A. Johnson

① 새로운 엘리베이터 안전 기능을 안내하려고
② 최근 엘리베이터 오작동에 대해 사과하려고
③ 예정된 엘리베이터 유지·보수 일정을 알리려고
④ 입주자들에게 주 승강기 사용을 줄여 달라고 요청하려고

어휘

• tenant 세입자, 임차인
• notification 알림, 통보
• regarding ~에 관하여, 관련하여
• passenger 승객, 이용자
• mandatory 의무적인, 필수적인
• maintenance 정비, 유지 보수
• shutdown 가동 중단, 폐쇄
• allocate 할당하다, 배분하다
• disruption 중단, 혼란

16 [독해 – 문장 제거] ▶ ③

난이도 하

정답 해설

이 글은 '과잉 교육' 현상이 가족 배경과 같은 사회적 요인과 어떻게 연결되는지를 설명한다. ①번 문장은 과잉 교육이 무작위적으로 발생하는 것이 아니라 가정 배경의 영향을 받는다고 문제를 제기하고, ②번 문장은 부모의 소득이나 인맥이 특권층 자녀에게 유리한 취업 기회를 제공한다는 점을 구체적으로 설명한다. ④번 문장은 이러한 불평등 구조의 결과로, 경제적으로 불리한 배경의 졸업생이 자신의 능력을 충분히 활용하지 못하는 일자리로 더 자주 밀려난다고 지적한다. 그러나 ③번 문장은 고등 교육 기관이 실용 기술과 인턴십을 강조하는 교육과정 개편 노력을 언급하는데, 가정 배경이 고용 결과에 미치는 영향과 직접적인 관련이 없다. 따라서 글의 흐름상 어색한 문장은 ③이다.

해석

'과잉교육'－즉, 어떤 직업이 요구하는 수준보다 더 높은 학력을 갖는 현상－은 오늘날 노동시장에서 점점 더 큰 문제로 여겨지고 있다. ① 최근 연구에 따르면, 이러한 현상은 무작위로 발생하는 것이 아니라 졸업생의 가정 배경이 과잉학력 상태에 놓일 가능성에 큰 영향을 미친다고 한다. ② 부모의 소득이나 직업적 인맥은 유리한 배경을 가진 졸업생들에게 자신의 능력에 맞는 일자리에 접근할 수 있는 더 나은 기회를 제공한다. (③ 대학들은 실용적 기술과 인턴십을 강조하는 방향으로 교육과정을 점차 개편하고 있다.) ④ 그 결과, 동일한 학위를 가지고 있어도 경제적으로 덜 여유로운 가정 출신의 졸업생은 자신의 능력을 충분히 활용하지 못하는 일자리로 더 자주 밀려나게 된다. 이러한 부조화는 개인의 경력과 소득뿐 아니라, 사회 전체의 인적 자원이 효율적으로 활용되는 데에도 부정적인 영향을 미친다.

어휘

• overeducation 과잉교육
• likelihood 가능성, 확률
• privileged 특권을 가진, 유리한
• institution 기관, 단체
• emphasize 강조하다, 중시하다
• qualification 자격, 능력
• frequently 자주, 빈번히
• mismatch 불일치, 부조화
• human capital 인적 자본

17 [독해 – 문장 삽입] ▶④

정답 해설

이 글은 미세플라스틱이 인체 내 다양한 장기에서 검출되며 심각한 건강 위협이 되고 있음을 경고한다. ①번부터 ③번 뒤 문장에서 혈액, 폐, 간을 넘어 태반과 고환에 이르기까지 인체 내에서 발견된 미세플라스틱의 구체적 사례와 질병 위험을 일관되게 나열한다. 이때 ④번에 주어진 문장이 들어가면, '증거가 또한 쌓이고 있다'는 표현을 통해 인체 데이터에 이어 동물 실험이라는 추가 근거를 제시하며 논의의 범위를 효과적으로 확장한다. 특히 ④번 위치가 결정적인 이유는 마지막 결론 문장의 '임상 및 실험실 결과'라는 표현 때문인데, 여기서 '임상'은 앞선 인체 사례를, '실험실'은 주어진 문장의 쥐 실험을 각각 지칭하며 논리적 완결성을 완성한다. 따라서 주어진 문장이 들어갈 위치로 가장 적절한 것은 ④이다.

해석

미세 플라스틱 오염이 우리 일상 곳곳에 깊숙이 퍼져 있다는 사실이 점점 더 명확해지고 있다. 최근 연구에 따르면, 이러한 미세 플라스틱이 인체 내부로 놀랄 만큼 깊이 침투하고 있음이 드러났다. (①) 과학자들은 이미 이 미세한 입자들이 인간의 혈액 속을 순환하고, 폐에 축적되며, 심지어 간 깊숙한 부위에까지 자리 잡고 있다는 사실을 확인했다. (②) 더 나아가 최근 연구들은 미세 플라스틱이 태반과 고환에서도 발견된다는 사실을 확인했으며, 이는 태아 발달과 생식 건강에 잠재적인 위험을 제기한다. (③) 이러한 축적은 심장마비, 뇌졸중, 염증성 장 질환 등 심각한 건강 문제와 연관이 있는 것으로 알려져 있다. (④ 또한 동물 실험에서도 증거가 쌓이고 있는데, 2025년 쥐를 대상으로 한 연구는 미세플라스틱이 뇌를 통과해 이동하며 혈관을 막는 것을 보여주었다.) 이러한 건강 위험의 전체 스펙트럼이 아직 완전히 분류되지는 않았지만, 최근의 임상 및 실험실 결과에서 얻은 상당한 데이터는 시급한 규제 조치를 위한 설득력 있는 근거를 제공한다.

어휘

- pervasive 만연한, 퍼지는
- penetration 침투, 관통
- circulating 순환하는, 돌고 있는
- confirmed 확인된, 입증된
- presence 존재, 출현
- accumulation 축적, 누적
- inflammatory 염증의, 염증을 일으키는
- mounting 증가하는, 커져가는
- vessel 혈관, 도관

18 [독해 – 순서 배열] ▶③

정답 해설

주어진 글은 AI의 발전으로 인해 '의식'이라는 오래된 철학적 질문이 시급한 과학적 탐구 과제로 부상했음을 알린다. (C)는 "이 탐구"라는 표현으로 제시문을 자연스럽게 이어받으며, 의식 연구가 단순한 학문적 호기심을 넘어 윤리적·규제적 판단을 위해 필수임을 강조한다. 이어서 (A)는 (C)에서 제기된 '생물학적 기반에 대한 이해'의 필요성을 구체화하며, 과학자들이 의식과 관련된 신경적 신호를 찾는 연구, 즉 측정 가능한 벤치마크를 마련하려는 노력을 설명한다. 마지막으로 (B)는 "그러나"라는 연결어를 통해 (A)의 논의를 전환시키며, 이렇게 마련된 벤치마크조차 비생물학적 시스템인 AI에는 적용하기 어렵다는 근본적 문제를 제기하며 마무리한다. 따라서 글의 순서로 가장 적절한 것은 ③이다.

해석

인공지능, 특히 인간의 대화와 추론 방식을 모방하는 시스템의 급속한 발전은, 오랫동안 철학적 논제로 여겨졌던 의식의 본질이라는 질문을 시급한 과학적 탐구의 영역으로 끌어올렸다.

(C) 이제 이 문제는 더 이상 이론적 논의에 그치지 않는다. 인공지능이 사회 곳곳에 깊이 통합되면서, 이러한 기술이 주관적 경험을 가질 가능성이 있는지 파악하는 일은 윤리적·규제적 차원에서 매우 중요해졌다. 이를 위해서는 인간 의식의 생물학적 기반에 대한 이해가 필요하다.

(A) 이러한 이유로 과학자들은 의식과 연관된 신경 신호를 찾아내기 위한 연구를 강화하고 있다. 인간에게서 이러한 패턴을 규명함으로써, 의식을 측정할 수 있는 기준을 마련하고자 하는 것이다.

(B) 그러나 여전히 중요한 문제가 남아 있다. 그러한 기준점이 있다 하더라도, 실리콘 기반 시스템은 생물학적 뇌와 매우 다르게 작동하기 때문에 이를 AI에 적용하는 것은 어렵다.

어휘

- rapid 빠른, 급격한
- mimic 모방하다, 흉내 내다
- philosophical 철학적인, 이론적인
- embedded 내재된, 깊게 자리 잡은
- possess 소유하다, 가지다
- conscious 의식적인, 자각하는
- establish 설립하다, 확립하다
- benchmark 기준점, 표준
- operate 작동하다, 기능하다

19 [독해 – 빈칸 추론] ▶③

정답 해설

이 글은 '진정한 경청'이 얼마나 높은 인지적 노력을 요구하는가를 설명하고 있다. 빈칸은 문장의 주어 자리이며 뒤의 "심오한 수준의 인지적 훈련을 요구한다"는 서술어와 자연스럽게 연결되어야 한다. 본문에서는 먼저 '듣기'를 단순하고 수동적인 생리적 과정으로, '경청'을 능동적이고 심리적인 과정으로 대조한다. 이어서 진정한 경청을 위해서는 우리가 가진 '내적 독백', 즉 뇌가 자동적으로 생성하는 판단·반박·기억을 일시적으로 멈추고, 나아가 자아와 인지적 편향을 침묵시키는 의도적 자기 억제가 필요하다고 강조한다. 따라서 밑줄 친 부분에 들어갈 말로 가장 적절한 것은 ③이다.

해석

진정성 있고 적극적인 경청에 참여하려면 심오한 수준의 인지적 규율이 필요하다. 대부분의 사람들은 청각을 듣는 것과 동일시하지만, 이는 근본적으로 다른 과정이다. 청각은 수동적인 생리적 행위인 반면, 진정한 경청은 능동적인 심리적 행위이다. 이는 뇌가 자연스럽게 생성하는 끊임없는 판단, 반박 및 관련 기억의 흐름인 자신의 내적 독백을 일시적으로 중단할 것을 요구한다. 이러한 내적 소음은 종종 화자의 실제 메시지를 흐리게 한다. 따라서 진정한 이해를 달성하려면 화자의 의도한 의미보다는 화자의 의도에 전적으로 초점을 맞춘 자아와 인지적 편견을 침묵시켜야 한다. 이러한 의도적인 자기 억제 행위는 단순히 청각 신호를 처리하는 것보다 훨씬 더 많은 세금을 부과한다.

① 대중 연설 불안을 극복하려면
② 다양한 그룹 내에서 합의 구축하려면
③ 진정성 있고 적극적인 경청에 참여하려면
④ 설득력 있는 주장을 공식화하려면

어휘

- profound 깊은, 심오한
- equate 동일시하다
- passive 수동적인, 소극적인
- physiological 생리적인
- psychological 심리적인
- suspend 중단하다, 보류하다
- monologue 독백, 혼잣말
- rebuttal 반박, 반론
- interpretation 해석, 설명
- deliberate 의도적인, 신중한
- taxing 힘든, 고된
- auditory 청각의, 소리의

난이도 중

정답 해설

이 글은 연말에 소비자들이 과소비에 빠지는 심리적 메커니즘을 설명하고 있다. 본문은 과소비의 원인을 한편으로는 즉각적 만족을 추구하는 내재적 충동, 다른 한편으로는 소매업자의 판촉 전략과 물질적 선물로 애정을 보여야 한다는 외부적 압박으로 제시한다. 빈칸이 포함된 마지막 문장은 이러한 "내적 충동과 외적 압박의 결합"에 소비자가 굴복했을 때 나타나는 결과를 요약하는 자리다. 사회적 기대를 충족시키기 위한 단기적 인정 욕구를 재정 안정이라는 장기 목표보다 앞세우게 되면, 결국 예산을 초과하는 지출로 이어지고, 이는 곧 단기적 사회적 인정을 우선하다가 빚을 지게 되는 상황으로 귀결된다. 따라서 밑줄 친 부분에 들어갈 말로 가장 적절한 것은   이다.

해석

연말연시 시즌은 축제 분위기와 함께 역설적인 소비자 불안감의 급증을 유발하는 경우가 많다. 관대함에 동기부여를 받았지만 많은 사람들이 과도한 지출에 대한 타고난 충동의 희생양이 된다. 전문가들은 선물의 즉각적이고 가시적인 만족은 종종 금융 안정이라는 추상적이고 장기적인 목표를 무색하게 만든다고 지적한다. 이러한 인지적 편향은 외부 요인에 의해 더욱 악화된다. 소매업체는 긴급감을 조성하는 프로모션을 전략적으로 배포하여 원래 예산을 초과하는 지출을 장려한다. 또한 자재를 통해 애정을 표현하려는 암묵적인 사회적 기대가 있다. 결과적으로 많은 소비자가 내부 충동과 외부 압력의 혼합에 굴복하여 단기적인 사회적 검증을 우선시하여 빚을 쌓게 된다.

물질적 소유보다 경험을 더 우선시하다
새해를 맞아 더 엄격한 예산 관리 방식을 채택하다
비금전적인 방식으로 애정을 표현하려고 한다
단기적인 사회적 검증을 우선시하여 빚을 쌓게 된다

어휘

trigger 유발하다, 촉발하다
paradoxical 역설적인, 모순된
fall prey to   의 희생양이 되다
tangible 구체적인, 실질적인
overshadow 압도하다,   를 덮어버리다
deploy 배치하다, 활용하다
expenditure 지출, 비용
implicit 암묵적인, 내포된
succumb 굴복하다
adopt 채택하다, 입양하다
affection 애정, 호감
validation 인정, 확증

제7회 모의고사

01 ③	02 ②	03 ④	04 ②	05 ④
06 ②	07 ④	08 ③	09 ②	10 ②
11 ②	12 ④	13 ④	14 ②	15 ①
16 ②	17 ②	18 ②	19 ④	20 ①

01 [어휘 – 빈칸]　　　　▶ ③

난이도 중

정답 해설

승진이 객관적인 성과 지표에 따라 이루어진 것이 아니라는 점과, 그로 인해 직원들이 깊은 좌절감을 느꼈다는 점을 고려하면, 승진이 '임의적인' 기준에 따라 이루어졌다는 내용이 자연스럽다. 따라서 밑줄 친 부분에 들어갈 말로 가장 적절한 것은 ③이다.

해석

> 승진이 객관적인 성과 지표가 아니라 <u>임의적인</u> 기준에 좌우된다는 사실을 깨닫자 직원들은 좌절감을 느꼈다.

어휘

★ arbitrary 임의적인, 제멋대로인, 독단적인
● logical 논리적인, 타당한
● impartial 공정한
● cautious 조심스러운, 신중한

02 [어휘 – 빈칸]　　　　▶ ②

난이도 중

정답 해설

새로운 정책이 실질적인 이익 없이 업무 부담만 증가시킬 것이라는 직원들의 우려로 보아, 해당 정책의 도입을 '꺼리고' 있다는 내용이 자연스럽다. 따라서 밑줄 친 부분에 들어갈 말로 가장 적절한 것은 ②이다.

해석

> 많은 직원들은 그 정책이 실질적인 이익 없이 업무량만 늘릴 것이라 우려하여 도입을 <u>꺼렸다.</u>

어휘

★ reluctant 꺼리는, 마지못한, 주저하는
● eager 열렬한, 간절히 바라는, 열심인
● qualified 자격이 있는
● composed 침착한, 차분한

03 [문법 – 빈칸]　　　　▶ ④

난이도 중

정답 해설

④ **[적중포인트 082] 관계대명사의 선행사와 문장 구조**

빈칸은 명사를 수식하는 수식어 자리이다. 수식어 자리에 쓰일 수 있는 관계대명사는 선행사에 따라 달라지는데 사람을 수식하며 주어가 없는 불완전한 절을 이끄는 것은 주격 관계대명사 who가 적절하다. 따라서 밑줄 친 부분에 들어갈 말로 가장 적절한 것은 ④이다.

해석

> 최근 여론조사에 따르면 '조용한 사직'이 특히 상사로부터 인정받지 못한다고 느끼는 젊은 직원들 사이에서 추세로 남아 있음을 보여준다.

04 [생활영어 – 빈칸]　　　　▶ ②

난이도 하

정답 해설

Ben이 학자금 대출을 갚기 위해 투잡을 하며 지쳐 있는 상황이다. 빈칸 뒤에서 Ben이 감사 인사를 전하는 것을 보면, Anna는 그의 노력을 인정하면서도 건강을 걱정하는 따뜻한 위로와 조언을 건넸음을 짐작할 수 있다. 따라서 밑줄 친 부분에 들어갈 말로 가장 적절한 것은 ②이다.

해석

> Anna: 안녕, Ben! 이번 주 금요일에 저녁 먹을 시간 있어?
> Ben: 그러고 싶은데, Anna. 안 돼. 금요일 밤에는 배달 일을 해야 해.
> Anna: 또? 주말마다 계속 두 번째 일을 하는 것 같아. 너 정말 지쳤겠구나.
> Ben: 진짜 그래. 그런데 학자금 대출을 좀 더 빨리 갚으려고 하는 거야. 부업으로 버는 돈이 도움이 돼.
> Anna: 정말 대단한데, 그래도 몸은 좀 챙겨. 번아웃 오지 않게.
> Ben: 고마워, Anna. 큰 힘이 된다. 일요일에는 제대로 좀 쉬어볼게.

① 그 부업이 더 돈을 많이 준다면 본업을 그만둬야지.
② 정말 대단한데, 그래도 몸은 좀 챙겨. 번아웃 오지 않게.
③ 그냥 부모님께 돈을 빌리면 되잖아?
④ 네가 나를 만나기 싫어서 핑계 대는 거라고 생각해.

어휘

• grab 붙잡다, (재빨리) 먹다
• gig (특히 임시로 하는) 일[직장]
• pay off (빚을) 모두 갚다, (노력이) 결실을 맺다
• extra 추가의, 여분의

05 [생활영어 – 빈칸]　　　　▶ ④

난이도 하

정답 해설

B가 믿고 공유하려던 기사가 가짜 뉴스일 수 있다고 A가 지적한 상황에서, 빈칸에는 B가 스스로 속았다는 사실을 깨닫고 당황하거나 부끄러움을 드러내는 말이 자연스럽게 이어져야 한다. 뒤에서 A가 "누구나 속을 수 있다"고 위로하며 "더 비판적으로 보자"고 조언하는 흐름을 볼 때, 이러한 반응과 가장 잘 맞는 선택지는 자신의 경솔함을 인정했음을 짐작할 수 있다. 따라서 밑줄 친 부분에 들어갈 말로 가장 적절한 것은 ④이다.

해석

> A: 과학자들이 일주일 만에 암을 치료하는 식물을 발견했다는 기사 봤어?
> B: 정말? 대단한데! 당장 가족 단톡방에 공유해야겠다.
> A: 잠깐만. 내가 찾아보니까 출처가 이름도 없는 블로그야. 주요 의학 학술지들은 증거가 전혀 없다고 하더라.
> B: <u>아, 뉴스에 너무 몰두해서 그걸 확인하지 못했어.</u>
> A: 누구나 속을 수 있어. 이런 '기적' 같은 주장은 사람들이 믿고 싶어 해서 더 빨리 퍼지거든. 그래서 더 비판적으로 볼 필요가 있어.
> B: 맞아. 글 삭제할게.

① 내가 그 의학 학술지를 더 일찍 구독했어야 했는데.
② 그럴 리 없어. 우리 이모가 이미 해봤는데 효과 있었다고 했어.
③ 난 주류 언론을 믿지 않아. 그 블로그가 아마 맞을 거야.
④ 아, 뉴스에 너무 몰두해서 그걸 확인하지 못했어.

어휘

• claim 주장하다, 요구하다
• incredible 믿을 수 없는, 놀라운
• journal 학술지, 정기 간행물
• evidence 증거, 근거
• convincing 설득력 있는, 믿을 만한
• mainstream 주류의
• foolish 어리석은, 바보 같은

난이도 하

정답해설

이 글은 디지털 환경에서 퍼지는 허위 정보의 문제점을 지적하고, 이를 해결하기 위한 방안으로 시민들의 디지털 분별력을 높이는 캠페인을 소개하고 있다. 따라서 글의 제목으로 가장 적절한 것은   이다.
현대 미디어에서 알고리즘의 역할
디지털 문해력을 통한 시민 사회의 회복력 강화
급변하는 디지털 시대에 적응하기
디지털 허위정보로부터 민주주의를 보호하기

07 [독해   세트형 문항(홈페이지 게시글   내용 불일치)]   ▶

난이도 중

정답해설

우리는 검열을 지지하지 않으며, 대신 정보 소비자인 개인을 스스로 판단할 수 있도록 강화하는 것을 목표로 한다고 언급하고 있다. 따라서 윗글의 내용과 일치하지 않는 것은   이다.

오답해설

디지털 정보가 지배하는 시대에, 온라인 콘텐츠를 비판적으로 평가하는 능력은 단순한 기술이 아니라 시민 참여에 필수적인 요소라고 언급하고 있으므로 글의 내용과 일치한다.
알고리즘으로 구성된 뉴스피드는 기존의 신념을 강화하고 다양한 관점에 대한 노출을 방해함으로써 흔히 반향실 효과를 만들어낸다고 언급하고 있으므로 글의 내용과 일치한다.
"시민 디지털 계획"은 시민들에게 디지털 분별력을 기르는 데 필요한 필수 도구를 제공하기 위해 만들어진 캠페인이라고 언급하고 있으므로 글의 내용과 일치한다.

해석

디지털 문해력을 통한 시민 사회의 회복력 강화

디지털 정보가 지배하는 시대에, 온라인 콘텐츠를 비판적으로 평가하는 능력은 단순한 기술이 아니라 시민 참여에 필수적인 요소입니다. 알고리즘으로 구성된 뉴스피드는 기존의 신념을 강화하고 다양한 관점에 대한 노출을 방해함으로써 흔히 반향실 효과를 만들어냅니다. 이러한 환경은 가짜 정보가 확산되기에 아주 좋은 온상이 되며, 이 가짜 정보는 여론을 조작하기 위해 정식 뉴스 매체의 형식을 의도적으로 흉내 냅니다.

"시민 디지털 계획"은 시민들에게 디지털 분별력을 기르는 데 필요한 필수 도구를 제공하기 위해 만들어진 캠페인입니다. 우리의 워크숍은 출처 검증, 신뢰할 만한 매체와의 교차 확인, 그리고 선전에 담긴 미묘한 신호를 파악하는 방법에 초점을 맞춥니다. 우리는 디지털 문해력을 갖춘 시민들이 민주적 담론이 약화되는 것을 막아낼 가장 강력한 방어선이라고 믿습니다. 우리는 검열을 지지하지 않으며, 대신 정보 소비자인 개인을 스스로 판단할 수 있도록 강화하는 것을 목표로 합니다.

어휘

necessity 필요성, 필수품
proliferation 급증, 확산
curated 선별된, 구성된
impede 방해하다
mimic 모방하다, 흉내 내다
discernment 분별력, 판단력
verification 확인, 검증
cross-reference 교차 검증하다
reputable 평판 좋은
robust 강건한, 튼튼한
censorship 검열

08 독해   단일형 문항(안내문   내용 불일치)   ▶

난이도 중

정답해설

서부 해안의 평균 가격은 갤런당 4.18달러로 가장 높았으며, 이는 2025년 10월보다 3.9% 상승한 수치라고 언급하고 있다. 따라서 윗글의 내용과 일치하지 않는 것은   이다.

오답해설

2026년 10월, 일반 자동차 휘발유의 전국 평균 가격은 갤런당 3.06달러였다고 언급하고 있으므로 글의 내용과 일치한다.
이 가격은 2026년 9월보다 3.3% 하락한 가격이라고 언급하고 있으므로 글의 내용과 일치한다.
걸프 해안의 평균 가격은 갤런당 2.62달러로 가장 낮았으며, 이는 2025년 10월보다 3.2% 하락한 수치라고 언급하고 있으므로 글의 내용과 일치한다.

해석

교통국 통계 보도 자료

날짜: 2026년 11월 4일

교통통계국(BTS)은 2026년 10월의 월간 자동차 연료 가격을 발표했습니다. 2026년 10월, 일반 자동차 휘발유의 전국 평균 가격은 갤런당 3.06달러였습니다. 이 가격은 2026년 9월보다 3.3% 하락했으며 2025년 10월과 비교하면 2.5% 하락한 가격입니다.

지역별로 일반 휘발유의 평균 가격은 크게 달랐습니다. 서부 해안의 평균 가격은 갤런당 4.18달러로 가장 높았으며, 이는 2025년 10월보다 3.9% 상승한 수치입니다. 반면 걸프 해안의 평균 가격은 갤런당 2.62달러로 가장 낮았으며, 이는 2025년 10월보다 3.2% 하락한 수치입니다.

2026년 10월 2번 디젤유의 평균 가격은 3.68달러로 2026년 9월보다 1.8% 하락했습니다.

2026년 10월 전국 평균 휘발유 가격은 갤런당 3.06달러였다.
2026년 10월 전국 평균 휘발유 가격은 전월 대비 하락했다.
지역별 비교에서 서부 해안의 휘발유 가격은 두 번째로 높은 수준이었다.
걸프 해안은 평균 휘발유 가격이 가장 낮은 지역이었다.

어휘

release 발표하다, 공개하다
average 평균, 평균의
vary 달라지다, 다르게 나타나다
represent 나타내다, 의미하다
previous 이전의
regional 지역의
comparison 비교

09 [문법   밑줄]   ▶

난이도 중

정답해설

[적중포인트 079] 명사절 접속사의 구분과 특징
이 자리는 문장 전체의 주어 역할을 하는 명사절 자리이다. 밑줄 뒤의 절을 보면 동사 concerns 앞에 주어가 없는 불완전한 구조임을 알 수 있다. 명사절 접속사 that은 뒤에 완전한 문장이 올 때만 쓰일 수 있는 반면, 관계대명사 what은 선행사를 포함하여 '   하는 것'이라는 의미로 쓰이며 뒤에 주어나 목적어가 빠진 불완전한 절을 이끈다. 따라서 밑줄 친 부분의 that을 what으로 고쳐야 한다.

오답해설

[적중포인트 014] 형용사와 부사의 차이
부사는 명사를 제외한 문장 성분이나 문장 전체를 수식할 수 있다. 이 문장에서 clearly는 'is a significant improvement'라는 서술 전체를 수식하는 문장 부사적 역할을 한다. 따라서 밑줄 친 부분은 올바르게 쓰였다.

[적중포인트 065] 조동사 뒤의 동사원형과 조동사의 부정형
조동사 뒤에는 항상 동사원형을 써야 한다. 따라서 밑줄 친 부분은 올바르게 쓰였다.

[적중포인트 055] 감정 분사와 분사형 형용사
hired는 '고용된'의 의미로 쓰인 분사형 형용사로 뒤에 명사를 수식한다. 따라서 밑줄 친 부분은 올바르게 쓰였다.

해석

새로운 정책은 회사의 안전 기준을 분명히 크게 개선한 조치이다. 경영진이 가장 우려하는 것은 직원들이 새로운 지침에 얼마나 빨리 적응할 것인가이다. 원활한 전환을 위해 회사는 새로 채용된 모든 직원들을 대상으로 추가 교육 시간을 제공할 계획이다.

10 [문법 – 밑줄] ▶②

난이도 중

정답 해설

② **[적중포인트 080] 부사절 접속사의 구분과 특징 ★★★☆☆**
despite는 전치사로 뒤에 명사가 온다. 뒤에 동사를 포함한 절을 이끄는 것은 접속사이다. 따라서 밑줄 친 부분의 despite를 although로 고쳐야 한다.

오답 해설

① **[적중포인트 082] 관계대명사의 선행사와 문장 구조 ★★★★☆**
앞의 명사(new electrode material)를 보충 설명하는 계속적 용법으로 쓰였고, 관계대명사 that은 계속적 용법(콤마 뒤)으로 사용할 수 없으므로 which를 써야 한다. 따라서 밑줄 친 부분은 올바르게 쓰였다.

③ **[적중포인트 056] 여러 가지 분사구문 ★★★★★**
'if successful'은 'if this research is successful'에서 주어와 be동사가 생략된 형태로, 문법적으로 올바른 조건절 축약이다. 따라서 밑줄 친 부분은 올바르게 쓰였다.

④ **[적중포인트 093] 원급, 비교급, 최상급 강조 부사 ★★☆☆☆**
'much'가 비교급 'lighter'를 수식하는 강조 부사로 쓰였다. 따라서 밑줄 친 부분은 올바르게 쓰였다.

해석

연구자들은 초기 안정성을 보인 새로운 전극 소재를 시험하고 있으며, 이 프로젝트가 작년에야 시작되었음에도 불구하고, 연구팀은 기존의 방법으로는 달성하기 어려운 성과를 거두었다. 이 연구는 성공한다면, 화석 연료에 대한 우리의 의존도를 크게 줄일 수 있다. 이 새로운 소재는 흑연보다 훨씬 가볍다.

11 [독해 – 세트형 문항(전자메일 – 목적)] ▶②

난이도 하

정답 해설

이 이메일은 SLA에 명시된 서비스 가동 시간 기준(99.9%)을 실제 측정값(99.5%)이 충족하지 못했다는 점을 지적하며 이를 계약 위반으로 밝히고 있다. 또한 문제의 원인과 재발 방지 방안을 포함한 시정 조치를 공식적으로 요청하고 있다. 따라서 글의 목적으로 가장 적절한 것은 ②이다.
① 분기별 서비스 지표의 정확성을 확인하려고
② 계약 위반을 보고하고 시정 조치를 요청하려고
③ 서비스 수준 계약(SLA) 조건의 개정을 요청하려고
④ 향후 서비스 성과 개선을 제안하려고

12 [독해 – 세트형 문항(전자메일 – 유의어)] ▶④

난이도 하

정답 해설

밑줄 친 'investigate'는 '조사하다, 살피다'의 뜻으로, 이와 문맥상 가장 가까운 의미는 ④ 'examine(조사하다, 검사하다)'이다.

오답 해설

① assign 맡기다, 배정하다
② incorporate 통합시키다, 통합하다, 설립하다, 포함하다
③ calculate 계산하다, 산출하다

해석

수신인: legal@innovatecorp.com
발신인: contracts@synergytech.com
날짜: 2026년 12월 7일
제목: 계약 관련 건

InnovateCorp 법무팀 귀하,

본 이메일은 2025년 1월 15일자 서비스 수준 계약(SLA) 제4조 B항에 규정된 바와 같이, 당사가 확인한 3분기 서비스 가동 시간 지표에 관한 중대한 불일치 사항을 공식적으로 제기하기 위한 것입니다. 당사의 내부 모니터링 로그에 따르면 서비스 가동률은 99.5%로 나타났으며, 이는 계약상 의무화된 99.9%에 미치지 못하는 수치입니다.

이러한 편차는 SLA 위반에 해당하며 운영 작업 속도에 상당한 영향을 미쳤습니다. 이 문제를 내부적으로 조사하고 중단 원인과 재발 방지를 위한 개선 조치를 설명하는 공식 보고서를 제공해 주시기를 요청드립니다. 우리는 신속하고 투명한 해결책이 우리의 파트너십을 지속하는 데 매우 중요하다고 믿습니다.

진심으로,
SynergyTech 계약 부서

어휘

• discrepancy 불일치, 차이
• identify 확인하다, 식별하다
• stipulated 규정된, 명시된
• mandated 의무화된, 규정된
• deviation 벗어남, 이탈
• breach 위반, 침해
• tangibly 명백하게, 실질적으로
• downtime 정지 시간, 가동 중단 시간
• prompt 즉각적인, 신속한
• extend 연장하다
• corrective 시정의, 수정의
• exceptional 뛰어난, 예외적인

13 [독해 – 중심 내용 추론(주제)] ▶④

난이도 중

정답 해설

이 글은 항생제 내성 '슈퍼버그'가 심각한 보건상의 위협이라는 점을 먼저 밝힌다. 이어 이러한 위기가 거의 잊혀졌던 치료법인 '파지 요법'의 재부상을 촉진했다고 설명한다. 파지는 특정 박테리아만을 표적으로 삼기 때문에 광범위 항생제에 비해 부작용이 적고 정밀성이 높다는 장점이 있다. 서구에서는 한때 사용이 중단되었지만, 현재는 항생제 내성 문제를 해결하기 위한 유력한 대안으로 다시 검토되고 있다는 점을 강조한다. 따라서 글의 주제로 가장 적절한 것은 ④이다.

해석

항생제 내성 '슈퍼버그'의 증가는 기존 치료법의 효과를 약화시키며 전 세계적으로 큰 건강 위협이 되고 있다. 이러한 도전 과제는 파지 요법이라는 오래된 의학적 접근 방식에 대한 관심을 다시 불러일으켰다. 파지는 유익한 미생물과 유해한 미생물을 모두 해치는 광범위한 항생제와 달리 박테리아를 표적으로 삼아 죽이는 바이러스이다. 이러한 정밀도는 숙주의 미생물군집에 대한 의도치 않은 손상을 줄여준다. 한때 서구에서는 간과되었지만 파지 요법은 동유럽에서 지속적으로 개발되어 현재 전 세계적으로 항균 내성에 대한 유망한 도구로 재고되고 있다.

① 파지 사용 증가로 인한 슈퍼버그 확산
② 박테리아의 항생제 내성 메커니즘
③ 파지가 슈퍼버그 확산에 기여하는 방식
④ 슈퍼버그에 대응하기 위한 파지 치료의 재부상

어휘

• antibiotic-resistant 항생제에 내성이 있는
• superbug 슈퍼버그(항생제로 쉽게 제거되지 않는 박테리아)
• weakening 약화시키는
• conventional 전통적인, 기존의
• broad-spectrum 광범위한
• precision 정밀함, 정확성
• overlook 간과하다
• promising 유망한, 촉망되는; 조짐이 좋은
• collateral 부수[부차]적인, 이차적인
• combat 싸우다, 방지하다

14 [독해 – 단일형 문항(안내문 – 내용 일치)] ▶ ②

정답 ②

난이도 하

정답 해설

'제출 안내 사항' 부분에서 모든 의견을 이메일로 제출해야 한다고 명시되어 있다. 따라서 윗글의 내용과 일치하는 것은 ②이다.
① 공개 의견 수렴 기간은 설문조사 전에 시작된 것이다.
② 의견은 이메일을 통해서만 접수된다.
③ 익명을 유지한 채로 의견을 보낼 수 있는 선택지가 있다.
④ 제출된 의견은 별다른 조건 없이 모두 비공개로 처리된다.

오답 해설

① 이번 의견 수렴이 2026 글로벌 벤치마크 정책 설문조사 결과 발표 이후에 진행된 절차라고 명시되어 있으므로 글의 내용과 일치하지 않는다.
③ '제출 안내 사항'에 따르면 의견 제출 시 이름과 소속 기관을 반드시 기재해야 한다고 명시되어 있으므로 글의 내용과 일치하지 않는다.
④ '참고' 문구에서 이메일 본문에 비공개 요청을 명시하지 않는 한 모든 의견이 ISS 웹사이트에 공개될 수 있다고 밝히고 있으므로 글의 내용과 일치하지 않는다.

해석

ISS 거버넌스: 공개 의견 요청
날짜: 2026년 11월 3일

ISS 거버넌스는 2026년 벤치마크 정책 변경안에 대한 공개 의견 수렴 기간을 시작했다고 발표했습니다. 이는 2026 글로벌 벤치마크 정책 설문조사 결과 발표에 이어 진행되는 절차입니다.

의견 제출 기간은 2026년 11월 11일 오후 5시(미 동부시간)까지 유지됩니다.

제출 안내 사항:
• 모든 의견은 이메일(policy@issgovernance.com)로 제출해야 합니다.
• 제출 시 이름과 소속 기관을 반드시 기재해 주시기 바랍니다.

□ 참고: 모든 의견은 이메일 본문에서 비공개 요청을 명시하지 않는 한 ISS 웹사이트에 공개될 수 있습니다. ISS는 모든 종류의 의견을 환영하지만, 제안된 변경안에 대한 우려 사항을 중심으로 피드백을 제공하는 것을 권장합니다.

어휘

• announce 발표하다, 알리다
• commencement 시작, 개시
• benchmark 기준, 표준
• remain 남아 있다, 유지되다
• submission 제출, 제출물
• confidentiality 비밀 유지, 기밀성
• anonymously 익명으로, 작자[저자]미상으로
• confidential 기밀의, 비밀의

15 독해 – 단일형 문항(안내문 – 내용 일치) ▶ ①

난이도 중

정답 해설

'등록 안내' 부분 중 첫 번째에서 본 행사는 9구역 거주자만 참석할 수 있다고 명시되어 있다. 따라서 글의 내용과 일치하는 것은 ①이다.

오답 해설

② 이번 워크숍이 진행되는 장소는 '시청 의회 회의실 1층'으로 명시되어 있으므로 글의 내용과 일치하지 않는다.
③ '등록 안내' 부분 중 세 번째에서 현장 접수는 받지 않는다고 명시되어 있으므로 글의 내용과 일치하지 않는다.
④ 워크숍 종료 후 간단한 간식과 음료가 제공된다고만 언급되어 있을 뿐, 시작 전에 정식 식사가 제공된다는 내용은 제시되어 있지 않으므로 글의 내용과 일치하지 않는다.

해석

SAFE CITY 2026:
주민 안전 워크숍

일시
2026년 12월 13일(토) 오후 2시 ~ 오후 4시

장소
시청 의회 회의실 1층

배울 내용
• 새로운 'CitySafe' 긴급 대응 앱 사용 방법
• 스마트 홈 기기를 위한 사이버 보안 요령
• 거주 지역의 비상 대피 경로

등록 안내
• 본 행사는 9구역 거주자만 참석할 수 있습니다.
• 12월 10일까지 www.safecity.gov에서 온라인으로 등록해 주시기 바랍니다.
• 현장 접수는 받지 않습니다. (사전 등록자만 참석 가능)

다과 제공
워크숍 종료 후 간단한 간식과 음료가 제공됩니다.

① 사전 등록한 9구역 거주자만 참석할 수 있다.
② 이번 워크숍은 지역 공원에서 진행되는 야외 안전 훈련에 주로 초점을 맞출 예정이다.
③ 온라인 등록 기한을 놓친 사람들을 위해 현장 등록이 가능하다.
④ 모든 참석자를 위해 워크숍 시작 전에 정식 식사가 제공된다.

어휘

• chamber (공공건물의) 회의실
• cybersecurity 사이버 보안
• evacuation 대피, 피난, 비우기
• district 구역, 지역
• walk-in 예약이 안 된, 예약이 필요 없는
• refreshment 다과, 가벼운 식사

16 [독해 – 문장 제거] ▶ ②

난이도 하

정답 해설

이 글은 소셜 미디어를 통해 멀리서 벌어지는 갈등과 재난 장면에 반복적으로 노출되는 젊은 성인들 사이에서 나타나는 '대리 외상'을 설명하고 있다. ①번 문장은 대리 외상이 직접적 충격이 아닌 타인의 고통에 대한 공감적 반응에서 비롯되며 불안·무기력·감정적 마비 같은 증상을 낳는다고 설명한다. ③번 문장은 필터링되지 않은 위기 이미지의 연속이 사용자의 안전감과 세계관을 어떻게 흔드는지 분석한다. ④번 문장은 이러한 지속적 노출이 심리적 자원을 소진시켜 전통적으로 고위험 직종에서 나타나던 외상 반응과 유사한 영향을 줄 수 있음을 논의한다. 그러나 ②번 문장은 소셜 미디어 알고리즘이 자극적인 콘텐츠를 우선 배치하는 기술적 작동 방식을 설명하는 데 집중해, 대리 외상의 심리적 메커니즘을 서술하는 내용과는 맞지 않다. 따라서 글의 흐름상 어색한 문장은 ②이다.

해석

최근 심리학 연구들은 소셜 미디어에서 그래픽 갈등 관련 콘텐츠에 많이 노출된 젊은 성인의 '대리 트라우마'를 조사하고 있다. ① 직접적인 트라우마와 달리 대리 트라우마는 타인의 고통에 공감하는 것에서 발생하며, 불안과 정서적 무감각 같은 증상을 만들어낸다. (② 소셜 미디어 플랫폼은 종종 참여 기반 알고리즘을 통해 선정적이거나 감정적으로 충전된 게시물을 증폭시킨다.) ③ 연구자들은 이러한 끊임없는 필터링되지 않은 위기 이미지가 젊은 사용자의 안전 감각을 약화시켜 세상을 더 위협적으로 만든다고 경고한다. ④ 이러한 해결책 없는 장시간 노출은 일선 직업에서 볼 수 있는 심리적 부담과 유사하게 감정 자원을 압도할 수 있다.

어휘

• psychological 심리학의, 심리적인
• vicarious 대리의, 간접적인
• expose 노출시키다, 드러내다
• empathize 공감하다
• numbness 무감각, 마비
• amplify 확대하다, 증폭시키다
• constant 끊임없는, 지속적인
• undermine 약화시키다
• prolonged 장기간의, 오래 지속되는
• overwhelm 압도하다, 어쩔 줄 모르게 만들다
• frontline 최전선의

17 [독해 – 문장 삽입]　　　　　　　　　　　　▶ ②

난이도 상

정답 해설

이 글은 AI가 노동시장에 미치는 영향, 특히 대규모 일자리 대체 가능성을 중심으로 펼쳐진다. ①번 뒤 문장에서는 AI가 최대 3억 개의 일자리를 대체할 수 있다는 포괄적이고 일반적인 주장이 먼저 제시된다. 주어진 문장은 그 뒤를 이어, 이러한 대체가 모든 직무에 동일하게 적용되는 것이 아니라, 특히 반복적이고 감정·사회적 지능이 덜 요구되는 업무에 집중된다는 점을 명확히 한다. 이어지는 ②번 뒤 문장은 예시로 시작하며, 방금 제시된 기준에 부합하는 고객 서비스 직종을 구체적 사례를 든다. 따라서 주어진 문장이 들어갈 위치로 가장 적절한 것은 ②이다.

해석

> 인공지능이 노동 시장에 미치는 경제적 영향은 격렬한 논쟁의 대상이며, 일부 보고서에서는 대규모 일자리 이동을 예측하고 있다. (①) 투자 은행 분석에 따르면 AI가 3억 개의 정규직 일자리를 대체하여 미국과 유럽에서 업무의 4분의 1을 자동화할 수 있을 것으로 예상된다. (② <u>이러한 대체는 균일하지 않으며, 주로 반복적이고 높은 감정적 또는 사회적 지능이 필요하지 않은 작업에 영향을 미친다.</u>) 예를 들어, 반복적인 문의를 처리하는 고객 서비스 담당자와 같은 역할은 이러한 자동화에 매우 취약하다. (③) 데이터 입력 및 스케줄링이 주요 업무인 많은 백오피스 및 관리 기능에도 동일한 논리가 적용된다. (④) 그러나 이러한 자동화는 새로운 일자리를 창출하고 상당한 생산성 향상을 촉진하여 고용에 미치는 순 효과를 복잡하게 만들 것으로 예상된다.

어휘

- substitution 대체, 치환
- uniform 균일한, 고른
- intense 강렬한, 치열한
- predict 예측하다
- displacement 대체, 축출, 내몰림
- susceptible 영향을 받기 쉬운, 민감한
- administrative 행정의
- primary 주요한, 기본적인
- complicate 복잡하게 만들다

18 [독해 – 순서 배열]　　　　　　　　　　　　▶ ②

난이도 중

정답 해설

주어진 글은 북시나이 지역에서 신왕국 시대의 군사 요새가 발견되었다는 사실을 소개하며 시작한다. 이어지는 (B)는 이러한 발견 직후 이루어진 초기 발굴 과정을 서술하며, 남쪽 벽의 규모와 방어탑 등 요새의 기본 구조를 처음으로 밝힌다. (A)는 "발굴이 진행되면서"라는 문구로 (B)의 후속 단계임을 분명히 하면서, 같은 남쪽 벽에서 발견된 추가 출입구와 서쪽 지역의 지그재그 구조 등 더 세부적인 건축 요소를 소개한다. 마지막으로 (C)는 "이 독특한 건축 설계"라는 표현을 통해 앞서 (B)와 (A)에서 언급된 구조적 특징들을 종합하여, 이러한 형태가 신왕국 군사 건축의 대표적 특징임을 설명하며 발견의 역사적·전략적 의의를 정리한다. 따라서 글의 순서로 가장 적절한 것은 ②이다.

해석

> 북시나이에 있는 이집트 고고학 사절단이 텔 알 카루바 유적지에서 중요한 발견을 발표했다: 신왕국 시대의 군사 요새이다.
> (B) 초기 작업에서는 약 105미터에 달하고 11개의 방어용 탑으로 보강된 남쪽 벽을 조사했는데, 이는 이 요새의 전략적 중요성을 시사한다.
> (A) 발굴이 진행되면서 같은 벽에서 2차 출입구가 발견되었고, 서쪽에는 군인들을 위한 주거 지역을 둘러싸고 있는 75미터의 지그재그 벽이 드러났다.
> (C) 이 지그재그 디자인은 신왕국 군사 건축의 특징이며, 건축가들이 이집트의 동쪽 국경을 방어하기 위해 사막 조건에 어떻게 적응했는지를 보여준다.

어휘

- archaeological 고고학의
- major 주요한, 큰
- excavation 발굴
- uncover 드러내다, 발굴하다
- likely 그럴듯한, 가능성 있는
- enclose 둘러싸다, 에워싸다
- span 걸치다[걸쳐 이어지다]
- architecture 건축 양식

- adapt 적응시키다, 조정하다
- border 국경, 경계

19 [독해 – 빈칸 추론]　　　　　　　　　　　　▶ ④

난이도 중

정답 해설

이 글은 감정에 휘둘리지 않고 감정적 충동을 이성적 판단에 종속시키는 능력이 전략적 힘의 핵심임을 설명한다. 전략적 판단에서 감정의 개입을 최소화해야 한다는 점을 일관되게 강조한다. 초반에서 "즉각적인 감정 반응은 영향력을 행사하는 데 가장 큰 장애물"이라고 못박으며, 감정이 판단을 흐리고 통제력과 예측력을 약화시킨다고 지적한다. 분노는 특히 파괴적이며, 적대감을 숨기고 우호적인 태도를 가장하는 편이 더 효과적이라고까지 말한다. 심지어 긍정적 감정도 타인의 숨은 의도를 보지 못하게 하는 위험 요소로 제시된다. 글 전체의 핵심은 감정을 이성적 계산 아래에 두는 능력, 즉 감정의 통제가 전략적 힘의 기초라는 것이다. 따라서 밑줄 친 부분에 들어갈 말로 가장 적절한 것은 ④이다.

해석

> <u>감정적 충동을 합리적 계산에 종속시키는 능력은 전략적 힘의 초석이다.</u> 즉각적인 감정적 반응은 영향력에 대한 가장 큰 장애물이며, 이는 자신의 감정을 표현함으로써 얻는 짧은 안도감을 능가하는 전술적 실수이다. 감정은 판단을 흐리게 하며, 일단 인지가 왜곡되면 적절한 절제력이나 선견지명을 가지고 행동할 수 없다. 분노는 특히 부식성이 있어 긴장을 고조시키고 상대방의 결의를 강화한다. 적대감을 드러내는 것보다 친근한 태도를 유지하는 것이 더 효과적인 경우가 많다. 긍정적인 감정도 다른 사람의 숨겨진 동기를 무시할 수 있기 때문에 위험할 수 있다. 진정한 숙달은 그 순간에서 한발 물러나, 야누스의 객관적인 관점으로 상황을 평가하는 것을 요구한다.

① 자신의 감정을 즉각적이고 투명하게 표현하기
② 동맹을 구축하기 위한 사랑과 애정의 함양
③ 자신의 판단에 근거해 신속하게 행동하려는 의지
④ 감정적 충동을 합리적 계산에 종속시키는 능력

어휘

- cornerstone 초석, 기초
- impediment 방해물, 장애
- tactical 전술적인
- cloud (기억력·판단력 등을) 흐리다
- distort 왜곡하다
- foresight 예지력, 앞을 내다보는 능력
- corrosive 부식성의, 점점 해로운
- escalate 확대되다, 격화되다
- opponent 상대, 반대자
- facade 외관, 겉모습
- detached 분리된, 냉정한
- cultivation 배양, 양성
- heightened 고조된, 강화된
- subordinate 종속시키다, 억누르다

난이도 중

정답 해설

이 글은 '편승 효과'가 어떻게 사람들의 판단을 흐리고 군중을 무비판적으로 따르게 만드는지를 설명한다. 본문은 편승 효과를 '많은 사람이 하기 때문에' 특정 행동이나 신념을 받아들이는 인지 편향으로 규정하며, 이 용어가 어떤 움직임이 성공적으로 보일 때 합류한다는 관용구에서 기원했다고 밝힌다. 마지막 문장은 이 효과가 정치 영역에서 특히 강하게 작동함을 보여 준다. 유권자들은 후보자의 정책적 일치 때문이 아니라, 편승 효과의 정의 그대로 '성공하는 편' 또는 '이기는 편'에 속하고자 하는 욕구 때문에 특정 후보를 지지하게 된다. 따라서 밑줄 친 부분에 들어갈 말로 가장 적절한 것은 ①이다.

해석

"편승 효과"는 개인이 특정 행동이나 신념을 채택하는 현상을 설명하는 인지 편향으로, 주로 많은 사람들이 그렇게 하기 때문에 발생한다. 이는 운동이 성공적으로 보일 때만 참여한다는 의미의 "시류에 편승하다"는 관용구에서 비롯된다. 이러한 "군중을 따라가는" 경향은 종종 선택의 근본적인 증거나 본질적인 장점에 대한 비판적인 검토 없이 발생한다. 아이디어에 대한 집착이 커지면 인지된 타당성이 증가하여 더 많은 사람들을 끌어들이는 피드백 루프가 만들어진다. 이 메커니즘은 모멘텀이 결정적일 수 있는 정치 분야에서 특히 강력하다. 어떤 후보자가 대중의 지지를 받고 있다고 인식될 때, 그들은 정책적 일치감이 아니라 <u>성공하거나 승리하는 쪽과 일치하려는</u> 욕구에 의해 결정이 좌우되는 유권자들을 끌어들인다.

① 성공하거나 승리하는 쪽과 일치하려는
② 그들의 독특하고 독립적인 정치적 의견을 표현하려는
③ 정책의 근본적인 증거를 비판적으로 검토하려는
④ 군중의 증가하는 기세에 저항하려는

어휘

• bandwagon effect 편승 효과
• cognitive bias 인지 편향
• adopt 채택하다, 받아들이다
• imply 암시하다, 의미하다
• underlying 근본적인, 기저의
• intrinsic 고유한, 본질적인
• adherence 고수, 집착, 지지
• validity 타당성, 정당성
• sway 흔들다, 영향을 미치다
• independent 독립적인
• momentum 추진력, 탄력

영어 정답 및 해설

제8회 모의고사

01 ④	02 ②	03 ③	04 ③	05 ④
06 ①	07 ②	08 ④	09 ①	10 ②
11 ②	12 ④	13 ②	14 ②	15 ③
16 ②	17 ③	18 ④	19 ④	20 ②

01 [어휘 – 빈칸]　　　　　　　　　　　▶ ④

난이도 중

정답 해설

회사가 데이터 유출 사고 이후 신중하게 작성한 사과문을 발표했다는 점에서, 여론의 비판을 '진정시키려'는 목적이 자연스럽다. 따라서 밑줄 친 부분에 들어갈 말로 가장 적절한 것은 ④이다.

해석

회사는 데이터 유출 사고 이후 여론의 비판을 <u>진정시키기</u> 위해 신중하게 작성된 사과문을 발표했다.

어휘

★ mollify 진정시키다, 달래다
● clarify 명확하게 하다, 깨끗하게[맑게] 하다
● belittle 폄하하다, 하찮게 만들다
● fabricate 조작하다, 날조하다, 제작[조립]하다

02 [어휘 – 빈칸]　　　　　　　　　　　▶ ②

난이도 중

정답 해설

건설 회사가 안전 기준을 준수하지 않았다는 이유로 현장 작업의 즉각적인 중단을 명령할 수 있는 권한을 가진 기관이어야 하므로, 지역 '당국'을 의미하는 내용이 자연스럽다. 따라서 밑줄 친 부분에 들어갈 말로 가장 적절한 것은 ②이다.

해석

건설 회사가 안전 기준을 준수하지 않았기 때문에, 지역 <u>당국</u>은 모든 현장 작업을 즉각 중단하라고 명령했다.

어휘

★ authority 당국, 권한, 권위, 재가
● regulation 규정, 규제, 단속
● coverage 보도[방송], 범위, 보급(률)
● component 부품, (구성) 요소

03 [문법 – 빈칸]　　　　　　　　　　　▶ ③

난이도 중

정답 해설

③ **[적중포인트 069] 다양한 도치 구문 ★★★★☆**

앞 문장의 내용이 긍정일 경우에는 so를, 부정일 경우에는 neither를 사용한 도치 구문으로 이어 쓴다. 이 문장에서 앞 문장은 긍정의 내용이므로 so did가 적절하다. 또한 문장에 주어와 동사가 각각 두 번 나타나 두 절이 연결되는 구조이므로 접속사 and가 반드시 필요하다. 따라서 밑줄 친 부분에 들어갈 말로 가장 적절한 것은 ③이다.

해석

관리자는 수정된 예산안을 즉시 승인했으며, 이전에 그 안건에 대해 여러 가지 우려를 제기했던 이사회 구성원들 또한 그렇게 했다.

04 [독해 – 단일형 문항(안내문 – 내용 일치)]　　　▶ ③

난이도 중

정답 해설

점검 기간 동안 모든 온라인 및 디지털 서비스 이용이 중단된다고 명시되어 있다. 따라서 글의 내용과 일치하는 것은 ③이다.
① 점검 중에는 일부 지점만 영향을 받는다.
② 점검 중에는 온라인 검색은 가능하다.
③ 공급 정지 기간 동안에는 디지털 데이터베이스에 대한 접근이 중단된다.
④ 점검 기간 동안에는 신규 등록을 완료할 수 없다.

오답 해설

① 이 계획된 작업 기간 동안 모든 도서관 지점이 일시적으로 영향을 받게 된다고 언급하고 있으므로 글의 내용과 일치하지 않는다.
② 점검 기간 동안 이용할 수 없는 서비스 중 하나로 '온라인 자료 검색(검색, 대출 연장, 자료 예약 포함)'이 명시되어 있으므로 글의 내용과 일치하지 않는다.
④ 점검 기간 동안 이용할 수 있는 서비스 중 하나로 '도서관 회원 등록'이 명시되어 있으므로 글의 내용과 일치하지 않는다.

해석

피닉스 공공도서관 시스템 – 점검 안내

피닉스 공공도서관(PPL)은 온라인 서비스를 개선·업그레이드하기 위한 전면적인 시스템 점검을 실시합니다. 이 계획된 공급 정지 기간 동안 모든 도서관 지점이 일시적으로 영향을 받게 됩니다.

점검 기간:
약 60시간 동안 모든 온라인 및 디지털 서비스 이용이 중단됩니다.
점검 기간 동안 이용할 수 없는 서비스:
• 온라인 자료 검색 (검색, 대출 연장, 자료 예약 포함)
• 전자책, 오디오북, 모든 디지털 데이터베이스
• 도서관 내 공용 컴퓨터 및 Wi-Fi
점검 기간 동안 이용할 수 있는 서비스:
• 실물 자료 대여 및 반납 (도서관 카드 필요)
• 도서관 회원 등록

참고로, 모든 PPL 지점은 11월 15일 토요일 정규 운영 시간에 운영됩니다.

어휘

• conduct 수행하다, 실시하다
• maintenance 유지보수, 점검
• scheduled 예정된
• outage 공급 정지 기간, 사용 불능, 정전
• temporarily 일시적으로
• approximately 대략, 약
• regular 규칙적인, 정기적인
• branch 지사, 분점
• registration 등록, 가입

난이도　하

정답해설

David는 다음 달 회사에 AI 도구가 도입되면서 자신의 역할이 사라질까 걱정하고 있다. 그러나 Sarah의 반응을 들은 뒤, David는 "당황할 필요 없다"며 AI 덕분에 반복적인 업무가 줄고 더 전략적인 일에 집중할 수 있다고 생각을 바꾸게 된다. 이는 Sarah가 AI를 '대체물'이 아닌 '도구'로 바라보도록 조언하며 긍정적인 측면을 강조했음을 짐작할 수 있다. 따라서 밑줄 친 부분에 들어갈 말로 가장 적절한 것은 ④이다.

해석

David: 안녕, Sarah. 잠깐 시간 있어? 회사가 다음 달에 도입하는 새 AI 도구 때문에 좀 불안해서.
Sarah: 안녕 David. 무슨 일 있어?
David: 방금 데모를 봤는데, 내가 보통 일주일 내내 만드는 데이터 분석 보고서의 거의 80%를 자동화하더라. 솔직히 말해, 내가 필요 없는 사람이 될까 봐 걱정돼.
Sarah: 네 기분 이해해. 하지만 AI를 대체물이 아니라 도구로 보려고 해봐.
David: 맞아. 당황해서는 안 되겠네. AI가 도입되면 단순 반복 업무는 줄어들고, 우리가 더 가치 있다고 생각하는 전략적 업무에 집중할 수 있게 될 거라고 생각해.
Sarah: 맞아. 이건 우리를 대체하려는 게 아니라, 능력을 업그레이드할 기회야.

① 스트레스가 된다는 건 알지만, 이번 변화는 고용 안정성에 심각한 영향을 미칠 수 있을 거야.
② 도입이 다음 달이므로, 그 영향에 대해 아직은 걱정할 필요가 없어.
③ 자동화는 여러 산업 전반에 걸쳐 피할 수 없는 흐름이 되었어.
④ 네 기분 이해해. 하지만 AI를 대체물이 아니라 도구로 보려고 해봐.

어휘

• anxious 불안한, 걱정하는
• roll out 출시하다, 도입하다
• redundant 불필요한, 쓸모없는
• replace 대신[대체]하다
• manually 수동으로

06 [생활영어 – 빈칸]　　　　　　　　　　　▶①

난이도　하

정답해설

A가 이번 주 내내 야근하는 B를 걱정하며 프로젝트 상황을 묻자, B는 빠듯한 마감과 계속 바뀌는 요구사항 때문에 압도되고 있다고 털어놓는다. A가 "너 완전히 지쳐 보인다"고 걱정하자, 이후 A가 "이렇게 계속 버티기는 어렵다"며 해결책을 제시하는 흐름을 볼 때, B 역시 자신이 지쳐 있다는 점을 인정하며 A의 말에 공감했음을 짐작할 수 있다. 따라서 밑줄 친 부분에 들어갈 말로 가장 적절한 것은 ①이다.

해석

A: 저기, 너 이번 주 내내 매일 밤 늦게까지 일하고 있던데. 새 프로젝트는 괜찮아?
B: 솔직히 말하면, 너무 벅차. 마감도 빠듯한데, 의뢰인이 계속 요구사항을 바꾸고 있어.
A: 정말 엄청 스트레스 받겠네. 식사 거르지 않도록 해. 완전히 지쳐 보인다.
B: 그런 것 같아. 요즘 내내 기운이 없고 집중도 잘 안 돼.
A: 매니저와 얘기해보는 게 좋겠어. 이렇게 무리하는 건 오래 못 버텨.
B: 네 말이 맞는 것 같아. 내일 그녀와 미팅을 잡아볼게.

① 그런 것 같아. 요즘 내내 기운이 없고 집중도 잘 안 돼.
② 걱정하지 마. 내일 아침까지는 다 끝낼 거야.
③ 나 괜찮아. 그냥 커피 한 잔만 더 마시면 돼.
④ 별거 아니야. 이런 압박은 익숙해.

어휘

• overwhelmed 압도된, 감당하기 힘든
• deadline 마감 기한
• skip 건너뛰다, 거르다

난이도　중

정답해설

밑줄 친 'neutrality'는 '중립성'의 뜻으로, 이와 문맥상 가장 가까운 의미는 ② 'objectivity(객관성)'이다.

오답해설

① accuracy 정확(도)
③ proficiency 능숙함
④ liability 책임, 의무, 부채

08 [독해 – 세트형 문항(홈페이지 게시글 – 목적)]　　▶④

난이도　하

정답해설

이 글은 국경없는의사회(MSF)의 기본적인 활동을 간단히 소개한 뒤, 이 조직을 움직이는 핵심 신조인 '공정성'과 '중립성'의 원칙을 구체적으로 설명하고 있다. 즉, MSF가 어떠한 정치적·군사적·종교적 이해관계에도 얽매이지 않고, 오로지 필요에 근거해 의료 지원을 제공한다는 점을 강조한다. 따라서 글의 목적으로 가장 적절한 것은 ④이다.
① 국경없는의사회(MSF)가 다른 국제 구호 단체들과 어떻게 다른지를 설명하려고
② 분쟁 지역에서 의료 지원을 제공하는 것의 중요성을 강조하려고
③ MSF가 분쟁에서 어느 한쪽 편도 들지 않는 이유를 알리려고
④ 이 단체의 기본 원칙을 명확하게 설명하려고

해석

국경없는의사회 (MSF)

국경없는의사회는 국제 인도주의 단체로, 위기에 처한 사람들, 자연재해나 인위적 재해의 피해자들, 그리고 무력 분쟁의 피해자들에게 의료 지원을 제공합니다. 이 조직은 어떠한 정치적·군사적·종교적 목적에도 독립적으로 운영됩니다.

우리 활동의 핵심 원칙 중 하나는 공정성입니다. 우리는 인종, 종교, 성별, 정치적 성향과 관계없이 오직 필요를 기준으로 지원을 제공합니다. 피해자에게 접근하는 것이 우리의 최우선 관심사이며, 다른 구호 단체들이 닿기 어려운 지역에 도달하기 위해 노력합니다. 또한 중립성의 원칙에 따라 분쟁에서 어느 편도 들지 않으며, 정치·인종·종교·이념적 논쟁에 관여하지 않습니다. 이러한 원칙 덕분에 우리는 분쟁에 참여한 모든 당사자의 신뢰를 얻고, 그렇지 않으면 접근이 불가능한 지역에서도 활동할 수 있습니다.

어휘

• humanitarian 인도주의적인
• man-made 인공의, 인위적인
• tenet 신조, 원칙
• irrespective of ~와 관계없이
• affiliation 소속, 가입
• strive 노력하다, 분투하다
• neutrality 중립성
• controversy 논쟁, 논란
• recruit 모집하다, 뽑다

09 [문법 – 밑줄]　　　　　　　　　　　▶①

난이도　중

정답해설

① [적중포인트 038] 시제 관련 표현 ★★★★☆
'~하자마자 …했다'의 의미로 쓸 때는 'No sooner + had 주어 p.p.+than 주어 +과거시제 동사'의 도치 구문으로 쓸 수 있다. 따라서 밑줄 친 부분의 has를 had로 고쳐야 한다.

오답해설

② [적중포인트 080] 부사절 접속사의 구분과 특징 ★★★☆☆
until은 시간 부사절을 이끄는 접속사이고, 그 뒤에 주어와 동사가 오는 완전한 절을 취하고 있다. 따라서 밑줄 친 부분은 올바르게 쓰였다.
③ [적중포인트 038] 시제 관련 표현 ★★★★☆
'~하자마자 …했다'의 의미로 쓸 때는 'Scarcely + had 주어 p.p. + when/before 주어 + 과거시제 동사'의 도치 구문으로 쓸 수 있다. 따라서 밑줄 친 부분은 올바르게 쓰였다.

④ [적중포인트 014] 형용사와 부사의 차이 ★★★★★
문맥상 동사(cheered)를 수식하는 것은 형용사가 아닌 부사이다. 따라서 밑줄 친 부분은 올바르게 쓰였다.

해석

경기가 시작되자마자 곧바로 폭우가 쏟아지기 시작했다. 선수들은 몸을 피하려 달려갔고, 관중들은 우산을 펼쳤다. 심판은 비가 멈출 때까지 경기를 중단하기로 결정했다. 모두가 날씨가 개기를 바라며 초조하게 기다렸다. 비가 멈추자마자 다시 해가 떠올랐다. 경기는 재개되었고, 관중들은 큰 소리로 환호했다.

10 [독해 – 세트형 문항(안내문 – 제목)] ▶②

난이도 중

정답 해설

이 글은 한국은행의 핵심 임무인 물가 안정을 중심으로, 경제 상황에 따라 기준금리를 조정하는 통화정책의 운용 방식을 설명한다. 먼저 기준금리가 물가, 성장률, 금융 안정 등을 종합적으로 고려해 결정되며 금융시장의 기준 역할을 한다고 제시한 뒤, 경기 과열기에는 금리 인상으로 수요를 억제하고 침체기에는 금리 인하로 소비·투자를 촉진하는 조절 기능을 설명한다. 따라서 글의 제목으로 가장 적절한 것은 ②이다.
① 한국 중앙은행 시스템의 역사
② 물가 안정을 위한 유연한 기준금리 조정
③ 모든 상황에서 높은 이자율을 유지하기
④ 경제 성장을 지원하는 데 있어 금리의 역할

11 [독해 – 세트형 문항(안내문 – 내용 일치)] ▶②

난이도 중

정답 해설

금융통화위원회는 기준금리를 결정할 때 인플레이션 압력, 경제 성장 추세, 금융시장 안정성 등 경제 전반에 대한 종합적인 분석을 수행한다고 언급하고 있다. 따라서 윗글의 내용과 일치하는 것은 ②이다.
① 기준금리는 주로 고용 수준을 안정시키기 위해 조정된다.
② 금융통화위원회는 기준금리를 결정할 때 여러 경제 지표를 고려한다.
③ 경기가 과열될 때 기준금리는 이에 대응하여 인하된다.
④ 금리 조정의 주된 목적은 오직 단기적인 시장 변동에 대응하는 것이다.

오답 해설

① 기준금리는 시장금리의 기준점으로 작용하며, 금융 시스템의 유동성을 관리하는 핵심 정책 수단이라고 언급하고 있으므로 글의 내용과 일치하지 않는다.
③ 경기가 과열될 때는 과도한 차입을 억제하고 총수요를 진정시키기 위해 기준금리를 인상할 수 있다고 언급하고 있으므로 글의 내용과 일치하지 않는다.
④ 이러한 정책 조정의 궁극적인 목표는 안정적 틀 속에서 지속 가능한 경제성장을 이루는 것이라고 언급하고 있으므로 글의 내용과 일치하지 않는다.

해석

물가 안정을 위한 유연한 기준금리 조정

대한민국의 중앙은행인 한국은행의 가장 중요한 임무는 물가 안정 유지입니다. 금융통화위원회는 기준금리를 결정할 때 인플레이션 압력, 경제 성장 추세, 금융시장 안정성 등 경제 전반에 대한 종합적인 분석을 수행합니다. 기준금리는 시장금리의 기준점으로 작용하며, 금융 시스템의 유동성을 관리하는 핵심 정책 수단입니다.

경기가 과열될 때는 과도한 차입을 억제하고 총수요를 진정시키기 위해 기준금리를 인상할 수 있습니다. 반대로 경기 침체기에는 투자와 소비를 촉진하기 위해 금리를 인하합니다. 이러한 정책 조정의 궁극적인 목표는 안정적 틀 속에서 지속 가능한 경제성장을 이루는 것으로, 이를 통해 국가의 장기적인 경제적 안정과 번영을 도모합니다.

어휘

• foremost 가장 중요한[유명한], 맨 앞에 위치한
• price stability 물가 안정
• comprehensive 종합적인, 포괄적인
• liquidity 유동성
• curtail 줄이다, 억제하다
• downturn (매출 등의) 감소[하락], (경기) 하강[침체]
• flexible 탄력적인, 유연한
• adjustment 조정, 수정, 적응
• countermeasure 대책, 보호 조치

12 [문법 – 밑줄] ▶④

난이도 중

정답 해설

④ [적중포인트 021] 전치사가 필요 없는 대표 3형식 타동사 ★★★★☆
'접촉하다'의 의미인 contact는 3형식 타동사로 전치사 없이 바로 목적어를 취할 수 있으므로 전치사에 주의한다. 따라서 밑줄 친 부분의 to를 삭제해야 한다.

오답 해설

① [적중포인트 079] 명사절 접속사의 구분과 특징 ★★★★☆
앞에 형용사와 같은 선행 요소가 있고, 그 뒤에 주어와 동사가 모두 갖춰진 완전한 문장이 올 때에는 그 내용을 하나의 명사절로 연결해 주는 접속사 that이 적절하다. 따라서 밑줄 친 부분은 올바르게 쓰였다.
② [적중포인트 088] 전치사와 명사 목적어 ★★★☆☆
전치사는 뒤에 명사나 동명사를 목적어로 취할 수 있다. 따라서 밑줄 친 부분은 올바르게 쓰였다.
③ [적중포인트 014] 형용사와 부사의 차이 ★★★★★
make의 목적격 보어인 형용사(qualified)를 수식하는 것은 부사이다. 이 문장에서 well은 '제대로'의 의미인 부사로 쓰였다. 따라서 밑줄 친 부분은 올바르게 쓰였다.

해석

저는 저의 기술과 경험이 해당 직무에 적합한 지원자가 되게 한다고 확신합니다. 특히, 이전의 업무 경험은 문제 해결 능력을 강화함으로써 새로운 도전에 빠르게 적응할 수 있는 저의 역량을 키우는 데 기여해 왔습니다. 이러한 강점들은 귀 조직의 목표를 지원하는 데 있어 제가 제대로 자격을 갖추고 있음을 보여 줍니다. 추가로 필요한 정보가 있으시다면 언제든지 저에게 연락해 주시기 바랍니다.

13 독해 – 단일형 문항(안내문 – 내용 불일치)] ▶②

난이도 중

정답 해설

'입장' 부분에서 초청 언론과 VIP들은 우선 좌석이 제공되고 일반 관람객들은 입석 관람만 가능하다고 명시되어 있다. 따라서 글의 내용과 일치하지 않는 것은 ②이다.

오답 해설

① '장소' 부분에서 셔틀버스는 오전 9시 30분에 라스베이거스 시청에서 출발한다고 안내되어 있으므로 글의 내용과 일치한다.
③ '중요 안내 사항' 부분에서 사진 촬영은 허용되나, 영공 내 드론 사용은 엄격히 금지된다고 명시되어 있으므로 글의 내용과 일치한다.
④ '행사 일정' 중 오후 12시에 실시간 시험 운행을 하며 관람 무대에서 시청을 한다고 명시되어 있으므로 글의 내용과 일치한다.

해석

세계 첫 공연:
하이퍼루프 알파 제막식

교통의 미래를 직접 확인하세요

일시
2025년 12월 20일(토) 오전 11시 ~ 오후 2시

장소
네바다 사막 시험 시설
(셔틀버스는 오전 9시 30분에 라스베이거스 시청에서 출발합니다.)

행사 일정
• 오전 11시: CEO 기조 연설 및 기술 발표
• 오후 12시: 실시간 시험 운행 (관람 무대에서 시청)
• 오후 1시: 엔지니어링 팀과의 질의응답

입장
• 초청 언론 및 VIP: 우대석 제공
• 일반 관람객: 50달러 (입석 관람만 가능)

영공 내 드론 사용 금지!

① 행사가 시작되기 전에 셔틀버스가 라스베이거스 시청에서 출발할 것이다.
② 일반 관람객들에게는 행사 동안 지정 좌석이 제공될 것이다.
③ 행사에서는 사진 촬영이 허용되지만, 어떠한 경우에도 드론 조종은 허용되지 않는다.
④ 실시간 시험 운행은 지정된 관람 구역에서 볼 수 있다.

[어휘]
• premiere 첫 공연, 개봉
• unveiling 제막식, 첫 공개
• standing room 입석, 설 수 있는 자리
• waiver 면책, 포기
• ban 금(지)하다

14 [독해 – 문장 제거]　　▶ ③

[난이도] 중

[정답 해설]
이 글은 디지털 기술의 발달로 독서 방식이 '개인적 활동'에서 '사회적·상호작용적 활동'으로 변화했다는 점을 설명한다. ①번 문장에서는 디지털 기술로 인해 독서 습관이 변화했음을 제시하고, ②번 문장에서는 온라인 플랫폼을 통해 의견 공유와 토론이 가능해졌음을 설명한다. 이어 ④번과 마지막 문장은 이러한 변화로 독서가 더 사회적이고 역동적인 경험이 되었음을 정리하며 논지를 일관되게 이어 간다. 그러나 ③번 문장은 촉감적 이유로 종이책을 선호한다는 내용으로, '디지털 상호작용의 확대'라는 글의 핵심 논지와 직접적으로 연결되지 않는다. 따라서 흐름상 어색한 문장은 ③이다.

[해석]
과거에 독서는 주로 도서관이나 개인 주택과 같은 조용한 공간에서 이루어지는 개인적인 활동이었다. ① 그러나 디지털 기술의 등장과 함께 독서 습관은 큰 변화를 겪게 되었다. ② 이제 온라인 플랫폼을 통해 독자들은 자신의 의견을 즉시 공유하고, 전 세계의 다른 사람들과 토론에 참여할 수 있다. (③ 그 결과 오늘날 많은 사람들은 촉감적 경험 때문에 디지털 형식보다 종이책을 선호한다.) ④ 이러한 변화는 독서를 더욱 사회적이고 상호작용적인 활동으로 바꾸어 놓았으며, 사람들이 글을 소비하고 해석하는 방식까지 재구성하고 있다. 오늘날의 독서는 더 이상 개인적인 사색에만 머무르지 않고, 디지털 상호작용에 의해 형성되는 공유되고 역동적인 경험이 되었다.

[어휘]
• breakthrough 획기적 발전, 돌파구
• semiconductor 반도체
• superconductor 초전도체
• transformation 변화, 변형
• precise 정밀한, 정확한
• atomic 원자의
• modify 수정하다, 변형하다
• hallmark 특징, 상징
• notable 주목할 만한
• practical 실용적인, 현실[실질/실제]적인
• compatible 호환되는, 양립될 수 있는
• advance 발전시키다, 촉진하다

15 [독해 – 단일형 문항(전자메일 – 목적)]　　▶ ③

[난이도] 하

[정답 해설]
이 메일은 필라델피아 보건부가 지역 커뮤니티 파트너 기관들에게 보낸 공지로, 보조금 신청 마감이 임박했음을 강조하며 신속한 신청을 독려하는 것이 핵심 목적이다. 신청 기한과 마지막 정보 시간 일정을 반복적으로 안내하며, 모든 자격 요건과 질문을 마감 시각까지 완료해야 한다고 강조하고 있다. 따라서 글의 목적으로 가장 적절한 것은 ③이다.

[해석]

수신인 필라델피아 지역 파트너들
발신: 공중보건국
날짜: 2026년 11월 3일
제목: 긴급 안내

지역 파트너들에게 드리는 긴급 안내입니다.

공중보건국은 "One Philly SNAP Support Program"의 신청 절차를 시작했습니다. 이번 프로그램은 5,000달러에서 50,000달러까지의 보조금을 제공하며, SNAP 혜택을 이용하는 필라델피아 주민들을 지원하는 기관을 대상으로 합니다. 신청서 제출 마감 시간은 2026년 11월 4일 수요일 오후 5시입니다.

내일 11월 4일 오전 8시 30분부터 9시 30분까지(등록 필요) 마지막 Zoom 정보 시간을 개최하여 막바지 질문에 답변할 예정입니다.

고려하려면 모든 지원 질문을 마감일까지 완료해야 합니다. 모든 적격 파트너가 지원할 것을 권장합니다.

① 새로운 SNAP 혜택 프로그램의 설립을 발표하려고
② 주민들에게 도시 식량 기금 기부를 요청하려고
③ 마감일 전에 보조금을 신청하도록 촉구하려고
④ 자금 조달 기회를 위해 신청 마감일을 연기하려고

[어휘]
• issue 발행하다, 발표하다
• grant 보조금, 지원금
• intended 의도된
• required 필수인
• eligible 자격이 있는, 적격의
• urge 촉구하다, 강력히 권하다
• postpone 연기하다, 미루다

16 [독해 – 중심 내용 추론(주제)]　　▶ ②

[난이도] 중

[정답 해설]
이 글은 특정 미생물이 동물의 영양 흡수와 면역 반응을 증진시키는 사례를 제시하며, 생명체가 완전히 독립적으로 기능하기보다는 다른 생물과의 상호 협력적 관계에 의존해 살아간다는 관점을 강조한다. 개별 실험 결과들은 결국 생명 유지의 핵심이 자립성이 아니라 상호의존적 생물학적 관계에 있음을 뒷받침한다. 따라서 글의 주제로 가장 적절한 것은 ②이다.

[해석]
Keller 박사와 그녀의 연구팀은 의학 연구에 흔히 사용되는 실험용 동물에서 특정 박테리아 균주가 영양분 흡수를 향상시킨다는 사실을 예상치 못하게 발견했다. 이후 관련된 다른 박테리아 균주들을 대상으로 한 후속 실험에서도 여러 다른 동물 종에서 유사한 효과가 나타났다. Keller 박사는 현재 다양한 숙주에서 면역 반응을 강화하는 것으로 보이는 추가 미생물들에 대해 심층 연구를 진행하고 있다. 그녀는 서로 다른 미생물들이 자신이 서식하는 생물에게 제공할 수 있는 이점들을 더 포괄적으로 이해하는 것을 목표로 하고 있다. 이러한 발견들은 많은 생명체들이 완전히 독립적으로 기능하기보다는 협력적인 생물학적 관계에 의존한다는 생물학자들 사이의 확산되고 있는 관점을 뒷받침해 줄 것이다.

① 생명체의 생물학적 독립성
② 생명을 유지하는 데 있어 상호의존적 관계의 역할
③ 생명체의 면역 반응에 영향을 미치는 요인들
④ 자연 환경에서 생물의 자급자족

[어휘]
• strain 균주, 계통
• absorption 흡수, 통합
• microorganism 미생물
• host 숙주
• comprehensive 포괄적인, 종합적인
• independently 독립하여, 자주적으로

17 [독해 − 문장 삽입]　　▶ ③

난이도　중

정답 해설

이 글은 페로브스카이트 태양전지가 혁신적인 잠재력을 지니고 있지만, 습기와 열에 대한 취약성을 극복해야 상용화가 가능함을 강조한다. 먼저 ①, ②번 뒤 문장에서는 가벼움과 유연성, 높은 활용 가능성 등 장점을 제시하고 있다. 이어 주어진 문장은 이러한 장점에도 불구하고 상용화를 가로막아 온 한계를 언급하는 내용으로, 이후에 제시될 내구성 강화를 위한 보호 코팅 및 캡슐화 기술 연구가 왜 필요한지를 설명하는 연결 고리 역할을 한다. 연구 방향이 제시되기 직전에 들어가야 글의 흐름상 가장 자연스럽다. 따라서 주어진 문장이 들어갈 위치로 가장 적절한 것은 ③이다.

해석

페로브스카이트 태양전지는 기존의 실리콘 패널에 도전하는 2025년의 주요 혁신 기술로 떠오르고 있다. (①) 딱딱한 실리콘과 달리, 이들은 가볍고 유연하며 인쇄가 가능해 획기적인 효율을 제공한다. (②) 이러한 특성 덕분에 창문, 차량, 심지어 의류에까지도 통합될 수 있다. (③ 그러나 습기와 열에 대한 이러한 취약성은 역사적으로 상용화의 가장 큰 장벽이 되어, 광범위한 보급을 가로막아 왔다.) 따라서 현재의 주요 연구 초점은 내구성을 높이기 위한 보호 코팅과 캡슐화 기술을 개발하는 데 맞춰져 있다. (④) 만약 이러한 안정성 문제를 극복할 수 있다면, 페로브스카이트는 어디에나 적용 가능한 태양광 발전의 새로운 시대를 열 수 있을 것이다.

어휘

- vulnerability 취약성
- widespread 광범위한, 널리 퍼진
- solar cell 태양전지
- rigid 딱딱한, 엄격한
- encapsulation 캡슐화, 피포

18 [독해 − 순서 배열]　　▶ ④

난이도　중

정답 해설

주어진 글은 허위 정보가 민주주의와 공중 보건에 큰 위협이 되고 있으며, 이를 해결하기 위한 효과적인 대응책이 필요하다는 문제의식을 제기하며 시작한다. 먼저 (C)는 대표적인 대응 전략으로 '접종 이론'을 소개하며, 허위 정보를 약화된 형태로 미리 접하게 하고 그 안에 담긴 조작 기법을 이해하도록 함으로써 판단력을 높이는 방법임을 설명한다. 이어지는 (B)는 사실 확인처럼 사후에 대응하는 방식과 달리, 접종 이론은 허위 정보가 퍼지기 전에 미리 대비하는 예방 중심 전략임을 비교를 통해 보완한다. 마지막으로 (A)는 앞서 설명된 이 이론이 실제로 활용된 사례−조작적 전술을 인식하도록 돕는 짧은 교육 영상 실험−를 제시하며 마무리한다. 따라서 글의 순서로 가장 적절한 것은 ④이다.

해석

소셜 미디어와 생성형 AI로 가속화된 허위 정보의 확산은 민주적 절차와 공중 보건에 심각한 위협이 되고 있다. 이러한 문제로 인해 효과적인 대응책을 찾는 연구가 진행되고 있다.

(C) 그중 널리 연구된 접근법이 '접종 이론'인데, 이는 사람들이 허위 정보의 약화된 형태에 미리 노출되고 그 안에 사용된 조작 기법을 이해하면, 인지적 저항력을 키울 수 있다고 본다.

(B) 허위 정보가 퍼진 후에 이루어지는 팩트 체크와 달리, 접종은 백신과 유사하게 "감염"을 사전에 방지하는 것을 목표로 한다.

(A) 예를 들어, 최근 연구에서는 감정적 호소나 이분법 같은 흔한 조작 기법을 알아보는 방법을 가르치는 짧은 영상을 활용했는데, 그 결과 시청자들의 진위 판단 능력이 다양한 주제에서 향상된 것으로 나타났다.

어휘

- misinformation 허위 정보
- accelerate 가속하다
- pose 제기하다
- democratic 민주주의의
- prompt 촉발하다, 유도하다
- countermeasure 대응책
- recognize 인식하다, 알아보다
- dichotomy 이분법
- spread 퍼지다, 확산하다

- in advance 사전에
- inoculation theory 접종 이론(미리 약한 형태를 노출해 저항성을 기르는 심리 기법)
- expose 노출시키다

19 [독해 − 빈칸 추론]　　▶ ④

난이도　상

정답 해설

이 글은 보상(치즈)을 향해 나아가는 '접근 지향' 동기부여와 위협(올빼미)으로부터 벗어나려는 '회피 지향' 동기부여가 수행에 어떤 차이를 만드는지 비교한 실험을 소개한다. 실험 결과, 접근 지향 집단이 속도와 정확도 모두에서 훨씬 뛰어난 성과를 보였다. 본문은 그 이유를, 접근 지향은 분명한 목표가 주의를 한 점에 모아주는 반면, 회피 지향은 단지 위협을 피하는 데만 초점을 두어 행동이 분산되기 쉽기 때문이라고 설명한다. 빈칸에는 불이익을 피하기보다는 특정한 이익을 추구하는 것이 긍정적인 결과를 초래한다는 내용이 들어가야 자연스럽다. 따라서 밑줄 친 부분에 들어갈 말로 가장 적절한 것은 ④이다.

해석

심리학 연구에 따르면 과제의 제시 방식에 따라 동기의 형태가 크게 달라진다. 한 실험에서 참가자들은 두 가지 조건에서 미로를 통과했는데, 한 집단은 보상을 향해 나아가도록 설정되었고 다른 집단은 위협을 피하도록 설정되었다. 긍정적인 보상을 얻는 데 집중한 집단은 속도와 정확도 면에서 훨씬 뛰어난 성과를 보였다. 이는 사람들이 분명하고 원하는 목표를 추구할 때 전반적으로 더 좋은 수행을 한다는 점을 시사한다. 반면 회피 중심의 프레이밍은 행동을 촉발할 수는 있지만, 부정적 상황에서 벗어나는 데만 몰두하게 하여 행동이 산만하고 비효율적으로 흐르는 경향이 있다. 이에 비해 구체적인 목표는 주의 집중을 강화하는 정신적 기준점 역할을 하여 수행을 향상시킨다. 그러므로 보상을 설계하거나 개인적인 목표를 설정할 때, 특정한 이익을 추구하는 것이 단순히 불이익을 피하려고 노력하는 것보다 더 나은 결과를 낳는다는 점을 인식하는 것이 중요하다.

① 지각된 위협은 동기에 상당한 영향을 줄 수 있다
② 회피 중심의 제시 방식도 여전히 강한 참여를 유발할 수 있다
③ 인지적 제시 방식은 과제 수행에 거의 영향을 미치지 않는다
④ 특정한 이익을 추구하는 것이 단순히 불이익을 피하려고 노력하는 것보다 더 나은 결과를 낳는다

어휘

- psychological 심리학의, 심리적인
- pursue 추구하다, 뒤쫓다[추적하다]
- avoidance-based 회피 중심의
- scattered 산만한, 흩어진
- sharpen 날카롭게 하다, 강화하다
- perceived 지각된, 인식된
- engagement 참여, 몰입
- negligible 무시해도 될 정도의

[난이도] 상

[정답 해설]

이 글은 인간의 정신이 논리적 사고를 담당하는 '의식'과 원초적 감정을 관장하는 '무의식'으로 이분화되어 있음을 설명한다. 빈칸 앞 문장은 무의식이 사랑·두려움 같은 강한 감정의 영역이라는 점을 제시하고, 빈칸 뒤 문장은 이러한 감정이 이성적 의도를 압도해 강한 내적 갈등을 일으킨다고 말한다. 빈칸에는 무의식이 이러한 감정과 욕망을 실제로 움직이는 핵심 동력이라는 내용이 와야, 무의식이 왜 이성을 넘어서는 힘을 갖고 내적 갈등을 유발하는지 그 원인을 자연스럽게 연결할 수 있다. 따라서 밑줄 친 부분에 들어갈 말로 가장 적절한 것은 ②이다.

[해석]

> 인간의 정신은 두 갈래로 나뉘어 있다. 의식은 논리에 의존하지만, 무의식은 사랑·두려움·질투·기쁨과 같은 날것의 감정을 관장한다. <u>우리의 핵심 감정과 욕망을 이끄는 것은 바로 이 무의식이라는 원동력인데</u>, 종종 이성적인 의도를 압도하고 우리가 깨닫기도 전에 행동의 많은 부분을 형성한다. 그래서 의식적인 선택이 깊이 자리 잡은 무의식적 충동과 충돌할 때 강한 내적 갈등이 생긴다. 예를 들어, 누군가 논리적으로는 해로운 습관을 끊기로 결심하더라도, 마음속 깊은 곳의 지속적인 욕망 때문에 그 결심이 쉽게 흔들릴 수 있다. 이렇게 '멈추고 싶다'는 의지와 '계속하고 싶다'는 욕망이 갈라지는 순간, 상당한 심리적 고통이 발생한다. 더 나아가 신경과학은 무의식의 우위를 뒷받침한다. 뇌는 우리가 의식적으로 결정했다고 느끼기 몇 밀리초 전에 이미 행동 준비를 시작한다는 것이다. 이는 우리가 의식적 선택이라고 믿는 것이 사실은 무의식에서 먼저 내려진 결정을 의식이 뒤늦게 승인하는 것일 수 있음을 시사한다.

① 논리적 사고는 때때로 내적 갈등을 완화할 수 있는데
② 우리의 핵심 감정과 욕망을 이끄는 것은 바로 이 무의식이라는 원동력인데
③ 의식은 감정을 어느 정도만 통제할 수 있는데
④ 모든 의사결정에서 무의식이 의식적인 사고를 완전히 대체하는데

[어휘]

- **psyche** 정신, 영혼
- **unconscious** 무의식적인
- **raw** 가공되지 않은, 날것의
- **clash** 충돌하다
- **subconscious** 잠재의식, 무의식
- **drive** 이끌다, 몰다, 추진시키다
- **persistent** 지속적인, 끈질긴
- **deliberate** 숙고한, 의도적인
- **exert** 발휘하다, 행사하다

영어 정답 및 해설

✓ 제9회 모의고사

01 ①	02 ③	03 ②	04 ③	05 ②
06 ③	07 ③	08 ④	09 ②	10 ④
11 ②	12 ③	13 ②	14 ③	15 ③
16 ②	17 ④	18 ③	19 ①	20 ②

01 [어휘 – 빈칸] ▶①

난이도 중

정답 해설

많은 젊은 전문 인력들이 도시를 떠나는 현상의 이유로 임금은 장기간 '정체되면서' 생활비만 지속적으로 상승한다는 내용이 자연스럽다. 따라서 밑줄 친 부분에 들어갈 말로 가장 적절한 것은 ①이다.

해석

생활비가 지속적으로 상승하는 반면 임금 수준은 장기간 정체되면서, 많은 젊은 전문 인력들이 해당 도시를 떠나는 현상이 나타나고 있다.

어휘

- ★ stagnant 정체된, 침체된, 고여 있는
- ● insipid 맛이 없는, 재미없는
- ● competitive 경쟁력 있는, 뒤지지 않는
- ● versatile 다재다능한, 다용도의

02 [어휘 – 빈칸] ▶③

난이도 중

정답 해설

회계사가 서류를 제출하기 전, 보고된 수치가 실제 분기 수익과 일치하는지 '확인하는' 절차를 거친다는 내용이 자연스럽다. 따라서 밑줄 친 부분에 들어갈 말로 가장 적절한 것은 ③이다.

해석

회계사는 서류를 제출하기 전에, 보고된 수치들이 분기별 수익을 정확하게 반영하고 있는지 확인해야 한다.

어휘

- ★ verify 입증하다, 확인하다
- ● menace 위협하다
- ● doubt 확신하지 못하다, 의심하다
- ● diffuse 분산시키다, 퍼지다

03 [문법 – 빈칸] ▶②

난이도 중

정답 해설

② **[적중포인트 088] 전치사와 명사 목적어 ★★★☆☆**
& [적중포인트 010] 격에 따른 인칭대명사 ★★☆☆☆

전치사 at 뒤에는 반드시 명사(구)가 와야 한다. 이때 completion은 '완료'라는 명사이므로 전치사의 목적어로 적절하다. 또한 이 명사는 누가 완료했는지를 나타내기 위해 앞에서 수식해야 하는데, 명사를 수식하는 자리에는 형용사 기능을 하는 소유격 대명사를 써야 한다. 따라서 밑줄 친 부분에 들어갈 말로 가장 적절한 것은 ②이다.

해석

우리는 제한된 자원과 인력에도 불구하고 그가 프로젝트를 예정보다 앞서 완료한 것에 놀랐다.

04 [생활영어 – 빈칸] ▶③

난이도 하

정답 해설

사무실 복귀 정책으로 인해 출근 요일이 정해진 상황에서, David는 정기적인 허리 물리치료 때문에 수요일 출근이 어렵다고 밝혔다. Ji-won이 의료 일정은 예외로 인정된다며 해결책을 제시하자, David가 목요일 출근이 가능하다고 답한 점으로 보아 수요일 근무일을 목요일로 조정하는 제안이 이루어졌음을 짐작할 수 있다. 따라서 밑줄 친 부분에 들어갈 말로 가장 적절한 것은 ③이다.

해석

Ji-won: 안녕하세요, David. 새로운 사무실 복귀 정책 관련해서 확인차 연락드립니다. 다음 주부터 월·수·금 사무실 출근으로 일정 잡혀 있습니다.

David Kim: 안녕하세요, Ji-won. 그 부분 말인데요… 제가 허리 때문에 매주 수요일 아침에 정기적으로 물리치료 예약이 있습니다. 집 근처입니다.

Ji-won: 그렇군요. 새로운 정책이 꽤 엄격하긴 하지만, 의료 일정은 인정되는 예외입니다.

David Kim: 그럼 저는 어떻게 해야 할까요?

Ji-won: 사무실 근무일을 조금 조정하는 것이 어떨까요?

David Kim: 아, 다행이네요. 네, 그렇게 할 수 있어요. 그럼 목요일에는 하루 종일 출근할게요.

① 수요일마다 유급 휴가를 사용하셔야 합니다.
② 죄송하지만, 물리치료 일정을 다시 잡으셔야 할 것 같습니다.
③ 사무실 근무일을 조금 조정하는 것이 어떨까요?
④ 완전 재택 근무로 전환하셔야 하겠습니다.

어휘

- • return-to-office 사무실 복귀와 관련된
- • recurring 반복되는, 정기적으로 있는
- • valid 유효한, 정당한
- • paid time off 유급 휴가

05 [생활영어 – 빈칸] ▶②

난이도 하

정답 해설

신용카드 명세서를 확인한 A가 지출을 줄이기 위해 스트리밍 구독을 취소하려는 상황이다. 이에 B는 자신도 같은 서비스를 이용하지만, 최대 다섯 명까지 공유할 수 있는 요금제를 통해 훨씬 저렴하게 사용하고 있음을 언급하며 A에게도 동일한 방식을 제안한 것으로 짐작할 수 있다. 따라서 밑줄 친 부분에 들어갈 말로 가장 적절한 것은 ②이다.

해석

A: 방금 신용카드 명세서를 확인했는데, 완전히 감당이 안 될 정도야.
B: 무슨 말인지 알아. 물가 상승 때문에 가격이 계속 오르고 있잖아.
A: 맞아. 그래서 돈 좀 아껴보려고 음악 스트리밍 구독을 취소할까 생각 중이야.
B: 어떤 거 쓰고 있어? 나는 'TuneSphere' 이용해.
A: 나도 그거야. 좋은 서비스긴 한데, 나 혼자 쓰는데 월 15달러는 좀 아깝더라고.
B: 가족 요금제가 있는지 한번 확인해보는 게 어때?
A: 그런 게 있는지도 몰랐어. 어떻게 되는 거야?
B: 최대 다섯 명까지 추가할 수 있어. 나랑 친구들은 하나를 같이 쓰는데, 각자 약 4달러만 내면 돼.

① 나도 동의해, 아마 바로 취소하는 게 좋을 거야.
② 가족 요금제가 있는지 한번 확인해보는 게 어때?
③ 대신 광고가 있는 무료 버전을 듣는 게 좋겠어.
④ 나는 사실 15달러면 음악 값 치고 꽤 합리적인 가격이라고 생각해.

어휘

- • bill 명세서, 청구서, 계산서
- • subscription 구독, 가입
- • reasonable 합리적인, 적당한

난이도 중

정답 해설

이 글은 기업 임원들을 표적으로 한 고도로 정교한 스피어 피싱 캠페인이 급증하고 있음을 알리는 '경고' 성격의 글이다. 피싱 이메일의 특징, 주요 공격 방식, 악성코드 유포 과정, 기존 보안 필터의 한계, 그리고 직원 교육의 중요성 등을 구체적으로 제시하며 특정 보안 위협에 대한 위험성을 강조하고 있다. 따라서 글의 제목으로 가장 적절한 것은 ③이다.
① 기업 이메일 시스템에서의 데이터 유출 방지하기
② 사이버 위협 대응을 위한 임원 교육
③ 경고: 고도화된 스피어 피싱 위험
④ 민감한 기업 문서 처리 방법

07 [독해 − 세트형 문항(홈페이지 게시글 − 내용 일치)] ▶ ③

난이도 중

정답 해설

사용자가 해당 링크를 클릭하면 악성코드가 조용히 다운로드되고, 이 악성코드는 재무 기록과 지식재산권을 포함한 민감한 기업 데이터를 외부로 유출하도록 설계되어 있다고 언급하고 있다. 따라서 윗글의 내용과 일치하는 것은 ③이다.
① 최근 일반적인 대량 피싱 공격이 급증하고 있다.
② 공격 이메일은 매력적인 광고 형태로 위장한다.
③ 링크를 클릭하면 악성코드가 자동으로 다운로드된다.
④ 이러한 공격은 일반적인 보안 필터만으로도 충분히 탐지가 가능하다.

오답 해설

① 금융보안청은 최근 기업 임원을 겨냥한 정교한 스피어 피싱 공격이 급증하고 있다고 언급하고 있으므로 글의 내용과 일치하지 않는다.
② 공격 이메일은 종종 신뢰할 만한 동료나 평판 있는 비즈니스 파트너에게서 온 것처럼 위장된다고 언급하고 있으므로 글의 내용과 일치하지 않는다.
④ 이러한 공격은 대상에 맞춰 정교하게 만들어지기 때문에 일반적인 보안 필터로는 탐지가 어려울 수 있다고 언급하고 있으므로 글의 내용과 일치하지 않는다.

해석

경고: 고도화된 스피어 피싱 위험

금융보안청은 최근 기업 임원을 겨냥한 정교한 스피어 피싱 공격이 급증하고 있음을 확인했습니다. 일반적인 대량 피싱과 달리, 이러한 공격은 대상자에 대한 세밀한 정보 조사를 바탕으로 매우 그럴듯한 구실을 만들어낸다는 점이 특징입니다. 공격 이메일은 종종 신뢰할 만한 동료나 평판 있는 비즈니스 파트너에게서 온 것처럼 위장됩니다.

주요 공격 방식은 '분기 보고서'나 '기밀 인수·합병 제안서'와 같은 정상 문서로 가장한 악성 링크를 포함하는 것입니다. 사용자가 해당 링크를 클릭하면 악성코드가 조용히 다운로드되고, 이 악성코드는 재무 기록과 지식재산권을 포함한 민감한 기업 데이터를 외부로 유출하도록 설계되어 있습니다. 이러한 공격은 대상에 맞춰 정교하게 만들어지기 때문에 일반적인 보안 필터로는 탐지가 어려울 수 있습니다. 가장 중요한 방어 수단은 의심하는 문화를 조직 내에 조성하는 것입니다. 직원들은 특히 긴급성을 강조하며 민감한 정보를 요구하는 예기치 않은 요청에 대해, 반드시 독립적으로 사실 여부를 확인하도록 교육받아야 합니다.

어휘

- surge 급증, 폭증
- sophisticated 정교한, 고도화된
- spear-phishing 스피어 피싱(표적형 피싱 공격)
- executive 임원, 경영진
- pretext 구실, 핑계
- fraudulent 사기의, 거짓의
- malicious 악성의
- confidential 기밀의
- exfiltrate (몰래) 유출하다
- vigilant 방심하지 않는, 경계하는
- skepticism 회의, 의심
- advanced 고급의, 진보된

08 독해 − 세트형 문항(안내문 − 유의어)] ▶ ④

난이도 상

정답 해설

밑줄 친 'stipulate'는 '규정하다, 명기하다'의 뜻으로, 이와 문맥상 가장 가까운 의미는 ④ 'prescribe(규정하다, 지시하다, 처방하다)'이다.

오답 해설

① infringe 위반하다, 제한하다
② advocate 지지하다, 옹호하다
③ speculate 추측하다, 투기하다

09 독해 − 세트형 문항(안내문 − 목적)] ▶ ②

난이도 중

정답 해설

이 글은 국립과학재단 보조금 제안서를 제출하는 공식적인 절차를 상세히 설명하고 있다. 제안서 제출 방식, 포함해야 할 서류, 평가 기준, 심사 절차, 결과 통보 시기 등을 절차적으로 안내하고 있다. 따라서 글의 목적으로 가장 적절한 것은 ②이다.
① 연구 보조금 수령자를 발표하려고
② 보조금 신청을 위한 공식 프로토콜을 제공하려고
③ 검토 패널이 내린 결정에 항소하려고
④ 제안 평가 위원회에 전문가를 모집하려고

해석

정부 연구비 지원 신청 규정

본 문서는 국립과학재단(NSF) 연구비 지원을 위한 제안서 제출 절차를 공식적으로 명시한 것입니다. 모든 제출 서류는 검토를 위해 본 문서에 규정된 지침을 엄격히 준수해야 합니다.

제안서는 11월 30일 오후 5시 이전에 공식 포털을 통해 전자 방식으로 제출해야 합니다. 제출 서류에는 세부 연구 계획서, 예산 산출 근거서, 주요 연구진의 이력서가 반드시 포함되어야 합니다. 이후의 심사 절차는 독립적인 전문가 패널에 의해 진행됩니다.

평가 기준에는 과학적 가치, 실현 가능성 및 잠재적 영향력이 포함됩니다. 지원자들은 제출 마감일로부터 90일 이내에 결과를 통보받게 됩니다. 심사위원단에 의해 내려진 결정은 최종적이며 이의 제기를 할 수 없습니다..

어휘

- delineate 명확히 설명하다, 기술하다
- procedure 절차
- conform 따르다, 준수하다
- stipulate 규정하다, 명시하다
- justification 타당한[정당한] 이유
- curriculum vitae 이력서
- subsequent 이후의
- feasibility 실현 가능성
- notify 알리다
- appeal 항소하다, 이의를 제기하다
- recipient 받는 사람, 수령[수취]인

10 [문법 − 밑줄] ▶ ④

난이도 중

정답 해설

④ [적중포인트 067] 주의해야 할 조동사와 조동사 관용 표현 ★★★☆☆
need 바로 뒤에 부정어가 쓰인 것으로 보아 여기서 need는 일반동사가 아닌 조동사로 쓰였고, need not 뒤에는 to부정사가 아닌 동사원형이 와야 한다. 따라서 밑줄 친 부분의 to worry를 worry로 고쳐야 한다.

오답 해설

① [적중포인트 088] 전치사와 명사 목적어 ★★★☆☆
전치사(in) 뒤에 명사나 동명사를 목적어로 취할 수 있다. 따라서 밑줄 친 부분은 올바르게 쓰였다.

② **[적중포인트 054] 분사 판별법 [현재분사 VS 과거분사] ★★★★★**

문맥상 fearing은 두려워하는 주체가 주절의 주어와 일치하고, 학생들이 직접 '두려워하는' 능동적 관계에 있으며 뒤에 that절의 목적어가 있으므로 현재분사로 써야 한다. 따라서 밑줄 친 부분은 올바르게 쓰였다.

③ **[적중포인트 078] 등위접속사와 병렬 구조 ★★★★☆**

등위접속사 and 기준으로 앞에 동사인 현재완료 시제(have followed)와 병렬 구조를 이뤄야 한다. 참고로 뒤에 동사는 have가 생략되어 표현되었다. 따라서 밑줄 친 부분은 올바르게 쓰였다.

> **해석**
>
> 준비는 시험 불안을 극복하는 데 있어 가장 결정적인 요소다. 많은 학생은 중요한 것을 놓칠까 봐 두려워하며, 세부적인 내용 하나하나를 암기하느라 잠 못 이루는 밤을 보낸다. 하지만 여러분이 일관되게 체계적인 학습 계획을 따랐고 핵심 개념들을 이해했다면, 시험 결과에 대해 걱정할 필요가 없다.

11 [문법 – 밑줄]　　▶②

난이도 중

정답 해설

② **[적중포인트 081] 주의해야 할 부사절 접속사 ★★☆☆☆**

'~하지 않도록, ~할까봐'의 의미로 쓰이는 lest는 이미 부정의 의미가 있으므로 뒤에 부정부사 not을 쓰지 않는다. 따라서 밑줄 친 부분의 not worsen을 worsen으로 고쳐야 한다.

오답 해설

① **[적중포인트 060] to부정사의 명사적 역할 ★★★★☆**

'~할 여유가 있다'의 의미로 쓰이는 afford는 to부정사를 목적어로 취하는 3형식 타동사이다. 따라서 밑줄 친 부분은 올바르게 쓰였다.

③ **[적중포인트 040] 상관접속사와 수 일치 ★★★☆☆**

'not only A but (also) B'의 구조에서 only는 merely와 just로 대신할 수 있다. 따라서 밑줄 친 부분은 올바르게 쓰였다.

④ **[적중포인트 069] 다양한 도치 구문 ★★★★☆**

'Only+전치사+명사'가 문두에 오면 뒤에 '조동사+주어~'의 형태로 도치 구조로 쓴다. 따라서 밑줄 친 부분은 올바르게 쓰였다.

> **해석**
>
> 국제사회는 이러한 놀라운 기후 변화에 대한 대응을 지연시킬 여유가 없다. 상황이 돌이킬 수 없는 지점을 넘어 악화되지 않도록 우리는 즉각적인 조치를 취해야 한다. 지구를 보호하는 것은 단지 하나의 선택 사항이 아니라, 우리가 미래 세대에게 짊어진 근본적인 책임이다. 오직 집단적이고 결단력 있는 조치를 통해서만 우리는 지속 가능한 세상을 보장할 수 있다.

12 [독해 – 단일형 문항(전자메일 – 목적)]　　▶③

난이도 하

정답 해설

이 이메일은 Valdosta 시 주민들에게 발송된 공식 공지로, 허리케인 헬렌의 여파로 일시적으로 중단되었던 연체료 부과 및 서비스 중단 정책을 상황이 안정된 현재 시점부터 다시 시행하겠다는 내용을 전달하고 있다. 주민들에게는 불이익을 피하기 위해 제때 요금을 납부할 것을 권고하며, 경제적 어려움을 겪는 이들을 위한 분할 납부 및 지원 프로그램도 안내하고 있다. 따라서 글의 목적으로 가장 적절한 것은 ③이다.

> **해석**
>
> 수신인: Valdosta 시 주민 여러분께
> 발신인: Valdosta 시 수도·전력 공공요금 부서
> 날짜: 2026년 9월 25일
> 제목: 중요 안내 사항
>
> 이 안내문은 귀하의 시 공공요금 계정과 관련된 중요한 업데이트입니다.
>
> 허리케인 헬렌 이후 복구 기간 동안, Valdosta 시는 주민들을 지원하기 위해 연체료 부과와 서비스 중단 조치를 일시적으로 중단한 바 있습니다.
>
> 이제 중요한 서비스와 인프라가 안정화됨에 따라, 시는 모든 연체 계좌에 대한 연체료 및 서비스 중단 통지를 포함한 표준 청구 정책이 2026년 10월 1일부터 시행될 것이라고 발표하고 있습니다.

> 위약금을 피하기 위해 고객은 적시에 결제할 것을 강력히 권장합니다. 시는 재정적 어려움을 겪고 있는 고객을 위해 결제 수단과 지원 프로그램을 제공합니다. 도움이 필요한 고객은 즉시 유틸리티 고객 서비스 팀에 문의하시기 바랍니다.

① 주민들에게 공공요금 할인 혜택을 제공하려고
② 허리케인 헬렌의 임박한 도착을 경고하려고
③ 일시적으로 중단되었던 요금 정책의 재개를 알리려고
④ 모든 주민을 위한 새로운 요금 지원 프로그램을 소개하려고

어휘

- aftermath 여파, 후유증
- pause 중단하다, 잠시 멈추다
- standard 표준의, 기본의
- past-due 연체된, 기한이 지난
- resume 재개하다, 다시 시작하다
- penalty 벌금, 불이익
- urge 촉구하다, 재촉하다

13 [독해 – 중심 내용 추론(주제)]　　▶②

난이도 중

정답 해설

이 글은 일산화탄소(CO)라는 핵심 소재를 중심으로 '위험성 제시'와 '예방법 제안'이 결합된 전형적인 구조를 보여준다. 첫 문장을 통해 글의 전반부가 일산화탄소의 치명적인 위험성을 경고하고 있음을 알 수 있으며, 이어지는 To prevent CO poisoning이라는 결정적 전환 시그널을 기점으로 구체적인 안전 수칙(감지기 설치, 환기, 연례 점검)들이 나열된다. 따라서 글의 주제로 가장 적절한 것은 ②이다.

> **해석**
>
> 공공안전 및 비상대비부는 난방 시스템 사용이 잦은 추운 시기에 특히 주의해야 할 일산화탄소(CO) 중독의 위험성에 대해 경고를 발령했다. 일산화탄소는 무색, 무취의 기체로, 많은 양을 흡입할 경우 심각한 건강 문제나 심지어 사망에까지 이르게 할 수 있다. 해당 부처는 일산화탄소의 일반적인 발생원으로 고장 난 난방기, 가스레인지, 그리고 휴대용 발전기를 꼽았다. 일산화탄소 중독을 예방하기 위해, 부처는 주민들에게 가정 내 일산화탄소 감지기를 설치하고, 적절한 환기를 유지하며, 전문가에게 매년 난방 시스템 점검을 받을 것을 권고했다. 또한, 실내에서 휴대용 발전기나 그릴을 절대 사용하지 말 것을 강조했는데, 이는 치명적인 수준의 일산화탄소를 발생시킬 수 있기 때문이다.

① 무색 기체 감지 시 안전 센서의 한계
② 일산화탄소 중독의 위험성과 예방 전략
③ 일산화탄소 배출이 환경에 미치는 영향 평가
④ 실내 휴대용 발전기의 올바른 유지관리 절차

어휘

- preparedness 준비
- carbon monoxide 일산화탄소
- frequent 잦은, 빈번한
- colorless 무색의
- odorless 냄새가 없는, 무취의
- inhale 숨을 들이마시다, 빨아들이다
- portable 휴대[이동]가 쉬운, 휴대용의
- ventilation 환기
- inspect 점검하다, 조사하다
- emphasize 강조하다
- lethal 치명적인

난이도 중

정답 해설

'노점상 종류' 부분에서 현장에서 조리하는 음식은 불가하다고 명시되어 있다. 따라서 윗글의 내용과 일치하지 않는 것은 ③이다.

오답 해설

① '노점상 종류' 부분에서 특산 식품으로 잼, 구운 과자 등 포장 식품만 명시되어 있으므로 글의 내용과 일치한다.
② '신청 절차' 부분에서 환불이 불가한 신청비 $25를 납부하라고 명시되어 있으므로 글의 내용과 일치한다.
④ 선정된 노점상들은 12월 1일까지 부스비 $150를 납부해야 한다고 명시되어 있으므로 글의 내용과 일치한다.

해석

> **공급업체 모집 공고: 2026 올드타운 휴일 마켓**
> **신청 마감일: 2026년 11월 15일**
>
> 올드타운 상인회(OTBA)는 12월 6일부터 22일까지 주말 동안 열리는 제10회 연례 휴일 마켓에 참여할 공예·푸드 공급업체를 모집합니다. 우리는 고품질의 독창적이고 수작업으로 제작된 제품을 찾고 있습니다. 대량 생산 또는 재판매 품목은 해당되지 않으며 거부됩니다.
>
> **노점상 종류:**
> * 공예: 보석, 도자기, 섬유 제품 등
> * 특산 식품: 잼, 구운 과자 등 포장 식품 (현장에서 조리하는 음식은 불가)
>
> **신청 절차:**
> 1. 11월 15일까지 온라인 신청서를 제출합니다.
> 2. 환불 불가 신청비 $25를 납부합니다.
> 3. 제품 사진 고해상도 이미지 3~5장을 첨부합니다.
>
> 모든 신청서는 심사위원단에 의해 검토될 것입니다. 11월 20일까지 이메일로 승인 또는 불인가 결과가 안내됩니다. 선정된 노점상들은 12월 1일까지 부스비 $150를 납부해야 합니다.

① 특정 유형의 식품 항목만 판매가 허용된다.
② 지원자들은 신청이 거절되더라도 환불을 받지 못할 것이다.
③ 음식 노점상들은 자신의 부스에서 따뜻한 음식을 요리하고 제공하는 것이 허용된다.
④ 선정된 노점상들은 부스에 대한 추가 비용을 지불해야 한다.

어휘

- vendor 노점상, 판매자, 공급업체
- artisan 장인, 공예가
- handcrafted 손으로 만든, 수공예의
- mass-produced 대량 생산된
- eligible 자격이 있는
- reject 거절하다, 기각하다
- specialty food 특산 식품, 전문 음식
- non-refundable 환불 불가의
- high-resolution 고해상도의
- acceptance 승인, 합격
- rejection 불인가, 거절, 부결

난이도 중

정답 해설

'티켓 환불' 부분에서 온라인으로 티켓을 구매하신 분들은 5~7 영업일 이내에 원래 결제 수단으로 전액 자동 환불을 받으실 수 있다고 명시되어 있다. 따라서 윗글의 내용과 일치하는 것은 ③이다.

오답 해설

① 천문대 공원에서 열릴 예정이었던 "스타라이너 발사 관람 파티"가 무기한 연기되었음을 알리고 있으므로 글의 내용과 일치하지 않는다.
② 오늘 오전 항공우주국에서 발표한 우주선의 기술적 지연으로 인해 발사 일정이 현재 재검토 중이라고 언급하고 있으므로 글의 내용과 일치하지 않는다.
④ '대체 계획' 부분에서 파티는 취소되었으나, 천문대 공원은 이번 주 토요일 오후 8시부터 10시까지 일반인을 위한 정기 별자리 관측을 위해 개방될 예정이라고 언급하고 있으므로 글의 내용과 일치하지 않는다.

해석

> **중요 공지**
> **시립 스카이워치 파티 취소**
>
> 이번 주 토요일인 5월 25일, 천문대 공원에서 열릴 예정이었던 "스타라이너 발사 관람 파티"가 무기한 연기되었음을 알려드리게 되어 유감입니다.
>
> **취소 사유:**
> 오늘 오전 항공우주국에서 발표한 우주선의 기술적 지연으로 인해 발사 일정이 현재 재검토 중입니다. 결과적으로, 저희 지역 관람 행사는 계획대로 진행될 수 없습니다.
>
> **티켓 환불:**
> □ 온라인으로 티켓을 구매하신 분들은 5~7 영업일 이내에 원래 결제 수단으로 전액 자동 환불을 받으실 수 있습니다.
> □ 귀하께서 직접 조치를 취하실 부분은 없습니다.
>
> **대체 계획:**
> 파티는 취소되었으나, 천문대 공원은 이번 주 토요일 오후 8시부터 10시까지 일반인을 위한 정기 별자리 관측을 위해 개방될 예정입니다. 입장은 무료이나, 개인 쌍안경을 지참하시기 바랍니다.

① 파티는 예정대로 진행될 것이다.
② 우주선의 기술적 문제는 신속히 해결되었다.
③ 온라인으로 티켓을 구매한 사람들은 원래 결제 수단으로 환불받을 것이다.
④ 별자리 관측 행사 또한 취소되었다.

어휘

- cancellation 취소, 무효화
- scheduled 예정된
- indefinitely 무기한으로
- spacecraft 우주선
- business day 영업일, 평일
- stargazing 별자리 관측
- binoculars 쌍안경

난이도 하

정답 해설

이 글은 신장에서 유래한 대사물질인 베타인이 운동과 유사한 세포 재생 및 항노화 효과를 보일 수 있다는 최신 연구 결과를 다루고 있다. ①번 문장은 일반적으로 신체 활동을 통해 나타나는 이점과 유사한 효과를 보인다는 점을 설명한다. ③번 문장은 이러한 발견이 신체적 이유로 운동을 하지 못하는 사람들에게 운동의 일부 효과를 분자 수준에서 대체할 수 있는 치료적 가능성을 제시한다. ④번 문장은 베타인의 작용 방식과 장기적 안전성을 확인하기 위한 후속 연구가 진행 중임을 설명한다. 그러나 ②번 문장은 운동이 심혈관 건강과 근육량 증가에 가장 효과적이라는 일반적 사실을 언급하며 전체 흐름과 무관하다. 따라서 글의 흐름상 어색한 문장은 ②이다.

해석

> 최근의 연구는 운동과 유사한 효과를 가진 세포 재생의 핵심 요소로서 신장에서 유래한 대사물질인 베타인을 확인했다. ① 연구에 따르면 베타인을 투여했을 때 미토콘드리아 기능이 향상되고 염증이 감소했으며, 이는 일반적으로 신체 활동을 통해 완화되는 노화 관련 지표이다. (② 운동은 심혈관 건강을 개선하고 근육량을 늘리는 가장 효과적인 방법으로 남아 있다.) ③ 이번 발견은 신체적 이유로 운동을 할 수 없는 사람들에게 운동의 항노화 효과를 분자 수준에서 일부 대체할 수 있는 치료 옵션이 될 가능성을 제시한다. ④ 베타인이 세포 경로와 어떻게 상호작용하는지, 또 그 효과가 인간에게서 지속적이고 안전한지를 규명하기 위한 추가 연구가 진행 중이다.

어휘

- identify 확인하다, 밝혀내다
- kidney 신장, 콩팥
- metabolite 대사 산물
- cellular 세포의
- rejuvenation 재생, 회춘, 원기 회복

- inflammation 염증
- cardiovascular 심혈관의
- molecular 분자의
- anti-aging 노화 방지의
- long-lasting 오래 지속되는[지속될 수 있는]

17 [독해 – 문장 삽입] ▶ ④

이 글은 디지털 기기 알림의 방해로부터 집중력을 회복하기 위한 단계적 실천 방안을 제시하는 논리적 구조를 취하고 있다. ③번 뒤 문장에서 제시된 '의도적인 경계를 만들라'는 조언은 다소 추상적인 개념에 해당한다. 주어진 문장은 이러한 추상적인 개념을 '디지털 프리 존(digital-free zone) 설정'이라는 구체적인 행동 지침으로 연결하며 논리를 심화시킨다. 이어지는 ④번 뒤 문장에서는 '식탁이나 침실'이라는 실제 공간의 예시를 들어 이 지침의 구체적인 적용법을 설명하고 있다. 따라서 주어진 문장이 들어갈 위치로 가장 적절한 것은 ④이다.

스마트폰에서 끊임없이 쏟아지는 알림은 현대인들이 깊은 집중력을 발휘하는 것을 점점 더 어렵게 만들고 있다. (①) 주의력에 대한 통제권을 되찾기 위해서는, 의지력에만 의존하기보다는 물리적 환경을 선제적으로 관리해야 한다. (②) 제가 기술을 완전히 버리라거나 숲속의 은둔자처럼 살아야 한다고 제안하는 것은 아니다. (③) 대신에, 목표는 끊임없는 방해로부터 당신의 인지적 자원을 보호할 수 있는 의도적 경계를 만드는 것이다. (④ <u>정신적인 휴식을 보장하기 위해 모든 전자 기기가 엄격히 금지되는 "디지털 프리 존"을 집 안에 설정해라.</u>) 예를 들어, 식탁과 침실을 휴대폰이 허용되지 않는 구역으로 지정하여, 방해받지 않는 대화나 더 나은 수면이 가능하게 할 수 있다.

- establish 설립[설정]하다
- prohibit 금지하다
- notification 알림, 통고, 통지, 신고
- attention 주의 (집중),주목
- proactively 선행 학습에 영향받아, 사전 대책을 강구해
- willpower 의지력
- abandon 버리다, 포기하다
- hermit 은둔자
- intentional 의도적인, 고의로 한
- interruption 중단, 방해
- designate 지정하다, 지명하다

18 [독해 – 순서 배열] ▶ ③

주어진 글은 세계 경제 성장률이 둔화될 것이지만, 그 전망이 지역별로 다르게 나타난다고 밝히며 비교·대조 구조를 예고한다. 먼저 (C)는 '선진국'의 약 1.5% 수준의 낮은 성장 전망을 제시하며 첫 번째 사례를 설명한다. 이어 (A)는 '반면'이라는 대조를 통해 '신흥국 및 개발도상국'이 4%대 성장세를 보일 것임을 제시하며 선진국과 뚜렷한 대비를 이루게 한다. 마지막으로 (B)는 '두 그룹 모두'라는 표현으로 앞의 두 범주를 함께 받아서, 지정학적 불확실성·보호무역주의·금융시장 조정 가능성과 같은 공통의 하방 위험을 지적하며 글을 마무리한다. 따라서 글의 순서로 가장 적절한 것은 ③이다.

국제통화기금(IMF)의 최근 세계 경제 전망에 따르면, 내년에는 세계 경제 성장률이 둔화될 것으로 보이지만 지역별 전망에는 큰 차이가 있다.
(C) 선진국들은 인플레이션을 조절하기 위한 긴축 통화 정책과 지속적인 노동 공급 문제로 인해 주로 약 1.5%의 완만한 성장을 보일 것으로 예상된다.
(A) 이와 대조적으로, 신흥 시장과 개발도상국들은 여러 주요 국가의 강력한 내수 덕분에 4%를 약간 상회하는 성장을 할 것으로 예상되지만, 여전히 외부 충격에는 취약한 상태이다.
(B) 두 그룹 모두 여전히 상당한 위험에 직면해 있다. IMF는 지정학적 불확실성, 보호무역주의 확대, 금융시장 조정 가능성이 현재의 성장 경로와 관계 없이 경제 안정성을 위협할 수 있다고 경고한다.

- International Monetary Fund (IMF) 국제통화기금
- project 예상하다, 전망하다
- forecast 전망, 예측, 예측하다
- domestic demand 내수, 국내 수요
- geopolitical 지정학적
- protectionism 보호주의
- undermine 약화시키다
- modest 크지 않은, 완만한, 보통 정도의
- restrictive 억제하는, 제한적인
- monetary policy 통화[화폐] 정책

19 [독해 – 빈칸 추론] ▶ ①

이 글은 신뢰를 단순한 감정이나 모호한 미덕이 아니라, 협업의 속도와 질을 좌우하고 경제적 마찰을 줄여 성과를 높이는 '실질적이고 구축 가능한 자산'이자 현대 리더십의 핵심 역량으로 정의하고 있다. 빈칸이 포함된 첫 문장은 신뢰에 대한 '근본적인 오산'을 언급하며 글이 비판하는 잘못된 통념을 제시해야 하는 구조이다. 지문 후반부에서 신뢰가 "추상적인 것과는 거리가 멀다"고 강조하고 있으므로, 이와 반대로 신뢰를 실질적 가치가 없는 모호하고 추상적인 개념으로만 치부하는 태도를 지적하는 내용이 들어가야 한다. 따라서 밑줄 친 부분에 들어갈 말로 가장 적절한 것은 ①이다.

<u>신뢰를 단지 부드럽고 무형적인 이상향으로만 간주하는 것</u>은 조직과 개인 관계 역학에서의 근본적인 오판이다. 신뢰는 저절로 가지게 되는 수동적 특성이 아니라, 모든 의미 있는 상호작용의 토대이며 업무와 소통의 속도·질을 좌우하는 핵심 요소이다. 또한 신뢰는 조정 비용을 줄이고 협업을 가능하게 하는 경제적 동력으로도 작용한다. 추상적인 개념과는 달리, 신뢰는 의도적으로 구축할 수 있고 손상되었을 때는 세심하게 회복할 수 있는 실질적 자산이다. 기업 스캔들과 불신이 커지는 환경에서 신뢰를 형성하고 유지하는 능력은 회복력 있는 조직을 다른 조직과 구분 짓는 결정적인 리더십 역량이 되었다.

① 신뢰를 단지 부드럽고 무형적인 이상향으로만 간주하는 것
② 신뢰가 개인적인 관계에서 관련이 있다고 가정하는 것
③ 신뢰를 실행 가능하고 갱신 가능한 자원으로 믿는 것
④ 구조적 신뢰보다 개인적 매력에 더 집중하는 것

- fundamental 근본적인, 기본적인
- miscalculation 잘못된 판단, 오산
- passive 수동적인, 소극적인
- friction 마찰, 불협화음
- restore 회복하다, 복구하다
- skepticism 회의, 의심
- competency 역량, 능력
- distinguish 구별하다
- deliberate 의도적인, 신중한
- credibility 신뢰도, 신용

[난이도] 상

[정답 해설]

이 글은 자가면역 질환이 어떻게 발생하는지를 단계적으로 설명하고 있다. 먼저 외부 항원에 대한 작은 국소 면역 반응이 일어나지만, 이것이 충분하지 않으면 면역 체계는 항체를 동원한 더 강한 전신 반응으로 격상시킨다. 문제는 이 강화된 면역 반응이 '조절되지 않은 채' 오래 지속될 때이다. 본문은 이런 지속적 활성 상태가 '만성 염증'으로 이어지며, 이것이 병리적 결과를 초래한다고 밝힌다. 빈칸은 이 만성 염증이 구체적으로 어떤 해로운 결과를 유발하는지를 설명해야 한다. 따라서 밑줄 친 부분에 들어갈 말로 가장 적절한 것은 ②이다.

[해석]

> 자가면역은 면역체계가 실수로 몸의 자체 조직을 유해한 것으로 잘못 인식할 때 발생한다. 이러한 비정상적인 반응은 종종 미묘하게 시작된다. 환경 독소나 병원체가 체내로 침입하면 작은 국소적 면역 반응이 촉발된다. 이러한 초기 반응은 대체로 균형을 이루며, 우리가 자각하지 못하는 수준에서 진행된다. 그러나 이 반응이 침입한 위협을 제거하는 데 실패하면, 면역체계는 표적 항체를 방출하는 방식으로 대응을 강화한다. 이처럼 더 강한 반응은 보호를 위해 필수적이지만, 지속되면 오히려 해로워질 수 있다. 만약 이렇게 고조된 활동이 억제되지 않은 채 계속된다면, 그 결과로 나타나는 만성 염증은 <u>그것(면역체계)이 방어하려던 바로 그 조직들을 파괴하기 시작하며</u>, 이는 장기 손상과 자가면역 질환의 발병으로 이어진다.

① 초기 면역 반응을 의식적으로 느낄 수 있게 만들며
② 그것이 방어하려던 바로 그 조직들을 파괴하기 시작하며
③ 환경 독소를 더 효율적으로 제거하는 데 집중하며
④ 지속적인 영향을 남기지 않는 일시적인 방어 기제를 촉발하며

[어휘]

- autoimmunity 자가면역
- mistakenly 잘못하여
- abnormal 비정상적인
- toxin 독소
- pathogen 병원체
- localized 국소적인
- release 방출하다, 풀어 주다
- chronic inflammation 만성 염증
- inflict (괴로움 등을) 가하다, 입히다
- collateral damage 부수적 피해

✓ 제10회 모의고사

01 ②	02 ②	03 ③	04 ③	05 ①
06 ③	07 ②	08 ③	09 ②	10 ④
11 ④	12 ①	13 ④	14 ①	15 ①
16 ④	17 ②	18 ②	19 ④	20 ③

01 [어휘 − 빈칸] ▶②

난이도 중

정답 해설

입구에서 생체 인증을 요구하는 정도의 보안 시스템이라는 점을 고려할 때, 서버실에 대한 무단 접근을 실질적으로 '저지하도록' 설계되었다는 내용이 자연스럽다. 따라서 밑줄 친 부분에 들어갈 말로 가장 적절한 것은 ②이다.

해석

보안 시스템은 입구에서 생체 인증을 요구함으로써 서버실에 대한 무단 접근을 저지하도록 설계되었다.

어휘

★ deter 저지하다, 방해하다, 단념시키다
● infringe 위반하다, 제한[침해]하다
● depreciate 가치가 떨어지다[절하되다]
● authenticate 진짜임을 증명하다

02 [어휘 − 빈칸] ▶②

난이도 상

정답 해설

이사회는 두 기업 간의 문화적 충돌을 우려 사항으로 언급했다는 점을 고려하면, 두 기업 간의 합병에 대해 지지를 보내기보다는 '의구심'을 보였다는 내용이 자연스럽다. 따라서 밑줄 친 부분에 들어갈 말로 가장 적절한 것은 ②이다.

해석

이사회는 두 기업 간의 잠재적인 문화적 충돌에 대한 우려를 언급하며, 제안된 합병에 대해 의구심을 표명했다.

어휘

★ reservation 의구심, 예약, 보호구역
● transaction 거래, 매매, 처리 (과정)
● amenity 생활 편의 시설
● credential 자격, 적격, 자격증, 신임장

03 [문법 − 빈칸] ▶③

난이도 중

정답 해설

③ **[적중포인트 001] 문장의 구성 요소 ★★★★☆**
& [적중포인트 007] 불가산 명사의 종류와 특징 ★★★☆☆
문장의 주어 역할을 하는 there is 뒤에는 명사가 와야 한다. 문맥상 인사팀장이 '새로운 복지 패키지에 대해 혼란이 많다'는 점을 강조했고, 이를 명확히 하기 위해 세미나를 연다는 내용이 자연스럽다. 또한 양을 나타내는 형용사 much는 불가산 명사를 수식하므로 명사형이 들어가는 것이 적절하다. 따라서 밑줄 친 부분에 들어갈 말로 가장 적절한 것은 ③이다.

해석

인사과장은 새로운 복지 혜택 패키지에 대해 많은 혼란이 있다는 점을 강조했으며, 따라서 이에 대한 명확한 설명을 위해 다음 주 금요일에 유익한 세미나가 개최될 예정이다.

04 [생활영어 − 빈칸] ▶③

난이도 하

정답 해설

Sarah가 응급실 예약을 문의하자, Mark는 응급실이 예약제가 아닌 '의료적 우선순위'에 따라 운영됨을 알리며 구체적인 증상을 묻는다. 빈칸 뒤에서 Mark가 "그런 경우라면 즉시 데려오라"고 하며, 환자 분류 간호사의 진단이 필요하다고 강조한 것으로 보아, Sarah는 긴박한 응급 상황을 말했음을 짐작할 수 있다. 따라서 밑줄 친 부분에 들어갈 말로 가장 적절한 것은 ③이다.

해석

Sarah Chen: 병원에 가기 전에 응급실 빈자리를 예약하는 것이 가능한가요?
Mark Lee: 아니요, 환자들은 의학적 우선순위에 따라 진료받기 때문에 예약을 받지 않습니다. 현재 증상을 설명해 주시겠습니까?
Sarah Chen: 제 아들이 지금 숨쉬기 힘들어하고 있어요.
Mark Lee: 그런 경우라면, 저희 부상자 분류 간호사가 상태를 판단할 수 있도록 즉시 데려오십시오.
Sarah Chen: 알겠습니다, 지금 가는 중이니 준비해 주세요.

① 지금 병원 바로 근처예요.
② 저번에 병원에서 진료 본 기록이 있어요.
③ 제 아들이 지금 숨쉬기 힘들어하고 있어요.
④ 현재 응급실에는 자리가 하나도 비어 있지 않습니다.

어휘

• slot 자리, 틈
• reservation 예약
• symptom 증상, 징후
• triage (치료 우선순위를 정하기 위한) 부상자 분류

05 [생활영어 − 빈칸] ▶①

난이도 하

정답 해설

A의 제안에 대해 B는 텀블러를 사용하지 못하는 이유를 설명해야 한다. 이어지는 대화에서 A가 '잊어버리지 않도록 하는 방법'을 조언하고 있다는 점을 보면, B가 텀블러를 사용하지 못하는 가장 큰 이유는 집에서 챙겨 오는 것을 자주 잊기 때문임을 알 수 있다. 따라서 "계속 사용하려고 하지만, 집에서 가져오는 것을 항상 잊어버린다"는 내용이 들어가야 자연스럽다. 따라서 밑줄 친 부분에 들어갈 말로 가장 적절한 것은 ①이다.

해석

A: 이봐요 Clara, 커피 또 마시네요? 오늘 벌써 세 번째 일회용 컵이에요.
B: 알아요, 알아. 쓰레기 때문에 죄책감이 좀 들어요.
A: 그럼 텀블러를 사용하지 그래요? 대부분 카페에서는 할인도 해주잖아요.
B: 계속 그러려고 하는데, 집에서 가져오는 걸 항상 잊어버려요.
A: 현관문에 포스트잇을 붙여보도록 해요. 기억하는 데 도움이 될 거예요.
B: 그거 좋은 생각이네요. 내일 한번 시도해 볼게요.

① 계속 그러려고 하는데, 집에서 가져오는 걸 항상 잊어버려요.
② 저는 텀블러로 마시는 커피 맛을 별로 안 좋아해요.
③ 사실, 이 컵들은 전부 생분해돼요.
④ 나는 텀블러를 여러 개 가지고 있지만, 그중 어느 것도 내 차의 컵홀더에는 맞지 않아요.

어휘

• disposable 일회용의
• guilty 죄책감을 느끼는
• discount 할인, 할인하다
• recycling bin 재활용 쓰레기통

06 [독해 − 세트형 문항(홈페이지 게시글 − 제목)]　　▶ ③

난이도 중

정답 해설

이 글은 Northwood 산업 지구의 용도 변경 제안과 관련된 공청회 개최 안내이다. 공청회의 일정, 진행 절차, 발언 규정, 서면 제출 기한 등을 구체적으로 안내하고 있으며, 공청회를 통해 Northwood 산업 지구를 주거 및 상업 복합 용도로 '용도 지역 변경'하는 것에 대해 시민들의 의견을 듣겠다는 것이다. 따라서 글의 제목으로 가장 적절한 것은 ③이다.
① 산업 단지를 위한 환경 지침
② 사업 제안서 제출 절차
③ 토지 이용 변경에 대한 지역 사회 의견 수렴 기회
④ 도시 계획에 대한 입법 의결 결과

07 [독해 − 세트형 문항(홈페이지 게시글 − 내용 불일치)]　　▶ ②

난이도 하

정답 해설

이번 공청회는 먼저 개발업자가 마스터플랜을 발표하고, 이어서 독립 자문기관의 환경 영향 평가가 제시될 예정이라고 안내되어 있다. 따라서 윗글의 내용과 일치하지 않는 것은 ②이다.

오답 해설

① 이 공청회는 어떠한 입법 조치를 취하기 전에 공적 논의를 보장하기 위해 시 조례 7.14에 따라 의무적으로 실시되는 것이라고 언급하고 있으므로 글의 내용과 일치한다.
③ 시민 의견 발표는 1인당 3분으로 제한된다고 언급하고 있으므로 글의 내용과 일치한다.
④ 이번 공청회는 정보 제공 및 의견 수렴을 위한 자리일 뿐이며, 이 회의에서 최종 표결은 이루어지지 않는다고 언급하고 있으므로 글의 내용과 일치한다.

해석

> ### 토지 이용 변경에 대한 지역 사회 의견 수렴 기회
>
> 웨스트우드 시의회는 Northwood 산업 지구를 주거·상업 혼합 용도로 재지정하려는 안건과 관련하여 공청회 개최를 발표합니다. 이 공청회는 어떠한 입법 조치를 취하기 전에 공적 논의를 보장하기 위해 시 조례 7.14에 따라 의무적으로 실시되는 것입니다.
>
> 해당 시간은 10월 28일 오후 7시에 시청 회의실에서 개최될 예정입니다. 먼저 개발업자가 마스터플랜을 발표하고, 이어서 독립 자문기관의 환경 영향 평가가 제시될 예정입니다. 시민 의견 발표는 1인당 3분으로 제한되며, 내용은 재지정 제안 그 자체에 직접적으로 관련된 사항이어야 하고 그 외의 주변 문제에 대해서는 발언할 수 없습니다. 서면 제출은 당일 오후 5시까지 가능하며, 모두 공식 기록에 포함됩니다. 이번 공청회는 정보 제공 및 의견 수렴을 위한 자리일 뿐이며, 이 회의에서 최종 표결은 이루어지지 않습니다.

어휘

• public hearing 공청회
• rezoning 구역 재지정, 용도 변경
• residential 주거의
• mandate 의무화하다, 명령하다
• ordinance 법령, 조례
• chamber 회의실
• independent 독립적인
• ancillary 부차적인, 보조적인
• in accordance with ~에 따라서

08 [독해 − 단일형 문항(안내문 − 내용 불일치)]　　▶ ③

난이도 중

정답 해설

표 부분에서 청소년 대상자의 요건 부분에 '소설 5권 또는 500페이지 읽기' 중 선택할 수 있다고 명시되어 있다. 따라서 윗글의 내용과 일치하지 않는 것은 ③이다.

오답 해설

① 이 프로그램은 지역 사회가 여름 휴가 기간 동안 더 많은 책을 읽도록 권장한다고 언급하고 있으므로 글의 내용과 일치한다.
② 참가자들은 모바일 앱이나 종이 기록장을 사용하여 자신의 진행 상황을 기록

할 수 있다고 언급하고 있으므로 글의 내용과 일치한다.
④ 표 부분에서 성인 대상자의 요건 부분에 '서로 다른 장르의 책 3권 읽기'라고 명시되어 있으므로 글의 내용과 일치한다.

해석

> ### 여름 독서 챌린지 안내
>
> Metro 공립 도서관은 모든 연령대의 독자들을 "여름 독서 챌린지"에 초대합니다. 이 프로그램은 지역 사회가 여름 휴가 기간 동안 더 많은 책을 읽도록 권장하며, 독서 이정표(목표)에 도달할 때마다 흥미진진한 보상을 제공합니다.
>
> 참가자들은 모바일 앱이나 종이 기록장을 사용하여 자신의 진행 상황을 기록할 수 있습니다. 챌린지를 완료하면, 모든 참가자는 8월 말에 열리는 시상식에 초대됩니다.
>
> **챌린지 카테고리:**
>
> | 카테고리 | 요건 | 보상 |
> | --- | --- | --- |
> | 어린이 독자 | 그림책 10권 읽기 | 장난감 세트와 증서 |
> | 청소년 | 소설 5권 또는 500페이지 읽기 | 20달러 도서 상품권 |
> | 성인 | 서로 다른 장르의 책 3권 읽기 | 한정판 대형 손가방 |
>
> 등록은 6월 1일에 시작됩니다. 신청하시려면 도서관 웹사이트를 방문하거나 메인 데스크에 들러주세요. 이번 여름을 이야기로 가득 채워봅시다!

① 이 계획은 오직 여름에만 제공된다.
② 진행 상황은 디지털 방식이나 종이 기록물 중 하나로 기록될 수 있다.
③ 청소년 참가자들은 각각 최소 500페이지가 넘는 소설을 5권을 읽어야 한다.
④ 성인 챌린지는 오직 한 가지 장르의 책들만 읽는 것을 허용하지 않는다.

어휘

• milestone 이정표, 획기적인 사건
• log 기록, 일지
• completion 완료, 완성
• requirement 요건, 필요조건
• certificate 증서, 증명서, 자격증
• tote bag 여성용 대형 손가방

09 [독해 − 단일형 문항(전자메일 − 목적)]　　▶ ②

난이도 중

정답 해설

이 글은 'The Hamilton' 아파트 주민들에게 관리사무소가 보낸 긴급 공지로, 모든 세대 내부의 화재경보기 점검이 이루어질 예정임을 알리고 있다. 층별 점검 일정이 제시되어 있으며, 점검을 위해 기술자들이 각 세대에 출입해야 한다는 점을 강조하면서, 부재 시 열쇠를 맡기거나 이웃을 통해 출입을 가능하게 해 달라는 협조를 요청하고 있다. 따라서 글의 목적으로 가장 적절한 것은 ②이다.

해석

> 수신인: 'The Hamilton' 모든 입주민
> 발신인: 해밀턴 아파트 관리사무소
> 날짜: 2026년 11월 5일
> 제목: 긴급 공지
>
> 도시 안전 규정에 따라 실시되는 연례 화재경보기 시스템 점검에 관한 필수 공지입니다. 당사 공인 기술자들이 모든 세대 내부에 설치된 경보기(사이렌/섬광등)를 점검할 예정입니다.
>
> 점검 일정:
> • 1~10층: 11월 12일(수) 오전 9시 ~ 오후 5시
> • 11~20층: 11월 13일(목) 오전 9시 ~ 오후 5시
>
> 기술자들은 각 세대에 약 5~10분간 출입해야 합니다. 귀하가 집에 계시지 않을 경우, 다음 중 하나의 방법으로 출입하도록 조치를 취해야 합니다.
> 1. 봉인된 이름표가 있는 봉투에 열쇠를 프런트 데스크에 맡기기
> 2. 믿을 수 있는 이웃이 대신 있어 주도록 하기
>
> 참고: 복도와 로비 등 공용 구역의 경보기는 11월 14일(금)에 별도로 점검되며, 소음이 매우 클 예정입니다. 이 점검은 세대 출입이 필요하지 않습니다.

① 화재 발생 시 주민들에게 대피 지침을 제공하려고
② 각 세대 내 화재경보기 점검을 위한 협조를 요청하려고
③ 기술자가 출입할 수 없는 세대를 사전에 파악하려고
④ 도시 안전 규정 변경에 대한 주민들의 의견을 수렴하려고

- **mandatory** 의무적인
- **regulation** 규정, 규제
- **certified** 인증된, 공인의
- **audible** 들을 수 있는
- **trusted** 신뢰할 수 있는
- **separately** 별도로, 따로따로
- **inspection** 점검, 검사
- **identify** 확인하다, 찾다, 발견하다

10 [독해 – 세트형 문항(홈페이지 게시글 – 유의어)]   ▶④

난이도 하

정답 해설

밑줄 친 'foster'는 '촉진하다, 육성하다, 기르다'의 뜻으로, 이와 문맥상 가장 가까운 의미는 ④ 'promote(촉진하다, 홍보하다, 승진시키다)'이다.

오답 해설

① align 조정[조절]하다, 나란히 만들다
② repress 참다, 억누르다, 진압하다
③ coerce 강압하다, 강제하다

11 [독해 – 세트형 문항(홈페이지 게시글 – 내용 불일치)]   ▶④

난이도 중

정답 해설

심포지엄 발표 내용은 학술지(동료 평가 저널)에 논문집 형태로 출판될 예정이나, 심포지엄에서 발표했다고 해서 자동으로 출판이 보장되는 것은 아님을 유의해야 한다고 안내하고 있다. 따라서 윗글의 내용과 일치하지 않는 것은 ④이다.
① 이 행사는 첨단 연구 결과의 공유를 장려하기 위해 기획되었다.
② 양자 물리학 분야의 대학원생은 참석이 가능하다.
③ 참석자들은 양자 역학에 대한 기초 지식을 갖추어야 한다.
④ 행사에서 발표된 모든 연구는 학술지에 포함될 것이다.

오답 해설

① 이번 행사는 협력을 촉진하고 최신 연구 성과를 공유하는 것을 목표로 한다고 언급하고 있으므로 글의 내용과 일치한다.
② 참가 대상은 대학원생 및 양자물리학 및 관련 분야의 전문가라고 언급하고 있으므로 글의 내용과 일치한다.
③ 기술 시간을 충분히 이해하기 위해서는 양자역학에 대한 기초 지식이 필수라고 언급하고 있으므로 글의 내용과 일치한다.

해석

> **양자물리 심포지엄 초청 안내**
>
> 고등물리연구소는 여러분을 국제 양자 얽힘 심포지엄에 정중히 초대합니다. 이번 심포지엄은 해당 분야 연구자와 학계 전문가들에게 중요한 행사로, 협력을 촉진하고 최신 연구 성과를 공유하는 것을 목표로 합니다.
>
> 일간 진행되는 이번 행사는 노벨상 수상자인 Evelyn Reed 박사와 Kenji Tanaka 박사의 기조 연설을 비롯하여, 수많은 병행 시간과 포스터 발표로 구성될 예정입니다. 모든 발표는 영어로 진행됩니다. 참가 자격은 양자 물리학 및 관련 분야의 대학원생과 전문가들에게 열려 있습니다. 모든 참가자가 기술 세션의 내용을 충분히 이해하고 도움을 받기 위해서는 양자 역학에 대한 기초 지식이 필수 선행 조건입니다. 등록은 의무 사항이며 11월 1일에 마감됩니다. 심포지엄의 공식 기록은 동료 심사 학술지에 게재될 예정이나, 심포지엄에서 발표를 한다고 해서 게재가 보장되는 것은 아님을 유의하시기 바랍니다.

- **symposium** 심포지엄, 학술 회의
- **cordially** 정중하게, 진심으로
- **disseminate** 전파하다, 퍼뜨리다
- **cutting-edge** 최첨단의
- **keynote address** (정당·회의 등의) 기조 연설
- **laureate** 수상자
- **discipline** 분야, 규율
- **prerequisite** 전제 조건, 필수 조건
- **proceeding** 공식 기록, 회의[의사]록
- **eligible** 자격이 있는

12 [문법 – 밑줄]   ▶①

난이도 중

정답 해설

① **[적중포인트 044] 주어 자리에서 반드시 단수 또는 복수 취급하는 특정 표현 ★★★☆☆**
언어학(linguistics)과 같은 학문명은 단수 취급한다. 따라서 밑줄 친 부분의 require를 requires로 고쳐야 한다.

오답 해설

② **[적중포인트 063] to부정사의 동사적 성질 ★★★★☆**
일반적으로 to부정사의 의미상 주어를 따로 표시할 경우는 'for 목적격'을 써야 한다. 따라서 밑줄 친 부분은 올바르게 쓰였다.
③ **[적중포인트 014] 형용사와 부사의 차이 ★★★★★**
altogether는 '전적으로, 완전히'라는 의미로 부사로 형용사(indispensable)를 수식할 수 있다. 따라서 밑줄 친 부분은 올바르게 쓰였다.
④ **[적중포인트 062] to부정사의 부사적 역할 ★★☆☆☆**
문장 맨 앞에서 목적(~하기 위해서)을 나타내는 부사적 용법의 to부정사로 뒤에 오는 주절(a hybrid approach... is now the standard)과 논리적으로 잘 연결된다. 따라서 밑줄 친 부분은 올바르게 쓰였다.

해석

> AI 개발에서 언어학은 구문론과 의미론에 대한 정교한 이해를 필요로 한다. 일부 엔지니어들은 방대한 양의 데이터만으로도 기계가 학습하기에 충분하다고 주장하지만, 대부분의 전문가는 구조적 지식이 전적으로 필수적이라는 점에 동의한다. 결과적으로, 데이터 기반 학습과 언어학 이론을 결합한 하이브리드 접근 방식이 이제 표준이 되었다.

13 [문법 – 밑줄]   ▶④

난이도 중

정답 해설

④ **[적중포인트 088] 전치사와 명사 목적어 ★★★☆☆**
전치사 'in'의 목적어 자리에는 명사 또는 동명사가 와야 한다. 여기서 'narrow'는 동사로 쓰여 어법상 맞지 않다. '배출 격차를 줄이는 것'이라는 의미가 되어야 하므로 동명사로 써야 한다. 따라서 밑줄 친 부분의 narrow를 narrowing으로 고쳐야 한다.

오답 해설

① **[적중포인트 079] 명사절 접속사의 구분과 특징 ★★★☆☆**
that절의 주어(projections)는 복수형이므로 동사도 복수 형태로 써야 한다. 또한 문맥상 과거부터 지금까지의 변화 결과가 '현재 시점'에 반영되어 있기 때문에 현재완료형이 적절하다. 따라서 밑줄 친 부분은 올바르게 쓰였다.
② **[적중포인트 039] 현재시제 동사와 be동사의 수 일치 ★★★★★**
주어 'delays'가 복수형이므로 동사도 복수 형태로 써야 한다. 따라서 밑줄 친 부분은 올바르게 쓰였다.
③ **[적중포인트 039] 현재시제 동사와 be동사의 수 일치 ★★★★★**
주어 'The report'가 단수형이므로 동사도 단수 형태로 써야 한다. 따라서 밑줄 친 부분은 올바르게 쓰였다.

해석

> 2025년 배출 격차 보고서는 전 세계 온난화 전망치가 소폭 하락했다고 밝힌다. 그러나 지정학적 긴장과 경제적 불안정으로 인해 대폭적인 배출 감축이 지연되면서, 세계는 1.5℃ 한계를 일시적으로 초과하게 될 것임을 의미한다. 이 보고서는 배출 격차를 좁히는 데 있어 G20의 행동이 결정적인 역할을 할 것이라고 주장한다.

14 [독해 - 단일형 문항(안내문 - 내용 일치)] ▶ ①

난이도 하

정답 해설

일반 배송의 경우 50달러 이상 주문 시 무료라고 명시되어 있다. 따라서 윗글의 내용과 일치하는 것은 ①이다.

오답 해설

② 빠른 배송은 12월 18일(목) 오후 11시 59분(EST)까지 주문해야 한다고 명시되어 있으므로 글의 내용과 일치하지 않는다.
③ 익일 배송은 12월 22일(목) 오후 1시(EST)까지 주문해야 한다고 명시되어 있으므로 글의 내용과 일치하지 않는다.
④ 알래스카·하와이 및 국제 배송은 추가로 영업일 5~7일이 더 필요하며, 12월 24일까지 도착을 보장할 수 없다고 명시되어 있으므로 글의 내용과 일치하지 않는다.

해석

연말 배송 마감 안내: 12월 24일 도착을 원하신다면 지금 주문하세요
날짜: 2026년 11월 5일

연말 선물이 제때 도착하도록 하려면, 아래 기한까지 주문을 완료해 주세요.
☐ 일반 배송(Standard Shipping, $5.99 / $50 이상 주문 시 무료):
  12월 15일(월) 오후 11시 59분(EST)까지 주문
☐ 빠른 배송(Expedited Shipping, $12.99):
  12월 18일(목) 오후 11시 59분(EST)까지 주문
☐ 익일 배송(Overnight Shipping, $24.99):
  12월 22일(월) 오후 1시(EST)까지 주문

이 마감일은 미 본토(continental US) 배송에만 적용됩니다. 알래스카·하와이 및 국제 배송은 추가로 영업일 5~7일이 더 필요하며, 12월 24일까지 도착을 보장할 수 없습니다.

참고: 이니셜 각인 제품은 추가로 3영업일의 처리 기간이 필요하며, 익일 배송을 이용할 수 없습니다.

① 50달러가 넘는 주문에 대해서는 일반 배송이 무료로 제공된다.
② 빠른 배송은 12월 18일 오전까지 주문을 완료해야 한다.
③ 12월 22일 오후 2시에 주문하면 익일 배송을 이용할 수 있다.
④ 알래스카로 배송되는 주문은 12월 24일까지 반드시 도착한다.

어휘

• shipping 배송, 운송
• ensure 보장하다
• standard shipping 일반 배송
• expedited shipping 빠른 배송
• overnight shipping 익일 배송
• continental 대륙의
• business day 영업일
• guarantee 보장하다
• free 무료의
• unlikely 가능성이 낮은, ~할 것 같지 않은

15 [독해 - 중심 내용 추론(주제)] ▶ ①

난이도 상

정답 해설

이 글은 "장기적으로 효율적인 기술이 반드시 승리한다"는 전통 경제학의 지배적 가정을 '경로 의존성' 개념을 통해 정면으로 반박한다. 필자는 QWERTY 키보드 사례를 제시하며, 초기의 사소하거나 우발적인 선택이 강력한 '고착(Lock-in)' 효과를 형성함으로써 더 우월한 대안이 등장하더라도 비효율적인 표준이 지속될 수 있음을 설명한다. 결론적으로 기술의 발전 궤적은 항상 합리적인 완성을 향해 나아가는 것이 아니라, 전환 비용이나 네트워크 효과와 같은 과거의 우연한 사건들에 의해 제약될 수 있다는 점이 이 글의 핵심 주제이다. 따라서 글의 주제로 가장 적절한 것은 ①이다.

해석

경제학에서 널리 받아들여지는 가정은 장기적으로는 효율성이 결국 우세해진다는 것이다. 이런 관점에서 보면, 최적이 아닌 기술은 더 우수한 대안에 의해 빠르게 대체되어야 한다. 하지만 경제사에는 이와 상반되는 사례들이 가득하며, 그중에서 QWERTY(쿼티) 키보드가 가장 많이 인용된다. 이러한 현상을 '경로 의존성'이라 부르는데, 이는 초기 단계에서의 사소하거나 우연한 선택들이 강력한 '잠금(lock-in)' 효과를 만들어낼 수 있다는 개념이다. 전환 비용이 높거나 기존 인프라가 견고하게 자리 잡았을 때, 그리고 사용자가 많을수록 제품 가치가 커지는 네트워크 효과가 존재할 때, 열등한 표준조차 굳어져 지속될 수 있다. 따라서 기술 발전의 경로는 항상 완벽함을 향해 합리적으로 나아가는 것이 아니라, 그 기술이 지나온 과거의 우발적 사건들에 의해 제약되는 경우가 많다는 점을 보여준다.

① 낮은 품질의 기술 표준이 지속되는 이유들
② 차선의 기술을 신속하게 대체하는 방법
③ 기술 시장에서 선점하는 것의 중요성
④ 차선의 기술을 대체하는 효율적인 방법들

어휘

• dominant 지배적인, 우세한
• assumption 가정, 전제
• posit 단정하다, 제시하다
• prevail 우세하다, 지배하다
• suboptimal 차선의, 최적이 아닌
• replete 가득한[충분한]
• counterexample 반례
• stochastic 우연적인
• entrench 단단히 자리 잡게 하다
• trajectory 궤적, 경로
• constrained 제한된
• inevitable 불가피한

16 [독해 - 문장 제거] ▶ ④

난이도 하

정답 해설

이 글은 AI를 활용해 고객 데이터를 분석하고 개별화된 가격을 제시하는 '감시 기반 가격 책정'의 개념과 이를 둘러싼 논란을 다루고 있다. ①번 문장은 AI 분석을 통해 개인별로 동적 가격을 설정할 수 있다는 점을 설명하고, ②번 문장은 개별 가격 책정에 영향을 미치는 구체적 요소를 제시한다. 이어 ③번 문장은 이러한 방식을 정교한 시장 세분화로 보고, 충성 고객에게 혜택을 주는 긍정적 시각을 소개한다. 마지막 문장은 이 방식이 차별적이고 불투명하여 소비자 신뢰를 해칠 수 있다는 비판을 제시하며 ③번 문장과 대비된다. 그러나 ④번 문장은 플랫폼이 고객 데이터를 보호하기 위해 사이버보안에 투자한다는 내용으로 핵심 논지인 가격 차별 방식의 정당성·윤리성 논쟁과는 직접적 관련이 없다. 따라서 글의 흐름상 어색한 문장은 ④이다.

해석

전자상거래에서 점점 우려가 커지고 있는 것은 '감시 기반 가격 책정'의 확산이다. 이는 소매업자가 AI를 사용해 소비자의 개인정보와 온라인 행동을 분석하는 전략을 말한다. ① 이러한 방식은 기업이 소비자가 지불할 가능성이 있는 금액을 추정해, 개인별로 동적 가격을 설정할 수 있게 한다. ② 검색 기록, 위치, 기기 종류, 심지어 추정 소득 수준까지도 동일한 제품에 제시되는 가격에 영향을 미칠 수 있다. ③ 옹호자들은 이것이 단지 더 정교해진 시장 세분화 전략이며, 충성 고객에게 할인을 제공하는 방식이라고 주장한다. (④ 많은 플랫폼이 고객 데이터를 보호하기 위해 사이버 보안에도 투자하고 있다.) 그러나 비판론자들은 이러한 관행이 본질적으로 차별적이며, 소비자가 공정한 가격을 받고 있는지 알 수 없는 불투명한 시장을 만든다며 신뢰와 투명성을 훼손한다고 지적한다.

어휘

• e-commerce 전자상거래
• surveillance 감시
• retailer 소매업자, 소매상
• dynamic 역동적인, 변동적인
• perceived 인지된, 추정된
• reward 보상하다
• discriminatory 차별적인
• opaque 불투명한, 알기 어려운

17 [독해 – 문장 삽입]　　　　　　　　　　　　　▶ ②

난이도 중

정답 해설

이 글은 시각적인 만족감만 주는 '수동적 학습(형광펜)'의 허상과 '능동적 회상'의 실질적 효과를 대조하고 있다. ①번 뒤 문장에서 학생들이 시험 대비 시 본능적으로 행하는 '밑줄 긋기'라는 구체적인 통념이 제시된다. 주어진 문장은 "However"라는 강한 역접의 연결사를 사용하여 흐름을 뒤집으며, 앞선 행위가 정보 유지에 비효율적이라는 전문가의 견해를 도입한다. 이 문장은 통념과 그 뒤에 이어지는 구체적인 비판 및 대안을 잇는 결정적 전환점 역할을 한다. 이어지는 ②번 뒤 문장에서는 형광펜이 주는 '가짜 성취감'을 지적하며 '능동적 회상'이라는 구체적 대안을 제시하고 있으므로, 반박이 시작되어야 하는 부분에 들어가야 한다. 따라서 주어진 문장이 들어갈 위치로 가장 적절한 것은 ②이다.

해석

> 학생들은 시험을 준비할 때 본능적으로 몇 가지 인기 있는 학습 기술에 의존한다. (①) 두꺼운 교과서를 마주할 때, 여러분은 아마도 중요한 문장들을 표시하기 위해 형광펜을 집어 들 것이다. (② 하지만, John Dunlosky 박사에 따르면, 이것은 정보를 기억하는 가장 효과적인 방법과는 거리가 멀다.) 선명한 색상들(형광펜 칠하기)이 성취감은 만들어내지만, 지식을 머릿속에 각인시키는 데는 실패하며, 스스로 테스트하는 '능동적 회상'을 훨씬 더 우수한 전략으로 만든다. (③) 여러분의 뇌는 신경 경로를 강화하기 위해 인지적 노력을 필요로 하는데, 이는 오직 능동적인 인출 과정 동안에만 유발된다. (④) 이러한 정신적 노고 없이는 정보는 피상적인 수준에 머물게 되며, 여러분의 노력은 색깔만 화려하고 알맹이는 없는 교과서라는 결과만 낳을 뿐이다.

어휘

- retain 유지[보유]하다
- instinctively 본능적으로, 무의식적으로
- thick 두꺼운, (부피가) 굵은
- sentence 문장
- embed (단단히) 박대[끼워 넣다]
- superior 우수한, 상급의
- strengthen 강화되다, 강력해지다
- neural 신경(계통)의
- superficial 피상[표면]적인, 깊이 없는

18 [독해 – 순서 배열]　　　　　　　　　　　　　▶ ②

난이도 중

정답 해설

주어진 글은 2024년 이산화탄소 농도가 기록적으로 급증했다는 사실을 전달한다. 이어지는 (B)는 이러한 증가가 여러 요인 때문이라고 설명하면서, 첫 번째이자 가장 중요한 원인으로 화석 연료 사용을 제시한다. (A)는 "이에 더하여"라는 연결을 통해 (B)에서 언급된 인간 활동 외에도 산불과 같은 자연적 요인이 문제를 더욱 악화시키고 있음을 두 번째 원인으로 추가한다. 마지막으로 (C)는 "이 문제를 더욱 심화시키는 것은"이라는 연결로, 앞서 제시된 배출 문제에 더해 탄소 흡수원의 능력이 약해지고 있다는 세 번째 요인을 제시하며 글을 마무리한다. 따라서 글의 순서로 가장 적절한 것은 ②이다.

해석

> 세계기상기구(WMO)는 2024년 전 세계 이산화탄소 농도가 기록적으로 급증했다고 발표하며, 지구 온난화의 가속화에 대한 우려를 제기했다.
>
> (B) 이러한 증가 폭은 관측이 시작된 이후 가장 큰 것으로, 여러 요인이 복합적으로 작용한 결과라고 보고서는 설명한다. 그중에서도 가장 중요한 원인은 여전히 에너지 생산을 위한 화석연료의 광범위한 사용이다.
>
> (A) 인간 활동에서 배출되는 탄소 외에도 자연적 요인이 문제를 더욱 악화시키고 있다. 특히 건조하고 더운 조건으로 인해 확산된 산불이 막대한 양의 탄소를 대기 중에 방출했다.
>
> (C) 이 문제를 더욱 심화시키는 것은 해양과 숲과 같은 자연적 탄소 흡수원이 CO_2를 흡수하는 능력이 감소하고 있는 것으로 보인다. 흡수량이 줄어들면 배출된 탄소가 대기 중에 더 오래 남게 되고, 이는 결국 지구 온도를 더 빠르게 상승시키는 요인이 된다.

어휘

- record 기록적인, 기록을 깨는
- carbon dioxide 이산화탄소
- concentration 농도, 집중
- emission 배출물, 배기가스
- stored 축적된, 저장된
- alarming 심각한, 불안하게 만드는
- measurement 측정, 측량, 치수
- fossil fuels 화석 연료
- compound 악화시키다, 더 심각하게 만들다
- diminish 줄어들다, 약해지다

19 [독해 – 빈칸 추론]　　　　　　　　　　　　　▶ ④

난이도 중

정답 해설

이 글은 '수동적 수신'이라는 잘못된 경청 태도와 '능동적·추출적 과정'으로서의 올바른 경청 태도를 대조하고 있다. 첫 문장은 잘못된 태도의 기준을 화자의 유창함에만 두는 경향을 지적한다. 빈칸이 있는 두 번째 문장은 이와 같은 수동적 경청이 무엇을 의미하는지 구체적으로 설명하는 자리이다. 이어지는 문장들은 좋은 청자가 정보를 스스로 캐내고, 명확한 질문을 던지고, 화자를 탓하기보다 자신의 이해를 먼저 점검하며 책임을 지는 태도를 보여준다고 설명한다. 이러한 능동적 태도와 대비되는 수동적 경청의 핵심은 이해의 책임을 온전히 말하는 사람에게 떠넘기는 것이다. 따라서 밑줄 친 부분에 들어갈 말로 가장 적절한 것은 ④이다.

해석

> 우리는 흔히 화자의 말솜씨만으로 의사소통을 평가하곤 한다. 그러다 보니 <u>이해의 책임을 전적으로 말하는 사람에게 떠넘기는</u> 수동적 수용 방식에 머무르게 된다. 그러나 이런 수동적 태도는 결정적인 오류다. 훌륭한 경청자는 다르게 행동한다. 그들은 경청을 마치 금을 캐는 광업과 같이 능동적이고 추출적인 과정으로 취급한다. 말이 정돈되지 않았거나 전달 방식이 미흡하더라도 그 속에 중요한 통찰이 숨어 있을 수 있음을 알고 있기 때문이다. 따라서 청자는 파고들고, 명확한 질문을 던지고, 흩어진 아이디어들을 연결하는 것이 자신의 역할이라고 생각한다. 이해가 잘 되지 않을 때 화자를 탓하기보다, 효과적인 청자는 먼저 자기 이해가 충분한지 되짚어본다. 이런 '책임을 스스로 지는 태도'가 수동적 청취자와 능동적 학습자를 구분하며, 결국 어떤 상호작용에서 얼마나 많은 가치를 얻어내는지를 결정한다.

① 말의 내용보다 전달 방식에 더 주의를 돌리는
② 말의 이면에 있는 핵심 메시지를 적극적으로 찾아내는
③ 메시지를 이해하기 위해 피상적인 단서에만 의존하는
④ 이해의 책임을 전적으로 말하는 사람에게 떠넘기는

어휘

- eloquence 웅변, 유창한 이야기[화술], 설득력
- extractive 뽑아내는[추출하는]
- disparate 서로 다른, 이질적인
- blame 비난하다, 탓하다
- interrogate 질문하다, 캐묻다
- underlying 근본적인, 숨겨진
- surface-level 피상적인
- comprehension 이해
- transmit 전달하다, 전송하다

난이도 ┃ 중

정답 해설

이 글은 1880년대 캐나다 철도 건설의 주역이었던 중국인 이민자들이 공사 완료 후 직면한 사회·경제적 역풍을 다루고 있다. 정부는 자국민의 배타적 압력에 밀려 당시 거금이었던 500달러의 가혹한 인두세를 부과했으며, 이를 감당할 수 없었던 노동자들은 세금을 피하기 위해 비극적이게도 지하 터널로 숨어들어야 했다. 이러한 맥락에서 빈칸에 들어갈 내용은 재발견된 터널 유적지가 지닌 상징성이다. 이 터널은 단순한 구조물이 아니라 철도 완공 이후 노동자들이 견뎌야 했던 실질적인 고난을 생생하게 증언하고 있음을 나타내야 한다. 따라서 밑줄 친 부분에 들어갈 말로 가장 적절한 것은 ③이다.

해석

> 1880년대 약 17,000명에 달하는 중국인 이민자들의 유입은 캐나다 태평양 철도 건설에 핵심적인 역할을 했으나, 공사가 완료되자 사회·경제적 반발을 촉발했다. 1885년 경기 침체와 실업 증가 속에서 상당수 캐나다인들은 불안을 남아 있던 중국인 노동자들에게 돌렸다. 정부는 이러한 배타주의적 압력에 굴복하여, 당시로서는 어마어마한 금액인 50달러의 차별적인 인두세를 도입했다. 이러한 징벌적 조치에도 불구하고 많은 이민자가 잔류했다. 이에 정부는 세금을 점진적으로 인상하여, 대부분의 노동자에게 1년 치 임금을 상회하는 수치인 500달러까지 올리게 되었다. 이 억압적인 정책은 많은 중국인 공동체 구성원들을 지하로 숨어들게 만들었고, 그들은 세금을 피하기 위해 지하 터널에서 생활해야 했다. 1980년대에 재발견된 이 터널들은 이제 <u>철도 완공 이후 노동자들이 겪었던 고난을 반영하는</u> 역사적 장소 역할을 하고 있다.

① 철도 사업의 경제적 성공을 보여주는
② 이민 노동자들을 지원하기 위한 정부의 노력을 드러내는
③ 철도 완공 이후 노동자들이 겪었던 고난을 반영하는
④ 세계적인 도시 거주자 수의 현저한 증가를 반영하는

어휘

- influx 유입, 밀어닥침
- catalyze 촉발시키다, 촉진시키다
- backlash 반발
- unemployment 실업
- bend 강요하다[설득하다]
- institute 도입하다, 제정하다
- discriminatory 차별적인
- formidable 엄청난, 만만치 않은
- punitive 처벌적인
- oppressive 억압적인, 탄압하는
- subterranean 지하의
- demonstrate 보여주다, 입증하다
- hardship 어려움, 고난
- symbolize 상징하다

영어 정답 및 해설

✅ 제11회 모의고사

01 ①	02 ③	03 ③	04 ②	05 ③
06 ③	07 ①	08 ①	09 ①	10 ②
11 ③	12 ③	13 ①	14 ③	15 ①
16 ③	17 ②	18 ②	19 ②	20 ③

01 [어휘 – 빈칸]   ▶ ①

난이도 상

정답 해설

공무원이 단순한 표면적 문제에 그치지 않고 근본적인 문제까지 파악하고 있다는 점으로 보아, 해당 공무원은 '예리하다'는 내용이 자연스럽다 따라서 밑줄 친 부분에 들어갈 말로 가장 적절한 것은 ①이다.

해석

그 공무원은 단순한 표면적 문제에만 주목하는 것이 아니라, 그 기저에 있는 근본적 문제까지 파악할 만큼 충분히 예리하다.

어휘

★ sharp 예리한, 날카로운
● conservative 보수적인
● reserved 말을 잘 하지 않는, 내성적인
● spontaneous 자발적인, 즉흥적인

02 [어휘 – 빈칸]   ▶ ③

난이도 중

정답 해설

기억이 감정 상태나 외부적 암시에 따라 과거 사건을 자주 재구성한다는 점에서, 인간의 기억은 매우 '잘 변한다' 내용이 자연스럽다 따라서 밑줄 친 부분에 들어갈 말로 가장 적절한 것은 ③이다.

해석

인간의 기억은 매우 잘 변해서, 감정 상태나 외부적 암시에 따라 과거 사건을 빈번히 재구성한다.

어휘

★ mutable 변할 수 있는, 잘 변하는
● consistent 한결같은, 변함없는
● enduring 오래가는, 지속되는
● persuasive 설득력 있는

03 [문법 – 빈칸]   ▶ ③

난이도 중

정답 해설

③ [적중포인트 084] 관계대명사 주의 사항 ★★★☆☆

빈칸은 관계대명사 who의 수식을 받는 선행사이자 해당 절의 주어 자리이다. 관계대명사 바로 뒤에 나오는 동사는 수식하는 대상(선행사)의 수에 일치시켜야 하는데, 동사가 단수 형태이므로 빈칸에도 반드시 단수 취급을 하는 명사가 와야 한다. 선택지 중에 단수 취급을 하는 것은 everyone뿐이다. 따라서 밑줄 친 부분에 들어갈 말로 가장 적절한 것은 ③이다.

해석

그 이메일은 직원들에게 교육 시간에 참여하는 모든 사람이 떠나기 전에 출석부에 서명해야 함을 상기시켰다.

04 [생활영어 – 빈칸]   ▶ ②

난이도 하

정답 해설

시스템 장애로 항공편이 지연된 상황에서, A가 항공사의 "통제 불가능한 상황"이라는 변명을 언급하자 B는 포기하지 말라고 조언한다. 이어 A가 나 아직 탑승권이랑 지연 안내 이메일 가지고 있다고 반응하는 점을 보면, B가 지연을 증명할 자료를 갖고 공식적으로 보상을 청구하라고 조언했음을 짐작할 수 있다. 따라서 밑줄 친 부분에 들어갈 말로 가장 적절한 것은 ②이다.

해석

A: 야, 어제 시스템 사용 불능 때문에 항공편들이 지연된 거 들었어?
B: 응, 뉴스에 많이 나오더라. 너도 영향받았어?
A: 아쉽게도 그래. 런던발 비행기가 6시간 넘게 지연됐어. 하루 종일 공항에 묶여 있었지.
B: 정말 끔찍했겠다. 항공사에서 보상은 해준대?
A: 전혀 그렇지 않아. 자기들 통제 밖의 "특별한 상황"이라고 하더라.
B: 그런 변명 자주 쓰지. 그래도 포기하면 안 돼. 지연을 증명할 자료를 갖고 정식으로 보상 청구를 제기해야 해.
A: 정말 그렇게 해야 할까? 탑승권이랑 지연 안내 이메일은 가지고 있어.
B: 당연하지. 지금 규정상 기술적인 문제라도 3시간 이상 지연되면 보상받을 권리가 있어.

① 모든 국제선 여행객들에게는 유효한 신분증이 요구돼.
② 지연을 증명할 자료를 갖고 정식으로 보상 청구를 제기해야 해.
③ 출발 전에 예약을 확인하는 것이 좋아.
④ 공항 보안 측이 그 지연에 대해 책임을 져야 해.

어휘

• outage 사용 불능, 정전, (수돗물의) 단수
• extraordinary 보기 드문, 비범한
• circumstance 상황, 환경, 정황
• compensation 보상, 배상
• entitled 권리가 있는, 자격이 있는

05 [생활영어 – 빈칸]   ▶ ③

난이도 하

정답 해설

공기청정기를 중고로 거래하는 상황에서 Min-su가 40달러로 가격을 흥정한 후 Jane의 대답을 듣고 Min-su가 긍정적으로 반응하며 45달러로 구매하겠다고 답한 점을 보면, 판매자인 Jane이 40달러는 거절하면서도 가격의 중간 지점에서 타협하자고 제안했음을 짐작할 수 있다. 따라서 밑줄 친 부분에 들어갈 말로 가장 적절한 것은 ③이다.

해석

Min-su: 안녕하세요, 공기청정기 아직 판매 중인가요? 중고거래 앱에서 게시글을 봤어요.
Jane: 네, 아직 있어요. 상태도 아주 좋아요. 3개월만 사용했어요.
Min-su: 좋네요. 가격이 50달러 맞나요? 혹시 40달러로 내려주실 수 있나요? 오늘 바로 가지러 갈 수 있어요.
Jane: 가격이 확고하지만, 이번 한 번만 예외로 당신과 중간 지점에서 타협할게요.
Min-su: 좋아요. 45달러로 하죠. 어디서 만날까요?
Jane: 지하철역 근처 편의점 앞에서 오후 5시에 만나요.

① 최종 희망 판매 가격은 원래 게시글을 참조해 주세요.
② 제품 세부 사항은 앱 설명란에서 다시 확인할 수 있어요.
③ 가격이 확고하지만, 이번 한 번만 예외로 당신과 중간 지점에서 타협할게요.
④ 배달 기사가 최종 가격에 대해 책임을 질 거예요.

어휘

• available 이용 가능한, 구할 수 있는
• willing ~할 의향이 있는, 기꺼이 ~하려는
• lower 낮추다, 내리다

06 [독해 – 중심 내용 추론(주제)]　　　▶ ③

[난이도] 중

[정답 해설]

이 글은 수면 중 성장호르몬(GH) 분비를 조절하는 정확한 뇌 회로가 규명되었다는 내용을 설명한다. 비REM 수면이 GH 분비를 촉발하며, 이렇게 분비된 GH는 다시 각성과 관련된 신경 경로를 조절한다. 글의 핵심은 수면 부족이 이 회로를 교란시켜 GH 분비 결핍을 초래하고, 그 결과 대사 장애와 인지 기능 저하로 이어질 수 있다는 점이다. 따라서 글의 주제로 가장 적절한 것은 ③이다.

[해석]

> 신경과학자들은 최근 수면 중 성장호르몬(GH) 분비를 조절하는 정확한 뇌 회로를 밝혀냈다. 연구에 따르면, 이 과정에는 복잡한 피드백 시스템이 존재한다. 비(非) 렘(REM) 수면 동안 시상하부의 특정 뉴런이 활성화되면서 뇌하수체가 GH를 분비하도록 신호를 보낸다. 이 호르몬은 성장과 세포 회복을 촉진할 뿐 아니라, 각성(깨 있음)과 관련된 신경 경로를 조절하는 역할도 한다. 이번 발견은 나쁜 수면 패턴과 연쇄적인 건강 문제 사이의 중요한 연결고리를 밝히는 데 기여한다. 만성 불면증이나 수면 분절과 같은 요인으로 이 '수면 - GH 회로'가 붕괴되면 호르몬 분비가 부족해질 수 있다. 그리고 이러한 GH 결핍은 비만이나 당뇨 같은 대사 질환뿐 아니라, GH가 뇌 가소성과 기억 형성에 중요한 역할을 하기 때문에 인지 기능의 가속적인 저하와도 강하게 연관되어 있음이 드러나고 있다.

① 세포 회복에서 뇌하수체의 역할
② 성인 만성 불면증의 주요 원인
③ 수면의 질을 대사·인지 건강과 연결하는 신경 회로
④ 성장호르몬 결핍을 위한 새로운 의약 치료법

[어휘]

- precise 정확한, 정밀한
- release 분비, 방출
- activate 활성화하다
- trigger 유발하다, 촉발하다
- fuel 촉진하다, 자극하다
- cascade 연쇄
- chronic 만성적인
- insomnia 불면증
- deficient 부족한, 결함이 있는, 모자라는
- metabolic 신진대사의
- plasticity 가소성
- consolidation 공고화, 강화, 합동
- deficiency 부족, 결핍

07 [독해 – 세트형 문항(안내문 – 내용 일치)]　　　▶ ①

[난이도] 중

[정답 해설]

우리의 사명은 사고의 근본 원인을 밝혀내고, 공장·규제 기관·산업 단체에 안전 권고를 제시함으로써 화학 안전의 변화를 이끄는 것이라고 언급하고 있다. 따라서 윗글의 내용과 일치하는 것은 ①이다.
① 이 기관은 사고의 근본적인 원인을 파악하고 안전 지침을 제공한다.
② 이 기관은 위반자에 대해 재정적 제재를 부과할 권한이 있다.
③ 기관의 주요 목표는 화학 제품 제조 분야에서 세계를 선도하는 것이다.
④ 이 기관은 조사를 시작하기 전에 다른 기관으로부터 승인을 받아야만 한다.

[오답 해설]

② 벌금이나 처벌을 부과하지 않는다고 언급하고 있으므로 글의 내용과 일치하지 않는다.
③ 화학 사고 조사 분야에서 세계적인 선도 기관이 되는 것을 목표로 한다고 언급했을 뿐 화학 물질 제조 분야에 대해서는 언급되지 않았으므로 글의 내용과 일치하지 않는다.
④ 우리는 규제기관이나 집행기관의 압력으로부터 자유로운 상태에서 독립적이고 객관적으로 활동한다고 언급하고 있으므로 글의 내용과 일치하지 않는다.

08 [독해 – 세트형 문항(안내문 – 유의어)]　　　▶ ①

[난이도] 하

[정답 해설]

밑줄 친 'uncover'는 '밝혀내다, 알아내다, 덮개를 벗기다'의 뜻으로, 이와 문맥상 가장 가까운 의미는 ① 'disclose(밝히다, 드러내다)'이다.

[오답 해설]

② conceal 숨기다, 감추다
③ recover 회복되다, 되찾다
④ disregard 무시하다, 묵살하다

[해석]

> **미국 화학물질 안전 위원회**
>
> **사명**
> 우리는 고정식 산업 시설에서 발생한 주요 화학 사고를 조사하여 근로자, 대중, 그리고 환경을 보호합니다. 우리의 사명은 사고의 근본 원인을 밝혀내고, 공장·규제 기관·산업 단체에 안전 권고를 제시함으로써 화학 안전의 변화를 이끄는 것입니다. 우리는 벌금이나 처벌을 부과하지 않습니다.
>
> **비전**
> 우리는 화학 사고 조사의 글로벌 리더가 되는 것을 목표로 하며, 우리의 조사 결과와 권고 사항이 체계적인 안전 개선으로 이어지도록 보장합니다. 우리는 산업계, 근로자, 그리고 대중에게 이익이 되는 객관적이고 과학적인 분석을 보장함으로써 이를 촉진합니다.
>
> **핵심 가치**
> ☐ 정직 & 진실성: 우리 조사 결과에는 완전한 정직성과 투명성이 반드시 담겨야 합니다.
> ☐ 독립성 & 객관성: 우리는 규제기관이나 집행기관의 압력으로부터 자유로운 상태에서 독립적이고 객관적으로 활동하여, 조사에 대한 신뢰를 구축합니다.

[어휘]

- protect 보호하다, 지키다
- root 근본적인, 기초적인
- regulatory 규제의, 관리의
- impose 부과하다, 강요하다
- objective 객관적인, 사실에 기반한
- integrity 진실성, 온전함
- independence 독립성, 자주성
- authority 권한, 권위
- approval 승인, 허가

09 [문법 – 밑줄]　　　▶ ①

[난이도] 중

[정답 해설]

① **[적중포인트 053] 암기해야 할 동명사 표현 ★★★★★**
'~에 전념하다'의 의미인 'be committed to'에서 to는 전치사로 뒤에 명사나 동명사로 써야 한다. 따라서 밑줄 친 부분의 expand를 expanding으로 고쳐야 한다.

[오답 해설]

② **[적중포인트 076] if 생략 후 도치된 가정법 ★★★★☆**
'Should 주어'로 시작한다면 if가 생략된 가정법으로 가정법 공식을 확인해야 한다. 가정법 미래의 주절에 '(please) 명령문'으로 쓸 수 있으며, 이때 동사는 동사원형으로 써야 한다. 따라서 밑줄 친 부분은 올바르게 쓰였다.

③ **[적중포인트 087] 관계사, 의문사, 복합관계사의 구분 ★★☆☆☆**
whoever는 'anyone who'의 의미를 갖는 복합관계대명사로, 여기서는 전치사 to의 목적어 역할을 하는 명사절을 이끈다. 이때 명사절 내부(whoever is assigned…)에서 주어 역할을 수행해야 하므로 주격을 써야 한다. 따라서 밑줄 친 부분은 올바르게 쓰였다.

④ **[적중포인트 057] 분사의 동사적 성질 ★★★★☆**
주절의 시점인 '현재(is now ready)'보다 앞선 시점에 분석이 완료되었음을 나타내기 위해 완료 분사구문이 쓰였다. 이는 분석을 먼저 끝낸 후(과거/현재완료) 비로소 발표할 준비가 되었다(현재)는 논리적 선후 관계를 명확히 보여준다. 따라서 밑줄 친 부분은 올바르게 쓰였다.

[해석]

> 최근의 경기 침체에도 불구하고, 우리 회사는 자사의 세계 시장 점유율을 확대하는 데 여전히 전념하고 있습니다. 새로운 프로젝트와 관련하여 어떠한 도움이라도 필요하시다면, 기획 부서로 언제든지 편하게 연락해 주십시오. 우리는 태스크포스(TF)팀에 배정되는 누구에게나 필요한 자원을 제공할 것입니다. 더불어 예비 시장 조사를 마친 팀은 이제 이사회에 최종 제안서를 발표할 준비가 되었습니다.

난이도 하

정답 해설

이 글은 National Park Trust의 "Buddy Bison School Program"을 소개하며, 자연 체험 기회가 부족한 아이들을 국립공원과 연결하기 위해 독자들에게 기부나 자원 봉사 참여를 요청하고 있다. 따라서 글의 제목으로 가장 적절한 것은 ②이다.
① 도시와 농촌 학교 시스템의 비교하기
② 도시 청소년과 대자연 사이의 간극을 메우기
③ 환경 관리자를 위한 전문 교육
④ 정화 활동을 통한 신체 건강 증진하기

11 [독해 − 세트형 문항(홈페이지 게시글 − 내용 불일치)]　▶ ③

난이도 중

정답 해설

이 프로그램은 어린이들이 미국의 국립공원과 공공 자연지의 경이로움과 연결될 수 있도록 돕는 것을 목표로 한다고 언급하고 있을 뿐, 전문 여행 가이드를 교육한다는 내용은 지문에 언급되지 않았다. 따라서 윗글의 내용과 일치하지 않는 것은 ③이다.

오답 해설

① 이 대표 프로그램은 특히 교육 · 지원 여건이 부족한 학교의 어린이들이 미국의 국립공원과 공공 자연지의 경이로움과 연결될 수 있도록 돕는 것을 목표로 한다고 언급하고 있으므로 글의 내용과 일치한다.
② 우리는 이 노력이 차세대 환경 관리인을 길러내는 데 중요한 역할을 한다고 믿는다고 언급하고 있으므로 글의 내용과 일치한다.
④ 하고 싶은 활동을 선택하는 부분에 복수 선택이 가능하다고 명시되어 있으므로 글의 내용과 일치한다.

해석

도시 청소년과 대자연 사이의 간극을 메우기

매년 National Park Trust는 전국의 학교들을 "Buddy Bison School Program"에 참여하도록 초대합니다. 이 주요 프로그램은 특히 교육 · 지원 여건이 부족한 학교의 어린이들이 미국의 국립공원과 공공 자연지의 경이로움과 연결될 수 있도록 돕는 것을 목표로 합니다. 우리는 이 노력이 차세대 환경 관리인을 길러내는 데 중요한 역할을 한다고 믿습니다.

이 프로그램은 아이들 사이에서 커지고 있는 "자연 결핍" 문제에 대응하기 위해 시작되었습니다. 특히 도시 지역의 많은 청소년들은 공원을 방문할 기회를 갖기 어렵습니다. 이러한 단절은 그들의 신체 건강, 정신적 웰빙, 그리고 환경 보존에 대한 이해에 영향을 미칩니다. 버디 바이슨 프로그램은 이러한 변화를 이끌어 줄 체험 기회를 제공합니다.

당신도 아이들이 자연과 연결될 수 있도록 도울 수 있습니다.

당신이 하고 싶은 활동을 선택하세요 (복수 선택 가능)
☐ 국립공원 현장체험학습 지원하기
☐ 공원 프로그램 운영 지원 자원봉사 참여하기
☐ 지역 공원 환경 정화 활동 참여하기
☐ Kids to Parks Day 교통비 후원하기

어휘

• flagship 주요한
• lack 부족하다, 결핍되다
• cultivate 기르다, 함양하다
• stewards 관리인, 책임자
• disconnect 단절, 분리
• conservation 보존, 보호
• transformative 변화시키는, 혁신적인

12 [문법 − 밑줄]　▶ ③

난이도 중

정답 해설

③ **[적중포인트 093] 원급, 비교급, 최상급 강조 부사 ★★☆☆☆**
　very는 형용사 또는 부사의 원급을 수식한다. 형용사 또는 부사의 비교급을 수식하는 것은 even, much, far, by far, a lot, still 등이 있다. 따라서 밑줄 친 부분의 very를 even, much, far, by far, a lot, still 등으로 고쳐야 한다.

오답 해설

① **[적중포인트 071] 강조 구문과 강조를 위한 표현 ★☆☆☆☆**
　강조하고자 하는 핵심 요소인 '신재생 에너지원으로의 전환'을 It be와 that 사이에 배치한 강조구문이다. 본래 aim to accelerate 뒤에 위치해야 할 목적어가 강조를 위해 문두로 나간 구조이며, that절은 목적어가 없는 불완전 구조를 취하고 있다. 따라서 밑줄 친 부분은 올바르게 쓰였다.
② **[적중포인트 049] 5형식 동사의 수동태 구조 ★★★★☆**
　consider가 5형식 동사고 5형식 동사가 수동태가 되면 뒤에 형용사 주격 보어가 그대로 남아 있는다. 따라서 밑줄 친 부분은 올바르게 쓰였다.
④ **[적중포인트 097] 「전치사 + 관계대명사」 완전 구조 ★★★★☆**
　'전치사 + 관계대명사' 구조로 관계절 내의 문장(they can manage the budget… through the strategies)에서 전치사 through가 관계대명사 which 앞으로 이동한 형태이다. 뒤에 완전한 절을 취하고 있다. 따라서 밑줄 친 부분은 올바르게 쓰였다.

해석

최근 정부의 계획들이 가속화하고자 목표하는 것은 바로 재생 에너지원으로의 전환이다. 이러한 변화는 기후 목표를 달성하기 위해 필수적인 것으로 간주된다. 하지만 요구되는 투자 규모가 초기 예상보다 훨씬 더 커서, 예산에 큰 도전 과제가 되고 있다. 당국은 예산을 더 효율적으로 관리할 수 있는 새로운 전략들을 모색하고 있다.

---

13 [독해 − 단일형 문항(안내문 − 목적)]　▶ ①

난이도 중

정답 해설

이 글은 NPS 본부에서 발송한 내부 공지로, 혼잡한 국립공원 10곳에 새로 도입되는 ParkPass 시간 지정 예약 시스템의 변경 사항을 직원들에게 안내하고 있다. 업데이트된 세부 내용을 설명한 뒤, 모든 직원이 이를 반드시 숙지해야 한다고 강조하고 있다. 따라서 글의 목적으로 가장 적절한 것은 ①이다.

해석

내부 공지 − NPS 본부

날짜: 2026년 11월 3일
제목: 새로운 ParkPass 시간 지정 입장 시스템 시행 안내

국립공원관리청(NPS)은 방문객 수를 조절하고 혼잡을 완화하기 위해, 혼잡도가 높은 10개 국립공원에서 새로운 시범 예약 시스템인 'ParkPass'를 도입합니다. 이 시스템은 2027년 1월 1일부터 운영될 예정입니다.

방문객은 최대 60일 전에 Recreation.gov 에서 온라인으로 정시 예약을 해야 하며, 환불이 불가능한 2달러의 요금을 지불해야 합니다.
• 예약 플랫폼: Recreation.gov
• 예약 가능 기간: 최대 60일 전
• 수수료: 예약당 2달러(환불 불가)

이 프로그램은 기존의 연간 패스인 "America the Beautiful" 패스를 대체하지 않으며, 해당 패스는 입장료만 면제할 뿐, 예약료 2달러는 포함하지 않는다는 점도 명확히 하고 있습니다. 이러한 정보는 업데이트된 정책을 반영하며, 모든 직원은 이러한 변경 사항을 검토하고 숙지해야 합니다.

---

① 직원들에게 새로운 시스템의 변화를 알리려고
② 방문객들에게 새로운 온라인 시스템 사용법을 가르쳐주려고
③ 사람들에게 국립공원 연간 이용권을 구매하도록 권장하려고
④ 예약 수수료가 왜 2달러로 인상되었는지 설명하려고

어휘

• launch 시작하다, 출시하다
• pilot 시험적인, 시범적인
• reservation 예약, 보류
• congestion 혼잡, 정체
• non-refundable 환불 불가의

- exempt 면제하다, 면제되는
- familiar 익숙한, 친숙한
- suspension 중단, 정지, 연기, 보류

14 [독해 – 순서 배열] ▶ ③

난이도 중

정답 해설

주어진 글은 팬데믹 이후 업무 환경이 유연성과 기술 중심으로 변화하고 있음을 설명한다. 이어지는 (C)는 '변화'를 '이러한 진화'라는 표현으로 받아 유연성을 구체화하며, 하이브리드 모델이 확산되어 유연성과 협업을 함께 추구하게 되었음을 보여준다. (A)는 이러한 하이브리드 작업 공간의 성공을 지원하기 위해 기업들이 VR·AR 등 새로운 기술에 투자하고 있음을 덧붙인다. 마지막으로 (B)는 'Still'이라는 전환어를 통해, 이러한 긍정적인 변화 뒤에 숨은 번아웃과 고립감 같은 새로운 과제를 지적하며, 이것이 원격·하이브리드 근무 모두에서 해결해야 할 숙제임을 강조하며 글을 마무리한다. 따라서 글의 순서로 가장 적절한 것은 ③이다.

해석

조직들이 팬데믹 이후의 환경을 헤쳐 나가면서, 업무 방식은 더욱 높은 유연성과 기술 중심의 형태로 변화하고 있다. 이는 팀이 협업하고 연결되는 방식을 새롭게 재편하고 있다.
(C) 이러한 진화는 하이브리드 모델에 의해 가장 잘 나타나며, 이 모델은 팀의 결속력을 유지하는 동시에 유연성과 협업 사이의 균형을 맞추기 위해 사무실 출근과 재택근무를 결합한다.
(A) 통합형 업무 공간의 성공을 촉진하기 위해, 기업들은 표준적인 화상 회의를 넘어 가상 협업을 강화하고 더 몰입감 있는 공유 업무 공간을 만들기 위해 VR(가상현실) 및 AR(증강현실)과 같은 기술에 투자하고 있다.
(B) 그럼에도 불구하고, 원격 및 하이브리드 설정 모두 어려움을 수반하며, 이는 조직으로 하여금 분산된 근무 환경에서 더욱 두드러지게 나타나는 직원의 복지 문제를 해결하고 번아웃이나 고립을 방지할 것을 요구하고 있다.

어휘

- post-pandemic 팬데믹 이후의
- flexibility 유연성
- operate 운영하다, 작동하다
- remote 원격의, 먼
- address 해결하다, 다루다
- isolation 고립, 분리, 격리
- widespread 광범위한, 널리 퍼진
- balance 균형을 유지하다
- cohesion 응집력, 결합

15 [독해 – 단일형 문항(안내문 – 내용 불일치)] ▶ ①

난이도 중

정답 해설

글의 제목 아래에는 게시일이 2026년 11월 2일로 명시되어 있다. 축제는 2026년 11월 28일에 시작되므로, 이 안내문은 축제 개막 26일 전에 게시되었음을 알 수 있다. 따라서 윗글의 내용과 일치하지 않는 것은 ①이다.

오답 해설

② 이 사랑받는 지역 축제에서는 200만 개 이상의 조명이 설치되어 있다고 언급하고 있으므로 글의 내용과 일치한다.
③ '티켓' 항목에서 일반 입장은 11월 28~30일, 12월 1~4일로 총 7일간 무료라고 명시되어 있으므로 글의 내용과 일치한다.
④ '특별 이용' 항목에서 "ZIP 패스트 패스"($25)를 이용하면 오후 6시에 조기 입장할 수 있으며 전용 라운지를 이용할 수 있다고 명시되어 있으므로 글의 내용과 일치한다.

해석

오스틴 'Trail of Lights' 축제, 61번째 시즌으로 돌아오다

(게시일: 2026년 11월 2일)

61번째를 맞이하는 오스틴 Trail of Lights 행사가 2026년 11월 28일부터 12월 23일까지 Zilker Park에서 개최됩니다. 이 사랑받는 지역 축제에서는 200만 개 이상의 조명, 90개의 홀리데이 트리, 그리고 새로운 상호작용 전시물이 선보일 예정입니다.

시간: 야간 영업 시간은 오후 7시부터 10시까지입니다.

티켓: 일반 입장은 총 7일간 무료입니다(11월 28~30일, 12월 1~4일). 다른 모든 밤에는 사전 티켓 구매가 필요합니다($10). 티켓은 공식 이벤트 웹사이트를 통해 온라인으로 구매해야 하며, 게이트에서는 티켓이 판매되지 않습니다.

특별 이용: "ZIP 패스트 패스"($25)를 이용하면 오후 6시에 조기 입장할 수 있으며 전용 라운지를 이용할 수 있습니다.

참고: 연례 Fun Run 행사는 공식 개막 이틀 전인 11월 26일에 열립니다.

① 이 안내문은 축제 개막 이틀 전에 게시되었다.
② 이번 축제는 수많은 조명으로 꾸며져 진행된다.
③ 일반 입장은 축제 기간 내내 모든 날에 적용되지는 않는다.
④ 방문객들은 추가 요금을 지불하고 특별 조기 입장권을 구매할 수 있다.

어휘

- feature 특징으로 삼다, 포함하다
- admission 입장, 입장료
- purchase 구매하다, 구입하다
- exclusive 독점적인, 전용의
- announcement 공지, 발표
- decorated 장식된, 훌륭하게 꾸민
- entry 입장, 들어감, 가입

16 [독해 – 문장 제거] ▶ ③

난이도 중

정답 해설

이 글은 '녹색 수소' 생산을 가능하게 하는 전기분해 기술의 발전과 그 중요성을 중심으로 전개된다. ①번 문장에서는 전기분해 기술의 효율 향상을 위한 연구 동향을 제시하고, ②번 문장에서는 이러한 기술 혁신이 높은 생산 비용을 낮추기 위한 노력임을 설명한다. ④번 문장 역시 녹색 수소가 철강, 운송 등 탄소 배출 감축이 어려운 산업 분야에서 중요한 역할을 한다는 점을 강조한다. 그러나 ③번 문장은 높은 생산 비용이 경쟁력을 제한한다는 사실과 정면으로 배치되는 모순된 내용이다. 따라서 글의 흐름상 어색한 문장은 ③이다.

해석

전 세계적인 탈탄소화 흐름은 그린 수소를 유망한 청정 에너지 운반체로 주목하게 만들었다. 그린 수소는 재생에너지를 사용해 물을 분해하는 전해조를 가동함으로써 생산된다. ① 최근에는 전해조의 효율을 개선하기 위한 연구가 활발하며, 기존의 알칼라인 방식에서 벗어나 PEM(양성자교환막)과 고체 산화물 전해조 같은 더 효율적인 기술로 전환이 이루어지고 있다. ② 이러한 기술 혁신은 현재 그린 수소의 경쟁력을 떨어뜨리는 높은 생산 비용을 줄이는 데 초점을 맞추고 있다. (③ 사실, 많은 사람들은 그린 수소가 다른 연료들보다 생산 비용이 훨씬 저렴하기 때문에 그것을 사용하는 것을 선호한다.) ④ 여러 생산상의 어려움에도 불구하고, 그린 수소는 철강 제조나 중공업 운송 등 탄소 배출 감축이 어려운 분야의 탈탄소화를 위해 필수적인 에너지원으로 여겨지고 있다.

어휘

- decarbonization 탈탄소화, 탄소 제거
- renewable 재생 가능한
- power 동력을 공급하다, 작동시키다
- split 분해하다, 나누다
- advancement 발전, 진보
- competitiveness 경쟁력
- extraction 추출, 뽑아냄
- high-pressure 고압의, 강압적인
- underground 지하의
- formation 지층, 형성
- steelmaking 제강

난이도 중

정답 해설

이 메일은 시애틀 교통국이 주민들에게 보낸 공지문으로, '여러분의 의견을 듣고자 합니다'와 '온라인 주민 의견 설문조사를 작성해 주시기 바랍니다.'와 같은 표현을 통해, 교통 계획 초안에 대한 주민 의견을 수렴하려는 목적임을 알 수 있다. 따라서 글의 목적으로 가장 적절한 것은 ②이다.

해석

> 수신인: 시애틀 주민 전체
> 발신인: 시애틀 교통국
> 날짜: 2026년 11월 5일
> 제목: 2030 교통계획 초안
>
> 친애하는 시애틀 주민 여러분,
>
> 시애틀 교통국(SDOT)은 향후 10년을 위한 비전을 담은 2030 교통계획 초안을 공개했습니다. 이 계획은 안전성, 지속 가능성, 교통 형평성에 중점을 두고 있습니다.
>
> 우리는 이 중요한 문서를 최종 확정하기 전에 여러분의 의견을 듣고자 합니다. 주민 여러분의 참여는 이 계획이 모든 지역사회의 필요를 반영하는 데 매우 중요합니다. 공식 웹사이트에서 전체 초안을 검토하신 후, 온라인 주민 의견 설문조사를 작성해 주시기 바랍니다. 이 설문은 2026년 11월 30일까지 참여 가능합니다.
>
> 여러분의 참여는 시애틀의 미래 교통 시스템에 직접적인 영향을 미치게 됩니다. 또한, 다음 주에는 두 차례의 온라인 타운홀 미팅이 열려 실시간 질의응답이 진행될 예정입니다.
>
> 참여와 관심에 감사드립니다.

① 새로운 교통 계획의 최종안을 발표하려고
② 2030 교통 계획 초안에 대한 주민 의견을 수렴하려고
③ 최근 발생한 교통사고의 원인에 대해 사과하려고
④ 2030년까지의 교통 안전 정책을 홍보하려고

어휘

- release 발표하다, 공개하다
- draft 초안, 원고
- decade 10년
- equity 형평성, 공정성
- finalize 마무리짓다, 완결하다
- review 재검토하다, 되새기다
- influence 영향을 주다[미치다]
- engagement 참여, 관여
- promote 촉진하다, 홍보하다

18 [독해 – 문장 삽입] ▶ ②

난이도 상

정답 해설

이 글은 특정 박과 채소에 존재하는 쓴맛 화학물질로 인해 발생할 수 있는 심각한 중독 위험을 설명한다. ①번 뒤 문장에서 먼저 실제 환자 사례를 통해 문제의 심각성을 드러낸 뒤, 이어서 "이 생명을 위협하는 상태가 무엇 때문에 발생하는지(쿠쿠르비타신이라는 화합물)"를 밝혀 주는 주어진 문장이 오는 것이 자연스럽다. 그 후에 ②번 뒤 문장에서 이 물질이 보통은 무해한 농도로 존재하지만, 교잡 수분이나 환경적 스트레스에 의해 농도가 급격히 증가할 수 있다는 설명이 뒤따른다. 따라서 주어진 문장이 들어갈 위치로 가장 적절한 것은 ②이다.

해석

> 2025년 11월 12일에 보고된 최근의 의료 사례는, 일상적으로 먹는 몇몇 채소에서 드물지만 매우 심각한 위험이 발생할 수 있음을 보여주었다. (①) 한 여성은 박과 채소로 만든 집에서 직접 갈아 만든 주스를 마신 뒤 생명을 위협하는 증상을 겪었다. (② 이러한 부작용은 쿠쿠르비타신에 의해 발생하는데, 이는 호박이나 주키니와 같은 박과 식물에서 천연적으로 발견되는 쓴맛을 내는 화합물 종류이다.) 이러한 고유 성분들은 평상시 재배된 식물 속에 인체에 무해한 수준으로 존재하지만, 교잡 수분이나 환경적 스트레스와 같은 요인으로 인해 농도가 급격히 높아질 수 있다. (③) 주스가 비정상적으로 쓰게 느껴지는 것은 중요한 경고 신호지만, 과일 같은 다른 재료와 섞이면 그 쓴맛이 쉽게 가려질 수 있다. (④) 보건 당국은 호박이나 주키니가 평소보다 지나치게 쓰거나 맛이 "이상하다"고 느껴진다면, 중독을 막기 위해 즉시 버릴 것을 권고하고 있다.

어휘

- recent 최근의
- rare 드문, 희귀한
- severe 심각한, 엄격한
- life-threatening 생명을 위협하는
- harmless 무해한
- dramatically 극적으로, 급격하게
- ingredient 재료, 성분
- discard 버리다, 폐기하다
- prevent 막다, 예방하다
- poisoning 중독
- compound 화합물, 복합체
- bitter 맛이 쓴

19 [독해 – 빈칸 추론] ▶ ②

난이도 중

정답 해설

이 글은 맛이나 냄새처럼 언어로 형용하기 어려운 추상적인 감각을 설명할 때, 청각이나 시각 등 다른 감각의 어휘를 빌려와 표현하는 '공감각적 은유' 현상을 다룬다. 신맛을 '높다'고 하거나 쓴맛을 '낮다'고 표현하는 행위는 우리가 이미 잘 알고 있는 익숙한 감각(청각/음악)을 도구 삼아 설명하기 어려운 무형의 감각(미각)을 더 구체적으로 이해하기 위한 시도이다. 이러한 감각 간의 연결은 단순히 언어적 유희에 그치지 않고, 소비자의 잠재의식과 본능에 호소하려는 마케팅 전략으로까지 확장되어 시각적 디자인(날렵한 선)을 속도감이라는 신체적 느낌으로 치환하기도 한다. 따라서 밑줄 친 부분에 들어갈 말로 가장 적절한 것은 ②이다.

해석

> 맛을 묘사하는 것은 흔히 우리의 언어에 도전 과제를 안겨주며, 그래서 우리는 다른 감각 영역으로부터 용어를 빌려옴으로써 이러한 간극을 메운다. 예를 들어, 우리는 보통 음악의 음조를 위해 남겨둔 어휘를 사용하여, 신맛을 "높다"라고 하거나 쓴맛을 "낮다"라고 특징지을 수 있다. 공감각적 은유라고 알려진 이 현상은 우리가 무형의 경험에 대한 이해를 깊게 하기 위해 <u>익숙한 감각적 개념을 사용하여 서로 다른 경험을 이해하게</u> 해준다. 광고주들은 특히 이 메커니즘을 활용하는 데 능숙하다. 추상적인 모양이나 소리를 특정 제품과 연결함으로써, 그들은 다차원적인 소비자 경험을 만들어낸다. 매끈한 선을 가진 자동차는 단지 시각적으로뿐만 아니라 본능적으로 더 빠르다고 직관적으로 인식될 수 있다. 여러 감각을 동시에 관여시킴으로써, 마케터들은 잠재의식적인, 거의 본능적인 수준에서 소비자들에게 호소할 수 있다.

① 순수한 지각에 집중하기 위해 각 감각을 고립시키게
② 익숙한 감각적 개념을 사용하여 서로 다른 경험을 이해하게
③ 모순된 감각 신호로 소비자들을 혼란스럽게
④ 명확성을 확보하기 위해 오직 문자 그대로의 묘사에만 의존하게

어휘

- bridge the gap 간극을 메우다
- sour (맛이) 신, 시큼한
- bitter 맛이 쓴
- pitch 음의 높이
- synesthetic 공감각의
- metaphor 은유, 비유
- intangible 무형의
- abstract 추상적인, 관념적인
- dimensional 차원의, 치수의
- appeal 호소하다, 항소하다
- subconscious 잠재의식적인

난이도 　중

정답 해설

이 글은 기술 발전이 대량 실업을 불러온다는 통념을 반박한다. 기술 발전이 생산성과 소득 증가 → 상품·서비스 수요 확대 → 신규 고용 창출로 이어진다는 점을 거시경제적 증거로 제시한다. 마지막 문장 역시 이러한 흐름을 정리하며, 장기적 효과는 일자리의 순감소가 아니라 오히려 다른 형태의 고용으로 이어진다는 점을 강조한다. 특정 산업에서 일시적으로 밀려난 노동자들이 기술이 만들어낸 새로운 역할과 산업으로 이동하는 현상에 대한 내용이 들어가야 한다. 따라서 밑줄 친 부분에 들어갈 말로 가장 적절한 것은 ③이다.

해석

기술 발전이 결국 대량 실업을 초래한다는 서사는 오래된 역사적 오류이다. 자동화가 특정 부문에서 육체 노동자들을 대체할 수 있는 것은 분명하지만, 거시 경제적 증거는 직관에 반하는 이야기를 들려준다. 기술적 진보는 전반적인 생산성을 향상시키고 국민 소득을 증대시킨다. 이러한 집단적 부의 실질적인 상승은 단순히 사라지는 것이 아니라, 궁극적으로는 광범위한 상품과 서비스에 대한 더 높은 수요로 이어진다. 이러한 새로운 수요를 충족시키기 위해 기업들은 흔히 기술 그 자체에 의해 새롭게 만들어진 직책에 더 많은 노동자를 고용해야만 하는데, 이는 마치 자동차 산업의 부흥이 결과적으로 이전에는 존재하지 않았던 교외 소매업과 관광업 분야에서 수백만 개의 일자리를 창출했던 것과 같다. 따라서 과도기적 어려움은 존재하지만, 장기적인 효과는 일자리의 순감소가 아니라 새로운 산업으로 인력을 재분배하는 것이다.

① 사회가 자동화 시스템에 의존하게 되는 것
② 숙련 노동자와 비숙련 노동자 간 임금 격차의 확대
③ 새로운 산업으로 인력을 재분배하는 것
④ 전체 상품 수요의 영구적인 감소

어휘

- inevitably 불가피하게, 필연적이다시피
- unemployment 실업
- persistent 지속적인, 끈질긴
- fallacy 오류, 잘못된 믿음
- displace 대체하다, 쫓아내다
- macroeconomic 거시경제의
- boost 증가시키다, 북돋우다
- translate 바꾸다, 옮기다
- meet 충족시키다, 부응하다
- net loss 순손실
- dependence 의존, 의지
- overall 전체적인, 종합적인

영어 정답 및 해설

> ⊘ **제12회 모의고사**
>
> | 01 ③ | 02 ① | 03 ② | 04 ③ | 05 ③ |
> | 06 ③ | 07 ② | 08 ② | 09 ③ | 10 ② |
> | 11 ② | 12 ④ | 13 ② | 14 ③ | 15 ① |
> | 16 ② | 17 ④ | 18 ④ | 19 ① | 20 ① |

01 [어휘 – 빈칸] ▶ ③

난이도 중

정답 해설

원격 지점에서 근무하는 직원들의 더 높은 생활비를 상쇄해준다는 점으로 보아, 회사가 매달 주거 '보조금'을 지급한다는 내용이 자연스럽다. 따라서 밑줄 친 부분에 들어갈 말로 가장 적절한 것은 ③이다.

해석

> 개정된 회사 정책에 따라, 원격 지점에서 근무하는 직원들은 이제 더 높은 생활비를 상쇄하기 위한 월 주거 보조금을 받을 자격이 있다.

어휘

- ★ subsidy 보조금, 장려금
- ● withdrawal 철회, 취소, 회수
- ● compliance 준수, 따름
- ● discrepancy 차이, 불일치

02 [어휘 – 빈칸] ▶ ①

난이도 하

정답 해설

종합 보험이 사고 피해는 보상하지만, 'although'라는 역접 접속사를 기점으로 자연적인 마모 등은 보상 범위에서 '제외된다'는 내용이 자연스럽다. 따라서 밑줄 친 부분에 들어갈 말로 가장 적절한 것은 ①이다.

해석

> 종합 보험 정책은 건물에 대한 우발적인 손상을 보장하지만, 자연적인 마모로 인해 발생한 수리는 보장 범위에서 특별히 제외된다.

어휘

- ★ exclude 제외하다, 배제하다, 거부하다
- ● commend 칭찬하다, 추천하다
- ● adopt 채택하다, 입양하다
- ● expedite 더 신속히 처리하다

03 [문법 – 빈칸] ▶ ②

난이도 중

정답 해설

② **[적중포인트 045] 능동태와 수동태의 차이** ★★★★★
문장의 주어(A legal document)를 수식어구(essential for the merger…)가 길게 설명하고 있는 구조이다. 문장 전체에서 본동사가 빠져 있으므로, 주어인 문서가 서명되었다는 수동의 의미가 들어가야 자연스럽다. 또한 타동사 뒤에 목적어가 없으므로 수동태 형태가 적절하다. 따라서 밑줄 친 부분에 들어갈 말로 가장 적절한 것은 ②이다.

해석

> 양사 CEO가 신중하게 검토했던 합병 필수 법적 문서는 비공개 기자회견 도중 서명되었다.

04 [생활영어 – 빈칸] ▶ ③

난이도 하

정답 해설

음악 스트리밍 서비스 요금 인상에 대해 고객이 문의하는 상황이다. B는 기존 10달러에서 15달러로 오른 요금 때문에 다른 플랫폼으로 옮기는 것을 고려하고 있다고 말한다. 그러나 A의 답변을 들은 뒤 B가 "원래 가격으로 이용할 수 있다면 계속 쓰겠다"고 말하는 점을 보면, A가 이전 요금인 10달러로 계속 사용할 수 있는 프로모션을 제안했음을 짐작할 수 있다. 따라서 밑줄 친 부분에 들어갈 말로 가장 적절한 것은 ③이다.

해석

> A: 안녕하세요, 고객지원 센터입니다. 무엇을 도와드릴까요?
> B: 안녕하세요, 음악 스트리밍 서비스 구독료 때문에 전화드렸습니다. 이번 달에 15달러가 청구됐는데, 예전에는 10달러였거든요.
> A: 네, 그렇습니다. 라이선스 비용 상승으로 인한 가격 조정과 관련하여 지난달에 이메일을 보내드렸습니다. 못 받으셨나요?
> B: 아마 놓쳤나 봅니다. 솔직히 말해서 50% 인상은 저에게 좀 과한 것 같아요. 다른 플랫폼으로 옮기는 걸 고려 중입니다.
> A: 12개월 동안 요금을 10달러로 유지하는 장기 사용자 할인을 제공해 드릴 수 있습니다.
> B: 정말요? 그럼 1년 동안 원래 가격 그대로 사용할 수 있다는 말이군요. 그렇다면 계속 이용하겠습니다.

① 계정 해지 전에 환불 절차를 안내해 드릴 수 있습니다.
② 안타깝지만, 이번 요금 인상은 예외 없이 모든 이용자에게 적용됩니다.
③ 12개월 동안 요금을 10달러로 유지하는 장기 사용자 할인을 제공해 드릴 수 있습니다.
④ 월 5달러를 추가하면 가족 요금제로 업그레이드하실 수 있습니다.

어휘

- • subscription 구독료, (서비스) 사용
- • adjustment 조정, 수정, 적응
- • steep 가파른, 급격한
- • cancellation 취소, 무효화

05 [생활영어 – 빈칸] ▶ ③

난이도 하

정답 해설

월간 마케팅 보고서를 준비하는 과정에서 Ji-soo가 고객 피드백 데이터를 요약하기 위해 생성형 AI 도구 사용을 해보겠다고 말하며 개인정보가 포함되어 있지만 익명화 후 업로드할 수 있다고 말한다. 그러나 David의 반응을 듣자 Ji-soo가 "정책이 그렇게 엄격한 줄 몰랐다"며 수동으로 요약하겠다고 태도를 바꾸는 점을 보면, David가 익명화 여부와 관계없이 내부 데이터를 외부 AI 서버에 업로드하는 것이 회사 정책상 금지되어 있다는 내용을 전달했음을 짐작할 수 있다. 따라서 밑줄 친 부분에 들어갈 말로 가장 적절한 것은 ③이다.

해석

> Ji-soo: 안녕하세요, Johnson 씨. 지금 월간 마케팅 보고서를 작성 중인데요. 새로운 생성형 AI 도구를 사용해서 고객 피드백 데이터를 요약해볼까 생각 중입니다. 그러면 시간을 많이 절약할 수 있을 것 같아요.
> David Johnson: 안녕하세요, Ji-soo 씨. 효율성을 높이려는 당신의 노력은 고맙게 생각해요. 그런데 그 데이터에 우리 고객들의 개인정보가 포함되어 있나요?
> Ji-soo: 네, 이름과 이메일 주소 포함되어 있는데, 업로드 전에 익명화하는 방법을 시도해볼 수는 있어요.
> David Johnson: 하지만, 회사 정책상 내부 데이터를 공개된 AI 서버에 업로드하는 것은 엄격히 금지되어 있어요.
> Ji-soo: 알겠습니다. 회사 정책이 그렇게 엄격한 줄은 몰랐어요. 안전하게 수동으로 요약할게요.
> David Johnson: 이해해줘서 고마워요. 보안이 우리에게 가장 중요한 사항이에요.

① 좋아요, 이름만 지우면 그 AI 도구를 마음껏 사용해도 돼요.
② IT 부서에 그 소프트웨어 설치를 요청해야 한다고 생각해요.
③ 하지만, 회사 정책상 내부 데이터를 공개된 AI 서버에 업로드하는 것은 엄격히 금지되어 있어요.
④ 그 대신 데이터를 처리할 프리랜서를 고용하는 게 어떻겠나요?

어휘

- summarize 요약하다
- anonymize 익명화하다
- manually 수동으로
- forbid 금지하다

06 [문법 – 밑줄] ▶ ③

난이도 중

정답 해설

③ **[적중포인트 045] 능동태와 수동태의 차이 ★★★★★**
동사 expect는 '~을 예상하다'라는 의미의 타동사이다. 하지만 이 문장의 주어 (the situation)는 스스로 예상할 수 없으며, 사람들에 의해 '예상되는' 대상으로 수동태로 써야 한다. 따라서 밑줄 친 부분의 expects를 is expected로 고쳐야 한다.

오답 해설

① **[적중포인트 079] 명사절 접속사의 구분과 특징 ★★★☆☆**
emphasizes의 목적어 역할을 하는 완전한 절을 취하므로 명사절 접속사 that은 적절하다. 따라서 밑줄 친 부분은 올바르게 쓰였다.

② **[적중포인트 034] 완료시제와 잘 쓰이는 시간 부사 ★★★☆☆**
문맥상 '이미 혹독한 홍수를 경험했다'는 최근의 경험이나 완료된 사실을 나타내므로 현재완료 시제로 쓰였고, 완료시제를 나타내는 시간부사 already와 함께 쓰는 것이 적절하다. 따라서 밑줄 친 부분은 올바르게 쓰였다.

④ **[적중포인트 009] 관사의 종류와 생략 ★☆☆☆☆**
response는 가산 명사로 쓰일 수 있으며, '하나의 세계적인 대응'이라는 의미로 앞에 'a'를 붙이고 형용사(global)를 수식하는 것은 적절하다. 따라서 밑줄 친 부분은 올바르게 쓰였다.

해석

> 최근 기후 보고서는 상승하는 해수면이 지구 온난화의 직접적인 결과임을 강조한다. 많은 해안 지역 사회는 이미 심각한 홍수를 경험했으며, 즉각적인 개입 없이는 상황이 더욱 악화될 것으로 예상된다. 이 도전 과제는 세계적인 대응을 필요로 한다.

07 [문법 – 밑줄] ▶ ②

난이도 중

정답 해설

② **[적중포인트 044] 주어 자리에서 반드시 단수 또는 복수 취급하는 특정 표현 ★★★☆☆**
문장의 주어(ensuring full compliance)는 동명사구로 항상 단수 취급한다. 따라서 밑줄 친 부분의 are를 is로 고쳐야 한다.

오답 해설

① **[적중포인트 054] 분사 판별법 [현재분사 VS 과거분사] ★★★★★**
분사의 수식을 받는 명사가 행동한다는 능동의 의미일 경우 현재분사로 써야 한다. 따라서 밑줄 친 부분은 올바르게 쓰였다.

③ **[적중포인트 065] 조동사 뒤의 동사원형과 조동사의 부정형 ★☆☆☆☆**
문맥상 가능성을 나타내며 뒤에 동사원형이 나온 것으로 보아 조동사 can이 적절하다. 따라서 밑줄 친 부분은 올바르게 쓰였다.

④ **[적중포인트 056] 여러 가지 분사구문 ★★★★★**
앞 문장의 결과(편견이 내재되어 있어 차별적 결과를 초래함)를 나타내는 분사구문이다. 'as biases can be... data, (and they) lead to...'를 분사구문으로 바꾼 형태로, 능동의 의미를 가지는 현재분사로 써야 한다. 따라서 밑줄 친 부분은 올바르게 쓰였다.

해석

> AI 윤리를 조사하는 연구원들은 알고리즘이 투명하고, 책임감 있으며, 공정성을 보장해야 한다고 주장한다. 하지만 최근 국제 위원회에 의해 수립된 다양한 법적 체계와 윤리 지침을 완전히 준수하도록 보장하는 것은 매우 어려운데, 이는 편향성이 학습 데이터에 깊이 박혀 있어 차별적인 결과로 이어질 수 있기 때문이다.

08 [독해 – 세트형 문항(홈페이지 게시글 – 제목)] ▶ ②

난이도 하

정답 해설

이 글은 매년 3월에 진행되는 826 National의 학생 글쓰기 캠페인 'Amplify'에 참여하도록 안내하고 있다. 이 캠페인은 학생들의 목소리를 널리 알리고 스스로의 힘을 기르는 것을 목표로 하며, 예술 교육 예산 축소라는 배경 속에서 공립학교 학생들을 지원하기 위해 마련되었다. 이러한 취지를 설명한 뒤, 글쓰기 멘토링, 원고 편집, 행사 운영 등 구체적인 자원봉사 참여 방법과 일정을 제시하고 있다. 따라서 글의 제목으로 가장 적절한 것은 ②이다.
① 창의적 글쓰기 실력을 향상시키는 방법
② 학생 글쓰기를 지원할 자원봉사자 모집
③ 학생의 글쓰기 능력을 향상시키기 위한 전략들
④ 일대일 전문가 멘토링의 혜택

09 [독해 – 세트형 문항(홈페이지 게시글 – 내용 불일치)] ▶ ③

난이도 하

정답 해설

우리는 맞춤형 쓰기 지원을 제공하고 창의적 표현을 장려하는 성인 멘토와 학생들을 연결함으로써 읽고 쓰는 능력의 격차를 줄이는 것을 목표로 한다고 언급하고 있을 뿐, 공립학교의 법적 체계를 관리할 책임이 있다고는 지문에서 언급되지 않았다. 따라서 글의 내용과 일치하지 않는 것은 ③이다.
① 이 프로그램은 매년 봄에 연례적으로 개최된다.
② 이 프로그램은 예술 프로그램에 대한 재정적 지원 축소로 인해 수립되었다.
③ 성인 멘토들은 공립학교의 법적 체계를 관리할 책임이 있다.
④ 자원봉사자들은 위치에 상관없이 프로그램에 참여할 수 있다.

오답 해설

① 매년 3월, 826 National은 지역사회와 함께 학생 글쓰기의 힘을 기념한다고 언급하고 있으므로 글의 내용과 일치한다.
② 예술 교육 예산 삭감에 대응하여 시작된 이 캠페인은 자원이 부족한 공립학교 학생들을 지원한다고 언급하고 있으므로 글의 내용과 일치한다.
④ 자원봉사자들의 선호하는 시간 항목에서 대면과 가상 둘 중 하나를 선택할 수 있다고 명시되어 있으므로 글의 내용과 일치한다.

해석

> ### 학생 글쓰기를 지원할 자원봉사자 모집
>
> 매년 3월, 826 National은 지역사회와 함께 학생 글쓰기의 힘을 기념합니다. "Amplify"라는 이 캠페인은 학생들의 목소리를 세상에 알리고, 창의적 글쓰기를 자기 표현과 자립의 도구로 삼을 수 있도록 돕는 것을 목표로 합니다. 이것은 더 공감적이고 교양 있는 사회를 만들기 위한 중요한 단계입니다.
>
> 예술 교육 예산 삭감에 대응하여 시작된 이 캠페인은 자원이 부족한 공립학교 학생들을 지원합니다. 우리는 맞춤형 쓰기 지원을 제공하고 창의적 표현을 장려하는 성인 멘토와 학생들을 연결함으로써 읽고 쓰는 능력의 격차를 줄이는 것을 목표로 합니다.
>
> **자원봉사 역할 선택**
> ☐ 글쓰기 멘토: 학생 결과물에 대해 1:1 피드백 제공
> ☐ 편집 보조: 출판을 위한 원고 편집
> ☐ 행사 코디네이터: 지역사회 워크숍 조직
> ☐ 초청 연사: 전문적인 글쓰기 경험 공유
>
> **선호하는 시간 유형**
> ☐ 대면 (지역 학교 또는 센터에서 진행)
> ☐ 가상 (Zoom을 통한 온라인 멘토링)
>
> **활동 가능 시간**
> ☐ 평일 오전 (오전 9시 – 오후 12시)
> ☐ 평일 오후 (오후 1시 – 오후 5시)
> ☐ 주말 시간

어휘

- aim to ~을 목표로 하다
- empathetic 공감하는, 감정 이입의
- literate 문해력이 있는, 글을 읽고 쓸 줄 아는
- under-resourced 자원이 충분히 제공되지 않는
- expression 표현, 표출, 표정

• manuscript 원고, 사본
• in-person 대면, 직접

10 [독해 – 세트형 문항(안내문 – 유의어)]　　　▶ ②

난이도 중

정답 해설

밑줄 친 'profound'는 '심오한, 엄청난, 깊은'의 뜻으로, 이와 문맥상 가장 가까운 의미는 ② 'abstruse(심오한, 난해한)'이다.

오답 해설

① ingenuous 순진한, 천진한, 사람을 잘 믿는
③ explicit 분명한, 솔직한, 노골적인
④ peripheral 주변적인, 지엽적인

11 [독해 – 세트형 문항(안내문 – 목적)]　　　▶ ②

난이도 하

정답 해설

이 글은 'The Hastings Center'의 비전(윤리적 가치 존중), 문제 인식(의료 기술 접근의 불평등), 그리고 주요 활동(생명윤리적 쟁점 분석, 다양한 주체와의 협력)을 구체적으로 소개하고 있다. 즉, 이 기관이 사회 속에서 어떤 역할을 수행하는지 알리는 데 초점이 맞추어져 있다. 따라서 글의 목적으로 가장 적절한 것은 ②이다.
① 더 많은 생명윤리 지원의 필요성을 강조하려고
② 이 기관의 역할을 설명하려고
③ 새로운 의료 윤리 캠페인을 제안하려고
④ 의료용 윤리 교육의 필요성을 강조하려고

해석

The Hastings Center

사람들은 건전한 윤리적 가치에 기반하여 건강하고 풍요로운 삶을 살아야 합니다. 의학과 기술이 발전함에 따라, 이러한 강력한 도구들이 책임감 있게 사용되는 것은 필수적입니다. 윤리적 숙고는 사회적 안녕에 중요한 기여를 하며, 과학적 진보가 인류에 이바지하도록 보장합니다.

그러나 새로운 의학 기술에 대한 접근과 그 적용은 항상 공평하지 않습니다. 이러한 혁신은 사회가 반드시 논의해야 할, 삶과 죽음, 그리고 정의에 관한 <u>심오한</u> 윤리적 질문을 제기합니다.

Hastings Center는 이러한 필요를 지원하기 위해 존재합니다. 비당파적 생명 윤리 연구기관으로서, 보건·과학·기술 분야에서 제기되는 어려운 윤리적 쟁점들을 규정하고 분석하는 것을 목표로 합니다. 또한 정책 입안자, 자선가, 과학계 등 다양한 주체들과 협력하여 공적 논의와 정책 형성에 기여함으로써 이러한 비전을 실현하고자 합니다.

어휘

• prosperous 번영하는, 풍요로운
• ethical 윤리적인, 도덕적인
• responsibly 책임감 있게
• equitable 공평한, 형평성 있는
• non-partisan 비당파의, 중립적인
• bioethics 생명 윤리
• committed 헌신적인, 전념하는
• policymaker 정책 입안자
• philanthropist 자선가
• propose 제안하다, 제시하다

12 [독해 – 중심 내용 추론(주제)]　　　▶ ②

난이도 중

정답 해설

이 글은 우리가 흔히 믿는 '평판의 신뢰성'에 강력한 의문을 제기하며 시작한다. 필자는 인격이 한 번 형성되면 변하지 않는다는 고정관념 때문에 평판에 의존하는 판단은 위험하다고 경고한다. 인간은 선과 악이라는 단순한 이분법으로 나눌 수 있는 존재가 아니며, 실제로는 상황에 따라 실용적인 선택을 내리는 존재이기 때문이다. 정직함이란 변하지 않는 기념비처럼 고정된 것이 아니라, 어떤 보상이나 압박이 주어지는가에 따라 언제든 변화하고 요동칠 수 있는 역동적인 상태임을 강조하고 있다. 따라서 글의 주제로 가장 적절한 것은 ②이다.

해석

평판에 의거하여 정직성을 판단하는 것은 인격이 정체되어 있다고 가정하기 때문에 결함이 있는 전략이다. 과거의 행동을 바탕으로 사람을 근본적으로 "선"하거나 "악"하다고 분류하는 것은 인간 심리의 복잡한 난해함을 무시하는 처사이다. 대부분의 사람은 실용주의자로 행동하며, 특정 맥락 속에서 잠재적인 이익과 위험 사이의 미묘한 균형을 토대로 도덕적 선택을 내린다. 그러므로 한 상황에서 정직했던 개인이라도 압도적인 압박이나 유혹적인 보상에 직면했을 때는 다르게 행동할 수 있다. 결과적으로, 정직은 고정된 특성이 아니라 가변적인 특성이다. 정직성은 고정된 실체가 아니라, 시간의 흐름과 서로 다른 상황에 따라 변하는 역동적인 상태이다.

① 도덕적 선택에 있어서 개인적 이익의 역할
② 정직성이 영구적이지 않고 상황 맥락적인 이유
③ 과거의 평판: 정직성을 예측하는 핵심 열쇠
④ 인간 심리의 본질적인 복잡성

어휘

• reputation 평판, 명성
• integrity 정직성, 진실성
• flawed 결함[결점/흠]이 있는
• intricate 복잡한
• pragmatist 실용[실익]주의자
• overwhelming 압도적인, 너무도 강력한[엄청난]
• tempt 유혹하다, 부추기다
• variable 변동이 심한, 가변적인
• dynamic 역동적인, 활발한
• circumstance 상황, 환경

13 [독해 – 단일형 문항(안내문 – 내용 불일치)]　　　▶ ②

난이도 중

정답 해설

'시설 폐쇄' 안내 중 급수 시설인 식수대와 RV 폐수 처리장은 운영이 중단된다고 명시되어 있다. 따라서 윗글의 내용과 일치하지 않는 것은 ②이다.

오답 해설

① 추운 날씨가 다가오면서, 그린밸리 주립공원은 방문객의 안전과 공원 시설 보호를 위해 '겨울철 준비 작업'을 시작한다고 언급하고 있으므로 글의 내용과 일치한다.
③ 공원 내 트레일은 계속 개방되지만 제설이나 제빙 작업은 하지 않는다고 언급하고 있으므로 글의 내용과 일치한다.
④ 보트 경사로는 개방되지만, 부두는 겨울 동안 철수된 상태라고 언급하고 있으므로 글의 내용과 일치한다.

해석

그린밸리 주립공원: 겨울 시즌 안내

추운 날씨가 다가오면서, 그린밸리 주립공원은 방문객의 안전과 공원 시설 보호를 위해 '겨울철 준비 작업'을 시작합니다.

시설 폐쇄:
☐ 캠프장: 메인 캠프장(1~50번 사이트)은 2025년 11월 10일부터 2026년 4월 15일까지 전면 폐쇄됩니다.
　※ 캠핑장 대신 오두막집은 연중 내내 이용할 수 있습니다.
☐ 현대식 화장실 & 샤워장: 공원 내 모든 현대식 화장실과 샤워 시설이 현재 폐쇄되었으며, 물을 빼고 동절기 대비 작업을 진행합니다.
☐ 급수 시설: 식수대와 RV 폐수 처리장은 운영이 중단됩니다.

무엇이 열려 있나요?
☐ 트레일: 공원 내 트레일은 계속 개방됩니다. 다만 제설이나 제빙 작업은 하지 않습니다. 방문객은 각별한 주의를 기울여 본인의 책임하에 이용해야 합니다.
☐ 호수 접근: 보트 경사로는 개방되지만, 부두는 겨울 동안 철수된 상태입니다.

① 공원은 추운 계절에 대비하여 시설들을 정비하는 조치를 취하고 있다.
② 방문객들이 사용 후 세척한다는 조건하에, 식수대는 여전히 이용 가능하다.
③ 지면에 눈과 얼음이 남아 있겠지만, 하이킹 코스는 개방 상태를 유지한다.
④ 부두는 사용 중이지 않지만, 보트 경사로는 이용 가능하다.

- **winterize** 겨울철 준비를 하다
- **closure** 폐쇄, 닫힘
- **cabin** 오두막집, 객실
- **throughout** ~내내, 전 기간에 걸쳐
- **restroom** 화장실
- **drain** 배수하다, 물을 빼다
- **remain** 남다, 계속 ~한 상태이다
- **dock** 부두, 선착장
- **reservation** 예약

14 [독해 – 문장 제거]　　　　▶③

난이도 중

정답 해설

이 글은 2025년 말 제안된 암흑 물질에 대한 '새로운 가설'을 소개하고 있으며, 그 핵심은 암흑 물질이 빛과 미세하게 상호작용할 수 있다는 주장에 있다. ①번 문장은 광자가 에너지를 얻거나 잃는 현상, ②번 문장은 먼 은하의 빛이 붉거나 푸른 색조를 띠는 변화, ④번 문장은 이 현상이 암흑 물질의 '비중력적 증거'가 될 수 있다는 점을 언급하며 모두 이 새로운 가설의 내용과 의의를 구체적으로 설명한다. 그러나 ③번 문장은 초기 우주의 암흑 물질의 '양(비율)'에 대한 논쟁을 언급하는 내용으로, 새 가설에서 제시하는 색조 현상과 직접적인 관련이 없다. 따라서 글의 흐름상 어색한 문장은 ③이다.

해석

> 요크대학교 연구진의 최근 분석은 암흑 물질에 대한 새로운 가설을 제시하고 있다. 이 가설은 암흑 물질이 완전히 '어둡고' 중력으로만 상호작용한다는 기존의 믿음에 도전한다. ① 이 이론에 따르면 암흑 물질은 빛과 아주 미세하게 상호작용할 수 있으며, 이 과정에서 광자는 극소량의 에너지를 얻거나 잃을 수 있다. ② 이것은 먼 은하계에서 오는 빛에 미미한 '색조'를 만들어내어, 그 빛을 붉은색이나 푸른색 쪽으로 약간 치우치게 할 것이다. (③ 초기 우주에서 암흑 물질의 정확한 비율은 우주론자들 사이에서 치열한 논쟁의 대상이다.) ④ 만약 이 가설이 입증된다면, 이는 암흑 물질의 최초의 비중력적 '지문'을 제공하게 되며, 이 신비한 물질을 연구할 새로운 관측 통로를 열게 될 것이다. 궁극적으로 이 새로운 관점은 우주의 보이지 않는 질량을 구성하는 것이 무엇인지에 대한 오랜 수수께끼를 푸는 데 도움이 될 수 있다.

- **hypothesis** 가설
- **dark matter** 암흑 물질
- **gravity** 중력, 심각성
- **subtly** 미묘하게, 약하게
- **photon** 광자, 광양자
- **faint** 희미한, 약한
- **tint** 색조, 빛깔
- **standard** 표준의, 일반적인
- **fingerprint** 지문, 현저한 특징
- **unseen** 보이지 않는, 관측되지 않는
- **mass** 질량, 덩어리, 무리

15 [독해 – 단일형 문항(안내문 – 내용 일치)]　　　　▶②

난이도 중

정답 해설

표 부분에서 초록색 수거함에 배출할 품목(유리병 및 단지)은 '뚜껑을 제거하고 내부를 깨끗이 헹굴 것'이라고 명시되어 있다. 따라서 윗글의 내용과 일치하는 것은 ②이다.

오답 해설

① 시의회는 다음 달부터 시행되는 새로운 색상별 재활용 시스템을 도입한다고 언급하고 있으므로 글의 내용과 일치하지 않는다.
③ 표 부분에서 노란색 수거함에 수용 가능한 품목으로 '알루미늄 캔, 플라스틱 병'으로 명시되어 있으므로 글의 내용과 일치하지 않는다.
④ 수거 요일은 변동 없이 유지된다고 언급하고 있으므로 글의 내용과 일치하지 않는다.

해석

> ### 새로운 주거 지역 재활용 지침
>
> 매립 쓰레기를 줄이고 지속 가능성을 증진하기 위해, 시의회는 다음 달부터 시행되는 새로운 색상별 재활용 시스템을 도입합니다. 모든 거주자는 새로운 지침에 따라 가정 쓰레기를 분류해야 합니다.
>
> 재활용 프로세스가 효과적으로 작동하려면 정확한 분류가 필수적입니다. 각 재료 유형에 맞는 올바른 수거함을 사용하고 있는지 확인하기 위해 아래 도표를 참조해 주십시오.
>
> | 수거함 색상 | 수용 가능 품목 | 비고 |
> | --- | --- | --- |
> | 파란색 | 종이, 판지, 잡지 | 깨끗하고 건조한 상태여야 함 |
> | 초록색 | 유리병, 유리 단지 | 뚜껑을 제거하고 깨끗이 헹굴 것 |
> | 노란색 | 알루미늄 캔, 플라스틱 병 | 공간 절약을 위해 쭈그러뜨릴 것 |
>
> 수거 요일은 변동 없이 유지됩니다. 하지만, 혼합되거나 오염된 품목을 포함하고 있는 수거함은 수거되지 않을 것입니다.

① 새로운 시스템은 내년부터 공식적으로 시작된다.
② 초록색 수거함을 사용하기 전에는 항상 뚜껑을 제거해야 한다.
③ 노란색 수거함은 모든 종류의 재활용품을 수용한다.
④ 수거 일정은 상당히 변경될 것이다.

- **landfill** 쓰레기 매립지
- **implement** 시행하다
- **sort** 분류하다, 구분하다
- **below** 아래에
- **crush** 으스러[쭈그러]뜨리다, 밀어 넣다
- **contaminated** 오염된

16 [독해 – 문장 삽입]　　　　▶②

난이도 상

정답 해설

이 글은 2억 4천만 년 전 발견된 새로운 악어 조상 화석을 소개하며, 현대 악어와의 뚜렷한 차이점과 진화적 다양성을 설명하는 흐름으로 전개된다. ①번 뒤 문장에서 이 화석 생물이 공룡과 닮았고 몸 전체가 갑옷처럼 덮여 있었다는 외형적 특징을 제시한다. 주어진 문장은 이러한 갑옷 외형이 연구자들이 이를 "전사" 조상이라 부르게 된 이유를 설명하는 내용으로, ①번 뒤 문장에서 제시된 특징에 대한 해석과 의미 부여를 자연스럽게 이어 준다. 이어지는 ②번 뒤 문장부터는 서식 환경과 생태적 특성에 대한 설명으로 넘어가기 때문에, 외형 제시 → 외형의 의미 부여 → 환경 설명이라는 논리적 흐름이 형성된다. 따라서 주어진 문장이 들어갈 위치로 가장 적절한 것은 ②이다.

해석

> 2억 4천만 년 전의 놀라운 화석 발견이 2025년 11월 12일에 발표되었으며, 이는 초기 악어 조상에 대한 우리의 이해에 도전장을 던지고 있다. (①) 화석은 놀랍게도 공룡처럼 보이는 생물을 보여주는데, 몸 전체가 장갑판으로 뒤덮여 있었다. (② 이러한 갑옷 같은 외형 때문에 연구자들은 이 생물을 현대의 악어와 뚜렷이 구별되는 "전사" 조상이라고 불렀다.) 과학자들은 이 종이 수백만 년 전 육지에 살았다는 점에 주목하는데, 이는 현대 악어들의 수중 서식지와는 매우 다른 환경이다. (③) 그 신체 구조는 이 생물이 물이 아닌 육지 생활에 적응한 육상 포식자였을 가능성을 시사한다. (④) 이 발견은 익숙한 수생 형태가 지배적이 되기 전, 악어 계통 파충류가 얼마나 다양한 진화 경로를 거쳤는지를 보여준다.

- **remarkable** 놀라운, 주목할 만한
- **fossil** 화석
- **challenge** 도전하다, 의문을 제기하다
- **ancestor** 조상, 선조
- **creature** 생물, 생명이 있는 존재
- **plated armor** 판금 갑옷, 장갑판
- **terrestrial** 육상의
- **predator** 포식자, 약탈자

- **dominant** 지배적인, 우세한
- **appearance** 외형, 모습, 출현
- **differentiate** 구별하다, 차별화하다

17 [독해 – 단일형 문항(전자메일 – 목적)] ▶ ④

정답률 중

정답 해설

이 메일은 본문 전반에서 참석자들이 행사장에 도착하기 전에 공식 앱을 다운로드할 것을 강력히 요청하고 있다. 특히 앱이 체크인, 실시간 일정 확인, 질의응답(Q&A) 등 행사 운영의 핵심 기능을 담당한다는 점과 종이 일정표가 제공되지 않는다는 사실을 강조하고 있다. 따라서 글의 목적으로 가장 적절한 것은 ④이다.

해석

> 수신인: 모든 등록 참가자
> 발신인: 운영팀
> 날짜: 2026년 10월 10일
> 제목: 중요 안내
>
> 참가자 여러분께,
>
> 저희는 11월 10일 월요일에 열리는 Innovate 2026에 여러분을 모시게 되어 기쁘게 생각합니다. 보다 나은 컨퍼런스 경험을 제공하기 위해, 행사 기간 동안 주요 안내 역할을 할 Innovate 2026 공식 모바일 앱을 출시했습니다.
>
> 이번 메일을 통해 행사장 도착 전에 앱을 반드시 다운로드해 주시길 강력히 권장드립니다. 이 앱은 다음과 같은 기능을 제공합니다:
> - 체크인: 앱의 QR 코드를 사용하면 빠르고 간편하게 디지털 체크인이 가능합니다.
> - 네트워킹: 참가자 목록을 확인하고 메시지를 보낼 수 있습니다.
> - 일정 확인: 최신 일정과 마지막 순간의 강의실 변경 사항 등을 실시간으로 확인할 수 있습니다.
> - 라이브 Q&A: 세션 진행 중 발표자에게 직접 질문을 제출할 수 있습니다.
>
> 인쇄된 일정표는 제공되지 않으니 유의해 주시기 바랍니다. 지도와 연사 정보 등 모든 필수 정보는 앱에서만 확인하실 수 있습니다. 앱 스토어나 구글 플레이 스토어에서 "Innovate 2026"을 검색하여 다운로드하실 수 있습니다.
>
> 감사합니다,
> 'Innovate 2026' 운영팀

① 컨퍼런스 등록비 변경 사항을 공지하려고
② 참가자들로부터 사전 피드백을 수집하려고
③ 행사장의 종이 없는 정책을 강조하려고
④ 디지털 행사 플랫폼의 사용을 장려하려고

어휘

- **registered** 등록된
- **organize** 조직하다, 준비하다
- **thrilled** 아주 기쁜, 신이 난
- **launch** 출시하다, 공개하다
- **venue** 장소, 개최지
- **browse** 둘러보다, 훑어보다
- **up-to-date** 최신의
- **exclusively** 오로지, 독점적으로
- **urge** 촉구하다, 권고하다

18 [독해 – 순서 배열] ▶ ④

정답률 중

정답 해설

주어진 글은 먼저 JWST를 이용해 외계행성 WASP-18b의 3차원 대기 지도가 제작되었다는 결과를 밝힌다. 이어지는 (C)는 이러한 결과가 어떻게 얻어졌는지를 설명하며, 행성이 별 뒤로 사라졌다가 다시 나타나는 과정을 관찰해 대기 정보를 수집한 방법을 제시한다. (B)는 이렇게 확보된 데이터가 드러낸 내용을 설명하는 부분으로, 극단적인 온도차와 별을 향하는 지점에서 벗어난 뜨거운 지역 등 흥미로운 발견을 보여준다. 마지막으로 (A)는 앞선 관측 과정과 발견을 종합해, 이와 같은 정밀한 지도 제작이 이전에는 불가능했으며 새로운 관측 기술의 가능성을 입증하는 중요한 의의를 정리한다. 따라서 글의 순서로 가장 적절한 것은 ④이다.

해석

> 제임스 웹 우주망원경(JWST)을 사용한 천문학자들이 외계행성 WASP-18b의 최초 3차원 대기 지도를 만드는 데 성공했다.
> (C) 연구팀은 JWST의 강력한 적외선 관측 장비를 이용해 이 행성을 한 주기 동안 추적함으로써 이를 이루어냈다. 행성이 별 뒤로 넘어갔다가 다시 나타날 때 빛이 미세하게 변하는 양상을 분석해 대기의 온도와 조성을 파악할 수 있었다.
> (B) 데이터에 따르면 극명한 온도 차이가 나타났는데, 여기에는 항성을 향하는 지점으로부터 치우쳐 위치할 정도로 극심한 낮 지역의 핫스팟이 포함되어 있으며, 이는 강력한 바람의 증거이다.
> (A) 특정 분자들의 검출을 포함한 이러한 획기적인 발견들은 이전의 망원경들로는 불가능했을 것이다. 이는 WASP-18b에 대한 이해를 심화시킬 뿐만 아니라, 먼 행성들을 연구하는 새로운 방법을 제시한다.

어휘

- **astronomer** 천문학자
- **atmospheric** 대기의, 대기와 관련된
- **detection** 발견, 탐지
- **molecule** 분자
- **deepen** 심화시키다, 더 깊게 하다
- **distant** 먼, 멀리 떨어진
- **contrast** 대비, 차이
- **dayside** 햇빛을 받는 측면
- **extreme** 극단적인, 매우 강한
- **orbit** 궤도
- **reappear** 다시 나타나다
- **temperature** 온도, 기온

19 [독해 – 빈칸 추론] ▶ ①

정답률 중

정답 해설

이 글은 인간의 두 이중 경보 시스템인 공포와 불안이 갖는 '시간적 지향점'의 차이를 통해 두 감정의 본질적 차이를 규명하고 있다. 공포는 현재의 즉각적인 위협에 대응하여 생존을 위한 신속한 행동을 유발하는 반면, 불안은 아직 실현되지 않은 미래의 불확실한 위협을 탐색하는 탐조등과 같다. 빈칸 바로 뒤에서 "걱정의 근원을 정확히 밝히는 데 애를 먹는다"고 명시한 것은, 곧 불안이 공포와 달리 '상황적 구체성'이 결여된 모호한 감정임을 의미하기 때문이다. 따라서 밑줄 친 부분에 들어갈 말로 가장 적절한 것은 ①이다.

해석

> 공포와 불안의 반응은 상당히 갈리기 때문에 그 둘을 구분하는 것이 매우 중요하다. 공포와 불안은 종종 동시에 발생하지만, 결코 동의어는 아니다. 공포는 현재의 위험에 대한 즉각적인 신호로 작용하여, 생존을 위한 신속한 행동을 강요한다. 반대로 불안은 미래의 흐린 지평선을 살피며, 나타날 수도 있고 그렇지 않을 수도 있는 잠재적 위협을 식별한다. 결과적으로, 불안은 공포가 가진 상황적 구체성이 부족하다. 우리는 걱정의 정확한 원인을 찾아내느라 애를 먹을 수도 있으며, 미래의 본질적인 예측 불가능성 때문에 특정 위협이 주의를 기울일 만한 가치가 있는지 판단하기 어렵게 만든다. 그럼에도 불구하고, 불안은 우리에게 발생 가능한 재앙을 경고함으로써, 재난을 피하거나 그 결과를 완화하기 위한 필수적인 대비책을 마련하도록 촉구하는 중요한 역할을 한다.

① 불안은 공포가 가진 상황적 구체성이 부족하다
② 공포는 불안보다 더 지속적인 상태이다
③ 불안은 공포보다 더 빠른 생리적 반응을 유발한다
④ 이중 경보 시스템은 그것들의 공통된 진화적 뿌리를 암시한다

어휘

- **distinction** 구분, 차이
- **diverge** 갈리다, 나뉘다
- **synonymous** 동의어, 유의어
- **compelling** 설득력 있는, 강력한
- **murky** 흐린, 탁한, 어두운
- **materialize** 구체화되다[실현되다]
- **unpredictability** 예측 불가능성
- **catastrophe** 재난, 참사

난이도 중

정답 해설

이 글은 남을 돕는 행위가 오히려 시간이 더 많다고 느끼게 만든다는 역설적인 연구 결과를 설명한다. 물리적으로는 남을 위해 시간을 썼으므로 시간이 부족해져야 마땅하지만, 실제로는 그 과정에서 얻은 유능감과 효율성이 심리적으로 시간이 확장되는 결과를 낳으며, 이러한 효능감은 내가 시간을 통제하고 있다는 느낌을 주어 시계의 구속으로부터 자유롭게 만든다. 마지막 문장의 '역설적이게도'라는 표현은 시간을 소모했는데 오히려 시간이 늘어났다는 반직관적인 결론을 유도하므로, 지문 전체를 관통하는 핵심인 '시간의 심리적 풍요'를 담은 내용이 들어가야 한다. 따라서 밑줄 친 부분에 들어갈 말로 가장 적절한 것은 ①이다.

해석

시간 인지의 심리학을 탐구하는 일련의 실험에서, Cassie Mogilner는 이타주의와 시간 사이의 반직관적인 관계를 입증했다. 피험자들은 두 그룹으로 나뉘었다. 한 그룹은 학생의 에세이를 교정해 주는 것과 같이 다른 사람을 돕는 데 시간을 쓰라는 지시를 받았고, 다른 그룹은 자신을 위한 일을 하거나 시간을 낭비하는 활동을 하라는 지시를 받았다. 논리적으로는 시간을 내어주는 것이 고갈된 느낌으로 이어져야 하지만, 결과는 그 반대로 나타났다. 다른 사람을 도와준 사람들은 오히려 자신이 가용할 수 있는 시간이 더 많아진 것처럼 느꼈다. 이러한 현상은 베푸는 행위가 한 개인의 유능감과 효율성을 높여주어, 심리적인 시간의 확장을 만들어낸다는 점을 시사한다. 우리가 다른 사람을 돕는 데 유능하다고 느낄 때, 우리는 시계(시간)에 의해 덜 구속받는다고 느낀다. 따라서, 만약 당신이 (할 일에) 압도당해 휴식을 찾고 있다면, 최선의 해결책은 나태함으로 물러나는 것이 아니라 손을 뻗어 누군가를 돕는 것이다. 역설적이게도, 시간을 내어주는 것은 <u>자신을 위해 시간을 아끼는 것보다 당신을 더 시간적으로 풍요롭게 느끼게 만든다</u>.

① 자신을 위해 시간을 아끼는 것보다 당신을 더 시간적으로 풍요롭게 느끼게 만든다
② 탈진 때문에 당신 자신의 업무를 소홀히 하게 만든다
③ 당신의 일상적인 압박으로부터 일시적인 기분 전환을 제공한다
④ 정신적 업무량을 증가시킴으로써 시간을 가속화한다

어휘

- perception 인지, 지각, 통찰력
- counterintuitive 반직관적인
- altruism 이타주의, 이타심
- divide 나뉘다, 갈라지다
- depletion 고갈, 소모
- competence 능숙함, 능숙도
- overwhelmed 압도된
- idleness 게으름, 나태
- distraction 기분 전환, 주의 산만

수고하셨습니다.
당신의 합격을 응원합니다.

영어 빠른 정답 찾기

제1회

| 01 ③ | 02 ① | 03 ④ | 04 ① | 05 ③ | 06 ③ | 07 ② | 08 ② | 09 ② | 10 ④ |
| 11 ③ | 12 ① | 13 ② | 14 ② | 15 ③ | 16 ② | 17 ④ | 18 ② | 19 ① | 20 ④ |

제2회

| 01 ③ | 02 ② | 03 ① | 04 ③ | 05 ④ | 06 ② | 07 ② | 08 ③ | 09 ③ | 10 ③ |
| 11 ④ | 12 ③ | 13 ③ | 14 ③ | 15 ③ | 16 ③ | 17 ④ | 18 ② | 19 ④ | 20 ② |

제3회

| 01 ② | 02 ③ | 03 ① | 04 ③ | 05 ③ | 06 ③ | 07 ④ | 08 ② | 09 ① | 10 ② |
| 11 ② | 12 ④ | 13 ③ | 14 ④ | 15 ③ | 16 ② | 17 ② | 18 ④ | 19 ③ | 20 ① |

제4회

| 01 ① | 02 ③ | 03 ② | 04 ② | 05 ③ | 06 ④ | 07 ③ | 08 ④ | 09 ② | 10 ④ |
| 11 ④ | 12 ④ | 13 ② | 14 ② | 15 ② | 16 ③ | 17 ③ | 18 ④ | 19 ④ | 20 ① |

제5회

| 01 ② | 02 ③ | 03 ④ | 04 ③ | 05 ① | 06 ④ | 07 ③ | 08 ④ | 09 ④ | 10 ② |
| 11 ③ | 12 ② | 13 ③ | 14 ④ | 15 ④ | 16 ④ | 17 ④ | 18 ③ | 19 ② | 20 ② |

제6회

| 01 ③ | 02 ② | 03 ③ | 04 ④ | 05 ② | 06 ④ | 07 ② | 08 ① | 09 ① | 10 ① |
| 11 ③ | 12 ② | 13 ② | 14 ③ | 15 ③ | 16 ③ | 17 ④ | 18 ③ | 19 ③ | 20 ④ |

2026 공무원 시험 대비 실전동형 모의고사 제7회 ~ 제12회
영어 빠른 정답 찾기

제7회

| 01 ③ | 02 ② | 03 ④ | 04 ② | 05 ④ | 06 ② | 07 ④ | 08 ③ | 09 ② | 10 ② |
| 11 ② | 12 ④ | 13 ④ | 14 ② | 15 ① | 16 ② | 17 ② | 18 ② | 19 ④ | 20 ① |

제8회

| 01 ④ | 02 ② | 03 ③ | 04 ④ | 05 ④ | 06 ① | 07 ② | 08 ④ | 09 ① | 10 ② |
| 11 ② | 12 ④ | 13 ② | 14 ③ | 15 ③ | 16 ② | 17 ③ | 18 ④ | 19 ④ | 20 ② |

제9회

| 01 ① | 02 ③ | 03 ② | 04 ③ | 05 ② | 06 ③ | 07 ③ | 08 ④ | 09 ② | 10 ④ |
| 11 ② | 12 ③ | 13 ② | 14 ③ | 15 ① | 16 ② | 17 ② | 18 ③ | 19 ① | 20 ② |

제10회

| 01 ② | 02 ② | 03 ③ | 04 ③ | 05 ① | 06 ③ | 07 ② | 08 ③ | 09 ② | 10 ④ |
| 11 ④ | 12 ① | 13 ④ | 14 ① | 15 ① | 16 ④ | 17 ② | 18 ② | 19 ④ | 20 ③ |

제11회

| 01 ① | 02 ③ | 03 ③ | 04 ② | 05 ③ | 06 ③ | 07 ① | 08 ① | 09 ① | 10 ② |
| 11 ③ | 12 ③ | 13 ① | 14 ③ | 15 ① | 16 ③ | 17 ② | 18 ② | 19 ② | 20 ③ |

제12회

| 01 ③ | 02 ① | 03 ② | 04 ③ | 05 ③ | 06 ③ | 07 ② | 08 ② | 09 ③ | 10 ② |
| 11 ② | 12 ② | 13 ② | 14 ③ | 15 ② | 16 ② | 17 ④ | 18 ④ | 19 ① | 20 ① |

수고하셨습니다.
당신의 합격을 응원합니다.

9급 국가공무원 공개경쟁채용시험 필기시험 답안지

컴퓨터용 흑색사인펜만 사용

책형	【필적감정용 기재】
가	* 아래 예시문을 옮겨 적으시오
나	본인은 ○○○(응시자성명)임을 확인함
	기 재 란

성 명	
자필성명	본인 성명 기재
응시직렬	
응시지역	
시험장소	

직렬코드

응시번호

전화번호

※ 시험감독관 서명
(성명을 정자로 기재할 것)

적색 볼펜만 사용

문번	제 회
1	① ② ③ ④
2	① ② ③ ④
3	① ② ③ ④
4	① ② ③ ④
5	① ② ③ ④
6	① ② ③ ④
7	① ② ③ ④
8	① ② ③ ④
9	① ② ③ ④
10	① ② ③ ④
11	① ② ③ ④
12	① ② ③ ④
13	① ② ③ ④
14	① ② ③ ④
15	① ② ③ ④
16	① ② ③ ④
17	① ② ③ ④
18	① ② ③ ④
19	① ② ③ ④
20	① ② ③ ④

(답란표 6개 동일: 각 표 문번 1~20, ① ② ③ ④)

9급 국가공무원 공개경쟁채용시험 필기시험 답안지

컴퓨터용 흑색사인펜만 사용

책형: 가 / 나

【필적감정용 기재】
* 아래 예시문을 옮겨 적으시오
본인은 ○○○(응시자성명)임을 확인함

기 재 란

성 명	
자필성명	본인 성명 기재
응시직렬	
응시지역	
시험장소	

직렬코드

응시번호

전화번호

※ 시험감독관 서명
(성명을 정자로 기재할 것)

적색 볼펜만 사용

문번	제 회
1	① ② ③ ④
2	① ② ③ ④
3	① ② ③ ④
4	① ② ③ ④
5	① ② ③ ④
6	① ② ③ ④
7	① ② ③ ④
8	① ② ③ ④
9	① ② ③ ④
10	① ② ③ ④
11	① ② ③ ④
12	① ② ③ ④
13	① ② ③ ④
14	① ② ③ ④
15	① ② ③ ④
16	① ② ③ ④
17	① ② ③ ④
18	① ② ③ ④
19	① ② ③ ④
20	① ② ③ ④

9급 국가공무원 공개경쟁채용시험 필기시험 답안지

컴퓨터용 흑색사인펜만 사용

책형	【필적감정용 기재】
㉮	* 아래 예시문을 옮겨 적으시오
㉯	본인은 ○○○(응시자성명)임을 확인함 기 재 란

성 명	
자필성명	본인 성명 기재
응시직렬	
응시지역	
시험장소	

직렬코드

응시번호

전화번호

※ 시험감독관 서명
(성명을 정자로 기재할 것)

적색 볼펜만 사용

문번	제 회			
1	①	②	③	④
2	①	②	③	④
3	①	②	③	④
4	①	②	③	④
5	①	②	③	④
6	①	②	③	④
7	①	②	③	④
8	①	②	③	④
9	①	②	③	④
10	①	②	③	④
11	①	②	③	④
12	①	②	③	④
13	①	②	③	④
14	①	②	③	④
15	①	②	③	④
16	①	②	③	④
17	①	②	③	④
18	①	②	③	④
19	①	②	③	④
20	①	②	③	④

(위 답안 기입란은 6개 열로 동일하게 반복됨: 문번 1–20, 각 문항 ① ② ③ ④)